Greg Perry

SAMS

Teach Yourself

Beginning
Programming

in 24 Hours

SECOND EDITION

SAMS

201 West 103rd Street, Indianapolis, Indiana, 46290 USA

Sams Teach Yourself Beginning Programming in 24 Hours
Copyright ©2002 by Sams Publishing

All rights reserved. No part of this book shall be reproduced, stored in a retrieval system, or transmitted by any means, electronic, mechanical, photo-copying, recording, or otherwise, without written permission from the pub-lisher. No patent liability is assumed with respect to the use of the information contained herein. Although every precaution has been taken in the preparation of this book, the publisher and author assume no responsibility for errors or omissions. Neither is any liability assumed for damages resulting from the use of the information contained herein. For information, address Sams Publishing, 201 N. 103rd Street, Indianapolis, IN 46290.

International Standard Book Number: 0-672-32307-9

Library of Congress Catalog Card Number: 2001094916

Printed in the United States of America

First Printing: November 2001

06   05   9   8   7

Trademarks

All terms mentioned in this book that are known to be trademarks or service marks have been appropriately capitalized. Sams Publishing cannot attest to the accuracy of this information. Use of a term in this book should not be regarded as affecting the validity of any trademark or service mark.

Windows is a registered trademark of Microsoft Corporation.

Warning and Disclaimer

Every effort has been made to make this book as complete and as accurate as possible, but no warranty or fitness is implied. The information provided is on an "as is" basis. The authors and the publisher shall have neither liability nor responsibility to any person or entity with respect to any loss or damages aris-ing from the information contained in this book.

EXECUTIVE EDITOR
Michael Stephens

ACQUISITIONS EDITOR
Carol Ackerman

DEVELOPMENT EDITOR
Christy A. Franklin

TECHNICAL EDITOR
Devan Shepherd

MANAGING EDITOR
Matt Purcell

PRODUCTION EDITOR
Theodore Young, Jr.
Publication Services, Inc.

COPY EDITOR
Michael Kopp,
Publication Services, Inc.

INDEXER
Joanna Keyes,
Publication Services, Inc.

PRODUCTION
Publication Services, Inc.

COVER DESIGNER
Aren Howell

BOOK DESIGNER
Gary Adair

Contents at a Glance

Contents

About the Author

GREG PERRY is a speaker and writer on both the programming and the application sides of computing. He is known for his skills at bringing advanced computer topics down to the novice's level. Perry has been a programmer and trainer since the early 1980s. He received his first degree in computer science and a master's degree in corporate finance. Perry's books have sold more than 2 million copies worldwide. He has authored best-selling books that include *Sams Teach Yourself Office XP in 24 Hours, Absolute Beginner's Guide to C, Teach Yourself Visual Basic 6 in 21 Days,* and *Sams Teach Yourself Windows XP in 24 Hours.* He has written about rental-property management and loves to travel. His favorite place to be when away from home is either at New York's Patsy's or in Italy because he wants to practice his fractured, broken Italian (if a foreign language were as easy as a computer language, he'd be fluent by now).

Dedication

I dedicate this book to Ray Comfort, a man I first heard in New Zealand and who, years later, fell directly into my family's path once again. Your writings at RayComfort.com contain more truth in each sentence than about a billion other Web pages combined.

Acknowledgments

The people at Pearson Education and Sams Publishing make the best books possible in the industry for a good reason: they take their jobs seriously. They want readers to have the best books possible. They accomplish that goal. Among the Sams editors and staff who produced this book, I want to send special thanks to Carol Ackerman who asked me to do this project and for whom I am grateful. Sams has a jewel and her name is Carol. In addition, Christy Franklin helped put my words together and formed this finished product. With the mess I always turn in, she had her hands full and did splendidly.

The people at Pearson Education and Sams Publishing make the best books possible in the industry for good reason: they take their jobs seriously. They want readers to have the best books possible. They accomplish that goal. Among the Sams editors and staff who produced this book, I want to send special thanks to Carol Ackerman who asked me to do this project and for whom I am grateful. Sams has a jewel and her name is Carol. In addition, Christy Franklin helped put my words together and formed this finished product. With the mess I always turn in, she had her hands full and did splendidly. In addition, Devan Shepherd made this book more accurate. If errors still exist, they are solely mine.

The best parents in the universe, Glen and Bettye Perry, still, after about 70 books, encourage and support my writing in every way. Thanks to both of them. My lovely and gracious bride Jayne continues to wait by my side while I finish just "one more page." Thanks, my love.

Introduction

Introduction to Programming

Learning how to program computers is easier than you might think. If you approach computers with hesitation, if you cannot even spell *PC*, if you have tried your best to avoid the subject altogether but can do so no longer, the book you now hold contains support that you can depend on in troubled computing times.

This 24-hour tutorial does more than explain programming. This tutorial does more than describe the difference between Visual Basic, C++, and Java. This tutorial does more than teach you what programming is all about. This tutorial is a *training tool* that you can use to develop proper programming skills. The aim of this text is to introduce you to programming using professionally recognized principles, while keeping things simple at the same time. It is not this text's singular goal to teach you a programming language (although you will be writing programs before you finish it). This text's goal is to give you the foundation to become the best programmer you can be.

These 24 one-hour lessons delve into proper program design principles. You'll not only learn how to program, but also how to *prepare* for programming. This tutorial also teaches you how companies program and explains what you have to do to become a needed resource in a programming position. You'll learn about various programming job titles and what to expect if you want to write programs for others. You'll explore many issues related to online computing and learn how to address the needs of the online programming community.

Who Should Use This Book?

The title of this book says it all. If you have never programmed a computer, if you don't even like them at all, or if your VCR's timer throws you into fits, take three sighs of relief! This text was written for *you* so that, within 24 hours, you will understand the nature of computer programs and you will have written programs.

This book is aimed at three different groups of people:

- Individuals who know nothing about programming but who want to know what programming is all about.
- Companies that want to train non-programming computer users for programming careers.
- Schools—both for introductory language classes and for systems analysis and design classes—that want to promote good coding design and style and that want to offer an overview of the life of a programmer.

Readers who seem tired of the plethora of quick-fix computer titles cluttering today's shelves will find a welcome reprieve here. The book you now hold talks to newcomers to programming without talking down to them.

What This Book Will Do for You

In the next 24 hours, you will learn something about almost every aspect of programming. The following topics are discussed in depth throughout this 24-hour tutorial:

- The hardware and software related to programming
- The history of programming
- Programming languages
- The business of programming
- Programming jobs
- Program design
- Internet programming
- The future of programming

Can This Book Really Teach Programming in 24 Hours?

In a word, yes. You can master each chapter in one hour or less. (By the way, chapters are referred to as "hours" in the rest of this book.) The material is balanced with mountains of shortcuts and methods that will make your hours productive and hone your programming skills more and more with each hour. Although some chapters are longer than others, many of the shorter chapters cover more detailed or more difficult issues than the shorter ones. A true attempt was made to make each hour learnable in an hour. Exercises at the end of each hour will provide feedback about the skills you learned.

If you run across a term that you don't know, check the glossary in Appendix A. All terms introduced in the book are explained there.

Conventions Used in This Book

This book uses several common conventions to help teach programming topics. Here is a summary of those typographical conventions:

- Commands and computer output appear in a special `monospaced` computer font.
- Words you type also appear in the `monospaced` computer font.
- If a task requires you to select from a menu, the book separates menu commands with a comma. Therefore, this book uses File, Save As to select the Save As option from the File menu.

In addition to typographical conventions, the following special elements are included to set off different types of information to make it easily recognizable.

Special notes augment the material you read in each hour. These notes clarify concepts and procedures.

You'll find numerous tips that offer shortcuts and solutions to common problems.

The cautions warn you about pitfalls. Reading them will save you time and trouble.

Tell Us What You Think!

As the reader of this book, *you* are our most important critic and commentator. We value your opinion and want to know what we're doing right, what we could do better, what areas you'd like to see us publish in, and any other words of wisdom you're willing to pass our way.

As the Executive Editor for the Programming team at Macmillan Computer Publishing, I welcome your comments. You can fax, email, or write me directly to let me know what you did or didn't like about this book, as well as what we can do to make our books stronger.

Please note that I cannot help you with technical problems related to the topic of this book, and that, due to the high volume of mail I receive, I might not be able to reply to every message.

When you write, please be sure to include this book's title and author as well as your name and phone or fax number. I will carefully review your comments and share them with the author and editors who worked on the book.

Fax: 317-581-4770

E-mail: `feedback@samspublishing.com`

Mail: Michael Stephens
          Executive Editor
          Sams Publishing
          201 West 103rd Street
          Indianapolis, IN 46290 USA

Part I

Start Programming Today

Hour

Hour 1

Hands-on Programming with Liberty BASIC

You have this book because you want to go farther than the typical computer user. You don't just want to use computers; you want to write programs for them. You want the skills necessary to make computers do exactly what you want.

This 24-hour tutorial shows that you don't have to be a wizard to become a proficient (or even an expert) programmer. By the time you finish this one-hour lesson, you will have entered your first computer program, run it, and looked at the results. This chapter springboards you into programming so you can get a feel for programming right away. Once you've had this hands-on experience, subsequent hours will explain more of the background you need to understand how to design and write programs.

The highlights of this hour include:

- Learning what a program does
- Understanding the truth behind common programming myths

- Mastering source code concepts
- Using a compiler
- Entering and running your first program

Get Ready to Program

You'll find this hour divided into these two areas:

- An introduction to the nature of programming
- A hands-on practice with your first programming language

Most new programmers want to start programming right away. Yet, some background is necessary as well. This hour attempts to take care of both demands by offering an introductory background look at programming and then quickly jumping head-first into hands-on programming. If you went straight into a new programming language with absolutely no background first, you might miss the entire point of programming in the first place. So, the next few pages bring all readers up to a level playing field so that everyone who takes this 24-hour course can begin to write programs right away.

What a Computer Program Does

Most people today have some understanding of a computer's purpose. For example, a computer can help people balance their books or track their inventory. If you want to begin programming, chances are you have probably been using a computer for some time. Nevertheless, as a future programmer, you should review some fundamental computing concepts before mastering the ins and outs of a new computer language.

At its simplest level, a computer *processes data*. Figure 1.1 shows this as the primary goal of all computer programs. Many businesses call their computer programming departments *data processing departments* because computers process data into meaningful information. You may not have considered the difference between the words *data* and *information* before, but there is a tremendous difference to a computer professional. Raw data consists of facts and figures, such as hundreds of days of stock prices. A program might process that data into meaningful information, such as a line chart that shows the overall trend of the stock prices over time. It is the computer *program* that tells the computer what to do. Sometimes, a program might simply process data from another program without showing any output for the user. The processed data is still information because the program's output, stored on the disk, is changed in some way. For example, a program that closes monthly account balances may collect data from various accounting systems in a company and combine and balance and close that data, resetting the data for the following month.

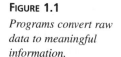

FIGURE 1.1

Programs convert raw data to meaningful information.

A *program* is a list of detailed instructions that the computer carries out. The program is the driving force behind any job that a computer does. The computer cannot do anything without a program. It is the job of the programmer to design and write programs that direct the computer to take raw data and transform that data into meaningful information for the end-user. The *end-user* (usually just called the *user*) of the computer is generally the nontechnical, nonprogramming person who needs the results (the information) that the program provides.

You, as the programmer, are responsible for guiding the computer with the programs you write. Learning to program computers takes a while, but it is certainly rewarding. Computer programming offers the advantage of instant feedback, unlike a lot of other jobs you can train for.

Common Programming Misconceptions

This text aims directly at the heart of the matter: Computers are easy to use and easy to program. A computer is nothing more than a dumb machine that "knows" absolutely nothing. You must supply the program that tells the computer what to do. A computer is like a robot that waits on your every command and acts out your instructions exactly as you give them. Sometimes your program instructions are incorrect. If they are, the computer goes right ahead and attempts them anyway.

> Don't fear computer programming. Computers are tools to help you get your job done. You can learn to program.

Many misconceptions about computers exist and stem from a lack of understanding about how computers work and what computers are physically capable of doing. This book wants to shoot down the myths and improve your understanding of these machines. You'll be programming computers in no time. The computer is nothing more than a tool that helps you do certain types of work. The computer itself is not bad or good. A hammer is a tool you can use for good (to build houses) or for bad (to break things). A computer in the wrong hands can be used for bad purposes, but that isn't the computer's fault any more than it is the hammer's fault if someone misuses it.

The next three sections attack the three most popular computer myths. Have you heard any of them? Did you think some were true?

Myth 1: Only Math Experts Can Program Computers

Thank goodness this is a myth and not reality—thousands of people would be out of work (including most computer book authors!). Computers would be elitist machines used by only the best engineers and scientists; the casual user could not master them. Computers would still be beneficial in some areas but they would not provide the benefits that so many people can enjoy.

Not only can you be poor at math—you don't even have to like math or have the desire to learn math to be a good computer programmer. The computer does all the math for you; that's one of its jobs. There are countless expert computer programmers in the world who cannot tell you the area of a circle or the square root of 64. Relax if you thought this myth was reality.

Programming can provide beneficial side effects. It turns out that, as you become a better programmer, you may find your math skills improving. Developing programming skills tends to improve your overall capability for logical thinking, which underlies many skills in math as well. Developing programming skills tends to improve your overall capability for logical thinking, which underlies many skills in math as well. Therefore, being better in math might be a result of programming but it's not a prerequisite.

> People who favor logic puzzles, crosswords, anagrams, and word-search games seem to adapt well to programming, but again, liking these gaming activities is not a programming prerequisite. You will find that you can learn to program computers, and actually become extremely good at it, without liking math, being good at math, or having any flair at all for puzzles or word games.

Myth 2: Computers Make Mistakes

You might have heard the adage, "To err is human, but to *really* foul things up takes a computer!" This might be accurate, but only in that a computer is so very fast that it duplicates a person's mistakes rapidly.

Computers do not make mistakes—people make mistakes. If you have heard a bank teller tell you that $24 was incorrectly deleted from your savings account because "the computer program made an error," the teller probably has no idea what really happened. People program computers, people run them, and people enter the data that the computer processes.

The odds of a computer randomly fouling up a customer's bank balance are minute. Computers simply do not make random mistakes unless they are programmed incorrectly.

Computers are finite machines; when given the same input, they always produce the same output. That is, computers always do the same things under the same conditions. Your job, as you learn to program, will be to reduce the chance of computer mistakes.

When a computer malfunctions it does not make a simple mistake; rather, it *really* messes things up. When a computer fails, it typically breaks down completely, or a storage device breaks down, or the power goes out. Whatever happens, computers go all out when they have a problem and it is usually very obvious when they have a problem. The good news is that computers rarely have problems.

Before people invented computers, banks kept all their records on ledger cards. When a teller found a mistake (possibly one that the teller had made), do you think the teller said, "The ledger card made a mistake"? Absolutely not. Computers can have mechanical problems, but the likelihood of small mistakes, such as an incorrect balance once in a while, is just too small to consider. Such mistakes are made by the people entering the data or by (gulp) the programmers.

Myth 3: Computers Are Difficult to Program

Computers are getting easier to use, and to program, every day. If you used a microwave or drove a car recently, then chances are good that you used a computer when you did. Yet, did you know you were using a computer? Probably not. The makers of computers have found ways to integrate computers into your everyday life to monitor and correct problems that might otherwise occur without them.

Of course, if you are reading this book, you want to learn enough about computers to write your own programs. Writing computer programs does take more work than using a microwave oven's computerized timer functions. The work, however, primarily involves getting down to the computer's level and learning what it expects.

Not only are computers getting easier to program every day, but you have more opportunities to learn about them than ever before. Cable television channels are loaded with educational shows about using and programming computers. Books and videos on the subject are all around you. The Internet itself contains scores of classes on all aspects of computers and other topics. There is probably a computer programming class now in session somewhere within 15 minutes of your house as you read this.

Many Programs Already Exist

Although there are many programs already written for you to use, sometimes you need a program that fills a specific need and you cannot find one that does exactly what you want. When you are done with this book, you will know exactly what you need to design and write your own programs.

Programmers Are in Demand

Look in your Sunday newspaper's help-wanted professional section. You'll find that there is a shortage of computer programmers. Amidst the requests for Java programmers, C++ programmers, Visual Basic programmers, systems analysts, senior systems analysts, object-oriented programmers, systems programmers, HTML coders, and application programmers, you may find yourself lost in a sea of uncertainty and *TLAs* (three-letter acronyms) that might, at first, seem hopeless. Do not fret; this book will help direct you toward areas of programming that might be right for you.

Hour 22's lesson, "How Companies Program," explores the chain of computer jobs and describes what each type of programming job is all about. If you are just starting out, you probably won't be able to go to work as the most senior-level programmer, but you will be surprised at the salary your programming skills can bring you.

The Real Value of Programs

Although individual computer programs are going down in price, companies and individual computer owners invest more and more in programs every year. Not only do people purchase new programs as they come out, but they update the older versions of programs they already have.

Businesses and individuals must factor in the cost of programs when making computer decisions. Whereas an individual usually buys a computer—called *hardware* because the machine isn't changed often or easily—and is done with the hardware purchasing for a while, the purchasing of programs—the *software*—never seems to end, because software changes rapidly. As a future programmer, this is welcome news because you have a secure career. For the uninformed computer purchaser, the cost of software can be staggering.

A business must also factor in the on-staff and contract programmers and the time needed to write the programs it uses. More information on the programming and support staff appears in the next section.

Users Generally Don't Own Programs

When a company purchases software, it most often purchases a *software license*. If a company wants to buy a word processing program for 100 employees, legally it must purchase 100 copies of the program, or at least buy a *site license* that allows the company to use the software on more than one machine. When a company buys a program, it does not own the program. When you buy a record, you do not own the music; you have only purchased the rights to listen to the music. You cannot legally alter the music,

1

record it, give away recordings of it, and most importantly, you cannot sell recordings that you make of it. The same is true for software that you buy. The license for individual software grants you permission to use the software on one computer at any one time.

Giving Computers Programs

Figure 1.2 shows a computer screen with a computer program in the center. As a matter of fact, this is the program you will be entering into the Liberty BASIC programming system very soon. Liberty BASIC is a programming system that enables you to create programs and run them using a simple Windows interface with menus and help files available. Liberty BASIC is based on an introductory programming language named BASIC which stands for *Beginner's All-purpose Symbolic Instruction Code*. Notice that the program is composed of lines of words somewhat like text in English. These are the program instructions. Although you will recognize many of the words in the program, the use of those words is somewhat cryptic. The words have special, specific meanings in the Liberty BASIC programming language.

FIGURE 1.2

A program's instructions are somewhat cryptic, but readable by people.

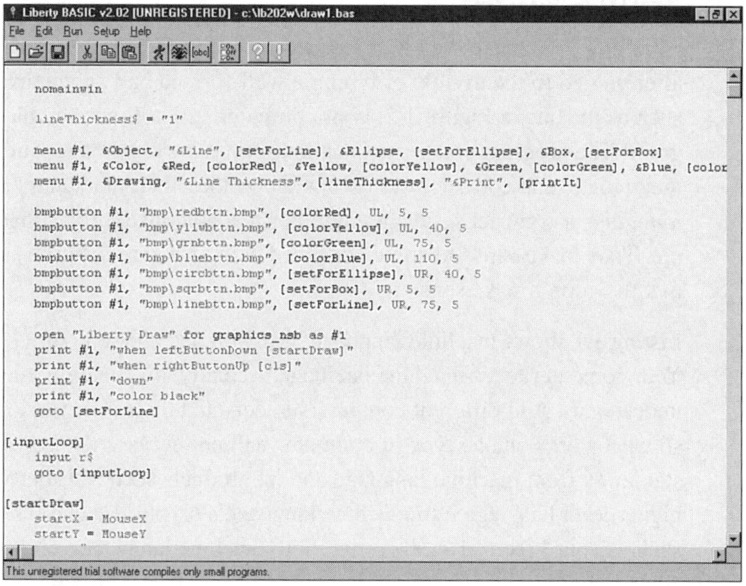

```
Liberty BASIC v2.02 [UNREGISTERED] - c:\lb202w\draw1.bas

File  Edit  Run  Setup  Help

    nomainwin

    lineThickness$ = "1"

    menu #1, &Object, "&Line", [setForLine], &Ellipse, [setForEllipse], &Box, [setForBox]
    menu #1, &Color, &Red, [colorRed], &Yellow, [colorYellow], &Green, [colorGreen], &Blue, [color
    menu #1, &Drawing, "&Line Thickness", [lineThickness], "&Print", [printIt]

    bmpbutton #1, "bmp\redbttn.bmp", [colorRed], UL, 5, 5
    bmpbutton #1, "bmp\yllwbttn.bmp", [colorYellow], UL, 40, 5
    bmpbutton #1, "bmp\grnbttn.bmp", [colorGreen], UL, 75, 5
    bmpbutton #1, "bmp\bluebttn.bmp", [colorBlue], UL, 110, 5
    bmpbutton #1, "bmp\circbttn.bmp", [setForEllipse], UR, 40, 5
    bmpbutton #1, "bmp\sqrbttn.bmp", [setForBox], UR, 5, 5
    bmpbutton #1, "bmp\linebttn.bmp", [setForLine], UR, 75, 5

    open "Liberty Draw" for graphics_nsb as #1
    print #1, "when leftButtonDown [startDraw]"
    print #1, "when rightButtonUp [cls]"
    print #1, "down"
    print #1, "color black"
    goto [setForLine]

[inputLoop]
    input r$
    goto [inputLoop]

[startDraw]
    startX = MouseX
    startY = MouseY
```

This unregistered trial software compiles only small programs.

A computer is only a machine. To give a machine instructions, your instructions might be fairly readable, as Figure 1.2's are, but the *code* (another name for a program's instructions) must be fairly rigid and conform to a predefined set of rules and regulations according to the programming language you use. Therefore, to write a program in the Liberty BASIC programming language, you must conform to Liberty BASIC's rules of proper command spelling and placement. This programming language grammar is called *syntax*. (And you thought syntax was just a levy placed on cigarettes and liquor!)

Although Figure 1.2's program listing is comprised of text, many programs rely on both text commands as well as graphic elements such as commandbuttons, scroll bars, and other Windows controls. The text part of a program can control these visual elements. You'll see how the visual elements work with the text program as you learn more about programming throughout this 24-hour tutorial.

Liberty BASIC programs are based on the BASIC programming language, which has been around for 40 years. Visual Basic, one of the most popular languages used today, is also based on BASIC. When you learn Liberty BASIC in this tutorial, you will be well on your way to knowing Visual Basic. As a matter of fact, the more of any programming language you learn, the more easily you will be able to learn a completely different language. Although computer languages have different goals, syntaxes, and reasons for being, they are often similar in structure.

Source Code

Even after you make the effort to learn a computer language such as Liberty BASIC, and after you go to the trouble of typing a well-formed and syntactically accurate program such as the one in Figure 1.2, your computer still will not be able to understand the program! The program you write is called *source code*. It is the source code that you write, manipulate, and correct. Your computer, on the other hand, can understand only *machine language*, a compact series of computer-readable instructions that make no sense to people. They make sense to some advanced computer gurus, but my general assertion stands that they don't make sense to people.

Listing 1.1 shows machine language. Can you decipher any of it? Your computer can. Your computer loves machine language. Actually, it's the only language your computer understands. And different computers understand their own version of a machine language so what works on one type of computer will not necessarily work on another. It's best to stay away from machine language and let products such as Liberty BASIC convert your higher-level language into machine language's cryptic 1's and 0's. To convert source code such as your Liberty BASIC program to machine language you need a *compiler*.

LISTING 1.1   Machine Language Is Extremely Difficult for People to Decipher.

```
01100100
10111101
10010011
10010100
00001111
01010101
11111110
```

All programs you run on your computer, including Microsoft Word, Internet Explorer, and even Liberty BASIC, are already converted into machine language. That's why you can click a program's icon and the program begins immediately. No compilation is required. By providing you with the machine language only, software vendors serve two purposes:

1. They give you programs that execute quickly without the intervening compiling step.
2. They ensure that you don't change the source code, thereby protecting their intellectual property.

The Compiler

A compiler converts human-readable source code, formed from a programming language you want to use, into machine language that your computer understands and can respond to. Given that a program is a set of instructions that tells the computer what to do, it's vital that you eventually get your program into the language of the machine. The compiler does just that.

You will need to select a compiler that understands the language you want to program in. With this book you'll get a Liberty BASIC compiler that converts your Liberty BASIC source code into machine language. You'll also get a Java compiler, which runs your Java source code after converting the code to an executable format. If you wanted to write a program in the C++ language you will need to locate a C++ compiler, which converts any C++ programs you write to machine language.

The bottom line is, you select whatever programming language you want to learn and write. The compiler for that language ensures that the programs you write are converted to the computer's machine language so the computer can understand and execute your program.

Your First Program

If you have not yet installed Liberty BASIC, take a moment to do so. Once you've installed the Liberty BASIC language and compiler, you'll be ready to complete this hour.

The first program that you write will be simple. You may not understand much of it, and that's fine. The goal here is not to explain the program details, but to walk you through the entire process of the steps that are typical of computer programming:

1. Type a program's source code and save it.

2. Compile the source code into machine language.

3. Run the program, which is now in machine language, and see what happens.

4. If the program has errors, called *bugs*, you'll need to fix those bugs in your source code and repeat these steps starting at Step 2. Hour 7, "Debugging Tools," explains how to locate and fix common bugs. You may need to do some bug hunting earlier than Hour 7 if you experience problems with your programs in these first few hours. If a program does not work as described, you will need to compare your source code very carefully to the code in the book and fix any discrepancies before recompiling.

Start Liberty BASIC

You will write your Liberty BASIC source code inside the Liberty BASIC system, which you should have installed. Liberty BASIC, like most programming languages these days, includes not only a compiler but also a *program editor* (often just called an *editor*). A program editor is a lot like a simple word processor. You type and correct your source code inside the editor.

Unlike word processors, your editor will not wrap the end of a line down to the subsequent line. It's important that programming instructions (called *statements*) remain separate and stay on their own lines in many cases. Even if a programming language allows multiple program statements per line, you'll find that your programs are more readable and easier to debug if you keep your statements one per line. Sometimes, a single statement can get lengthy and you may span long statements over two or three lines, but rarely would you want multiple statements to appear on the same line.

To start Liberty BASIC, follow these steps:

1. Click your Windows Start button.

2. From the Programs (or All Programs if you use Windows XP) menu, select the entry for Liberty BASIC v2.02.

3. Select the menu entry for Liberty BASIC v2.02 and the screen shown in Figure 1.3 appears.

FIGURE **1.3**

Liberty BASIC first displays a welcome screen that describes Liberty BASIC.

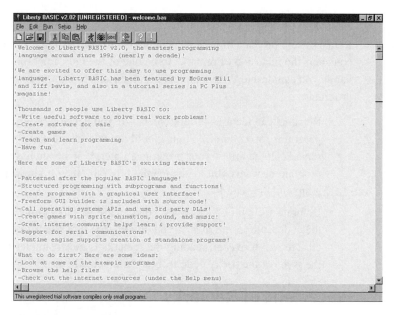

Remarkable Remarks

Your screen and Figure 1.3 show not only Liberty BASIC's opening screen, but also the Liberty BASIC program editor. As a matter of fact, the lengthy text that you see inside the editor is a valid Liberty BASIC program written in the BASIC programming language. Sure, it looks like written text and does not look like programming code, but you'll notice that each line begins with an apostrophe, '.

Lines beginning with apostrophes in Liberty BASIC are called *remarks*. All languages support remarks, which are also called *comments*, although not all languages use the apostrophe. Although you'll find many remarks in programs, and you'll put many remarks in the programs you write, remarks are not for the compiler or for the computer. Remarks are for people. In Liberty BASIC, for example, the compiler ignores all text to the right of the apostrophes. The computer knows that remarks are for you and not for it.

You can use the keyword Rem in place of any apostrophe appearing at the start of a line. Rem is an equivalent synonym for the apostrophe in BASIC-like languages.

Reasons for Remarks

Remarks help produce more understandable program listings. The programming industry considers the inclusion of remarks to be one of the most important of good programming habits you can develop. Here are common reasons programmers put remarks in their programs:

- Remarks can identify programmers—If you develop programs with others or write programs for a company, you should put your name and contact information in remarks at the top of your programs. Later, if someone has a question about the program or wants you to change the program, they'll know that you wrote the program and they can locate you.

- Before a section of tricky code you can use remarks to include your explanation of the code's purpose. Later, if you or someone else needs to change the program, the change will be easier; reading the remarks is much simpler than trying to figure out the goals of the tricky code from uncommented code.

Placement of Remarks

As long as you use an apostrophe rather than the Rem keyword to signal a remark, remarks can appear on the same line as code. The following code shows remarks to the right of lines of other program instructions. Notice that apostrophes precede the remark text. These remarks explain what each line of code does.

```
if hours > 12 then     ' Test the hour for AM/PM indicator
   hours = hours - 12  ' Convert 24-hour time to 12-hour
   amOrPm$ = "PM"       ' Set indicator that will print
```

Look once again at your Liberty BASIC editor. The three lines at the bottom of the editor contain executable commands that are not remarks but programming instructions. The remarks are the easy part. Learning to create and use the executable commands is the challenge before you.

Most programming languages are *free-form*, meaning that you can indent lines and add as many spaces and blank lines as you like. Doing so makes a program more readable. In Hour 7, "Debugging Tools," you'll learn how to use this *whitespace* (extra spaces and lines in code) to improve your programs' readability by separating one program section from another and, thereby, making it easier for programmers to understand your code.

Sure, as a programmer, you will often understand code without the need to put a remark to the right of each line. But at the time you write a program, the program is clearest to you. When you later go back to edit a program, what may have been clear before is no longer clear because time has passed. A few remarks will go a long way toward reminding you of your original intent.

However, do not overdo remarks. Some remarks are redundant, as the following shows:

```
Print "Martha"    ' Prints the word Martha
```

Such a remark is not helpful and serves only to cloud an already-understandable instruction. Don't overuse remarks, but use them generously when needed to clarify your code.

Loading a Sample Program

Instead of typing a program from your keyboard, first take a few moments to load an existing example program that comes with Liberty BASIC. Remember that to run a program you must enter (from the keyboard or disk) source code and then compile and run that code. All Liberty BASIC programs, like most programs written in languages derived from BASIC, use the filename extension .BAS or .bas for source code files.

> Liberty BASIC hides the compilation step from you somewhat. Once you get a source code program into the Liberty BASIC editor, either by typing the code or loading the code from disk, you can then run that program from Liberty BASIC's menus. When you run the program, Liberty BASIC quickly compiles the code and begins executing the resulting machine language.

Follow these steps to load your first program into Liberty BASIC:

1. Select File, Open.
2. Select draw1.bas and click OK. The source code located in the draw1.bas file will appear in the Liberty BASIC editor. Now that the program resides in the editor, you could make changes to the source code here if you wanted to—even though you loaded a program that someone else wrote. One advantage to source code, unlike the compiled machine language code, is that you can change the source code and run the program to see the results. Until you become more familiar with the language, do not change the program.

3. Select Run from the menu named Run. You can also press Shift+F5 or click the toolbar's Run button (it has a bank robber on it running) to choose this option. Liberty BASIC compiles the program and runs it in one step. When you write your own programs, if errors reside in the program, Liberty BASIC will tell you about the errors and will not be able to finish the compilation until you fix the errors.

4. To draw a line, click the line icon. To draw a circle or square, click one of those icons. To complete the drawing of a square or circle, click and hold your mouse button while moving your mouse. When you release your mouse button, the circle or square will appear.

5. Click a different color and draw more circles, squares, and lines. Your drawing will begin to take on a life of its own, not unlike the one in Figure 1.4.

FIGURE 1.4

You're running a program that you loaded and compiled.

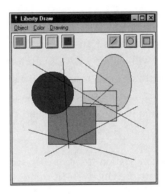

To stop the program, click the drawing window's Close button.

Entering Your Own Program

You're now ready to type and run your own program from scratch. The program will be simple. No color graphics like the ones in the drawing program you ran in the previous section. The goal here is to get you used to using the editor.

Follow these steps to enter and run your own program:

1. Select File and then New File to clear the source code window and prepare the editor for a new program.

2. Type the program in Listing 1.2 into the editor. Be careful that you type the program exactly as you see it in the listing. If you make a typing mistake, you will not

be able to run the program. The program is intentionally simple and easy to type. Notice the second line is nothing but an empty remark.

LISTING 1.2   Type Your First Program Into the Editor.

```
' Filename: First.bas
'
' Prints a countdown from 10 to 1
For i = 10 To 1 Step -1
  Print i
Next i
Print "Blast Off!"
End
```

3. Press Shift+F5 to compile and run the program. You should see the output window shown in Figure 1.5.

FIGURE 1.5

The results of your first program are impressive! Where did those numbers come from?

At this point, it might seem as though the program took quite a bit of work just to print 10 numbers in the window and a closing message. To give you a taste of the power of programming, if you change the number 1 in the fourth line to 10000, that one simple change is enough (when you rerun the program) to print numbers from 10,000 down to 1.

If your program contained an error, you would not be able to run the program. When you press Shift+F5, Liberty BASIC would refuse to run the program and would highlight the offending line. Figure 1.6 shows a source code window that highlights a line with the command Print misspelled.

FIGURE 1.6

*This compiler will let
you know which line
has a problem.*

Error on This Line

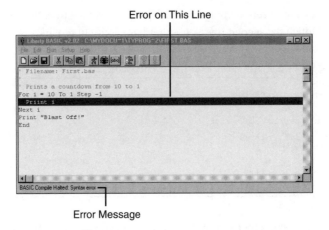

Error Message

Save your program under the filename First.bas by selecting File, Save, and typing the
filename. When you click OK, Liberty BASIC saves your first program.

You can find the First.bas program, as well as all other source code in this
24-hour tutorial, on this book's CD-ROM.

Summary

Now that you know a bit more about the computer industry as a whole, you have a better
idea of where programmers fit into the picture. Computers can do nothing without programs and programmers are responsible for providing those programs.

You already got a taste of programming this hour by starting Liberty BASIC and running
a couple of programs. Liberty BASIC includes several sample programs, such as the
draw1.bas program you ran. As you saw by typing your own program into the editor,
entering and running a program is not painful at all. As a matter of fact, the quick feedback that programming offers is a rewarding experience. Programmers often like their
profession very much because they can see the results of their work quickly.

Q&A

Q Once I write a program, is my job finished?

A It is said that a program is written once and modified many times. Throughout this
24-hour tutorial, you will learn the importance of maintaining a program after it is

written. As businesses change and computing environments improve, the programs that people use must improve as well. Companies provide upgrades to software as new features are needed. The programs that you write today will have to change in the future to keep up with the competition as well as with new features that your users require.

Q Why do I need a compiler to run the programs I write?

A You will write programs in a programming language, such as Liberty BASIC. Your computer does not understand programming languages, however. That's why you need a compiler to convert the programming language's code to machine language. A machine language program is your program's instructions compiled to a language your computer can understand.

Workshop

The quiz questions are provided for your further understanding. See Appendix B, "Quiz Answers," for answers to these questions.

Quiz

1. What is the difference between data and information?

2. What is a program?

3. What is a programming language?

4. True or false: Computers never make mistakes.

5. Why should people not fear the computer replacing their jobs?

6. What do programmers use editors for?

7. What is Liberty BASIC doing automatically when you run a program you've entered?

8. True or false: The output appears in a separate window when you run your source program.

9. What does Liberty BASIC do when you attempt to run a program that contains a bug?

10. What filename extension is used for all Liberty BASIC (and most other cousins of the BASIC language)?

HOUR 2

Process and Techniques

The words *program* and *programmer* are mentioned throughout each of these 24 lessons and you've undoubtedly heard them before you picked up this book. Before going back into specifics of Liberty BASIC and other programming languages, this hour explains what a program really is. A firm grasp of this hour's material is a prerequisite for moving on to the more advanced programming concepts that appear throughout this book.

As you read this hour's lesson, keep in mind that programming is rewarding, not only financially, but also mentally and emotionally. Programmers often feel the same sense of creative rush that artists and skilled craftspeople feel while honing their projects. Writing a program, however, can be tedious. It is often a detailed task and ample frustration comes with the territory. The computer's quick feedback on your mistakes and results, however, often provides a sense of accomplishment that keeps you programming until you get it right.

The highlights of this hour include

- Directing the computer with programs
- Detailing programs enough so that a computer can follow the instructions
- Executing programs in memory rather than from the disk drive

- Looking at whether programming is an art or science
- Learning why computers cannot yet understand a human language

Understanding the Need for Programs

When individuals and companies need a program, they can obtain it in one of three ways:

- Buy a program that's already written
- Buy a program and modify it so that the customized version does exactly what they need
- Write their own program

There are advantages and disadvantages to each option (see Table 2.1). The first two options are much quicker than the third and also are much less expensive.

TABLE 2.1   Advantages and Disadvantages of Obtaining Programs

Option	Advantages	Disadvantages
Buy	The program can be obtained quickly and inexpensively.	The program may not be exactly what is needed.
Buy and customize	A usable program that does what is needed can be obtained fairly quickly. Also, the program is relatively inexpensive, depending on the changes needed.	It isn't always possible to modify the program.
Write	The program (after proper design and testing) does exactly what you want it to do.	This option can be very expensive and takes a lot longer than the other options.

Most computer users (of both PCs and Macs) choose the first option because the programs are fairly inexpensive given their power. Because companies such as Intuit, Microsoft, and Symantec sell so many of the same programs, they can do so at reasonable prices. Individual computer users simply don't have the resources that companies have to write the many programs they need.

Companies, on the other hand, do not always choose the first option, although you may question why. The reason is that companies spend many years developing products and services to distinguish themselves from other companies, and they learn to keep records in specific ways so that they can manage those services effectively. When a company computerizes any of its record keeping, it is vital that new programs reflect exactly what the company already does. The company should not have to change the way it does business just so it can use programs found in stores or in mail-order software outlets. On the other hand, programs that can be purchased off the shelf have to be generic so that the producers of the programs can sell them to more than one customer. The second option—buy a program and customize it—might seem like the smartest option, but it is chosen least often. If companies could buy a program that is already written they would have a framework in which to quickly adapt the program to their specific needs. The problem is that software is rarely sold, as you learned in the previous hour; software is *licensed*. When you buy a program, you do not own the program; you only own the right to use it. You often cannot legally change it, sell it, or copy it (except for backup purposes). Some software does come with the license to revise the code but most software that you purchase off the shelf does not allow the modification of code.

Not only are there legalities involved, but also sometimes you cannot physically change the software. Programs come in two formats:

- Source code, such as the Liberty BASIC program you created in the previous hour
- Compiled, executable code, such as what you get when you run a program from the Liberty BASIC system

Once a program is written and compiled, programmers can no longer modify the program. Programs that are sold in stores do not usually include the source code. Therefore, companies cannot modify the programs they buy to make the program conform to their specific business. (Of course, programs that you write and compile, you can modify and re-compile because you will have access to your source code.)

So although it is expensive and time-consuming to write programs from scratch, many businesses prefer to do so, keeping large programming departments on hand to handle the programming load. A company might have several members of its data processing staff spend a full year writing a program that is close, but not identical, to one that the company could buy. Companies also might utilize contract programmers for specific projects.

Despite the cost and effort involved, it is worth it to some companies not to have to conform to a program they buy from someone else. The program, once written, conforms to the company's way of doing business.

2

Some companies have found that they can sell programs they develop to other firms doing similar business thereby recapturing some of their development costs. As you write programs for your company or for individuals, keep in mind the possible subsequent sale of your program to others.

Companies often measure the amount of time it takes to write programs in *people years*. If it takes two people years to write a single program, it is estimated that two people could write it in a single year, or one person would take two years. A 20-people-year project would take 20 people one year, or one person 20 years, or 10 people two years, and so forth. This measurement is only an estimate, but it gives management an idea of how it should allocate people and time for programming projects.

If you become a contract programmer, the people-year measurement is a great tool to use when pricing your service. You might give a customer an estimate of the price per people year (or, for smaller projects, perhaps you would estimate the job in people months or weeks). If you hire programmers to help you finish the program, you may finish early but you can still charge fairly for each person's labor due to the fact that you priced the programming job in people years and not in calendar time.

Recently, a lot of attention has been given to the mythical people years. Critics of this measurement state that computer firms do not generally estimate people-year measurements properly and that such a measurement is rarely meaningful. That may be, but just because people misuse the measurement does not make the measurement a bad way to gauge a project's completion when it is estimated correctly.

Programs, Programs, Everywhere

Why aren't all the programs ever needed already written? Walk into any software store today and you'll see hundreds of programs for sale. There are programs for everything: word processing, accounting, drawing, playing games, designing homes, going online, and planning and creating trip itineraries. It seems as if any program you need is within reach. Because computers have been around for 50 years, you would think that everybody would be about done with all the programming anyone would need for a long time.

To make matters worse, many Web sites contain thousands of programs you can download and run. Some of these programs are free and some are for sale. A quick look using a software search engine for software and shareware can produce countless sites filled to the brim with programs you can download.

> *Shareware* is a term applied to software you can download from the Internet and use free for an unlimited time or a limited time depending on the license. Sometimes, a shareware author will make the source code available so you can modify the program and customize it for your own use. You must have the right compiler, however, before you can customize software. For example, if a shareware program is written in C++, then you cannot use Java or Liberty BASIC to change the code. You must always use a compiler for the programming language you need to change.

If all the programs needed were already written, you would not see the large listings of "Programmer Wanted" ads in today's newspapers and on job listing Web sites. The fact is that the world is changing every day, and businesses and people must change with it. Programs written 10 years ago are not up-to-date with today's practices. Also, they were written on computers much slower and more limited than today's machines. For example, companies often want today's programs to interact with the Web so remote users in other company divisions can access data from headquarters. As hardware advances are made, the software must advance with it.

There is a tremendous need for good programmers, today more than ever. As computers become easier to use, some people believe that programmers will become relics of the past. What they fail to realize is that it takes top-notch programmers to produce those easy-to-use programs. More importantly it takes programmers to modify and improve upon the vast libraries of programs in use today. Even with economic slumps, the world is becoming more digitized daily and the demand for programmers will see an average increase as more people use computers more often.

Programs as Directions

If you have ever followed a map into unfamiliar territory, you know what it is like for your computer to follow a program's instructions. With only the map, you feel blind as you move from place to place, turning left and right, until you reach your destination or find that you made a wrong turn somewhere. Your computer, as the previous hour explained, is a blind and dumb machine waiting for you to give it directions. When you do, the computer acts out the instructions you give it without second-guessing your desires. If you tell your PC to do something incorrectly, it does its best to do so. Recall this definition of a program (from Hour 1):

   A program is a list of detailed instructions that the computer carries out.

The term *detailed* in the previous definition is vital to making a machine follow your orders. Actually, the job of programming is not difficult; what is difficult is breaking the computer's job into simple and detailed steps that assume nothing.

Practice with Detailing Your Instructions

To get an idea of the thinking involved in programming, consider how you would describe starting a car to someone from the past. Suppose a cowboy named Heath, from the Old West, appears at your doorstep bewildered by the sights around him. After getting over the future shock, Heath wants to adapt to this new world. Before learning to drive your car Heath must first learn to start it. When he is comfortable doing that you will teach him to drive. Unlike a 16-year-old learning to drive, Heath has not grown up seeing adults starting cars so he really needs to master this process before going any further. Being the busy programmer you are, you leave him the following set of instructions taped to the car key:

1. Use this key.
2. Start the car.

How far would Heath get? Not very far. You gave correct instructions for starting a car but you assumed too much knowledge on his part. You must remember that he knows nothing about these contraptions called automobiles and he is relying on you to give him instructions that he can understand. Instead of assuming so much these might be better instructions:

1. Attached is the key to the car. You need it to start the car.
2. With the key in hand, go to the car door that is closest to the front door of our home.
3. Under the door's black handle you will see a round silver-dollar-sized metal place into which you can insert the key (with its rough edge pointing down).
4. After sticking the key into the hole as far as it will go, turn it to the right until you hear a click.
5. Turn the key back to the left until it faces the same way as it did when you inserted it, and remove the key.
6. Pull up on the black handle to open the door and get into the car. Be sure to sit in front of the round wheel (called a *steering wheel*) on the left-hand side of the front seat.
7. Close the door.
8. On the right side of the column holding the steering wheel, you will see a slot in which you can put the key.

Are you beginning to get the idea? This list of eight items is very detailed, and Heath hasn't even started the car yet. You still have to describe the gas pedal that he might have to press while he turns the key, in the correct direction of çourse. You also don't want to assume that Heath will turn *off* the car when he is done practicing, so you have to give him those directions as well. (Perhaps you should also warn your neighbors to stay off the streets for a while!)

If you are beginning to think this car-starting analogy is going a little too far, consider what you must do to tell a nonthinking piece of electronic equipment—a computer—to perform your company's payroll. A payroll program cannot consist of only the following steps:

1. Get the payroll data.
2. Calculate the payroll and taxes.
3. Print the checks.

To the computer, these instructions lack thousands of details that you might take for granted. It is the detailing of the program's instructions that provides for the tedium and occasional frustration of programming. Programming computers isn't difficult but breaking down real-world problems into lots of detailed steps that a computer can understand is hard.

A typical payroll program might contain 20,000 or more lines of instructions. Don't let this deter you from learning to program, however. Large programming projects are written by teams of programmers; you will have plenty of help if you ever write such programs for a living. Also, new programming techniques and programming environments for today's computer languages make programming, even for the individual programmer working alone, much easier than ever before.

Closer to Home: A Liberty BASIC Example

Consider the program output window shown in Figure 2.1. A Liberty BASIC program produced this output.

FIGURE 2.1

It takes detailed instructions to produce simple output.

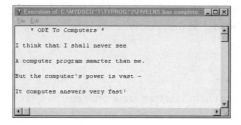

What does it take to produce the five simple lines of output? It takes detailed instructions in the Liberty BASIC programming language. The computer cannot read your mind to know what you want. You must specifically tell Liberty BASIC to print those five lines and even tell Liberty BASIC that you want a blank line between each of them. Listing 2.1 shows the program that produced this output window.

LISTING 2.1 You Must Supply Detailed Instructions When You Want the Computer to Do Something.

```
' Filename: FiveLns.bas
'
' Prints five lines to the output window
Print "    * ODE To Computers *"
Print " "
Print "I think that I shall never see"
Print " "
Print "A computer program smarter than me."
Print " "
Print "But the computer's power is vast -"
Print " "
Print "It computes answers very fast!"
End
```

Even though you don't yet know the Liberty BASIC programming language, you've got to admit that the program in Listing 2.1 is rather simple to understand. Nine `Print` statements tell the computer to print nine lines of output, four of which are blank. All Liberty BASIC program output from the `Print` statement goes to the output window unless you reroute the output to another location such as a disk file.

> The `End` statement is optional, but most programmers supply `End` so there is no doubt as to where the programmer intended the program to end.

Sure, if you want to see the words in Figure 2.1, all you need to do is start WordPad or some other word processor and type the text into the document window. Nevertheless, a lot of programming work went into that word processor to allow you to put text in the document so easily. The idea in these early hours is to focus on creating programs that produce results.

Tools That Help

Many design tools exist to help you take large problems and break them down into detailed components that translate into programming elements. Hour 3, "Designing a Program," explains many of the methods that programmers use to get to a program's needed details. You'll find that programming is simple as long as you approach it systematically, as this text attempts to do. By combining theory with as much early, hands-on examples as possible, you'll understand what you're doing and learn how to program faster. If programming were truly difficult, there is no way so many computer advances could have been made over the last 50 years.

Programs Are Saved Instructions

The nice thing about programs you write is that you save them to disk after you write them. As with word-processed text, you store the programs you write in disk files as you did in the previous hour's lesson with the First.bas program. A program is to a computer as a recipe is to a cook. When a cook wants to make a certain dish, he or she finds the correct recipe and follows the instructions. When someone wants to execute a program, she or he instructs the computer to load the program from disk into memory and then run the program's instructions.

The computer's internal memory is vital for holding program execution. Your computer's CPU cannot execute a program's instructions directly from the disk. Just as you cannot know what is in a book lying on a table until you read the book's contents into your memory (using your own CPU—your mind), your CPU cannot process a program's instructions until it loads the program from disk into main memory. Figure 2.2 shows the process of loading a program from the computer's disk (or disklike storage such as a CD-ROM) into memory. As the figure shows, the CPU has direct access to memory but has no access to the disk drive. The disk is the long-term storage, and the memory is the short-term storage, where programs temporarily reside while the CPU executes them.

FIGURE 2.2

A program must be in memory before the CPU can execute the program's instructions.

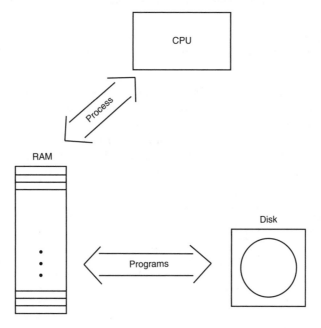

2

As you already know, the program differs greatly from the output itself. The program is a set of instructions and the *output* is the result of those instructions. A recipe's output is the finished dish and the program's output is the printed output once the instructions are running.

Perhaps a specific example will further clarify what it means to a programmer for a user to use a program. If you use a word processor, then you probably follow steps similar to these:

1. You load the word processing program from the disk into the computer's main memory. When you select the word processing program's name from the menu or select the word processor's Windows icon, you are instructing the computer to search the disk drive for the program and load it into main memory.

2. What you see onscreen is output from the program. You can produce more output by typing text on the screen. Everything that appears onscreen throughout the program's execution is program output.

3. After you type text, you may interact with other devices. You will probably issue a command to print the document (more than likely using the standard Windows File, Print menu option) to the printer and save the document in a data file on the disk.

4. When you exit the word processor, your operating system regains control. The word processing program is no longer in memory, but it is still safely tucked away on disk.

As you can see, the results of a program's execution make up the output. The instructions themselves are what produce those results. Figure 2.3 gives an overview of the program-to-output process. Modern-day programs produce output in many different ways. Programs play music, talk to other computers over the phone lines, and control external devices. Output sent to the screen and printer still makes up the majority of today's program output.

FIGURE 2.3

The program comes from disk, executes, and then sends its results to any of the many output devices, such as the disk, screen, or printer (or more than one of them from within the same program).

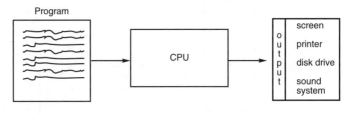

When a program is in memory, it is not there alone. Your operating system always resides in memory. If it did not, you could neither load a program from disk nor run it because the operating system itself is what actually loads programs to and from memory when you issue the correct command. Limited memory often poses a problem for larger programs. Recall that a program processes data and the data and the program must be in memory before the program can easily process the data.

Figure 2.4 shows what a typical computer installation's memory looks like when a program is running. The operating system takes a big chunk, the program must be there too, and finally there must be room for data.

2

FIGURE 2.4

A typical memory layout shows that the operating system shares memory with executing programs.

The more memory your PC has, the faster your programs run. The extra memory means that the operating system will have to swap less to and from disk as the program operates. Some programs are even contained in memory in their entirety the whole time that the program runs. As a programmer, you should run with ample memory, as much as 256MB or 512MB, so that you can properly test your running programs while still keeping your programming environment loaded.

Art or Science?

A debate that you often see in computer literature is whether programming is an art or a science. Through the years, there have been advances made in programming that, if followed, improve a program's accuracy, readability, and *maintainability* (the process of changing the program later to perform a different or additional set of tasks). Most of these advances are nothing more than suggestions; that is, programmers don't have to use them to write programs that work.

Two of the most important advances in programming have been more philosophically based than engineered. They are *structured programming* and *object-oriented programming*. This book explores these two programming advances thoroughly in the hours that follow. They both offer ways that a programmer can write a program to make it better. Again, though, these are just suggested approaches to programming; programmers can (and many do) ignore them.

There are many ways to write even the smallest and simplest programs. Just as authors write differently and musicians play differently, programmers each have a unique style. Therefore, you would think that programming is more of an art than a science. On the continuum of science to art, you would be closer to being correct than those few who argue that programming is more of a science.

Nevertheless, as more advances are made in developing programming approaches, as has already been done with structured programming and object-oriented programming, you should see a shift in thinking. With the proliferation of computers in today's world there is a massive educational effort in process to train tomorrow's programmers. Because programming is still a young industry, many advances are still left to be made.

Some of the biggest proponents of moving away from the artful approach to a more scientific approach, using structured and object-oriented programming, are the companies paying the programmers. Companies need to react quickly to changing business conditions, and they need programs written as quickly and as accurately as possible. As advances in computer programming are discovered, more companies are going to adopt policies that require their programmers to use more scientific and time-proven methods of writing better programs.

Speak the Language

The instructions you give in your programs must be in a language the computer understands, which as you learned from Hour 1 is machine language. At its lowest level, a computer is nothing more than thousands of switches flipping on and off lightning fast. A switch can have only one of two states; it can be *on* or *off*. Because either of these two states of electricity can be controlled easily with switches, many thousands of them control what your computer does from one microsecond to another.

If it were up to your computer, you would have to give it instructions using switches that represent on and off states of electricity. Actually, that is exactly the way that programmers programmed the early computers. A panel of switches, such as the one shown in Figure 2.5, had to be used to enter all programs and data. The next time you find yourself cursing errors that appear in programs you write, think of what it would have been like programming 50 years ago.

FIGURE 2.5

Programmers used a panel of switches to program early computers.

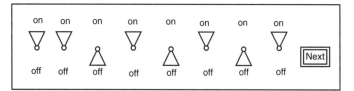

The on and off states of electricity are represented as 1s and 0s at the computer's lowest level. This representation has a name: *binary*. You can control what your computer does if you know the correct pattern of 1s and 0s required to give it commands. You can program a computer simply by issuing 1s and 0s if you have the correct system tools. Of course, programming in the binary digits of 1s and 0s is not much better than flipping up and down switches on the switch panel, so there has to be a better way.

Computers are not going to learn a human's spoken language any time soon, despite what you might see in science fiction movies. You have to learn a programming language if you want the computer to do what you want, and you must compile that language into machine language.

Computers Cannot Handle Ambiguity

Spoken languages are too ambiguous to computers. People's brains can decipher sentences intuitively, something a nonthinking machine cannot do. There are some inroads being made into *artificial intelligence*, which is the science of programming computers so that they can learn on their own. It also includes programming them to understand a spoken language such as English. Despite recent advancements, artificial intelligence is many years away (if it is even possible for computers to understand simple English commands).

Consider the following sentence:

Time flies like an arrow.

Your mind has no trouble understanding the parts of this sentence. You know that it is an analogy, and the parts of speech make total sense to you. *Time* is a noun that performs an action: it *flies*, and it does so *like an arrow*. If you teach the computer to accept these descriptions of this sentence, it will work fine until it runs into something like this:

Fruit flies like an orange.

Think about this for a moment. Again, you have no problem understanding this sentence, even though it is completely different from the other one. The computer taught to decipher the first sentence, however, is going to throw its cables up in frustration at the second sentence because none of the parts of the sentence are the same. The word *flies* is now a noun and not an action verb. The phrase *like an orange* is no longer a description of the action, but rather both the verb (*like*) and the object receiving the action (*an orange*). As you can see from these two sentences alone understanding simple sentences that most people take for granted poses a tremendous problem for programmers trying to "teach" a computer to understand a language such as English.

Here's another example.

> *The pop can has a lid.*

Computers have extreme problems with statements such as this one because the sentence appears to have a subject-verb agreement problem. Does the sentence state that the can of pop has a lid or that the pop can have a lid? If it's the latter, then *has* should be *have*. The human mind can easily distinguish these problems and knows that the can of pop has a lid, but given today's technology, machines simply cannot easily do so.

Therefore, computers and people are at opposite ends of the spectrum. People want to speak their own language but computers want to stick to their language comprised of 1s and 0s. There has to be some kind of go-between. Programming languages were created to try to appease both the computer and the person programming the computer. You've seen from Liberty BASIC that programming languages use words similar to those that people use, but programming languages have a highly specific syntax that allows little room for the ambiguity that is so prevalent in spoken languages. The computer can take a programming language and translate it to its machine language of 1s and 0s; the human programmer can learn, remember, and use the programming languages more effectively than 1s and 0s because programming languages appear similar to spoken languages, although more precise and simple.

Computers Speak Many Languages

You are going to learn a lot about several programming languages in this 24-hour course. You may have heard of some of the languages before. Over the years since the first computer language was invented, hundreds of programming languages have been written but there are only a handful that have prevailed to dominate the rest. Table 2.2 lists several programming languages that have gained more than obscure notoriety through the years.

TABLE 2.2 Many programming languages have appeared through the years.

Machine Language	Assembler
Algol	PL/I
PROLOG	LISP
COBOL	Forth
RPG	RPG II

continues

TABLE 2.2 Continued

Pascal	Object Pascal
HTML	Ada
C	C++
C#	FORTRAN
SmallTalk	Eiffel
BASIC	Visual Basic
APL	Java

Each programming language has its own dialects. BASIC has enjoyed tremendous popularity in all the following varieties:

BASICA

GW-BASIC (which stands for Gee-Whiz BASIC)

Quick BASIC

QBasic

Liberty BASIC

Visual Basic

The computer is like a modern-day tower of Babel, indirectly responsible for more programming languages than were ever needed. Most people considered to be computer experts might only know a handful of programming languages—from three to five—and they probably know only one or two very well. Therefore, don't let the large number of languages deter you from wanting to learn to program.

There are lots of reasons why there are so many programming languages. Different people have different preferences, some languages are better than others depending on the tasks, and some people have access to only one or two of the languages. For example, HTML is a language that programmers use for developing Web sites. FORTRAN was used in the past for highly mathematical applications, although other languages have supplanted FORTRAN in many programming departments. Java, combined with HTML, is great for putting interaction on Web pages.

Summary

There are several ways to obtain programs for computers, but to really make computers do what you want, you have to write the programs yourself. Most programs that you purchase are merely licenses to use but not customize the programs. Companies need programs that enable them to do business the way they prefer and do not force them to change their practices to conform to the programs.

Before you can program you must learn a programming language. You may want to learn several languages, but your work and interest goals will determine which languages you learn. Perhaps you want to specialize in Internet languages or perhaps you have a long-term Visual Basic contract. You'll find that the more languages you learn, the easier it will be for you to pick up additional languages.

The next hour describes some of the background needed for proper program design.

Q&A

Q Why do programs have to be so detailed?

A Programs are detailed because computers are machines. Machines do not have intelligence. A computer blindly follows your instructions, step by step. If you do not give detailed instructions, the computer can do nothing.

Workshop

The quiz questions are provided for your further understanding. See Appendix B, "Quiz Answers," for answers.

Quiz

1. What are the three ways to acquire a new program?
2. Why do businesses often write their own programs, despite the extra expense required?
3. Why must programmers know a programming language?
4. Why do computers not understand human language?
5. Which is more ambiguous, human language or computer language?
6. True or false: To be useful, a programmer should know at least five programming languages.
7. Why is RAM-based internal memory so important to a running program?
8. Which languages from Table 2.2 do you think are derived from the C programming language?
9. Name at least two dialects of the BASIC language.
10. Why might a programmer specialize in only one programming language?

HOUR 3

Designing a Program

Programmers learn to develop patience early in their programming careers. They learn that proper design is critical to a successful program. Perhaps you have heard the term *systems analysis and design*. This is the name given to the practice of analyzing a problem and then designing a program from that analysis. Complete books and college courses have been written about systems analysis and design. Of course, you want to get back to hands-on programming—and you'll be doing that very soon. However, to be productive at hands-on programming, you first need to understand the importance of design. This chapter attempts to cover program design highlights, letting you see what productive computer programmers go through before writing programs.

The highlights of this hour include

- Understanding the importance of program design
- Mastering the three steps required to write programs
- Using *output definition*
- Comparing top-down and bottom-up designs
- Seeing how flowcharts and pseudocode are making room for RAD
- Preparing for the final step in the programming process

The Need for Design

When a builder begins to build a house, the builder doesn't pick up a hammer and begin on the kitchen's frame. A designer must design the new house before anything can begin. As you will soon see, a program should also be designed before it is written.

A builder must first find out what the purchaser of the house wants. Nothing can be built unless the builder has an end result in mind. Therefore, the buyers of the house must meet with an architect. They tell the architect what they want the house to look like. The architect helps the buyers decide by telling them what is possible and what isn't. During this initial stage, the price is always a factor that requires both the designers and the purchasers to reach compromise agreements.

After the architect completes the plans for the house, the builder must plan the resources needed to build the house. Only after the design of the house is finished, the permits are filed, the money is in place, the materials are purchased, and the laborers are hired can any physical building begin. As a matter of fact, the more effort the builder puts into these preliminary requirements, the faster the house can actually be built.

The problem with building a house before it is properly designed is that the eventual owners may want changes made after it is too late to change them. It is very difficult to add a bathroom in the middle of two bedrooms *after* the house is completed. The goal is to get the owners to agree with the builder on the final house prior to construction. When the specifications are agreed on by all the parties involved, there is little room for disagreement later. The clearer the initial plans are, the fewer problems down the road because all parties agreed on the same house plans.

Sure, this is not a book on house construction, but you should always keep the similarities in mind when writing a program of any great length. You should not go to the keyboard and start typing instructions into the editor before designing the program any more than a builder should pick up a hammer before the house plans are finalized.

> The more up-front design work that you do, the faster you will finish the final program.

Thanks to computer technology, a computer program is easier to modify than a house. If you leave out a routine that a user wanted, you can add it later more easily than a builder can add a room to a finished house. Nevertheless, adding something to a program is never as easy as designing the program correctly the first time.

User-Programmer Agreement

Suppose you accept a job as a programmer for a small business that wants to improve its Web site. (After you've gone through these 24 hours, you'll understand programming better and you'll even learn how to write Web programs in Java.) The Web site changes that the owners want sound simple. They want you to write some interactive Java routines that enable their users to look at an online inventory and to print order lists that the users can bring into the store for purchases.

So, you listen to what they want, you agree to a price for your services, you get an advance payment, you gather the existing Web page files, and you go to your home office for a few days. After some grueling days of work you bring your masterpiece Web pages back to show the owners.

"Looks good," they say. "But where is the credit card processing area? Where can the user go to order our products online? Why don't you show the products we've back-ordered and that are unavailable? Why haven't you computed sales tax anywhere?"

You've just learned a painful lesson about user-programmer agreements. The users did a lousy job at explaining what they wanted. In fairness to them, you didn't do a great job at pulling out of them what they needed. Both of you thought you knew what you were supposed to do, and neither knew in reality. You realize that the price you quoted them originally will pay for about 10% of the work this project requires.

Before you start a job and before you price a job, you must know what your users want. Learning this is part of the program design experience. You need to know every detail before you'll be able to price your service accurately and before you'll be able to make customers happy.

Proper user-programmer agreement is vital for all areas of programming, not just for contract programmers. If you work for a corporation as a programmer, you also will need to have detailed specifications before you can begin your work. Other corporate users who will use the system must sign off on what they want so that everybody knows up front what is expected. If the user comes back to you later and asks why you didn't include a feature, you will be able to answer, "Because we never discussed that feature. You approved specifications that never mentioned that feature."

3

The program maintenance that takes place after the program is written, tested, and distributed is one of the most time-consuming aspects of the programming process. Programs are continually updated to reflect new user needs. Sometimes, if the program is not designed properly before it is written, the user will not want the program until it does exactly what the user wants it to do.

Computer consultants learn early to get the user's acceptance, and even the user's signature, on a program's design before the programming begins. If both the user and the programmers agree on what to do, there is little room for argument when the final program is presented. Company resources are limited; there is no time to add something later that should have been in the system all along.

Steps to Design

There are three fundamental steps you should perform when you have a program to write:

1. Define the output and data flows.
2. Develop the logic to get to that output.
3. Write the program.

Notice that writing the program is the *last* step in writing the program. This is not as silly as it sounds. Remember that physically building the house is the last stage of building the house; proper planning is critical before any actual building can start. You will find that actually writing and typing in the lines of the program is one of the easiest parts of the programming process. If your design is well thought out, the program practically writes itself; typing it in becomes almost an afterthought to the whole process.

Step 1: Define the Output and Data Flows

Before beginning a program, you must have a firm idea of what the program should produce and what data is needed to produce that output. Just as a builder must know what the house should look like before beginning to build it, a programmer must know what the output is going to be before writing the program.

Anything that the program produces and the user sees is considered output that you must define. You must know what every screen in the program should look like and what will be on every page of every printed report.

Some programs are rather small, but without knowing where you're heading, you may take longer to finish the program than you would if you first determined the output in detail. Liberty BASIC comes with a sample program called Contact3.bas that you can run. Select File, Open, and select Contact3.bas to load the file from your disk. Press Shift+F5 to run the program and then you should see the screen shown in Figure 3.1. No contacts exist when you first run the program, so nothing appears in the *fields* initially. A field, also known as a text box, is a place where users can type data.

Figure 3.1

Even Liberty BASIC's small Contact Management program window has several fields.

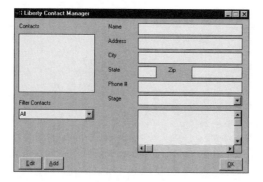

If you were planning to write such a contact program for yourself or someone else, you should make a list of all fields that the program is to produce onscreen. Not only would you list each field but you also would describe the fields. In addition, three Windows command buttons appear in the program window. Table 3.1 details the fields on the program's window.

Table 3.1 Fields That the Contact Management Program Displays

Field	Type	Description
Contacts	Scrolling list	Displays the list of contacts
Name	Text field	Holds contact's name
Address	Text field	Holds contact's address
City	Text field	Holds contact's city
State	Text field	Holds contact's state
Zip	Text field	Holds contact's zip code
Phone #	Text field	Holds contact's phone number
Stage	Fixed, scrolling list	Displays a list of possible stages this contact might reside in, such as being offered a special follow-up call or perhaps this is the initial contact
Notes	Text field	Miscellaneous notes about the contact such as whether the contact has bought from the company before

continues

TABLE 3.1 Continued

Filter Contacts	Fixed, scrolling list	Enables the user to search for groups of contacts based on the stage the contacts are in, enabling the user to see a list of all contacts who have been sent a mailing
Edit	Command button	Enables the user to modify an existing contact
Add	Command button	Enables the user to add a new contact
OK	Command button	Enables the user to close the contact window

Many of the fields you list in an output definition may be obvious. The field called Name obviously will hold and display a contact's name. Being obvious is okay. Keep in mind that if you write programs for other people, as you often will do, you must get approval of your program's parameters. One of the best ways to begin is to make a list of all the intended program's fields and make sure that the user agrees that everything is there. As you'll see in a section later this hour named "Rapid Application Development," you'll be able to use programs such as Visual Basic to put together a model of the actual output screen that your users can see. With the model and with your list of fields, you have double verification that the program contains exactly what the user wants.

Input windows such as the Contacts program data-entry screen are part of your output definition. This may seem contradictory, but input screens require that your program place fields on the screen, and you should plan where these input fields must go.

The output definition is more than a preliminary output design. It gives you insight into what data elements the program should track, compute, and produce. Defining the output also helps you gather all the input you need to produce the output.

Some programs produce a huge amount of output. Don't skip this first all-important step in the design process just because there is a lot of output. Because there is more output, it becomes more important for you to define it. Defining the output is relatively easy—sometimes even downright boring and time-consuming. The time you need to define the output can take as long as typing in the program. You will lose that time and more, however, if you shrug off the output definition at the beginning.

The output definition consists of many pages of details. You must be able to specify all the details of a problem before you know what output you need. Even command buttons and scrolling list boxes are output because the program will display these items.

In Hour 1, you learned that data goes into a program and the program outputs meaningful information. You should inventory all the data that goes into the program. If you're adding Java code to a Web site to make the site more interactive, you will need to know if the Web site owners want to collect data from the users. Define what each piece of data is. Perhaps the site allows the user to submit a name and e-mail address for weekly sales mailings. Does the company want any additional data from the user such as physical address, age, and income?

Object-Oriented Design

Throughout this 24-hour tutorial you will learn what *object-oriented programming (OOP)* is all about. Basically, OOP turns data values, such as names and prices, into objects that can take on a life of their own inside programs. Hour 14, "Java Has Class," will be your first detailed exposure to objects.

A few years ago some OOP experts developed a process for designing OOP programs called *object-oriented design* (*OOD*). OOD made an advanced science out of specifying data to be gathered in a program and defining that data in a way that was appropriate for the special needs of OOP programmers. Grady Booch was one of the founders of object-oriented design. It is his specifications from over a decade ago that help today's OOP programmers collect data for the applications they are about to write and to turn that data into objects for programs.

3

In the next hour, "Getting Input and Displaying Output," you'll learn how to put these ideas into a program. You will learn how a program asks for data and produces information on the screen. This *I/O* (*input and output*) process is the most critical part of an application. You want to capture all data required and in an accurate way.

Something is still missing in all this design discussion. You understand the importance of gathering data. You understand the importance of knowing where you're headed by designing the output. But how do you go from data to output? That's the next step in the design process—you need to determine what processing will be required to produce the output from the input (data). You must be able to generate proper data flows and calculations so that your program manipulates that data and produces correct output. The final sections of this hour will discuss ways to develop the centerpiece—the logic for your programs.

In conclusion, all output screens, printed reports, and data-entry screens must be defined in advance so you know exactly what is required of your programs. You also must decide what data to keep in files and the format of your data files. As you progress in your programming education you will learn ways to lay out disk files in formats they require.

When capturing data, you want to gather data from users in a way that is reasonable, requires little time, and has prompts that request the data in a friendly and unobtrusive manner. That's where rapid application development (discussed next) and prototyping can help.

Prototyping

In the days of expensive hardware and costly computer usage time, the process of system design was, in some ways, more critical than it is today. The more time you spent designing your code, the more smooth the costly hands-on programming became. This is far less true today because computers are inexpensive and you have much more freedom to change your mind and add program options than before. Yet the first part of this hour was spent in great detail explaining why up-front design is critical.

The primary problem many new programmers have today is they do absolutely no design work. That's why many problems take place, such as the one mentioned earlier this hour about the company that wanted far more in their Web site than the programmer ever dreamed of.

Although the actual design of output, data, and even the logic in the body of the program itself is much simpler to work with given today's computing tools and their low cost, you still must maintain an eagle-eye toward developing an initial design with agreed-upon output from your users. You must also know all the data that your program is to collect before you begin your coding. If you don't, you will have a frustrating time as a contract programmer or as a corporate programmer because you'll constantly be playing catch-up with what the users actually want and failed to tell you about.

One of the benefits of the Windows operating system is its visual nature. Before Windows, programming tools were limited to text-based design and implementation. Designing a user's screen today means starting with a programming language such as Visual Basic, drawing the screen, and dragging objects to the screen that the user will interact with, such as an OK button. Therefore, you can quickly design *prototype screens* that you can send to the user. A prototype is a model, and a prototype screen models what the final program's screen will look like. After the user sees the screens that he or she will interact with, the user will have a much better feel for whether you understand the needs of the program.

Although Liberty BASIC does not provide any prototyping tools, programming languages such as Visual C++ and Visual Basic do. Figure 3.2 shows the Visual Basic development screen. The screen looks rather busy, but the important things to look for are the Toolbox and the output design window. To place controls such as command buttons and text boxes on the form that serves as the output window, the programmer only has to drag that control from the Toolbox window to the form. So to build a program's output, the programmer only has to drag as many controls as needed to the form and does not have to write a single line of code in the meantime.

FIGURE 3.2

Program development systems such as Visual Basic provide tools that you can use to create output definitions visually.

Toolbox

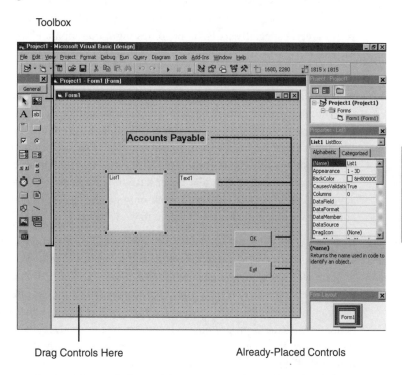

Drag Controls Here   Already-Placed Controls

Once you place controls on a Form window with a programming tool such as Visual Basic, you can do more than show the form to your users. You actually can compile the form just as you would a program and let your user interact with the controls. When the user is able to work with the controls, even though nothing happens as a result, the user is better able to tell if you understand the goals of the program. The user often notices if there is a missing piece of the program and can also offer suggestions to make the program flow more easily from a user's point of view.

The prototype is often only an empty shell that cannot do anything but simulate user interaction until you tie its pieces together with code. Your job as a programmer has only just begun once you get approval on the screens, but the screens are the first place to begin because you must know what your users want before you know how to proceed.

Rapid Application Development

A more advanced program design tool used for defining output, data flows, and logic itself is called *Rapid Application Development,* or *RAD* for short. Although RAD tools are still in their infancy, you will find yourself using RAD over the span of your career, especially as RAD becomes more common and the tools become less expensive.

RAD is the process of quickly placing controls on a form—not unlike you just saw done with Visual Basic—connecting those controls to data, and accessing pieces of prewritten code to put together a fully functional application without writing a single line of code. In a way, programming systems such as Visual Basic are fulfilling many goals of RAD. When you place controls on a form, as you'll see done in far more detail in Hour 16, "Programming with Visual Basic," the Visual Basic system handles all the programming needed for that control. You don't ever have to write anything to make a command button act like a command button should. Your only goal is to determine how many command buttons your program needs and where they are to go.

But these tools cannot read your mind. RAD tools do not know that, when the user clicks a certain button, a report is supposed to print. Programmers are still needed to connect all these things to each other and to data, and programmers are needed to write the detailed logic so that the program processes data correctly. Before these kinds of program development tools appeared, programmers had to write thousands of lines of code, often in the C programming language, just to produce a simple Windows program. At least now the controls and the interface are more rapidly developed. Someday, perhaps a RAD tool will be sophisticated enough to develop the logic also. But in the meantime, don't quit your day job if your day job is programming, because you're still in demand.

Teach your users how to prototype their own screens! Programming knowledge is not required to design the screens. Your users, therefore, will be able to show you exactly what they want. The prototyped screens are interactive as well. That is, your users will be able to click the buttons and enter values in the fields even though nothing happens as a result of that use. The idea is to let your users try the screens for a while to make sure they are comfortable with the placement and appearance of the controls.

Top-Down Program Design

For large projects, many programming staff members find that *top-down design* helps them focus on what a program needs and helps them detail the logic required to produce the program's results. Top-down design is the process of breaking down the overall problem into more and more detail until you finalize all the details. With top-down design, you produce the details needed to accomplish a programming task.

The problem with top-down design is that programmers tend not to use it. They tend to design from the opposite direction (called *bottom-up design*). When you ignore top-down design, you impose a heavy burden on yourself to remember every detail that will be needed; with top-down design, the details fall out on their own. You don't have to worry about the petty details if you follow a strict top-down design because the process of top-down design takes care of producing the details.

> One of the keys to top-down design is that it forces you to put off the details until later. Top-down design forces you to think in terms of the overall problem for as long as possible. Top-down design keeps you focused. If you use bottom-up design, it is too easy to lose sight of the forest for the trees. You get to the details too fast and lose sight of your program's primary objectives.

Here is the three-step process necessary for top-down design:

1. Determine the overall goal.
2. Break that goal into two, three, or more detailed parts; too many more details cause you to leave out things.
3. Put off the details as long as possible, then keep repeating steps 1 and 2 until you cannot reasonably break down the problem any further.

You can learn about top-down design more easily by relating it to a common real-world problem before looking at a computer problem. Top-down design is not just for programming problems. Once you master top-down design, you can apply it to any part of your life that you must plan in detail. Perhaps the most detailed event that a person can plan is a wedding. Therefore, a wedding is the perfect place to see top-down design in action.

What is the first thing you must do to have a wedding? First, find a prospective spouse (you'll need a different book for help with that). When it comes time to plan the wedding, the top-down design is the best way to approach the event. The way *not* to plan a wedding is to worry about the details first, yet this is the way most people plan a wedding. They start thinking about the dresses, the organist, the flowers, and the cake to serve at the reception. The biggest problem with trying to cover all these details from the beginning is that you lose sight of so much; it is too easy to forget a detail until it's too late. The details of bottom-up design get in your way.

What is the overall goal of a wedding? Thinking in the most general terms possible, "Have a wedding" is about as general as it can get. If you were in charge of planning a wedding, the general goal of "Have a wedding" would put you right on target. Assume that "Have a wedding" is the highest-level goal.

The overall goal keeps you focused. Despite its redundant nature, "Have a wedding" keeps out details such as planning the honeymoon. If you don't put a fence around the exact problem you are working on, you'll get mixed up with details and, more importantly, you'll forget some details. If you're planning both a wedding and a honeymoon, you should do two top-down designs, or include the honeymoon trip in the top-level general goal. This wedding plan includes the event of the wedding—the ceremony and reception—but doesn't include any honeymoon details. (Leave the honeymoon details to your spouse so you can be surprised. After all, you have enough to do with the wedding plans, right?)

Now that you know where you're heading, begin by breaking down the overall goal into two or three details. For instance, what about the colors of the wedding, what about the guest list, what about paying the minister...*oops*, too many details! The idea of top-down design is to put off the details for as long as possible. Don't get in any hurry. When you find yourself breaking the current problem into more than three or four parts, you are rushing the top-down design. Put off the details. Basically, you can break down "Have a wedding" into the following two major components: the ceremony and the reception.

The next step of top-down design is to take those new components and do the same for each of them. The ceremony is made up of the people and the location. The reception includes the food, the people, and the location. The ceremony's people include the guests, the wedding party, and the workers (minister, organist, and so on—but those details come a little later).

Don't worry about the time order of the details yet. The top-down design's goal is to produce every detail you need (eventually), not to put those details into any order. You must know where you are heading and exactly what is required before considering how those details relate to each other and which come first.

Eventually, you will have several pages of details that cannot be broken down any further. For instance, you'll probably end up with the details of the reception food, such as peanuts for snacking. (If you start out listing those details, however, you could forget many of them.)

Now move to a more computerized problem; assume you are assigned the task of writing a payroll program for a company. What would that payroll program require? You could begin by listing the payroll program's details, such as this:

- Print payroll checks.
- Calculate federal taxes.
- Calculate state taxes.

What is wrong with this approach? If you said that the details were coming too early, you are correct. The perfect place to start is at the top. The most general goal of a payroll program might be "Perform the payroll." This overall goal keeps other details out of this program (no general ledger processing will be included, unless part of the payroll system updates a general ledger file) and keeps you focused on the problem at hand.

Consider Figure 3.3. This might be the first page of the payroll's top-down design. Any payroll program has to include some mechanism for entering, deleting, and changing employee information such as address, city, state, zip code, number of exemptions, and so on. What other details about the employees do you need? At this point, don't ask. The design is not ready for all those details.

FIGURE 3.3

The first page of the payroll program's top-down design would include the highest level of details.

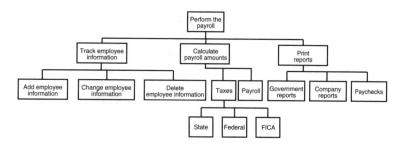

There is a long way to go before you finish with the payroll top-down design, but Figure 3.3 is the first step. You must keep breaking down each component until the details finally appear. Only after you have all the details ready can you begin to decide what the program is going to produce as output.

Only when you and the user gather all the necessary details through top-down design can you decide what is going to comprise those details.

Step 2: Develop the Logic

After you and the user agree to the goals and output of the program, the rest is up to you. Your job is to take that output definition and decide how to make a computer produce the output. You have taken the overall problem and broken it down into detailed instructions that the computer can carry out. This doesn't mean that you are ready to write the program—quite the contrary. You are now ready to develop the logic that produces that output.

The output definition goes a long way toward describing *what* the program is supposed to do. Now you must decide *how* to accomplish the job. You must order the details that you have so they operate in a time-ordered fashion. You must also decide which decisions your program must make and the actions produced by each of those decisions.

Throughout the rest of this 24-hour tutorial, you'll learn the final two steps of developing programs. You will gain insight into how programmers write and test a program after developing the output definition and getting the user's approval on the program's specifications.

> Only after learning to program can you learn to develop the logic that goes into a program, yet you must develop some logic before writing programs to be able to move from the output and data definition stage to the program code. This "chicken before the egg" syndrome is common for newcomers to programming. When you begin to write your own programs, you'll have a much better understanding of logic development.

In the past, users would use tools such as *flowcharts* and *pseudocode* to develop program logic. A flowchart is shown in Figure 3.4. It is said that a picture is worth a thousand words, and the flowchart provides a pictorial representation of program logic. The flowchart doesn't include all the program details but represents the general logic flow of the program. The flowchart provides the logic for the final program. If your flowchart is correctly drawn, writing the actual program becomes a matter of rote. After the final program is completed, the flowchart can act as documentation to the program itself.

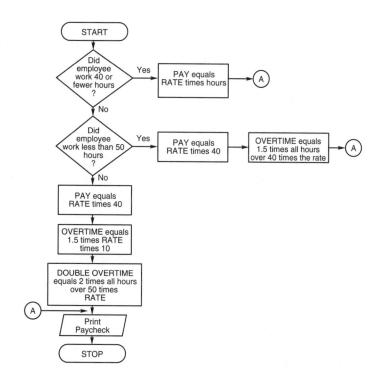

FIGURE 3.4

The flowchart depicts the payroll program's logic graphically.

Flowcharts are made up of industry-standard symbols. Plastic flowchart symbol outlines, called *flowchart templates*, are still available at office supply stores to help you draw better-looking flowcharts instead of relying on freehand drawing. There are also some programs that guide you through a flowchart's creation and print flowcharts on your printer.

Although some still use flowcharts today, RAD and other development tools have virtually eliminated flowcharts except for depicting isolated parts of a program's logic for documentation purposes. Even in its heyday of the 1960s and 1970s, flowcharting did not completely catch on. Some companies preferred another method for logic description called *pseudocode,* sometimes called *structured English,* which is a method of writing logic using sentences of text instead of the diagrams necessary for flowcharting.

Pseudocode doesn't have any programming language statements in it, but it also is not free-flowing English. It is a set of rigid English words that allow for the depiction of logic you see so often in flowcharts and programming languages. As with flowcharts, you can write pseudocode for anything, not just computer programs. A lot of instruction manuals use a form of pseudocode to illustrate the steps needed to assemble parts. Pseudocode offers a rigid description of logic that tries to leave little room for ambiguity.

Here is the logic for the payroll problem in pseudocode form. Notice that you can read the text, yet it is not a programming language. The indention helps keep track of which sentences go together. The pseudocode is readable by anyone, even by people unfamiliar with flowcharting symbols.

```
For each employee:
  If the employee worked 0 to 40 hours then
    net pay equals hours worked times rate.
  Otherwise,
    if the employee worked between 40 and 50 hours then
      net pay equals 40 times the rate;
      add to that (hours worked -40) times the rate times 1.5.
    Otherwise,
      net pay equals 40 times the rate;
      add to that 10 times the rate times 1.5;
      add to that (hours worked -50) times twice the rate.
  Deduct taxes from the net pay.
Print the paycheck.
```

Step 3: Writing the Code

The program writing takes the longest to learn. After you learn to program, however, the actual programming process takes less time than the design if your design is accurate and complete. The nature of programming requires that you learn some new skills. The next few hourly lessons will teach you a lot about programming languages and will help train you to become a better coder so that your programs will not only achieve the goals they are supposed to achieve, but also will be simple to maintain.

Summary

A builder doesn't build a house before designing it, and a programmer should not write a program without designing it either. Too often, programmers rush to the keyboard without thinking through the logic. A badly designed program results in lots of bugs and maintenance. This hour described how to ensure that your program design matches the design that the user wants. After you complete the output definition, you can organize the program's logic using top-down design, flowcharts, and pseudocode.

The next hour focuses on training you in your first computer language, Liberty BASIC.

Q&A

Q At what point in the top-down design should I begin to add details?

A Put off the details as long as possible. If you are designing a program to produce sales reports, you would not enter the printing of the final report total until you had

completed all the other report design tasks. The details fall out on their own when you can no longer break a task into two or more other tasks.

Q Once I break the top-down design into its lowest-level details, don't I also have the pseudocode details?

A The top-down design is a tool for determining all the details your program will need. The top-down design doesn't, however, put those details into their logical execution order. The pseudocode dictates the executing logic of your program and determines when things happen, the order they happen in, and when they stop happening. The top-down design simply determines everything that might happen in the program. Instead of pseudocode, however, you should consider getting a RAD tool that will help you move faster from the design to the finished, working program. Today's RAD systems are still rather primitive, and you'll have to add much of the code yourself.

Workshop

The quiz questions are provided for your further understanding. See Appendix B, "Quiz Answers," for answers.

Quiz

1. Why does proper design often take longer than writing the actual program?
2. Where does a programmer first begin determining the user's requirements?
3. True or false: Proper top-down design forces you to put off details as long as possible.
4. How does top-down design differ from pseudocode?
5. What is the purpose of RAD?
6. True or false: You will not have to add code to any system that you design with RAD.
7. Which uses symbols, a flowchart or pseudocode?
8. True or false: You can flowchart both program logic as well as real-world procedures.
9. True or false: Your user will help you create a program's output if you let the user work with an output prototype.
10. What is the final step of the programming process (before testing the final result)?

3

HOUR 4

Getting Input and Displaying Output

Input and output are the cornerstones that enable programs to interact with the outside world. In the previous hour, you learned how important the output process is to programming because through output, your program displays information. A program must get some of its data and control from the user's input, so learning how to get the user's responses is critical as well.

The highlights of this hour include

- Using Print to display output
- Printing multiple occurrences per line
- Separating output values
- Using variables to hold information
- Using Input to get data
- Prompting for data input
- Sending output to your printer

The `Print` Statement

In Liberty BASIC, the `Print` statement outputs data to the output window. `Print` is used in almost every Liberty BASIC program because displaying data on the screen is so important. Your users must be able to see results and read messages from the programs that they run.

There are several ways to use `Print`. The easiest way to print words on the output window is to enclose them in quotation marks after the `Print` statement. The following two statements print names on the screen:

```
Print "Sally Brown"
Print "John Wilson"
```

These statements produce the following output:

```
Sally Brown
John Wilson
```

Quotation marks never appear around printed *strings* (a string is data of one or more characters that is never used for calculation, such as names and addresses); in a line of code, the marks simply enclose the character strings to be printed. Whatever appears inside quotation marks prints exactly as it appears inside the quotation marks. The `Print` statement

```
PRINT "5 + 7"
```

doesn't print `12` (the result of `5 + 7`). Because quotation marks enclose the expression, the expression prints exactly as it appears inside the quotation marks. The `Print` statement produces this output:

```
5 + 7
```

If, however, you print an expression without the quotation marks, Liberty BASIC prints the result of the calculated expression:

```
Print 5 + 7
```

does print `12`.

> Don't be confused by the name `Print`. `Print` sends output to a window on the screen and not to the printer.

The `End` statement at the end of Liberty BASIC programs is optional. Most programmers put the `End` statement there so that others looking at the program know when they have reached the end instead of wondering if there might be another page to the program. In some instances, programmers insert End statements in program locations other than the very end to cause a premature termination of the program if a certain condition occurs, such as when a user wants to quit the running program early.

Consider the program in Listing 4.1. The program prints titles and results.

LISTING 4.1   Printing Results of Calculations

```
' Filename: AreaHalf.bas
' Program that calculates and prints the area
' of a circle and half circle
Print "The area of a circle with a radius of 3 is"
Print 3.1416 * 3 * 3
Print "The area of one-half that circle is"
Print (3.1416 * 3 * 3) / 2
End
```

Don't worry too much about understanding the calculations in this hour's programs. The next hour, "Data Processing with Numbers and Words," explains how to form calculations in Liberty BASIC.

Here is the output you see if you run the program in Listing 4.1:

```
The area of a circle with a radius of 3 is
28.2744
The area of one-half that circle is
14.1372
```

Notice that each Print statement causes a new line to be printed. Follow the program and see how its output is produced.

Capitalization does not affect commands in any way. You can use Print, PRINT, or print, and Liberty BASIC recognizes the command. In some languages, the capitalization does matter. For example, C++ requires all commands to appear in lowercase.

Clearing the Output Window

It is very easy to clear the output window in Liberty BASIC. The `Cls` statement is all you need. `Cls` stands for *clear screen*. When Liberty BASIC reaches a `Cls` statement in your program, it clears the contents of the output screen. So, the first part of your program might write to the output window and later parts of the program might need a freshly erased output window.

The following code erases the window and prints a message at the top of the cleared window:

```
Cls
Print "Liberty BASIC is fun!"
```

Advanced Printing

The `Print` statement can do far more than just print data values. You can use `Print` to output formatted data in columns that form tables of information. In addition, you can control the spacing of the values. The next several sections show you ways to use `Print` to display your program's output so that it looks exactly the way you want it to look.

Using the Semicolon

The following statement prints three numbers on three different lines:

```
Print 15
Print 20
Print 25
```

Here is the output produced by these `Print` statements when you run the program:

```
15
20
25
```

If you want to print several different values on the same line, you can do so by separating them with semicolons. Therefore, the statement

```
Print 15; 20; 25
```

prints all three values on a single line, like this:

```
152025
```

Obviously, you want some space between numbers. So the following prints the three numbers on a single line and inserts a space between them:

```
Print 15; " "; 20; " "; 25
```

Here is the output:

```
15 20 25
```

Using the semicolon, you can improve the program introduced earlier that calculated and printed the area of a circle. By making the values appear directly after the descriptions of the calculations instead of on the next line, your output will make more sense than before. Listing 4.2 shows the improved program.

LISTING 4.2   Use the Semicolon to Separate Printed Values on the Same Line.

```
' Filename: AreaHlSp.bas
' Program that calculates and prints the area
' of a circle and half circle
Print "The area of a circle with a radius of 3 is ";
Print 3.1416 * 3 * 3
Print "The area of one-half that circle is ";
Print (3.1416 * 3 * 3) / 2
End
```

Here is the output from this program:

```
The area of a circle with a radius of 3 is 28.2744
The area of one-half that circle is 14.1372
```

The semicolon can appear at the end of a `Print` statement with nothing following the semicolon:

```
Print "Sally ";
```

A subsequent `Print` will continue the output on the same line as the previous one. Therefore, you do not have to print all of a single line with a single `Print` statement.

Printing Blank Lines

To print a blank line, you only need to place a `Print` statement on a line by itself. A blank line appears in the middle of the output from the following three statements:

```
Print "First line"
Print
Print "Last line"
```

Here is the output that these three `Print` statements produce:

```
First line

Last line
```

Storing Data

As its definition implies, *data processing* means that your programs process data. That data must somehow be stored in memory while your program processes it. In Liberty BASIC programs, as in most programming languages, you must store data in *variables*. You can think of a variable as if it were a box inside your computer holding a data value. The value might be a number, character, or string of characters.

> Actually, data is stored inside memory locations. Variables keep you from having to remember which memory locations hold your data. Instead of remembering a specific storage location (called an *address*), you only have to remember the name of the variables you create. The variable is like a box that holds data, and the variable name is a label for that box so you'll know what's inside.

Your programs can have as many variables as you need. Variables have names associated with them. You don't have to remember which internal memory location holds data; you can attach names to variables to make them easier to remember. For instance, Sales is much easier to remember than the 4376th memory location.

You can use almost any name you want, provided that you follow these naming rules:

- Variable names must begin with an alphabetic character such as a letter.
- Variable names can be as long as you need them to be.
- Uppercase and lowercase variable names differ; the name MyName and MYNAME are two different variables.
- After the first alphabetic character, variable names can contain numbers and periods.

> Avoid strange variable names. Try to name variables so that their names help describe the kind of data being stored. Balance04 is a much better variable name for an accountant's 2004 balance value than X1y96a, although Liberty BASIC doesn't care which one you use.

Here are some examples of valid and invalid variable names:

Valid	*Invalid*
Sales04	Sales-04
MyRate	My$Rate
ActsRecBal	5ActsRec
row	Print

Don't assign a variable the same name as a Liberty BASIC command or
Liberty BASIC will issue an invalid variable name error message.

Variables can hold numbers or *character strings*. A character string usually consists of
one or more characters, such as a word, name, sentence, or address. If you follow the
naming rules just listed, the variables can hold numbers.

There is one special character that is useful to use at the end of variable names. If you
put a dollar sign ($) at the end of a variable name, the variable can hold one or more
alphabetic or special characters. These are called *string variables* because they can hold
strings of data. Therefore, the following variables can hold characters, words, and even
sentences:

```
nm$
```

```
Company$
```

```
show$
```

```
Employee$
```

Assigning Values

The majority of Liberty BASIC program statements use variable names. Liberty BASIC
programs often do little more than store values in variables, change variables, calculate
with variables, and output variable values.

When you are ready to store a data value, you must name a variable to put it in. You
must use an assignment statement to store values in your program variables. The assignment statement includes an equal sign (=) and an optional command Let. Here are two
sample assignment statements:

```
sales = 956.34
```

```
Let rate = .28
```

The Let keyword is optional and requires more typing if you use it.
Therefore, most programmers save typing time and leave off the Let from
their assignment statements. Probably there is not a good reason to use Let;
old versions of BASIC (in the 1960s) required it, so programmers who
learned it then might still use it. You should know what Let does in case you
run across an assignment statement that uses it.

Think of the equal sign in an assignment statement as a left-pointing arrow. Whatever is on the right side of the equal sign is sent to the left side to be stored in the variable there. Figure 4.1 shows how the assignment statement works.

FIGURE 4.1

The assignment state-ment stores values in variables.

If you want to store character string data in a variable, you must enclose the string inside quotation marks. Here is how you store the words *Liberty BASIC* in a variable named `lang$`:

```
lang$ = "Liberty BASIC"    ' Enclose strings in quotation marks
```

After you put values in variables, they stay there for the entire run of the program or until you put something else in them. A variable can hold only one value at a time. Therefore, the two statements

```
age = 67
age = 27
```

result in `age` holding 27, because that was the last value stored there. The variable `Age` cannot hold both values.

You can also assign values of one variable to another and perform math on the numeric variables. Here is code that stores the result of a calculation in a variable and then uses that result in another calculation:

```
pi = 3.1416
radius = 3
area = pi * radius * radius
halfArea = area / 2
```

Liberty BASIC zeroes all variables for you. This means that when you name a variable, Liberty BASIC assumes that the value of the variable is 0 (zero) until another value is assigned to it. Therefore, if you want a variable to begin with a zero, you don't have to assign a zero to it. Liberty BASIC initially stores *null strings* or *empty strings* in them to indicate that nothing has yet been assigned to the variables.

Use Print to print values stored in variables. Print the variable names without quotes around them. Listing 4.3 contains code similar to earlier listings in this hour's lesson, but instead of printing calculated results directly, the program first stores calculations in variables and prints the variables' values.

LISTING 4.3   Print Sends Output of Calculations and Other Data to the Screen.

```
' Filename: AreaVars.bas
' Program that calculates and prints the area
' of a circle and half circle
pi = 3.1416          ' Mathematical PI
radius = 3           ' Radius of the circle
area = pi * radius * radius     ' Compute circle area
halfArea = area / 2            ' Compute half the circle area
Print "The area of a circle with a radius of 3 is ";
Print area
Print "The area of one-half that circle is ";
Print halfArea
End
```

4

Getting Keyboard Data with Input

An Input statement is the opposite of Print. Input receives values from the keyboard. Those values typed by the user go into variables. In the previous section, you learned how to assign values to variables. You used the assignment statement because you knew the actual values. However, you often don't know all the data values when you write your program.

Think of a medical reception program that tracks patients as they enter the doctor's office. The programmer has no idea who will walk in next and so cannot assign patient names to variables. The patient names can be stored in variables only when the program is run.

When a program reaches an Input statement, it displays a question mark and pauses until the user types a value and presses the Enter key. Here is an Input statement:

```
Input age     ' Wait for user to type a value
```

When program execution reaches this statement, the computer displays a question mark in the output window. The question mark is a signal to the user that something is being asked and a response is desired. How does the user know what the question is? It is the programmer's responsibility to include before every Input statement a Print statement that asks the user for whatever type of value is needed. The Print statement prompts the user for the input. A prompt message is a question that you ask before a user's input is expected. The prompt message puts a complete question before the Input question mark. Consider these three lines from a program:

```
Print "What is your age";
Input age
Print "Thank you!"
```

When the computer reaches the first Print, it prints the message as usual. The semicolon at the end of the Print keeps the cursor on the same line so that whatever is printed next appears after the question. Do you remember what Input does? It prints a question mark. Because of the semicolon, however, the question mark appears after the question, and the user sees this:

```
What is your age?
```

The words appear because of Print, and the question mark appears because of Input. The program doesn't continue to the next Print statement until the user answers the question by typing a value and pressing Enter.

Follow the program in Listing 4.4 and study the output that appears below it. You can see how a variable with no value is assigned a value by an Input statement.

LISTING 4.4   Input **Receives a Value from the User at the Keyboard.**

```
' Filename: Input.bas
' Demonstrates the INPUT statement
'
Print "Before the INPUT, the variable named x is "; x
Print
Print "What value do you want x to have now";
Input x
' x now has the value entered by the user
Print
Print "After the Input, x is "; x
End
```

Liberty BASIC zeroes all variables for you when a program begins. This means that the value of x is zero until you give it a value via Input. Here is a sample output from the program. The user typed **27** for the value of x.

```
Before the Input, the variable named x is 0
What value do you want x to have now? 27
After the INPUT, x is 27
```

Liberty BASIC waits at the `Input` statement as long as it takes for the user to type a value in response to the `Input` statement. The `Input` is finished only when the user presses the Enter key.

Inputting Strings

Any type of variable, numeric or string, can be entered with `Input`. For example, these lines wait for the user to enter a string value:

```
Print "What is your first name";
Input first$
```

If the user types the name in response to the question, the name is put into the `first$` variable.

If the user only presses Enter, without entering a value in response to `Input`, Liberty BASIC puts a value called *null* into the variable. A null value is a zero for numeric variables, or an empty string for string variables. An empty string—a string variable with nothing in it—is literally zero characters long.

Combining `Print` and `Input`

You have seen the importance of printing an `Input` prompt message with `Print` before your `Input` statements. Your programs should not display an `Input`'s question mark without printing a message beforehand telling the user what kind of input you expect. The designers of Liberty BASIC realized the importance of displaying a prompt along with every `Input` in your program. They added a feature to the `Input` statement itself to include the prompt message along with the input. Instead of having pairs of `Print-Input` statements throughout your program, you can have single `Input` statements that both prompt the user and receive input.

A simple example shows how the prompt message works. The following statements should be old hat to you by now. The `Print` statement asks the user a question, and the `Input` statement gets the user's answer.

```
Print "What is the month number (i.e., 1, 5, or 11)";
Input monNum
```

The `Print statement` displays a message that tells the user what input is expected.

Here is an equivalent statement. It does the same thing as the previous `Print-Input`, but in a single line of code:

```
Input "What is the month number (i.e., 1, 5, or 11)"; monNum
```

This is what the user sees when Liberty BASIC reaches this line in the program:

```
What is the month number (i.e., 1, 5, or 11)
```

Notice that a question mark does not appear at the end of the prompt. Therefore, when combining the prompt text with `Input`, you must include the question mark:

```
Input "What is the month number (i.e., 1, 5, or 11)?"; monNum
```

The user can then answer the question, in effect supplying the variable `monNum` with a month number, and the program then continues with the rest of its execution.

> Some questions cannot be asked in a single `Input` prompt because they are too long. Therefore, you may have to put extra `Print` statements before an `Input` to hold the entire prompt. Here is an example that does just that:
>
> ```
> Print "You must now enter the last four digits of your "
> Input "extended zipcode.  What are those four digits?"; eZip
> ```
>
> If you placed the long prompt inside just the `Input` statement, the prompt would be very long. By printing the first half of the prompt with `Print`, with the rest following on the next line with the question mark from the `Input` statement, you make your program easier to read.

Listing 4.5 shows a program that a small store might use to compute totals at the cash register. The `Input` statements in this program are required; only at runtime will the customer purchase values be known. As you can see, getting input at runtime is vital for real-world data processing.

LISTING 4.5   You Can Use `input` to Simulate a Cash Register Program for a Small Store.

```
' Filename: StoreIn.bas
' Demonstrates INPUT by asking the user for several values
' at a store's cash register and prints a total of the sales
Print "** Mom and Pop's Store **"
Print
Input "How many bottles of pop were sold? "; pop
popTotal = pop * .75
Input "How many bags of chips were sold? "; chips
chipTotal = chips * 1.25
Input "How many gallons of gas were sold? "; gas
```

continues

LISTING 4.5 Continued

```
gasTotal = gas * 1.69

' Calculate total sale and add 7% sales tax
fullSale = popTotal + chipTotal + gasTotal    ' Total sale
sTax = .07 * fullSale
netSale = fullSale + sTax

' The following INPUT gets a null value just to pause the program
Input "Press Enter when you are ready for the invoice..."; ans
' Print an invoice on the screen
Print
Print
Print "** Invoice Mom and Pop's Store **"
Print
Print "*************************************************"
Print pop; " bottles of pop: "; popTotal
Print chips; " bags of chips: "; chipTotal
Print gas; " gallons of gas: "; gasTotal
Print "-----------------------"
Print "Total sale: "; fullSale
Print "Sales tax: "; sTax
Print "Final total: "; netSale
Print
Print "Thank the customer!"
End
```

Figure 4.2 shows the output of this program. As you can see, the program could be help-ful for a small store.

FIGURE 4.2

Running the cash reg-ister program produces this output.

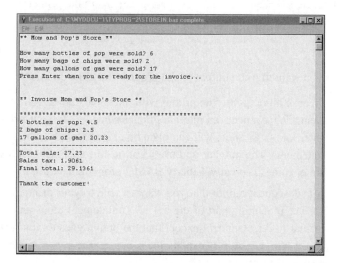

Where are the Windows controls such as text boxes?

You are well on your way to writing programs that display output and get the user's input! Nevertheless, you know that you work in a windowed computer environment and that most programs use a graphical user interface with command buttons, scrolling lists, and other controls. Hour 11, "Advanced Programming Issues," explains how to use these and other Windows controls in your Liberty BASIC window. They would actually get in the way at this point.

Your goal now should be to concentrate on learning the fundamentals of Liberty BASIC. By learning the fundamentals, you are honing more than just Liberty BASIC skills. You are readying yourself for all programming languages. All languages use calculations. All languages use variables. All languages use the program control statements you'll learn about in subsequent lessons. Yet, most languages interact with Windows controls in completely different ways. If you took a lot of time to learn how Liberty BASIC works with Windows controls, you would have to relearn how Java works with Windows controls. And then Visual BASIC would do it even differently.

The meat of traditional programming is the vital activity now because you've never programmed before. Once you gain more confidence in traditional programming, you'll be ready to see how languages support the various Windows controls, as discussed throughout the rest of this 24-hour tutorial.

Printing to Your Printer

Liberty BASIC does not have a command for sending output to your printer, but you can modify the Print statement to send output to your printer. The following three lines will send "This message appears on the printer" to the printer:

```
Open "Lpt1" For Output As #1
Print #1, "This message appears on the printer"
Close #1
```

When you want to route output to the printer, you must do this:

1. Precede all output to the printer with the Open "Lpt1" For Output As #1 statement. This connects an internal pointer named #1 to your printer, which your computer knows as Lpt1. You can open other items, such as files, with additional Open statements. The number you use identifies the statement with the device or file you are opening. Typically, Liberty BASIC programmers use #1 for the printer.

2. All subsequent output that you want to send to your printer must begin with Print #1. The remaining part of the Print #1 statement looks and behaves just like the regular Print statement except that the output goes to your printer. Therefore, Print #1, "Hello" is exactly the same as Print "Hello" but the former output goes to your printer.

3. When you're through sending output to your printer, you must issue the `Close #1` command to release the printer from your program.

> If your program does not fill the entire printed page, or the final page of multiple pages, you may have to press the Form Feed button on your printer to eject the page from your printer.

Summary

Proper input and output can mean the difference between a program that your users like to use and one they hate to use. If you properly label all input that you want so that you prompt your users through the input process, the user will have no questions about the proper format for your program. Getting the input data's format correct is important for Liberty BASIC because, unlike Windows programs, a Liberty BASIC program doesn't allow for fancy data-entry text boxes and edit fields that many Windows controls allow.

The next hour describes in detail how to use Liberty BASIC to program calculations using variables and the mathematical operators.

4

Q&A

Q What is the difference between Input and Print?

A Input gets values from the user and Print sends information to the user on the output window. Use Input to capture user input and store that input in variables.

Q Why doesn't Liberty BASIC have a command that prints to the printer?

A Liberty BASIC does support printing to your printer, but you must modify the Print command to do so. Other BASIC-based languages use the LPrint command to send output to the printer but Liberty BASIC does not support LPrint.

Workshop

The quiz questions and exercises are provided for your further understanding. See Appendix B, "Quiz Answers," for answers.

Quiz

1. How do you print words in the output window?

2. How would you write a Print statement that printed the sum of 10 and 20?

3. What does the semicolon do inside a Print statement?

4. True or false: Input is for getting input and Output is for displaying output.

5. What is a variable?

6. How do you print the contents of variables?

7. What is a prompt?

8. When does Liberty BASIC insert a question mark in an Input statement?

9. What is LPT1?

10. What statement must you use when you're through routing output to the printer?

Hour 5

Data Processing with Numbers and Words

Without an in-depth knowledge of characters, strings, and numbers, you won't be able to understand any programming language. This doesn't mean that you must be a math whiz or an English major. You must, however, understand how languages such as Liberty BASIC represent and work with such data.

In this hour, you will learn more about how Liberty BASIC performs its mathematical calculations. In addition, you will learn how Liberty BASIC represents and works with strings. Along the way, you will discover functions and powerful built-in routines that perform many of the programming chores for you.

The highlights of this hour include

- Merging strings together
- Understanding internal representation of strings

- Seeing the ASCII table work for you
- Mastering the programming operators
- Digging into Liberty BASIC's functions

Strings Revisited

The BASIC programming language and all its offshoots such as Liberty BASIC and Visual Basic have excelled in their support of strings. Hardly any programming language before BASIC was created in the 1960s supported string data except in a rudimentary form. BASIC was created for beginners, but it offered advanced support for strings.

Even since the first BASIC language, programming languages have been slow to adopt string support beyond a rudimentary level. C++, one of the newer programming languages of the past 50 years and one of the most-used, did not directly support strings. To work with strings in C++ (and its earlier rendition C), programmers had to do some fancy footwork to get around the fact that the fundamental string data type was not supported. Java, a language you will learn in Part III, "Stepping Up to Java," does support strings, but BASIC still rules in ease of string manipulation.

Merging Strings

You can merge or *concatenate* (programmers rarely use a simple word when a longer word will confuse more people) two strings together simply by placing a plus sign between them. Consider the short program in Listing 5.1. The program asks the user for the user's first and last names, using two Input statements, then prints the full name by concatenating them together with a space between them to separate the names.

LISTING 5.1 Merging Two Strings Together Is Simple.

```
' Filename: Merge.bas
' Program that asks the user for a first and
' last name and then prints the full name
Input "What is your first name? "; first$
Input "What is your last name? "; last$
'
' Store the combined strings
fullName$ = first$ + " " + last$
'
' Print the merged string
Print "Your full name is "; fullName$
End
```

Here is the output from the program:

```
What is your first name? Terri
What is your last name? Johnston
Your full name is Terri Johnston
```

The program stored the concatenated string in a string variable named `fullname$`. Remember that variable names ending with a dollar sign are string variables that hold character string data.

> You'll store lots of numbers, such as social security numbers, zip codes, and numerical inventory product codes in string variables. If you'll not do calculations with a number, or if a number does not represent a count of any kind, store those values in string variables, too. If you store the digits in a zip code using the zip+4 format, inside a numeric variable, the programming language might actually round the number. When rounding large numbers, your calculations will not be adversely affected in most cases. But when rounding occurs on numeric data that should not be rounded but that represents something such as a zip code or part number, the rounding will wreak havoc when you attempt to search or sort by that value.

You did not have to concatenate the first and last name into a single string to print the full name. Listing 5.2 produces the same output as Listing 5.1. Instead of concatenating the strings, the `Print` statement prints the first name followed by the last name.

LISTING 5.2   You Don't Have to Merge Strings to Print the Full Name.

```
' Filename: FullN.bas
' Program that asks the user for a first and
' last name and then prints the full name
Input "What is your first name? "; first$
Input "What is your last name? "; last$
'
' Print the two strings
Print "Your full name is "; first$; " "; last$
End
```

The advantage to merging strings is that you can work with the merged strings as a single variable and reuse that string variable later in the program. Perhaps you need to store the full name in a disk file or convert the name to all uppercase letters for some reason. Merging the strings together may come in handy.

The plus sign is used for concatenating strings as well as for adding numbers together. Liberty BASIC knows the difference because the context in which you use the plus sign determines what Liberty BASIC does. If you put a plus sign between two strings (or between two string variables), Liberty BASIC merges the strings. If you put a plus sign between two numbers (or between two numeric variables), Liberty BASIC adds the two values together.

The ASCII Table

To fully understand strings, you must understand how your computer represents characters internally. A concept that will come into major play while you program in any language is the *ASCII table* (pronounced *ask-ee*). Although the reason for the ASCII table and how to take advantage of your knowledge of the ASCII table will increase as you hone your programming skills, you should take a few moments for an introduction to this important character-based table.

Years ago, somebody wrote all the various combinations of eight binary 1s and 0s, from 00000000 to 11111111, and assigned a unique character to each one. The table of characters was standardized and is known today as the ASCII table. Table 5.1 shows a partial listing of the ASCII table that contains 256 entries. ASCII stands for *American Standard Code for Information Interchange*. Some ASCII tables use only the last seven *bits* (called the *7-bit ASCII table*) and keep the far left-hand bit off. As you might surmise, a bit is a 1 or a 0. Eight bits form a *byte,* which is a character in computer terminology due to the ASCII table. Seven-bit ASCII tables cannot represent as many different characters as can today's 8-bit ASCII tables.

TABLE 5.1 Every Character Possible Has Its Own Unique ASCII Value.

Character	ASCII Code	Decimal Equivalent
Space	00100000	32
0	00110000	48
1	00110001	49
2	00110010	50
3	00110011	51
9	00111001	57
?	00111111	63
A	01000001	65
B	01000010	66
C	01000011	67
a	01100001	97
b	01100010	98

Each ASCII value has a corresponding decimal number associated with it. These values are shown at the right of the eight-bit values in Table 5.1. Therefore, even though the computer represents the character "?" as 00111111 (two off switches with six on switches), you can refer, through programming, to that ASCII value as 63 and your computer will know you mean 00111111. One of the advantages of high-level programming languages is that they often let you use the easier (for people) decimal values and the programming language converts the value to the 8-bit binary value used inside the computer.

As you can tell from the ASCII values in Table 5.1, every character in the computer, both uppercase and lowercase letters, and even the space, has its own unique ASCII value. The unique ASCII code is the only way that the computer has to differentiate characters.

Every microcomputer uses the ASCII table. Large mainframe computers use a similar table called the *EBCDIC table* (pronounced *eb-se-dik*). The ASCII table is the fundamental storage representation of all data and programs that your computer manages. A new coding scheme called *Unicode* is now beginning to see some use. Unicode spans far more than the 256 character limit of the ASCII or EBCIDIC tables in order to take into account languages such as the Japanese-based *kanji* and others that require numerous characters to represent. Unicode assigns hundreds of numbers to hundreds and even thousands of possible characters depending on the language being represented.

When you press the letter *A*, that *A* is not stored in your computer; rather, the ASCII value of the letter *A* is stored. As you can see from the ASCII values in the previous table, the letter *A* is represented as 01000001 (all eight switches except two are off in every byte of memory that holds a letter *A*).

The ASCII table is not very different from another type of coded table you may have heard of. Morse code is a table of representations for letters of the alphabet. Instead of 1s and 0s, the code uses combinations of dashes and dots to represent characters.

As Figure 5.1 shows, when you press the letter *A* on your keyboard, the *A* does not go into memory, but the ASCII value of 01000001 does. The computer keeps that pattern of on and off switches in that memory location as long as the *A* is to remain there. As far as you are concerned, the *A* is in memory as the letter *A*, but now you know exactly what happens.

FIGURE **5.1**

The letter A is not an A after it leaves the keyboard.

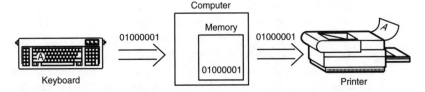

As Figure 5.1 illustrates, when you print a document from your word processor, the computer prints each "character" stored in that memory location, the computer's CPU sends the ASCII code for the letter *A* to the printer. Just before printing, the printer knows that it must make its output readable to people, so it looks up 01000001 in its own ASCII table and prints the *A* to paper. From the time the *A* left the keyboard until right before it printed, it was not an *A* at all, but just a combination of eight 1s and 0s that represents an *A*.

Performing Math with Liberty BASIC

Liberty BASIC performs mathematical calculations in the same way as most programming languages. Therefore, once you understand the way Liberty BASIC calculates, you'll understand how virtually every other computer language calculates. Table 5.2 lists the Liberty Basic math operators with which you should familiarize yourself.

TABLE 5.2   Liberty BASIC Math Operators Are Simple.

Operator	Description
( )	Groups expressions together
^	Exponentiation
*, /	Multiplication and division
+, −	Addition and subtraction

The order of the operators in Table 5.1 is important. If more than one of these operators appears in an expression, Liberty Basic doesn't always calculate the values in a left-to-right order. In other words, the expression

```
v = 5 + 2 * 3
```

stores the value 11 in v, not 21 as you might first guess. Liberty BASIC doesn't perform calculations in a left-to-right order, but rather in the order given in Table 5.2. Because multiplication appears before addition in the table, Liberty Basic computes the 2 * 3 first, resulting in 6; it then computes the answer to 5 + 6 to get the result of 11.

> The order in which operators are evaluated is often called *operator prece-*
> *dence.* Every programming language except APL computes expressions
> based on a precedence table. Different programming languages might use
> different operators from the ones shown in Table 5.2, although almost all of
> them use parentheses and the primary math operators (*, /, +, and -) in the
> same way as Liberty BASIC does.

Parentheses have the highest operator precedence. Any expression enclosed in parentheses is calculated before any other part of the expression. The statement:

```
v = (5 + 2) * 3
```

does assign the value of 21 to v because the parentheses force the addition of 5 and 2
before its sum of 7 is multiplied by 3.

The exponentiation operator raises a number to a particular power. In the following statement, 1,000 is placed in the variable x because 10^3 means raise 10 to the third power
(10 times 10 times 10):

```
x = 10 ^ 3
```

You can also raise a number to a fractional power with the ^ operator. For example, the
statement:

```
x = 81 ^ 0.5
```

raises 81 to the one-half power, in effect taking the square root of 81. If this math is getting deep, have no fear; some people program in Liberty BASIC for years and never need
to raise a number to a fractional power. But if you need to, you can thank Liberty
BASIC.

The forward slash (/) divides one number into another. The statement

```
d = 3 / 2
```

assigns 1.5 to d.

To sum up (pardon the pun) math operators, Listing 5.3 contains a program that prints
the result of calculations that use all the Liberty BASIC operators described in this lesson. The output of the program is shown in Figure 5.2 after the program listing.

5

LISTING 5.3   Liberty BASIC Calculations Follow the Order of Operator Precedence.

```
' Filename: OpPrec.Bas
' Program to demonstrate the Liberty Basic math operators
num1 = 12
num2 = 5
PRINT "num1 is "; num1
PRINT "num2 is "; num2
'
' Print the result of several calculations using 12 and 5
value = num1 + num2
PRINT "num1 + num2 equals "; value
value = num1 - num2
PRINT "num1 - num2 equals "; value
value = num1 * num2
PRINT "num1 * num2 equals "; value
value = num1 / num2
PRINT "num1 / num2 equals "; value
value = num1 ^ num2
PRINT "num1 ^ num2 equals "; value
value = num1 + num2 * 4
PRINT "num1 + num2 * 4 equals "; value
value = (num1 + num2) * 4
PRINT "(num1 + num2) * 4 equals "; value
END
```

FIGURE 5.2

Viewing the output of the calculations.

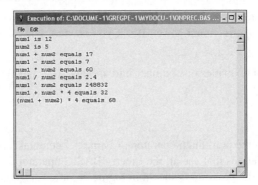

You don't have to be a math expert to use Liberty BASIC; it does all the math for you. You only have to understand how Liberty BASIC performs the math so that you can properly set up the equations you need to calculate.

How Computers Really Do Math

At their lowest level, computers cannot subtract, multiply, or divide. Neither can calculators. The world's largest and fastest supercomputers can only add—that's it. It performs the addition at the bit level. Binary arithmetic is the only means by which any electronic digital-computing machine can perform arithmetic.

The computer makes you think it can perform all sorts of fancy calculations because it is lightning fast. The computer can only add, but it can do so very quickly.

Suppose that you want the computer to add seven 6s together. If you asked the computer (through programming) to perform the calculation

```
6 + 6 + 6 + 6 + 6 + 6 + 6
```

the computer would return the answer 42 immediately. The computer has no problem performing addition. The problems arise when you request that the computer perform another type of calculation, such as this one:

```
42 - 6 - 6 - 6 - 6 - 6 - 6 - 6
```

Because the computer can only add, it cannot do the subtraction. However (and this is where the catch comes in), the computer can *negate* numbers. That is, the computer can take the negative of a number. It can take the negative of 6 and represent (at the bit level) negative 6. After it has done that, it can *add* –6 to 42 and continue doing so seven times. In effect, the internal calculation becomes this:

```
42 + (-6) + (-6) + (-6) + (-6) + (-6) + (-6) + (-6)
```

Adding seven –6s produces the correct result of 0. In reality, the computer is not subtracting. At its bit level, the computer can convert a number to its negative through a process known as *2's complement*. The 2's complement of a number is the negative of the number's original value at the bit level. The computer has in its internal logic circuits the ability to rapidly convert a number to its 2's complement and then carry out the addition of negatives, thereby seemingly performing subtraction.

 Here's another kind of 2's complement: *That's a very fine two you have there.*

Because the computer can add and simulate subtraction (through successive adding of negatives), it can simulate multiplying and dividing. To multiply 6 times 7, the computer actually adds 6 together seven times and produces 42. Therefore,

```
6 * 7
```

becomes this:

```
6 + 6 + 6 + 6 + 6 + 6 + 6
```

To divide 42 by 7, the computer subtracts 7 from 42 (well, it adds the *negative* of 7 to 42) until it reaches 0 and counts the number of times (6) it took to reach 0, like this:

```
42 + (-7) + (-7) + (-7) + (-7) + (-7) + (-7)
```

The computer represents numbers in a manner similar to characters. As Table 5.3 shows, numbers are easy to represent at the binary level. After numbers reach a certain limit (256 to be exact), the computer will use more than one byte to represent the number, taking as many memory locations as it needs to represent the extent of the number. The computer, after it is taught to add, subtract, multiply, and divide, can then perform any math necessary as long as a program is supplied to direct it.

TABLE 5.3   The First 20 Numbers Can Be Represented in Their Binary Equivalents.

Number	Binary Equivalent
0	00000000
1	00000001
2	00000010
3	00000011
4	00000100
5	00000101
6	00000110
7	00000111
8	00001000
9	00001001
10	00001010
11	00001011
12	00001100
13	00001101
14	00001110
15	00001111

continues

TABLE 5.3 Continued

Number	Binary Equivalent
16	00010000
17	00010001
18	00010010
19	00010011
20	00010100

The first 255 binary numbers overlap the ASCII table values. That is, the binary representation for the letter *A* is 01000001, and the binary number for 65 is also 01000001. The computer knows by the context of how your programs use the memory location whether the value is the letter *A* or the number 65.

To see an example of what goes on at the bit level, follow this example to see what happens when you ask the computer to subtract 65 from 65. The result should be 0, and as you can see from the following steps, that is exactly what the result is at the binary level:

1. Suppose you want the computer to calculate the following:

    ```
      65
    - 65
    ```

2. The binary representation for 65 is 01000001 and the 2's complement for 65 is 10111111 (which is –65 in *computerese*). Therefore, you are requesting that the computer perform this calculation:

    ```
     01000001
    +10111111
    ```

3. Because a binary number cannot have the digit 2 (there are only 0s and 1s in binary), the computer carries 1 any time a calculation results in a value of 2; 1 + 1 equals 10 in binary. Although this can be confusing, you can make an analogy with decimal arithmetic. People work in a base-10 numbering system. Binary is known as base-2. There is no single digit to represent 10; we have to reuse two digits already used to form ten, namely 1 and 0. In base 10, 9 + 1 is 10. Therefore, the result of 1 + 1 in binary is 10 or "0 and carry 1 to the next column."

    ```
     01000001
    +10111111
    100000000
    ```

5

Because the answer should fit within the same number of bits as the two original numbers (at least for this example—your computer may use more bits to represent numbers), the ninth bit is discarded, leaving the 0 result. This example shows that binary 65 plus binary negative 65 equals 0, as it should.

> You can see a complete ASCII table in Appendix C.

Using the ASCII Table

By understanding the ASCII table available, you can print any character by referring to its ASCII number. For instance, the capital letter *A* is number 65. The lowercase *a* is 96. Since you can type letters, numbers, and some special characters on your keyboard, the ASCII table is not needed much for these. However, you cannot use the keyboard to type the Spanish Ñ or the cent sign (¢), under normal circumstances. You print these with the Chr$ function, called the *character string function*. The format of Chr$ is

```
Chr$(ASCII number)
```

The following Print statement prints a quoted message, with the quotation marks showing in the output:

```
Print "She said "; Chr$(34); "I will go."; Chr$(34)
```

Here is the output:

```
She said "I will go."
```

Since 34 is the ASCII number that represents the quotation mark, Liberty BASIC replaces the Chr$(34) in the output with the quotation mark.

The ASCII number can be a numeric constant or a numeric variable. Chr$ is not a command, but a *function*. You do not use Chr$ by itself, as with most functions. It is combined with other statements. If you combine Chr$ with a Print statement, the character matching the ASCII number in the parenthesis will print.

The first 31 ASCII codes represent *nonprinting* characters. Nonprinting characters cause an action to be performed instead of producing characters. For instance, to form feed your printer paper, you could send the form feed ASCII code like this:

```
Print #1, Chr$(12)
```

12 is the ASCII number for form feed, so when you print Chr$(12) to your printer, the printer doesn't actually print a character but acts upon that ASCII code and ejects the sheet of paper currently being printed. Of course, this assumes that you've opened your printer for printing to #1 as you learned how to do in the previous hour. By placing this Print statement after you send your output to a printer, you ensure that the last page printed automatically ejects. You might recall from the previous hour that the last page printed does not always eject when you print from Liberty BASIC. As long as your final Print prints the ASCII Chr$(12) form-feed character, the page will always eject properly.

Now that you've seen a function in action, you are ready to learn more about functions.

Overview of Functions

Functions are built-in routines that manipulate numbers, strings, and output. Most strings have this in common: the function name is always followed by parentheses. The value in the parentheses determines what the function does. It is called an *argument*. The Chr$() functions in the statement

```
PRINT Chr(34); "Hi!"; Chr$(34)
```

each contain one argument, 34, and that argument is sent to the function. Without the argument, the function would have nothing on which to work.

Some functions have no arguments, some (such as Chr$()) have one argument, and others have more than one argument. A function never stands by itself in a statement; you always combine functions with other statements (assignment statements, output statements, and so on).

A function always *returns* a value. The numeric and string functions return either a number or a string based on the argument you send to it. When a numeric function returns a value, you must do something with that value—either print it, assign it to a variable, or use it in an expression. Because the purpose of a function is to return a value, you cannot put a function on the left side of an equal sign in an assignment statement.

A function name always has parentheses following it if it requires an argument, as most of them do.

5

The following sections walk you through the use of some Liberty BASIC numeric and string functions.

Numeric Functions

There are several functions supplied by Liberty BASIC that perform math routines, and this section introduces you to those. Lots of your own code is saved if you use these functions.

One common numeric function is the Int() function. Int() is the *integer* function (integers are whole numbers without decimal points). It returns the integer whole value of the numbers you put in the parentheses. If you put a decimal number inside the parentheses, Int() converts it to an integer. For example,

```
Print Int(8.93)
```

puts an 8 (the function's return value) on the screen. Int() returns a value that is equal to or less than the argument in the parentheses. Int() does not round numbers up. As with all math functions, you can use a variable or expression as the function argument.

These functions all print 8:

```
num = 8.93
Print Int(num)
num = 8
Print Int(num + 0.93)
num1 = 8.93
num2 = Int(num1)
Print num2
```

Int() works for negative arguments as well. The following line of code

```
Print Int(-7.6)
```

prints -8. This might surprise you until you learn the complete definition of Int(). It returns the highest integer that is less than or equal to the argument in parentheses. The highest integer less than or equal to -7.6 is -8.

You don't have to be an expert in math to use many of the mathematical functions that come with Liberty BASIC. Often, even in business applications, the following function comes in handy:

```
Abs(numeric value)
```

The Abs() function, called the *absolute value* function, can be used in many programs as well. Abs() returns the absolute value of its argument. The absolute value of a number is simply the positive representation of a positive or negative number. Whatever argument you pass to Abs(), its positive value is returned. For example, the line of code

```
Print Abs(-5); " "; Abs(-5.75); " "; Abs(0); " "; Abs(5);" "; Abs(5.76)
```

produces the following output:

```
5 5.76 0 5 5.76
```

The following advanced math functions are available if you need them:

```
Atn(numeric value)
Cos(numeric value)
Sin(numeric value)
Tan(numeric value)
Exp(numeric value)
Log(numeric value)
```

These are probably the least-used functions in Liberty BASIC. This is not to belittle the work of scientific and mathematical programmers who need them; thank goodness Liberty BASIC supplies these functions! Otherwise, programmers would have to write their own versions.

The `Atn()` function returns the arctangent of the argument in radians. The argument is assumed to be an expression representing an angle of a right triangle. If you're familiar with trigonometry (and who isn't, right?), you may know that the result of all arctangent calculations always falls between $-\pi/2$ and $+\pi/2$ and the `Arc()` function requires that its argument also fall within this range. `Cos()` always returns the cosine of the angle of the argument expressed in radians. `Sin()` returns the sine of the angle of the argument expressed in radians. `Tan()` returns the tangent of the angle of the argument expressed in radians.

If you need to pass an angle expressed in degrees to these functions, convert the angle to radians by multiplying it by $(\pi/180)$. (π is approximately 3.141592654.)

If you understand these trigonometric functions, you should have no trouble with the `Exp()` and `Log()`. You use them the same way. If you do not understand these mathematical functions, that's OK. Some people program in Liberty BASIC for years and never need them.

`Exp()` returns the base of natural logarithm (e) raised to a specified power. The argument to `Exp()` can be any constant, variable, or expression less than or equal to 88.02969. e is the mathematical expression for the value 2.718282. The following program shows some `Exp()` statements:

```
Print Exp(1)
Print Exp(2)
Print Exp(3)
Print Exp(4)
Print Exp(5)
```

Here is the output produced by these five Print statements:

```
2.71828183
7.3890561
20.0855369
54.59815
148.413159
```

Notice the first number; *e* raised to the first power does indeed equal itself.

Log() returns the natural logarithm of the argument. The argument to Log() can be any positive constant, variable, or expression. The following program shows the Log() function in use:

```
Print Log(3)
```

Here is the output:

```
1.098612
```

String Functions

Liberty BASIC's string functions work in a manner similar to numeric functions. When you pass them an argument, they return a value you can store or print. String functions enable you to print strings in ways you never could before, as well as look at individual characters from a string.

You have already seen one of the ASCII string functions, the Chr$() function. When you enclose an ASCII number inside the Chr$() parentheses (the argument), Liberty BASIC substitutes the character that matches that ASCII value. Two additional string functions work with the ASCII table also, and their formats are

```
Asc(string value)
Space$(numeric value)
```

Asc() returns the ASCII number of the character argument you give it. The argument must be a string of one or more characters. If you pass Asc() a string of more than one character, it returns the ASCII number of only the first character in the string. Therefore, you can obtain the ASCII number of a name's first initial. For example, the statement

```
Print Asc("A"); " "; Asc("B"); " "; Asc("C")
```

produces the following output:

```
65 66 67
```

You can look at the ASCII table to see that these three numbers are the ASCII values for A, B, and C. You can also use string variables as arguments:

```
letter1$ = "A"
letter2$ = "B"
letter3$ = "C"
Print Asc(letter1$); " "; Asc(letter2$); " "; Asc(letter3$)
```

This produces the same output as the previous example.

If you pass a string with more than one character to Asc(), it returns the ASCII value of only the first character. Therefore, the statement

```
Print Asc("Hello")
```

prints 72 (the ASCII value of H).

The Space$() function returns the number of spaces specified by its integer argument. Because a row of spaces is commonly required to make output more readable, Liberty BASIC includes this function. The following Print statement prints the letter *X* twice with 40 spaces between:

```
Print "X"; Space$(40); "X"
```

The Str$() and Val() functions are mirror-image functions. These two functions convert string data to numeric data and numeric data to string data. The Str$() converts the numeric variable, constant, or expression inside the parentheses to a string. If the number is positive, the string will have a leading space. The following statement is not a valid statement because you cannot put a number in a string variable:

```
s$ = 54.6    ' This is invalid
```

You can avoid an error by first using Str$() to convert the number to a string before assigning it to a string variable, as in

```
s$ = Str$(54.6)    ' This works
```

If you print s$, you see 54.5 in your output window. You must realize, however, that this is not a number; it is simply a string of characters with a period in the middle that looks like a number when it is printed. You cannot perform any math with s$ because it is not a number.

There might be times when you want to combine numbers and words into a string. You can enclose the number inside the Str$() function and concatenate it with other strings to build the longer string.

Val() converts the string variable, constant, or expression inside the parentheses to a number. The argument (the string in the parentheses) must start with a string of

5

characters that looks like a valid number (integer, decimal, or any other data type). `Val()` ignores any spaces that might be at the beginning of the string (called *leading blanks*). The following section of code illustrates the `Val()` function:

```
s1$ = "44 bottles"
n1 = Val(s1$)   ' Ignores everything after the number
Print n1
s2$ = "00012.5"
n2 = Val(s2$)   ' Converts the string to single-precision
Print n2
s3$ = "Sam is 68 years old"  ' No valid number at
n3 = Val(s3$)                '   beginning of string
Print n3
```

These lines of code produce the following output:

```
44
12.5
0
```

There are several more string functions that manipulate strings in many ways. They let you break one string into several smaller strings by removing portions of it. You can trim the leading spaces from strings and change the middle of a string without changing the rest of the string.

The `Len()` function is good to use when you want to know the length of a string. `Len()` also works with numbers to show you how much memory a numeric variable consumes. `Len()` returns the length (number of characters) of the string variable, constant, or expression inside its parentheses. The `Print` statement

```
Print Len("abcdef")
```

produces a 6 as its output.

If the string does not contain any data (it is a null string), `Len()` returns a value of 0. This lets you test to see if a user entered data in response to an `Input` request for string data.

`Left$()` requires two arguments: a string variable, constant, or an expression that is followed by an integer constant or a variable. The integer determines how many characters are stripped from the left of the string and returned. `Right$()` requires two arguments as well: a string variable, constant, or expression that is followed by an integer constant or a variable. The integer determines how many characters are stripped from the right of the string and returned. The following code demonstrates `Left$()`:

```
a$ = "abcdefg"
Print Left$(a$, 1)
Print Left$(a$, 3)
```

```
Print Left$(a$, 7)
Print Left$(a$, 20)
```

This produces the following output:

```
a
abc
abcdefg
abcdefg
```

Notice from the last Print statement that if you try to return more characters from the left of the string than exist, Left$() returns the entire string and not an error message.

Right$() works in the same manner, except that it returns the rightmost characters from a string, as shown here:

```
a$ = "abcdefg"
Print Right$(a$, 1)
Print Right$(a$, 3)
Print Right$(a$, 7)
Print Right$(a$, 20)
```

This produces the following output:

```
g
efg
abcefg
abcefg
```

The Mid$() function accomplishes what Left$() and Right$() cannot: Mid$() returns characters from the *middle* of a string. Mid$() uses three arguments: a string that is followed by two integers. The first integer determines where Mid$() begins stripping characters from the string (the position, starting at 1), and the second integer determines how many characters from that position to return. If you do not specify two integers, Mid$() uses 1 as the starting position.

Mid$() can pull any number of characters from anywhere in the string. The following example shows how the Mid$() function works.

```
a$ = "Basic FORTRAN COBOL C Pascal"
Print Mid$(a$, 1, 6)
Print Mid$(a$, 7, 7)
Print Mid$(a$, 15, 5)
Print Mid$(a$, 21, 1)
Print Mid$(a$, 23, 6)
```

This produces a listing of these five programming languages, one per line, as shown in the following output:

```
Basic
FORTRAN
```

5

```
COBOL
C
Pascal
```

Instr() is different from the others you've seen in this section. Instr() is a string search function. You use it to find the starting location of a string inside another string. Instr() returns the character position (an integer) at which one string starts within another string. The format of Instr() is different from most of the other string functions. It requires two or three arguments, depending on what you want it to do.

Instr() looks to see whether the second string expression (Instr()'s second argument) exists within the first string expression (Instr()'s first argument). If it is, Instr() returns the starting position of the string within the first string. Instr() assumes a beginning position of 1, unless you override it by including the option integer as Instr()'s third and optional argument. For example, if you give Instr() a starting value of 5, Instr() ignores the first four characters of the search string. If Instr() fails to find the first string within the search string, it returns a 0. The following lines make Instr()'s operation clear:

```
a$ = "Liberty Basic FORTRAN COBOL C Pascal"
Print Instr(a$, "FORTRAN")
Print Instr(a$, "COBOL")
Print Instr(a$, "C")
Print Instr(a$, "PL/I")
Print Instr(a$, "PL/I" 5)    ' Does not exist
```

Study the code to see how it produces the following output:

```
15
23
23
0
0
```

Summary

You now understand how Liberty BASIC calculations work. By utilizing the math operators and by understanding the math hierarchy, you will know how to compose your own calculations.

By understanding the ASCII table, you not only better understand how computers represent characters internally, but you also understand how to access those ASCII values by using the Chr$() function. Many of Liberty BASIC's functions are universal—similar functions exist in many languages that you'll learn throughout your programming career.

Q&A

Q **In Liberty BASIC, do I have to know all the values that I will assign to variables when I write the program?**

A Data comes from all sources. You will know some of the values that you can assign when you write your programs, but much of your program data will come from the user or from data files.

Q **What kinds of data can variables hold?**

A Variables can hold many kinds of data, such as numbers, characters, and character strings. As you learn more about programming, you will see that numeric data comes in all formats and, to master a programming language well, you must also master the kinds of numeric data that are available. Some programming languages, such as Visual Basic, support variables that hold time and date values as well.

Workshop

The quiz questions and exercises are provided for your further understanding. See Appendix B, "Quiz Answers," for answers.

Quiz

1. What is the result of the following expression?

   ```
   (1 + 2) * 4 / 2
   ```

2. What is the result of the following expression?

   ```
   (1 + (10 - (2 + 2)))
   ```

3. What is a function?

4. What is the output from the following `Print` statement?

   ```
   Print Int(-5.6)
   ```

5. What is the output from the following `Print` statement?

   ```
   Print Sqr(4)
   ```

6. Name a function that works both with numeric data and with character string data.

7. Name the three trigonometric functions mentioned in this hour.

8. True or false: `Chr$()` is the opposite of the `Asc()` function.

9. What does the following statement print?

   ```
   Print Chr$(Asc("A"))
   ```

10. What is the difference between the `Mid$()` function and the `Instr$()` function?

5

Hour **6**

Controlling Your Programs

This hour's lesson extends your knowledge of Liberty BASIC by showing you how to compare values and repeat sections of Liberty BASIC programs. A user's responses or calculated data can control the flow of your program. This lesson teaches you how to write programs that make decisions. The code sometimes needs to repeat sections in order to complete the processing of several data values. You'll learn how to create a loop to do just that.

With the concepts that you learn in this lesson, you can write powerful programs to do what you need done. You will find yourself thinking of new ideas and new ways to use your computer.

The highlights of this hour include the following:

- Making decisions with Liberty BASIC
- Using the `If` statement
- Changing decisions with the `Else` statement
- Repeating sections of code

- Using the `For` loop
- Using the `While...Wend` loop statement

Comparing Data with `If`

Liberty BASIC provides the ability for your program to make a choice and to perform one action or another depending on a condition. A Liberty BASIC decision statement has two possibilities. To decide which path to take in a Liberty Basic program, you must use the `If` statement. Most programming languages have an `If` statement that works exactly like Liberty BASIC's. Therefore, once you learn how Liberty BASIC supports the `If` statement, you will be able to apply the same principles for most other computer languages as well.

Listing 6.1 shows you an example of a program that contains an `If` statement. Even though you have never seen a Liberty BASIC `If` statement before, you will probably have little trouble figuring out what this program does.

LISTING 6.1   Use an `If` Statement When You Want Your Program to Make a Decision.

```
' Filename: If1.bas
' Deciding how much of a bonus to pay a salesperson
 Input "What is the salesperson's name? "; sName$
 Input "What were the total sales made last month? "; sales

 If (sales < 5000) Then
    bonus = 0
    daysOff = 0
 Else
    bonus = 25
    daysOff = 2
 End If

 Print
 Print sName$; " earned a bonus of "; bonus;
 Print " and gets "; daysOff; " days off."
End
```

Look at the following two sample runs of the program. Pay attention to the fact that the program calculates a different bonus based on the salesperson's total sales. The first sample run follows:

```
What is the salesperson's name? Jim
What were the total sales made last month? 3234.43
Jim earned a bonus of 0 and gets 0 days off.
```

The salesperson did not get a bonus because the sales were not high enough. Consider the difference in the following:

```
What is the salesperson's name? Jane
What were the total sales made last month? 5642.34 Jane earned a bonus of 25 and
gets 2 days off.
```

The program offers complete control over one of two options via the If statement. Figure 6.1 shows you the flowchart of this program. As Hour 3, "Designing a Program," explained, programmers rarely use flowcharts to design programs anymore, but flowcharts are helpful in teaching how statements logically work. The diamond in the flowchart represents a *decision symbol* and shows the operation of Liberty BASIC's If statement.

FIGURE 6.1

The flowchart's decision symbol illustrates the nature of the salesperson program's If *statement.*

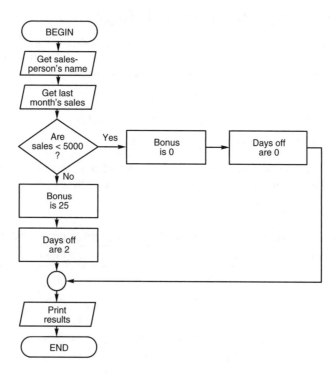

The If statement works just like it reads. If the statement to the right of the If is true, the block of statements following If executes. Notice that Then is required. If the statement to the right of If is not true, the block of statements following Else executes instead. The Else clause is optional; without it, you are testing to see whether you will execute a single block of statements. For example, the following is an If statement that prints a message only if the statement to the right of If is true. If it is not, and there is no Else, the program continues on the line after End If.

```
If (age < 18) Then
   Print "You are not old enough"
End If
```

End If always marks the end of the If set of statements. Whatever the result of the If is, the statements following End If always execute after the If finishes.

The parentheses around the statement to the right of the If are not required, but they clarify what exactly is being tested. This statement to the right of If, typically enclosed within parentheses, is called a *relational test*.

Writing the Relational Test

The If statement reads just as it does in plain English: *If something is true, do one thing; otherwise do something else.* You do not always add an *else* after a spoken *if*, and you do not have to have one in Liberty BASIC either. Consider the following statements:

If I make enough money, I'll retire early.

If you're out late, call me, else you'll get in trouble.

If you're in town, we'll eat dinner together.

As a programming language, Liberty BASIC is fairly strict about how you make the If test. The relational test, the statement to the right of the If, always includes one of the symbols from Table 6.1.

TABLE 6.1 If Statement Relational Operators Determine How the If Behaves.

Operator	Description	Example
<	Less than	If (sales < maxSales) Then
>	Greater than	If (amount > 100.00) Then
=	Equal to	If (age = 21) Then
>=	Greater than or equal to	If (grade >= 90) Then
<=	Less than or equal to	If (price <= 1.00) Then
<>	Not equal to	If (year <> 2004) Then

You learned about the math operators in Hour 5, "Data Processing with Numbers and Words." Liberty BASIC supplies these relational operators so you can test certain conditions with If statements. There are always two possibilities with the relational operators. Something is either less than something else, or it is not. Something is either greater than something else, or it is not. Something is either equal to something else, or it is not.

The two possibilities that the relational operators enable provide the means for duplicating the two-legged decision symbol in a flowchart. A decision symbol has two possible outcomes, and so does the If. If is either true or false.

The statements following Then and Else can be any Liberty BASIC statement or multiple statements. Else can even contain one more If in its block. Listing 6.2 contains a set of If statements that prints first or second depending on the number entered by the user.

LISTING 6.2 An If Within the Else Can Occur.

```
' Filename: If3.bas
' Prints a description based on user's number
 Input "How many years have you been in school? "; years
 If (years = 1) Then
    Print "This is your first year"
 Else If (years = 2) Then
    Print "This is your second year"
 End If
End
```

You can validate some input values to make sure the user entered what you expected. For instance, you can check an age to make sure it is greater than 0. There is not always a way to determine whether the user's input value is exactly correct, but you can check to see if it is reasonable. In addition, you might want to ensure that the user doesn't enter a number greater than 2 because doing so results in the same output as though the user entered 2.

Most languages allow for multiple If statements inside another If statement, but Liberty BASIC allows only one.

6

Looping Statements

Looping statements are another important feature of any programming language. Liberty BASIC supplies two statements that control loops. Your computer will never get bored. It will loop over and over, quickly repeating statements as long as you need it to.

Loops have many uses. You might need a loop to ask the user for several people's data, to calculate a combined total, or to print several lines of data. Liberty BASIC's two primary looping statements are

- For...Next loops
- While...Wend loops

The following sections describe these looping statements.

Using the For...Next Loop

The For...Next loop is actually a loop of statements enclosed between the For and the Next statements. Before you look at the For...Next loop, an analogy to things in everyday life might be helpful. As with the If, the For loops are natural ways of expressing an idea. Consider the following description:

```
For each of today's invoices:
```

➡   check the accuracy of the invoice,

➡   add the total amount to the daily sales total.

➡   Look at the next invoice.

You can sense from this description of invoice totaling that a repetitive process happens. If there are five invoices, the process repeats for each invoice.

The computer's For loop works just like the for-each concept in the invoice description (that's why it's called For). To ease you into the method of For loops, Listing 6.3 shows a simple loop that explains the For and Next statements.

LISTING 6.3   Use For and Next to Control a Counting Loop

```
' Filename: For1.bas
' First For...Next Program
' This program prints the number 1 through 5
For i = 1 To 5
    Print i
 Next i
End
```

Here is the output from Listing 6.3's program:

```
1
2
3
4
5
```

The For and Next statements work in pairs; they enclose one or more statements. The statements inside the For...Next loop repeat until the loop finishes. The loop is

controlled by the `For` statement's variable. In Listing 6.3's program, the control variable
is `i` (you can use any variable name). The `For` statement is saying the following: *For
each `i` (with `i` having a value of `1` the first time, `2` the second time, and so on until it
gets to `5`), perform the statement between `For` and `Next`.*

> As you can gather from Listing 6.3, the `For...Next` loop automatically incre-
> ments (adds 1 each time to) the control variable. The body of the `For` loop
> (the statement or statements between the `For` and `Next`) loops once for
> every increment of the variable until the variable reaches its final value spec-
> ified in the `For` statement.

Listing 6.4 shows a program that does exactly the same thing as Listing 6.3, but without
using a `For` loop. You can see that the `For` loop makes repetitive statements much easier
to code. (Consider how much easier it would be to use a `For...Next` statement to print
the numbers from 1 to 200, instead of writing two hundred lines of code to print those
numbers if you used the method in Listing 6.4.)

LISTING 6.4   Printing Without a `For...Next` Loop Gets Tedious.

```
' Filename: NoFor.bas
' Prints from 1 to 5 without a For...Next statement
i = 1
Print i
i = 2
Print i
i = 3
Print i
i = 4
Print i
i = 5
Print i
End
```

6

You do not have to print the value of the loop variable as done in Listing 6.4. Often, a
`For` loop controls a set of statements, determining the number of times those statements
repeat, without using the control variable for anything else. Listing 6.5, controlled by a
`For` loop, prints a message 15 times.

LISTING 6.5 Printing a Message Several Times in a Loop Is Efficient.

```
' Filename: For2.bas
' Message-printing program
For i = 1 To 15
    Print "Happy Birthday!"
 Next i
 End
```

Another example will make this clearer. Look at the program in Listing 6.6. A teacher might use it to print a grade sheet. The program asks the teacher how many test scores are to be entered. It uses that answer to loop through a series of statements asking for the next child's name and grade. As the teacher enters the data, the values are printed to the printer. At the end of the program, there is a complete listing of names and grades. (In Hour 9, "Programming Algorithms," you will learn how to program an accumulator to add all the grades together and to print a class average.)

LISTING 6.6 A Teacher's Grade-printing Program is Easy to Follow When You Use a Loop.

```
' Filename: Grade.bas
' Grade-printing program
 '
 Print  "** Grade-listing Program **"
 Print
 Input "How many tests are there today? "; numTests
 Print

 Open "Lpt1" For Output As #1
  Print #1, "** Grades for the Test **"
  Print #1, " "
  Print #1, "Names and Grades"
  For i = 1 To numTests
   Input "What is the next student's name? "; sName$
   Print "What is "; sName$; "'s grade";
   Input grade
   Print #1, "Name: "; sName$; ", Grade: "; grade
  Next i
  Close #1
 End
```

Here is the output from Listing 6.6 (the names and grades appear on the printed page as a grade sheet):

```
** Grade-listing Program **

How many tests are there today? 5

** Grades for the Test **

Names and Grades
What is the next student's name? Larry
What is Larry's grade?89
Name: Larry, Grade: 89
What is the next student's name? Susan
What is Susan's grade?62
Name: Susan, Grade: 62
What is the next student's name? Mary
What is Mary's grade?95
Name: Mary, Grade: 95
What is the next student's name? Kerry
What is Kerry's grade?82
Name: Kerry, Grade: 82
What is the next student's name? Joe
What is Joe's grade?99
Name: Joe, Grade: 99
```

If the teacher has 5 students, the For loop will loop 5 times. If the teacher inputs that there are 10 students, the program loops 10 times. Because the teacher's input value controls the For loop, the program is of general purpose and able to handle any number of students.

Controlling the For Loop

There are additional ways you can control a For loop. You can make the control variable increment by a value other than 1 each time through the loop. You can also make the count variable count down instead of up. By adding the Step option to the For statement, you can make the control variable change to a different value by either a positive or negative amount.

Listing 6.7 shows you a program that counts down from 10 to 1 and then prints "Blast Off!" at the end of the loop. You entered this same program in Hour 1 when you were first learning to use Liberty BASIC. To carry out the countdown, a negative Step value had to be used. The For statement says that a loop is requested, with i looping from 10 to 1. Each time through the loop, −1 is added to i, which causes the descending count.

6

LISTING 6.7   Counting Down from 10 to 1 is Simple with a `For` Loop.

```
' For3.bas
' A countdown program

For i = 10 To 1 Step -1
   Print i
Next i

Print "Blast Off!"
End
```

Here is the output from the program:

```
10
9
8
7
6
5
4
3
2
1
Blast Off!
```

You can specify any value for a `Step` amount. Listing 6.8 shows you a program that prints the even numbers below 15 and then the odd numbers below 15. Two loops control the counting. The first one begins counting at 2, and the second one begins counting at 1. Each loop adds a `Step` value of 2 to the initial `For` value to produce the sets of even and odd numbers.

LISTING 6.8   Print the First Few Even and Odd Numbers Using the `Step` Option

```
' Filename: For4.bas
' Print the first few even and odd numbers

Print "Even numbers from 2 to 14:"
For number = 2 To 15 Step 2
   Print number
Next number

Print "Odd numbers from 1 to 15:"
```

continues

LISTING 6.8   Continued

```
For number = 1 To 15 Step 2
   Print number
Next number
End
```

Figure 6.2 shows the output from this program.

FIGURE 6.2

*Printing some even
and odd numbers.*

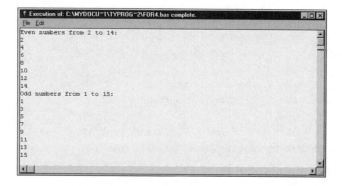

The `For` loop offers much loop control, but it is designed to count through the control loop's value. Not all your loops can be determined by a counting variable. Sometimes you need loops that loop while a certain condition is true or until a certain condition is met.

You can nest one loop inside another. Such nested constructs can seem rather advanced to beginning programmers, but the nested loops are simple to understand if you consider what happens when you need to perform a loop more than once. You *could* write the loop twice, back to back, or you could enclose the loop inside another loop that executes its body twice. Hour 9, "Programming Algorithms," explains nested loops in more detail.

Using the `While...Wend` Loop

The `While...Wend` loop supplies a way to control loops through a relational test. The loop's relational test uses the same relational operators used with `If` statements (refer back to Table 6.1 for a complete listing of relational operators).

Suppose the teacher with the grade-printing program doesn't know exactly how many students took the test, and doesn't want to take the time to count them. Because the total number of tests must be specified to control the `For` loop properly, another method is required. Listing 6.9 shows you the same program, but controlled by a `While...Wend` loop. Notice that the `While...Wend` continues looping while a certain condition is true. The condition is the teacher's answer in response to having more tests to enter.

6

LISTING 6.9   You Can Control the Grade Printing with a `While...Wend` **Loop.**

```
' Filename: Grade2.bas
' Grade-printing program
'
 Print  "** Grade-listing Program **"
 Print
 Open "Lpt1" For Output As #1
  Print #1,  "** Grades for the Test **"
  Print #1,  " "
  Print #1,  "Names and Grades"
  ' Loop until the teacher indicates no more grades
  Ans$ = "Y"   ' Yes to trigger at least one pass
  While (Ans$ = "Y")
   Input "What is the next student's name? "; sName$
   Print "What is "; sName$; "'s grade";
   Input grade
   Print #1, "Name: "; sName$; ", Grade: "; grade
   Input "Are there more grades (Y/N)"; Ans$
  Wend
End
```

This program keeps looping until the teacher indicates that there are no more grades to enter. Notice that the `While` is followed by a relational test, the result of which (true or false) determines whether the loop repeats again or quits. Before the loop first begins, the program assigns `Ans$` the value of "Y" to trigger the first pass through the loop. From that point, the final `Input` statement determines what goes into `Ans$` and whether or not the loop will repeat.

Summary

Congratulations! You can now enter data into a Liberty BASIC program and format the resulting output. You have also mastered the true power of any programming language—looping. The programs you saw in this lesson are getting to be powerful, yet you have seen that programming is easy. You have learned how the relational operators are used with the `If` statement so that a Liberty BASIC program can make decisions based on the data. In addition, the looping constructs enable sections of your program to repeat as long as necessary.

The next hour shows you how to analyze your programs to locate errors that might appear in them. You'll learn bug-catching secrets so that you can write more accurate programs more quickly.

Q&A

Q Does it matter whether I select `While` or `For` statements when I'm writing loops?

A Generally, `For` loops are useful when you must count values or iterate the loop's body for a specified number of times. The `While` loop is useful for iterating until or while a certain condition is met. If you are counting up or down, a `For` loop is easier to write and is slightly more efficient than an equivalent `While` loop.

Q How does an `If` loop compare to a `For` loop?

A Both the `If` statements and the `For` statements, as well as the `Do` statements, rely on conditional values to determine their job. Nevertheless, an `If` statement is never considered to be a loop. Always keep in mind that an `If` statement executes its body of code at mostly one time, and possibly never if the `If` is false to begin with. Even if the `If` condition is true, the `If` statement never executes its body more than one time, unlike the looping statements that can repeat their code bodies many times.

Workshop

The quiz questions and exercises are provided for your further understanding. See Appendix B, "Quiz Answers," for answers.

Quiz

1. How does a conditional operator differ from a mathematical operator?
2. What is a loop?
3. True or false: Code inside an `If` statement might never execute.
4. True or false: Code inside `For` loops always executes at least once.
5. How can you make a `For` loop count down?
6. How many times does the following `For` loop print?

```
For i = 2 To 19 Step 3
  Print i
Next i
```

7. Which loop, `While...Wend` or `For...Next`, is best to use when you want to execute the loop a fixed number of times?
8. Where does the conditional appear in the `While...Wend` loop?
9. How can you trigger the `While...Wend` loop the first time through the loop?
10. Which is easier to code: A loop or a counter that you increment each time you want something to occur? (Hint: See Listing 6.4.)

6

HOUR 7

Debugging Tools

Programs are easy to write. *Correct* programs are a different story. Locating program bugs can be difficult. Fortunately, most language distributors supply debugging tools to make your life easier as a programmer. Although the compiler locates syntax errors for you, logic errors often take extra time to locate, and you must be the one to locate such problems before your users locate the problems. For example, when a payroll amount comes out incorrectly due to a bug, you will need to locate the problem as soon as possible.

Although your debugging skills will improve as your programming skills improve, you can help reduce bugs that appear and make debugging simpler by learning to write programs in a way that will make them easier to maintain and update. When you write clear and concise code, you'll debug your programs faster. Many sophisticated debugging tools exist in today's programming languages. This hour shows you how to access some of Liberty BASIC's debugging tools so that you can try them yourself. Although in today's world the Liberty BASIC debugger is rather limited, you do get good exposure to the capabilities of debuggers by studying some of Liberty BASIC's bug-finding tools. More powerful debugging systems appear in languages such as Visual BASIC as you'll see later in this hour.

The highlights of this hour include

- Looking in the past to the first computer bug
- Learning the difference between logic and syntax errors
- Seeing the importance of writing clear and concise code
- Using the Debugging window to help locate errors
- Watching a program run one line at a time

The First Bug

The term *bug* has an interesting origin. The late U.S. Navy admiral Grace Hopper was one of the early pioneers of computer hardware and software. She helped to design and write the first COBOL compiler for the military. COBOL was a language later used by most business programmers of the 1960s and 1970s. Admiral Hopper was working on a military computer system in the early 1950s and, while printing a report, the printer stopped working. Admiral Hopper and her coworkers set out to find the problem.

After spending a lot of time without finding any problems in the program or in the data, Admiral Hopper looked inside the printer and noticed that a moth had lodged itself in a printer's relay switch, keeping the printer from operating properly. As soon as the *bug* (get it?) was removed, the printer worked perfectly. The moth did not fare as well, but it did go down in computer history as the first computer bug.

 Michael Crichton may have used Admiral Hopper's true story as the basis for his nail-biting suspense novel *Andromeda Strain*, a story that had a small printer problem that almost caused disaster.

Accuracy Is Everything

You are now well aware that the computer is a machine that cannot deal well with ambiguity. A programmer's plague is the collection of errors that show up in code. Perhaps as you've entered Liberty BASIC programs in the earlier hours, you've run across problems that occurred as you mistyped a character or two. Bugs can creep into code. Programmers must ensure that they do not write programs that contain errors, although this is not always as easy as it might seem.

When breaking the programming problem into detailed instructions, programmers often leave things out or code the wrong thing. When the program runs, errors appear because the programmer didn't plan for a particular event, used an incorrect calculation, or typed a line of code incorrectly.

The debugging process is what a programmer goes through to exterminate the bugs from a program. As a programmer writes a program, he or she often runs the program in its unfinished state (as much as it can be run) to catch as many bugs as possible during the program's development. Incrementally running the program as more and more of the code is completed helps eliminate bugs from the finished program. Still, the majority of the bugs can be found only after the program is completely written.

Beginning programmers often fail to realize how easy it is for bugs to creep into code. Expect them and you will not be surprised. Many early programming students have taken a program into the instructor saying, "the computer doesn't work right," when in reality, the program has a bug or two. When you begin to write programs, expect to have problems you will have to correct. Nobody writes a perfect program every time.

Depending on the length of a program, the time it takes the programmer (or programmers) to correct problems is often almost as long as the time taken to write the program originally. Some errors are very difficult to find.

There are two categories of computer bugs: syntax errors and logic errors. To learn the difference, take a few moments to find the two errors in the following statement:

There are two errrors in this sentence.

Found only one problem? Need a clue? Not yet; look again for two mistakes before going further.

The first error is obvious. The word *errrors* is misspelled; it should be spelled *errors*. The second problem is much more difficult to find. The second problem with the statement is that the entire premise of the statement is incorrect. There is only *one* error in the statement and that error is the misspelled word *errrors*. Therefore, the logic of the statement itself is in error.

This problem demonstrates the difference between a *syntax error* and a *logic error*. The syntax error is much easier to find. As you learned in Hour 1, "Hands-on Programming with Liberty BASIC," syntax errors often appear as misspelled programming language commands and grammatical problems with the way you use the programming language. Logic errors occur when your program is syntactically correct, but you told it to do something that is not what should really be done.

Compilers locate your program's syntax errors when you try to compile your program. This is another reason syntax errors are easier to spot: your computer tells you where they are. When a computer runs into a syntax error, it halts and refuses to analyze the program further until you correct the syntax error. Figure 7.1 shows a Liberty BASIC program that stopped because of a syntax error. You'll find this program under

7

the filename `bitmap.bas` in your Liberty BASIC folder. The Liberty BASIC compiler stops and highlights the exact line where the error occurred. The status line at the bottom of the screen describes the error.

FIGURE 7.1

Liberty BASIC finds a syntax error and refuses to continue until you fix the problem.

The Error Occurred Here

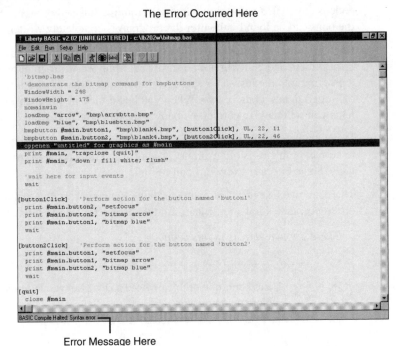

Error Message Here

Suppose you're writing a program to print invoices for your company's accounts receivable department. Because of an error, the computer prints all the invoices with a balance due of –$1000. In other words, according to the invoice, every customer has a $1000 credit. Your computer did its job, acting out your program's instructions. The program obviously contained no syntax errors because it ran without stopping. The logic errors, however, kept it from working properly.

Extensive testing is critical. The programmer wants to get all the errors out so the program will work correctly when the user finally uses it. The larger the program, the more difficult this is. Exterminating program bugs is just part of the daily job programmers tackle.

There is a third kind of error called a *runtime error*. Runtime errors are actually almost always caused by logic mistakes because the programmer failed to predict and therefore handle a potential problem. Runtime errors can occur if a program attempts to write to a disk without first checking to ensure that the disk door is closed and that a disk is inside the drive. A runtime error can occur, for instance, if the program divides by zero (division by zero is undefined mathematically). The more you program, the more you will learn to head off potential runtime errors that can occur.

Write Clear Programs

As you write programs, keep in mind the future maintenance that will be required. Sometimes, a program might be in use for a long time before a bug appears because a certain combination of factors occurred. Perhaps an unexpected data value appears, such as a negative value in an age field that should never be negative. Perhaps an operating system update causes a program to stop working.

Not only might bugs appear down the road, but programs often also need to be modified as the needs of the program change. When you write your programs, write clear and concise code. Every time you write a new line of code, consider whether a remark is needed to explain that line or to introduce a new section. Add extra whitespace characters to your program.

Consider the C program shown in Listing 7.1. The program is a valid, legal, C program that works on many C compilers that you might use. Yet, the program is horribly written. The program works and contains no syntax or logic errors, but the program is virtually impossible to maintain easily. The program is rather short but even advanced C programmers will have to hesitate to decipher the code if they are to make changes to it.

LISTING 7.1   This C Program Contains No Errors But Is Extremely Difficult to Maintain.

```
/* Filename: CFIRST.C Initial C program that
demonstrates the C comments and shows a few variables
 and their declarations */
#include <stdio.h>
main() {int i,j;/* These 3 lines declare 4 variables */
char c;float x;i=4;/* i and j are assigned integer values */
j=i+7;c='A';/* All character constants are enclosed in
single quotes */x=9.087;/* x requires a floating-point
value since it was declared as a floating-point variable */x=
x*4.5;/*Change what was in x with a formula */
/* Sends the values of the variables to the screen */printf("%d %d %c %f",i,
j,c,x);return 0;/* End programs and functions this way*/}
```

7

Whether you know C or not, you must admit that Listing 7.1 is bunched together and difficult to read. By adding whitespace and extra lines, the program automatically becomes easier to understand even for non–C programmers as Listing 7.2 demonstrates.

LISTING 7.2   This C Program With Better Spacing Is Far Clearer to Understand.

```
/* Filename: CFIRST.C
   Initial C program that demonstrates the C comments
   and shows a few variables and their declarations */
#include <stdio.h>

main()
{
   int i, j;      /* These 3 lines declare 4 variables */
   char c;
   float x;

   i = 4;         /* i and j are assigned integer values */
   j = i + 7;
   c = 'A';       /* All character constants are
                     enclosed in single quotes */
   x = 9.087;     /* x requires a floating-point value since it
                     was declared as a floating-point variable */
   x = x * 4.5; /* Change what was in x with a formula */

 /* Sends the values of the variables to the screen */
   printf("%d %d %c %f", i, j, c, x);

   return 0;    /* End programs and functions with return */
}
```

Practice Debugging with Liberty BASIC

Liberty BASIC contains some debugging tools that can help you locate and correct problems. As you know, Liberty BASIC informs you of syntax errors the moment you run a program that contains at least one syntax error. To see this in action, follow these steps:

1. Start Liberty BASIC.

2. Type the following code exactly as written here:
   ```
   Print "This program contains some buggs."
   PrintS "This line may have a problem."
   End
   ```

3. Press Shift+F5 to compile the program. Instantly, Liberty BASIC displays this statement in the status bar at the bottom of the screen: BASIC Compile Halted: Syntax error. Liberty BASIC has no problem with the first line, even though the

line has a misspelling (the word *buggs* contains an extra letter *g*) because the problem is not part of an instruction to Liberty BASIC. The problem is an error of misspelling and appears inside the quoted string. Liberty BASIC prints exactly what is in the string because the string is a properly-formed string, just misspelled.

4. To see a runtime error, select File, New.

5. Click No so your program with the bugs is not saved.

6. Type the following code exactly as written here:

```
Print "Error is coming"
a = 9 / 0
Print a
End
```

7. Press Shift+F5 to compile and run the program. The compiler process will complete, but as soon as Liberty Basic finishes compiling and attempts to run the program, a message box like the one in Figure 7.2 appears. (If you're running Windows 2000, you might get a bug when you attempt this. Liberty BASIC is not fully compatible with Windows 2000.)

FIGURE 7.2

Liberty BASIC lets you know that your program is attempting to do the impossible.

Output From Print Statement   Runtime Error

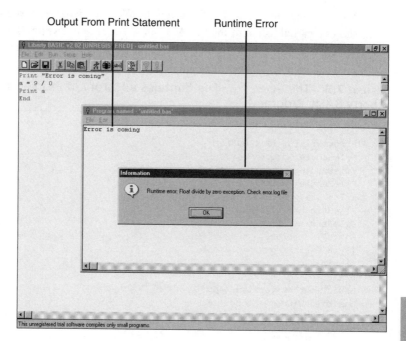

You'll notice that the Print statement worked. Liberty BASIC had no problem printing the message. The problem occurs in the division that comes next. Division by zero is undefined in the mathematics of real numbers. Therefore, even though the program is syntactically correct because you typed the code properly, when Liberty BASIC gets to the division by zero, Liberty BASIC has to give up and stop running the program. To let you know why it stopped, Liberty BASIC displays the error message box informing you that you cannot divide by zero.

8. Click OK to close the message box.

9. Click the Close button on the output window and answer Yes to terminate the program.

Liberty BASIC's Error Log

Every time an error occurs in Liberty BASIC, Liberty BASIC updates a file named error.log located in your Liberty Basic folder. The default Liberty BASIC folder is C:\LB202W. If you installed Liberty BASIC in another folder, the error.log file will appear in that folder.

You can open the error.log file using the Windows Notepad text editor. Listing 7.3 shows a partial listing of the file. Most of error.log is cryptic. But the first line under each date and time heading entry shows the error message you received at that point.

LISTING 7.3   The error.log File Contains a History of Problems You've Had With Liberty BASIC Programs.

```
Jul 17, 2003, 09:39:26
error writing file buffer
FileHandle(Object)>>error:
FileHandle>>writeFrom:toPage:for:pageSize:
FileHandle>>writeFrom:toPosition:for:
File>>writeBuffer:ofSize:atPosition:
FileStream>>writePage
FileStream>>close
BasicFile>>close
[] in BasicProgram>>closeAll
Set>>do:
BasicProgram>>closeAll
BasicProgram>>terminateApp
BasicTextWindow>>close:
BasicTextWindow(Object)>>perform:with:
TopPane>>event:
TopPane>>close

Jul 18, 2003, 20:14:40
Float divide by zero exception
Float class(Object)>>error:
```

continues

LISTING 7.3 Continued

```
Float class>>floatError
FloatCoprocessorDLL>>doesNotUnderstand:
Float>>/
Fraction>>asFloat
Fraction(Number)>>asFloatIfNonInt
BasicVariableManager>>assign:toBe:
BasicProgram>>assign:toBe:
[] in LetCommand>>assign:toBe:
BasicProgram>>begin
BasicProgram>>run
BasicSourcePane>>doIt
BasicSourcePane>>virtualKeyInput:withKeys:
Message>>perform
NotificationManager>>empty
```

Actually, the error.log file is so cryptic that you may rarely learn much more from it than you will know from the error message you received when you ran the program with a problem.

Debugging with Liberty BASIC

The Liberty BASIC error.log offers little help for most Liberty BASIC programmers. Fortunately, the authors of the Liberty BASIC system put better tools in the Liberty BASIC programming system that will help you locate bugs in your program. These debugging tools are most helpful when your program contains a difficult-to-locate logic error. For example, suppose you write a large program that calculates a daily report for a video rental store. During the testing of your program, you and the storeowners see that the sales tax computation does not compute correctly. Yet, you find the sales tax calculation and the math looks correct. Obviously, some data in variables is not correct before the tax computation.

To locate the bug, you can analyze the program code line-by-line to trace what the program does. With the whitespace and ample remarks you put in the program, you will be able to go through the code and locate the problem. The line-by-line check, however, is not usually required thanks to the debugging tools that Liberty BASIC provides.

7

Liberty BASIC's debugging tools are rather simple, but they do give you an idea of the kinds of tools you can find in other programming systems. For example, once you learn Liberty BASIC's debugging tools (described next), you will be able to learn those in Visual C++ and Visual Basic, two Microsoft language compilers, more quickly due to their similarities to Liberty BASIC's. Although a language such as Visual Basic provides much more powerful debugging tools, Liberty BASIC's tools provide a good introduction to the concept of variable inspection and the step-through process that other debuggers provide.

Liberty BASIC includes a Debug window that helps you debug your code by analyzing variables and by *single-stepping* through the program one line at a time. That means that instead of running your program from start to finish, you can make Liberty BASIC run your program one line at a time, stopping between lines so that you can look at data and make sure that the program is flowing properly.

By practicing with Liberty BASIC, you will gain insight into other tools available.

Entering the Sample Program

Type Listing 7.4 into Liberty BASIC. If you notice errors as you enter the program, keep them in the code. You'll use the debugger to help you debug the program.

LISTING 7.4   A Simple Liberty BASIC Program That Contains Errors.

```
' Filename: Bugs.bas
' This program contains a few bugs
'
 In put "What is your name? "; nam$

' The following code reverses the name
' and stores the reversed string in revStr$
  revStr$ = ""    ' String to build on
  For i = LEN(nam$) To 1 Step -1          ' Step back through the string
    revStr$ = revStr$ + Mid$(nam$, i, 1) ' Add one letter at a time
  Next i

' Show the user
  Print "your name backwards is "; revStr$
```

continues

LISTING 7.4 Continued

```
    Print

' Do some math to demonstrate debugger
' Initialize some payroll values
    hour = 40
    payRate = 6.70
    taxRate = .31
    Print "In a payrollll system, assume the following values:"
    Print "Rate: "; payRate
    Print "Hours: "; hours
    Print "Tax rate: "; taxRate
    grossPay = payRate * hours
    netPay = grossPay * (1 + taxRate)
    Print "The net will be "; netPay
End
```

Repairing the Syntax Error

The first Input statement contains the only syntax error in the program. Press Shift+F5 to run the program now and see the syntax error message. Liberty BASIC highlights the offending line. Repair the error by fixing the Input command, and rerun the program.

The program now runs without stopping because, assuming you typed the rest of the program just as Listing 7.4 shows, no more syntax errors exist.

You'll have to use some sleuthing skills to correct the logic errors that remain. When you run the program, you'll see output. The results are partially correct but not completely. Often, programs that contain almost correct results are the most difficult to correct because so much of the code works. It's your job to locate the code that does not work and exterminate the bugs.

The goal of this eclectic program is to accomplish these two tasks:

- Reverse the characters in the username and print the backward name.
- Calculate payroll values based on variables assigned in the program.

7

The program handles the reversal of the user's name just fine. The payroll figures, however, are incorrect, as Figure 7.3 illustrates. Although you might be able to correct these problems quickly without the aid of the debugger, use the debugger to help you locate the problems.

FIGURE 7.3

This output contains some bugs.

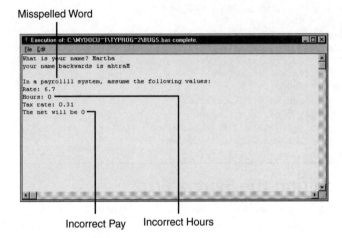

Misspelled Word

Incorrect Pay   Incorrect Hours

Single-Stepping

The first problem is the misspelled word, `payroll111`. Sure, you can quickly locate the word, but get used to using the debugging tools because some Windows programs that you work on might contain thousands of lines of code. One of the slowest, but most comprehensive, methods you can use to debug a program is to walk through the program one line at a time using the single-step feature.

To step through this program first close the output window. Click Liberty BASIC's Debug button (the one with the bug on it). Two things immediately take place:

- The program begins executing and the output window appears, although nothing resides there yet, as Figure 7.4 shows
- The Debugging window opens

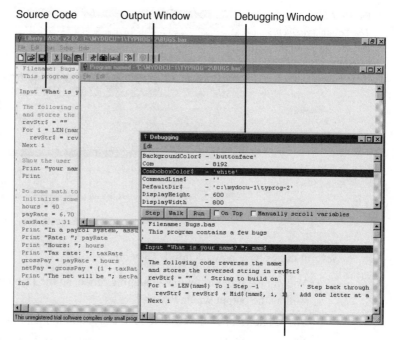

FIGURE 7.4

The debugger begins executing your program one line at a time.

Source Code Output Window Debugging Window

Next Line to Execute

The Debugging window is divided into two parts:

- The top half is the data description area where you can inspect the contents of variables and other program-related values
- The bottom half contains your program showing the next line to be executed as highlighted. The Debugging window skips over all remarks because remarks are never executed.

The Input statement is the next line to execute according to the Debugging window.

To execute the Input statement and only the Input statement, click the Debugging window's Step button. By clicking the button, you request that Liberty BASIC execute the current line. As soon as you click the button, the prompt "What is your name?" appears in the output window. Click the output window to make it the active window and type your first name at the prompt. When you press Enter, click the Debugging window to make it active and you'll see that the Debugging window now highlights the next statement to execute, the assignment to the revStr$ variable, as Figure 7.5 shows.

7

FIGURE 7.5

The Input *statement just executed and the assignment to* revStr$ *is about to execute.*

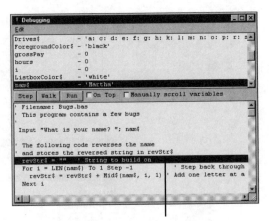

Next Line to Execute

Several things have now occurred. They are

- You ran the program in the debugging mode, so the Debugging window opened as well as the output window.
- You single-stepped through the first instruction in the program, the Input statement.
- You answered the Input statement's prompt. Even though the Debugging window was open, when you single-step through a program, the program behaves as it would if you ran the program normally—except the program runs only one statement at a time and you control the execution.
- The variable named nam$ has the value you typed.

Inspecting Data

Scroll the top half of your Debugging window to see every variable the program contains beginning with grossPay. The numeric variables are all zero because your program has not yet initialized them and Liberty BASIC (as do all BASIC renditions) automatically zeroes numeric variables when the program begins.

Many languages do not initialize variables to zero for you. Don't get in the habit of assuming that zero will be in your numeric variables. Popular languages such as C++ and Java do not initialize variables for you. Some hairy debugging sessions have resulted from programmers who had forgotten that the language they were using did not initialize variables to zero but had random values in them when the programs began. Even when using Liberty BASIC, if you want a variable to have zero in it, assign zero to that variable. By doing so, you clearly indicate your intent of the zero being in there.

As you continue scrolling, you'll see that the variable nam$ contains whatever value you entered in the Input statement. That's great! You expect the variable to contain the value you typed. The power of the debugger is revealing itself. The Debugging window shows values inside variables throughout the execution of the program. As you single-step through the code, the variables update to reflect their new values. You can inspect the variables at any time.

> If you are bug hunting and you locate a problem you were looking for while debugging, you can stop the debugger at any time by clicking the Debugging window's Close button or by clicking the Debugging window's Run button to finish the program from the current statement at the program's normal speed.

Keep stepping through the code. Each time you click Step, another line in the program highlights as Liberty BASIC runs the program except the remarks. The highlighted line is the line that is currently executing. Keep stepping through the program, clicking Step, watching the highlighter move through the code. When the program needs input, you will see the output screen and you can type the requested name. As you step through the program, you'll see the loops and the jumps that the program makes as it follows the Liberty BASIC instructions in the program.

Eventually, you'll get to the misspelled text in the Print statement as shown in Figure 7.6. Some debuggers actually let you change code during the debug process. Unfortunately, Liberty BASIC does not. Therefore, you'll have to make a note to yourself to fix the misspelling. The misspelling does not affect the code, however, as it's not a logic error or a syntax error because the misspelling occurs inside a quoted string; only misspellings of commands produce syntax error messages. Therefore, you can step through that Print statement and continue with the program.

7

FIGURE 7.6
*You'll eventually step
to the incorrect state-
ment.*

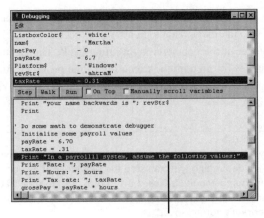

```
† Debugging                                              _ □ ✕
 Edit
ListboxColor$      - 'white'                                 ▲
nam$               - 'Martha'
netPay             - 0
payRate            - 6.7
Platform$          - 'Windows'
revStr$            - 'ahtraM'
taxRate            - 0.31                                    ▼
─────────────────────────────────────────────────────────
 Step │ Walk │ Run │ ☐ On Top  ☐ Manually scroll variables
─────────────────────────────────────────────────────────
   Print "your name backwards is "; revStr$                 ▲
   Print

' Do some math to demonstrate debugger
' Initialize some payroll values
   payRate = 6.70
   taxRate = .31
   Print "In a payrolll system, assume the following values:"
   Print "Rate: "; payRate
   Print "Hours: "; hours
   Print "Tax rate: "; taxRate
   grossPay = payRate * hours                               ▼
 ◀│                                                      ▶│
```

Next Line to Execute

Even in advanced debuggers such as the one offered in Visual Basic, your
ability to change programs while in single-step mode is sometimes limited.
For example, if you modify a statement that changes the structure of a program (such as changes in the structure of a loop or a definition of a new
variable in the middle of the program), some languages require that you
restart the program from the beginning. The program cannot incorporate
such a major change into the current execution.

In Listing 7.4's output, you know that a problem occurs when the hours worked are
printed because zero appears for the hours worked. Something about the initialization of
the variable that holds the hours worked, or something about the printing of that variable,
has a problem.

You can test the value of the variable named `hour` as soon as the program assigns `40` to it
in the following statement:

```
hour = 40
```

Of course, `40` must be in `hour` due to this direct assignment, but something's wrong
somewhere because the output of the `hour` value produces only a zero. Therefore, after
you single-step through the assignment of `40` to `hour`, scroll through the variable list in
the Debugging window and you'll see the problem: variables named both `hour` and
`hours` reside in this program. You assigned `hour` the value, but you use the plural, `hours`,
in the calculations and `Print` statements.

Bugs, such as omitting an *s* at the end of a variable name or using the letter *O* instead of the number *0* in an assignment, can be difficult to trace. The Debugging window, as you can see, often gives you clues to the problem. Two variables exist in the previous program—`hour` and `hours`–and there should only be one.

Therefore, you can terminate the program's execution and repair the bug easily. Change the assignment from `hour = 40` to `hours = 40`. After fixing the misspelled `payroll` word in the `Print` statement, rerun the program. You should see the results in Figure 7.7.

FIGURE 7.7

The program now runs correctly.

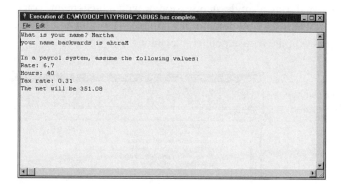

Advanced Debugging Tools

As mentioned earlier in this hour, when you use programming environments more powerful than Liberty BASIC, such as Visual C++ or Visual Basic, most of the debugging aids are similar to those that you now know. The Windows environment enables the debuggers to take on even more powerful features, however. For example, you can change source code during debugging to see how your changes immediately affect the output. Also, you can change variables as the program runs.

The following list is a partial sample of some of the features you'll find in most of today's Windows debugging systems that come with Windows programming languages:

- You can analyze variables at runtime (as you can do from Liberty BASIC's Debugging window) and view those variables in a window separate from the output. For Windows programming languages, you can also analyze the contents of control values. Therefore, you can easily check to see which value has been stored in a text box or command button property.

- You can change the contents of variables during the execution of the program (as you can do from Liberty BASIC's Immediate window) so that the rest of the program acts as though the code had assigned those values.

7

- You can set *breakpoints* throughout the program so that the program runs at normal speed until your preset breakpoint is reached. At that time, you can single-step through the rest of the code.

- You can set *watch variables* that halt the program's execution when the watch variables receive a specific value or range of values.

- You can skip statements that you don't want to execute during debugging.

Figure 7.8 shows one of the nicest features of Windows-based debuggers. When you halt a program during a single-step session or with a breakpoint, you can view the contents of a variable just by pointing to the variable. The value in the variable appears in a pop-up window at the mouse pointer's location.

FIGURE 7.8

The debugger can pop up a variable's value.

curGrosspay contains
312

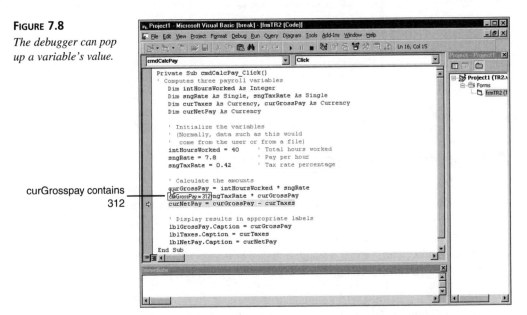

In addition to the usual fare of debugging features, you can also retrace your steps through a program. When you need to see exactly which parts of a program have executed up to a breakpoint, you can look at the *call stack*. The call stack appears in a dialog box and shows all procedures that have executed in the program to that point. If you double-click a procedure name, the code window opens to that procedure, and all variable values are still intact so that you can see what values have been computed.

Figure 7.9 shows a call stack dialog box that displays over a Visual Basic code window. In addition, a Debug toolbar appears so you have one-button access to common debug operations such as viewing watch window variables and stepping through code.

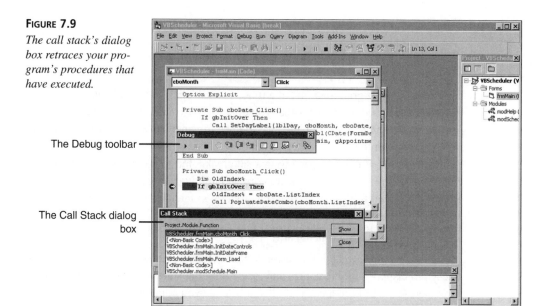

FIGURE 7.9

The call stack's dialog box retraces your program's procedures that have executed.

The Debug toolbar

The Call Stack dialog box

Summary

This hour showed how you can use powerful debugging tools to locate problems in your programs. You used the Liberty BASIC debugger to learn the skills related to debugging, but those same skills will transfer rapidly to other languages. Learning how to debug pays dividends when you need to track bugs. Although the debugging tools cannot locate specific logic bugs on their own, they make locating logic bugs easier for you to do.

One of the most powerful aspects of more advanced debuggers is their interactivity with the program during a breakpoint session. When your program reaches a breakpoint, all the values initialized and computed to that point are still live. Therefore, you can view variables to see whether their intermediate results contain the same values you expect. Also, you can change a variable's value in the middle of the program's execution and watch how the rest of the execution reflects that change.

7

Q&A

Q How can single-stepping help me debug a program when it takes so long to step through a large application?

A By executing a program one line at a time, you can analyze variable and control values at your pace. Remember that you don't have to single-step through every statement, but only the statements that you want to analyze. After you view values, you then can run the rest of the program or set a breakpoint later in the code and run the program at normal speed to that set breakpoint. Single-stepping not only helps you ensure that data values are correct, but you can also monitor the execution of a program to make sure that the program's statements execute in the order that you intended.

Q Can I debug a compiled program?

A Unfortunately, the debugging tools only work with source code. The source code is needed to display variable names and locate program statements. As a good programmer, you will keep a copy of all source code you compile into user's programs so you can locate and fix bugs that you or the user find later.

Workshop

The quiz questions are provided for your further understanding. For the answers, see Appendix B, "Quiz Answers."

Quiz

1. On what device did the first computer bug appear?

2. What is the difference between a logic error and a syntax error?

3. What kinds of errors does the programming language locate for you?

4. What kinds of errors can a programming language *not* locate for you?

5. What does single-stepping mean?

6. What is the purpose of the Liberty BASIC Debugging window?

7. What is the difference between the Debugging window's Step and Walk buttons?

8. What are watch variables?

9. If your program compiles without errors and executes without stopping at a run-time error, are you assured that the program is bug-free?

10. How does a Windows-based programming environment improve upon Liberty BASIC's debugging tools that you learned about this hour?

PART II

Programming Fundamentals

Hour

HOUR **8**

Structured Techniques

Now you are familiar with the steps to take before programming. You also know how to do some programming, having a little Liberty BASIC in your programming bag of tricks. In this hour's lesson, you begin honing your programming skills. From Hour 3, you now know that two steps must always precede writing the program—defining the output and data as well as developing the logic. After you develop the logic, you can write the program, using one of the many available programming languages.

This hour guides you into being a more structured programmer, writing clearer code, and writing code that is maintainable. Your future as a programmer depends on your being able to write code that others can change and manage.

The highlights of this hour include the following:

- Understanding the importance of structured programming
- Analyzing the three structured-programming constructs
- Testing a program
- Checking a program in stages
- Using parallel testing to eliminate downtime

Structured Programming

Structured programming is a philosophy stating that programs should be written in an orderly fashion without a lot of jumping to and fro. If a program is easy to read, the program is easier to change. People have known for many years that clear writing style is important, but it became obvious to computer people only after nearly 20 years of using nonstructured techniques.

In the late 1960s, programming departments began to wallow in programming backlogs that grew at tremendous rates. More people were writing more programs than ever, but many programmers had to be hired to maintain the previously written programs.

> You cannot hear the importance of writing readable and maintainable programs too often. By using a conscientious approach (instead of the old "throw a program together" approach that some programmers use), you help ensure your future as a programmer. Companies save money when a programmer writes code that is easily maintained.

When you finish a program, you are finished only for the time being. That program's assumptions about the job that it performs will change over time. Businesses never remain constant in this global economy. Data processing managers began to recognize that the programming maintenance backlog was beginning to take its toll on development. Programmers were pulled away from new projects in order to update older projects. The maintenance was taking too long.

By the way, the programming backlog of the 1960s has never really gotten better. Companies all around the world keep contract programmers and programming staff on hand to develop the new systems that they need. A backlog of computer projects seems to be the norm in the computer world. Constant change in the world means that an organization's data processing has to change as well.

Roots of Structured Programming

During the maintenance crisis of the 1960s, data processing people began looking for new ways to program. They weren't necessarily interested in new languages but in new ways to write programs that would make them work better and faster and, most important, make them readable so that others could maintain the programs without too much trouble. Structured-programming techniques were developed during this time.

There is some debate as to exactly when beginning programmers should be introduced to structured programming. Some people feel that programmers should be trained in structured programming from the beginning. Others feel beginners should learn to program any way that gets the job done, and then they should adapt to structured programming.

8

You've seen what flowcharts are, and the rest of this hour will use those tools to show you what structured programming is all about. As mentioned in Hour 3, flowcharts are not used so much anymore to design complete programs but are used for showing small logic flows. It is a good idea to incorporate structured-programming techniques into your code-writing process. Many of today's languages naturally lend themselves to structured-programming techniques because their commands and structure mirror the structured-programming rules you'll learn in the next sections.

Looking at Structure

Just because a program is well written and easily read doesn't necessarily mean it's structured. Structured programming is a specific approach to programming that generally produces well-written and easily read programs. Nothing can make up for a programmer rushing to finish a program by proceeding in what he thinks is the fastest way. You often hear "Later, I'll make it structured, but for now, I'll leave it as it is." *Later* never comes. People use the program until one day, when changes have to be made, the changes turn out to take as long as or longer than it would take to scrap the entire program and rewrite it from scratch.

Structured programming includes the following three constructs:

- Sequence
- Decision (also called *selection*)
- Looping (also called *repetition* or *iteration*)

A *construct* (from the word *construction*) is a building block of a language and one of a language's fundamental operations. As long as a programming language supports these three constructs (most modern languages do), you can write structured programs. The opposite of a structured program is known as *spaghetti code*. Like spaghetti that flows and swirls all over the plate, an unstructured program—one full of spaghetti code—flows all over the place with little or no structure. An unstructured program contains lots of *branching*. A branch occurs when a program goes this way and that with no particular order.

Jumping Around

Most programming languages enable you to branch with a Goto statement. The Goto works just as it sounds: it tells the computer to go to another place in the program and continue execution there. Having to search a program for the next instruction to execute makes you break your train of thought.

Listing 8.1 shows a Liberty BASIC program that uses Goto. The program prints three words—one, two, and three—but you've got to admit, it does so in a messy way. All those Goto statements make the program jump to the *label*, or bracketed word that precedes the section of code that the program is to execute next. Normally, execution flows line-by-line unless you jump around with Goto or use another control statement such as a loop. Listing 8.2 shows a better way to print the three words one, two, and three. Of course, Listing 8.1 resides here to demonstrate how *not* to program. In addition, Listing 8.1's Goto statements simply print one word. if the Goto takes the code to multiple complex commands, the lack of structure gets even more confusing.

Some programmers and programming textbooks warn you to completely stay away from the Goto statement. The Goto statement in itself isn't bad when used conservatively, but it can wreak havoc on a program's readability if you overuse it.

LISTING 8.1 Too Many Goto Statements Turn This Liberty BASIC Program Into Spaghetti Code.

```
' Filename: Goto.bas
'
' Demonstrates overuse of Goto statements
'
Goto [First]
'
[Second]
  Print "two"
  Goto [Third]
'
[First]
  Print "one"
  Goto [Second]
'
[Third]
  Print "three"
'
End
```

LISTING 8.2 Certainly No Goto Statements Are Required to Print Three Simple Words.

```
' Filename: NoGoto.bas
'
' No Goto statements are needed
'
  Print "one"
  Print "two"
  Print "three"
End
```

The three structured-programming constructs aren't just for programs. You will find that you can use them for flowcharts, pseudocode, and any other set of instructions you write for others, whether those instructions are computer-related or not. The three structured-programming constructs ensure that a program doesn't branch all over the place and that any execution is controlled and easily followed.

The following three sections explain each of the three structured-programming constructs. Read them carefully and you'll see that the concept of a structured program is easy to understand. Learning about structure before learning a language should help you think of structure as you develop your programming skills.

Sequence

Sequence is nothing more than two or more instructions, one after the other. The first few programs you wrote in Liberty BASIC use sequence, as does the simple program in Listing 8.2. The sequential instructions are the easiest of the three structured-programming constructs because you can follow the program from the first statement to the last within the sequence. Figure 8.1 shows a flowchart that illustrates sequence.

FIGURE 8.1

The sequence structured-programming construct executes the program in order.

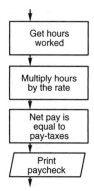

To show that you can represent any kind of logic using pseudocode as well as a flowchart, here is pseudocode that matches the sequence of the flowchart:

```
Get the hours worked.
Multiply the hours by the rate.
Subtract taxes to compute net pay.
Print paycheck.
```

Some programmers prefer to see pseudocode when looking at logic instead of flowcharts because of pseudocode's compact nature and its closeness to actual computer code.

Because computers must have the capability of making decisions and performing repetitive tasks, not all your programs can consist of straight sequential logic. When sequence is available, however, it makes for straightforward program logic.

Decision (Selection)

You have seen the *decision* construct before. In Liberty BASIC, when you wrote an If statement, you were using the structured-programming decision construct. At the point of such a decision, the program must take off in one of two directions. Obviously, a decision is a break from the sequential program flow, but it's a controlled break.

By its nature, a branch must be performed based on the result of a decision (in effect, the code must skip the code that is not to execute). A decision, however, as opposed to a straight branch using a command such as Goto, ensures that you don't have to worry about the code not performed. You won't have to go back and read the part of the program skipped by the decision. Based on new data, the program might repeat a decision and take a different route the second time, but again, you can always assume that the decision code not being executed at the time is meaningless to the current loop.

Figure 8.2 shows a flowchart that contains part of a teacher's grading program logic. The flowchart illustrates the use of the decision construct.

FIGURE 8.2.

The decision structured-programming construct offers one of two choices.

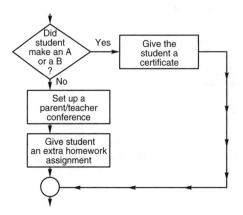

Here is the pseudocode for the decision shown in the flowchart:

```
If the student makes an A or B,
   give the student an achievement certificate.
Otherwise:
   set up a parent-teacher conference;
give the student extra homework.
```

Looping (Repetition and Iteration)

Perhaps the most important task of computers is *looping* (the term for repeating or iterating through lines of program code as you did in Hour 6's Liberty BASIC programs). Computers repeat sections of a program millions of times and never become bored. Computers are perfect companions for workers who have lots of data to process, because the computer can process the data, repeating the common calculations needed throughout all the data, and the person can analyze the results.

Looping is prevalent in almost every program written. Rarely do you write a program that is a straight sequence of instructions. The time it takes to design and write a program isn't always worth the effort when a straight series of tasks is involved. Programs are most powerful when they can repeat a series of sequential statements or decisions.

Figure 8.3 shows a flowchart that repeats a section in a loop. Loops only temporarily break the rule that says flowcharts should flow down and to the right. Loops within a flowchart are fine because eventually the logic will stop looping.

Be aware of the dreaded *infinite loop*. An *infinite loop* is a never-ending loop. If your computer goes into an infinite loop, it continues looping, never finishing, and sometimes it's difficult to regain control of the program without rebooting the computer. Loops should always be prefaced with a decision statement so that eventually the decision triggers the end of the loop and the rest of the program can finish.

FIGURE 8.3.

The looping structured-programming construct repeats parts of the program.

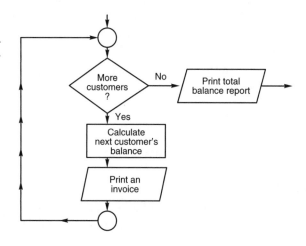

Here is the pseudocode for the flowchart:

```
If there are more customers,
  do the following:
    calculate the next customer's balance;
    print an invoice.
Otherwise,
  print the total balance report.
```

As you can see, eventually there won't be any customers, and the loop (beginning with do) will stop looping so that the rest of the logic can take over.

None of these structured-programming constructs should be new to you because you worked with them in the Liberty BASIC programs. As long as you keep these three constructs in mind while you develop your program's logic, and as long as you resist the temptation to start branching all over the program, you will write well-structured, easy-to-maintain programs and secure your position as a programmer for many years to come.

Testing the Program

When you finish writing the actual program code, you aren't completely done with the program. You must turn to the task of debugging the program using the methods described in Hour 7, "Debugging Tools." You know that you need to eliminate as many bugs from the program as possible. For obvious reasons, you don't want the user to do this. You don't want the user of your program finding all kinds of mistakes that you made. Therefore, you must thoroughly test the program.

Knowing how to debug is only the first step in writing trouble-free programs. You already know what to do if bugs appear, but before you release a program for use, you need to ensure that you have put that program through thorough testing so that few, if any, bugs ever appear.

Here are the typical testing steps that programmers should follow before distributing a final version of a program to users:

1. Perform desk checking.
2. Perform a beta test.
3. Compare the results of the beta test against the old system's parallel test results.

Desk Checking

Most programmers go through a series of desk checks on their programs. *Desk checking* is the process of sitting in front of a computer and checking the program by using as many different scenarios of data as possible to find weak spots and errors in the code. During desk checking, programmers should try extreme values, type bad input, and generally try their best to make the program fail. Programmers should also try every option available in the program, using different combinations to see what happens in all situations.

8

Beta Testing

When desk checking is completed and programmers are as confident as they can be about the program's correctness, programmers should set up a group of users to try the program. This is known in the industry as the *beta testing* stage. The more beta testers (test users of the program) you find to test the program, the better the chance that errors will be found. Users often try things the programmer never thought of while writing the program.

Beta Testing Now Exists on a Grand Scale

More and more companies are openly inviting the public to help beta-test products. Microsoft, for example, is extremely open about distributing beta test copies of its applications and operating systems long before the final release is available for sale. Most of these beta versions are available for download over the Internet. These beta test products give reviewers and testers an early peek at the software, which also helps Microsoft because these testers can inform Microsoft of bugs they find.

As the beta audience grows, so does the time a company takes for the test. The problem is that today's software is highly complex, requiring as many as a few hundred programmers to produce a product, such as a new version of Windows. A large-scale beta test is about the only way that these companies can discover some of the bugs that must be fixed before the product is released.

Parallel Testing

The user should never abandon an old system and switch to the new program right away. *Parallel testing* should be performed. For instance, if you write a payroll program to replace the manual payroll system for a dry cleaner, the dry cleaner shouldn't receive a copy of your program and use only that. Instead, the dry cleaner should continue its manual payroll system and use your program at the same time. Although this means that the payroll function takes a little longer each pay period, you can compare the results of the program with those of the manual system to see whether they match.

Only after several pay periods of well-matched parallel testing should the user feel confident enough to use the program without the manual backup.

During this testing period, programmers might have to make several changes to the program. Expect that changes will be necessary, and you won't feel disappointed or lose your programming confidence. Programmers rarely write a program correctly the first time. It usually takes many attempts to make programs correct. The thorough testing described in this section doesn't ensure a perfect program. Some errors might appear only after the program has been used for a while. The more testing you do, the less likely it is that errors will creep up later.

Profiling Code

A *profiler* is a program that monitors the execution of your program, looking for sluggish code that might be optimized for speed or size. Many of today's compilers are optimizing compilers that try to take your code and turn it into the fastest possible machine code, but there is always room for improvement. On average, 5% of a program takes 95% of the program's execution time. The profiler can help you improve the speed and efficiency of your program.

Advanced programming systems such as Visual C++ come with profiling tools that help you locate sluggish areas of your program. You cannot always speed up a program, but if parts of a program are slowing down the overall operation, you might be able to optimize the code to keep the program flowing smoothly. A profiler can also help you pinpoint when files get so large that faster disk drives and more memory might be beneficial to the operation of a program.

Getting Back to Programming

You're probably ready to get back into the foray of programming. That's good, because it's time to do just that. You now have some groundwork that many newcomers to programming never get. You know the importance of writing clear and concise code. You also know the importance of testing the program before you put the program into production, and you know how to debug any problems that you might find.

The rest of this part of the book focuses on improving your programming skills by teaching you some fundamental programming topics such as data searching, graphics, and programming for the Windows environment.

Summary

The programming process requires more than sitting at the keyboard. Proper design is important, as are structured-programming techniques and proper testing. You and others can easily maintain a well-written program. Because of the changing world and the high maintenance requirements of programs, you should attempt to learn structured-programming techniques that help clarify programs. The three structured-programming constructs that you are now familiar with are sequence, decision, and looping.

The next hour explains some advanced programming concepts that you can apply to search for data. You'll be back in front of the keyboard for a few more hours with Liberty BASIC to get you ready for the next step, which begins the third part of this book: Java programming.

Q&A

8

Q **How much testing is enough?**

A You can never test too much, but resources and the user's request for the program certainly bear on the decision to stop testing. If you know bugs exist in the program, you must remove them, so testing will help ensure that you've fixed all that you can fix.

Q **What tools are available to help me test my program?**

A Most of today's integrated debuggers are highly efficient at helping you spot and remove errors in your programs. You saw some of these in the previous hour when you used Liberty BASIC's debugger to locate problems, examine values, and test programs.

Workshop

The quiz questions are provided for your further understanding. For the answers, see Appendix B, "Quiz Answers."

Quiz

1. Why is the programming backlog still around?
2. Why do some programmers prefer to use and view pseudocode for logic design instead of flowcharts?
3. What is the opposite of spaghetti code?
4. What are the three structured-programming constructs?
5. What statement does Liberty BASIC use for branching?
6. What is a Liberty BASIC label used for?
7. Why can excessive branching be bad?
8. Which comes first, desk checking or beta testing?
9. What is the difference between parallel testing and beta testing?
10. What is a profiler?

HOUR 9

Programming Algorithms

In this hour, you will learn about programming algorithms that are common across all programming languages. An *algorithm* is a common procedure or methodology for performing a certain task. In mathematics, algorithms provide step-by-step methods for solving a problem in a finite number of steps that can require some repetition. To keep things simple, you'll see the algorithms in Liberty BASIC, but the concepts you learn here are important no matter which programming language you use.

You will learn how to use your programs to count data values and accumulate totals. The computer is a perfect tool for counting values such as the number of customers in a day, month, or year or the number of inventory items in a department's warehouse. Your computer also is capable of lightning-fast accumulations of totals. You can determine the total amount of a weekly payroll or the total amount of your tax liability this year.

Computers are masterful at sorting and searching for data. When you sort data, you put it in alphabetical or numerical order. There are different methods for doing this, and this hour presents the most common one. There are also many ways to search a list of data for a specific value. You might give the computer a customer number, have it search a customer list, and then have it return the full name and account balance for that customer. Although computers are fast, it takes time to sift through thousands of data items, especially when searching through disk files (your disk is much slower than memory). Therefore, it behooves you to gain some insight into some efficient means of performing a search.

After you master the sorting and searching techniques, this hour finishes by introducing you to the most important programming tool at your disposal in any programming language: the subroutine.

The highlights of this hour include:

- Counting with counter variables
- Storing data in array variables
- Totaling with accumulator variables
- Swapping the values of two variables
- Understanding ascending and descending sorts
- Using the bubble sort
- Searching for values in unsorted lists
- Searching by the binary search
- Using subroutines
- Nesting loops to improve a program's effectiveness

Counters and Accumulators

When you see a statement such as the following, what do you think?

```
number = number + 1
```

Your first impression might be that the statement isn't possible. After all, nothing can be equal to itself plus one. Take a second glance, however, and you will see that in a programming language such as Liberty BASIC, the equal sign acts like a left-pointing arrow. The assignment statement, in effect, says "take whatever is on the right side of the equal sign, evaluate it, and put it in the variable to the left of the equal sign." Most of the other programming languages also use assignment statements that work like the Liberty BASIC assignment. Hour 17, "Programming with C and C++," explains how special C operators can shortcut this section's calculations.

When Liberty BASIC reaches the statement just shown, it adds 1 to the contents in the variable named number. If number has a 7 to begin with, it now holds an 8. After it adds the 1 and gets 8, it then stores 8 in number, replacing the 7 that was originally there. The final result is one more than the initial value.

When you see a variable on both sides of an equal sign, and you are adding 1 to the variable, you are *incrementing* that variable's value. You might wonder how adding 1 to a variable is useful. It turns out to be extremely useful. Many programmers put such an assignment statement inside a loop to count items. The variable used is called a *counter*. Every time the loop repeats, 1 is added to the counter variable, incrementing it. When the loop finishes, the counter variable has the total of the loop.

The program in Listing 9.1 uses such a counter. The program lets the user keep guessing at a number until it is guessed correctly. This program gives the user a hint as to whether the guess was too low or too high. The program counts the number of guesses. The Tries variable holds the count.

LISTING 9.1   A Number-Guessing Game Can Use a Counter Variable

```
' Filename: Guess1.bas
' Number-guessing game
'
 compNum = 47    ' The computer's number
'
 Print "I am thinking of a number..."
 Print "Try to guess it."
'
 Tries = 0
'
' Zero guess to force loop through the first time
 guess = 0
 While (guess <> compNum)
    Print
    Input "What is your guess (between 1 and 100)? "; guess
    If (guess < compNum) Then
       Print "Your guess was too low, try again."
    Else
        If (guess > compNum) Then Print "Your guess was too high, try again."
    End If
    Tries = Tries + 1    ' Add one to the counter
 Wend
 Print "You got it in only "; Tries; " tries!"
End
```

Figure 9.1 shows a sample run of this program. Without the counter, the program would be unable to tell the user how many guesses were tried.

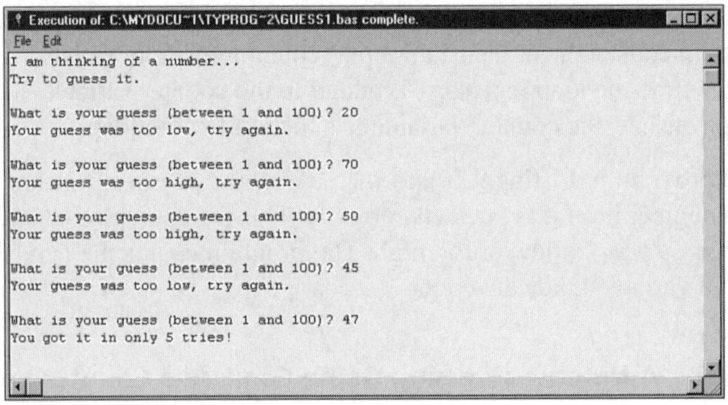

FIGURE 9.1

The number-guessing game's counter keeps track of the number of tries.

```
 Execution of: C:\MYDOCU~1\TYPROG~2\GUESS1.bas complete.         _□×
 File  Edit
I am thinking of a number...
Try to guess it.

What is your guess (between 1 and 100)? 20
Your guess was too low, try again.

What is your guess (between 1 and 100)? 70
Your guess was too high, try again.

What is your guess (between 1 and 100)? 50
Your guess was too high, try again.

What is your guess (between 1 and 100)? 45
Your guess was too low, try again.

What is your guess (between 1 and 100)? 47
You got it in only 5 tries!
```

Array Variables

Often, you must keep track of several items that are the same kind of data. For example, a teacher might need to keep track of 30 test scores, a company might need to track 150 products, or you might need to keep track of the money you've invested monthly into your retirement account. Although you could do so, it would be time-consuming to store similar data in the kind of variables you have seen. To keep track of them, you would have to give each one a different name.

For example, consider a teacher's test scores. If there are 30 pupils, the teacher might call the variables holding the scores `score1`, `score2`, `score3`, and so on. The teacher must know what student's name goes with each score, so there would also have to be 30 separate string variables, probably called something like `Sname1$`, `Sname2$`, `Sname3$`, and so on. Such variable names make for tedious processing and program writing. Listing 9.2 shows you a partial listing of what is involved in such a program.

LISTING 9.2   Requesting Several Student Names and Grades without Using Arrays Can Get Tedious.

```
' Filename: NoArrays.bas
' Program that begs to have arrays instead of regular variables
Input "What is the next student's name? "; Sname1$
Input "What is the test score for that student? "; score1
Print                    ' Prints a blank line
Input "What is the next student's name? "; Sname2$
Input "What is the test score for that student? "; score2
Print                    ' Prints a blank line
Input "What is the next student's name? "; Sname3$
Input "What is the test score for that student? "; score3
Print                    ' Prints a blank line
Input "What is the next student's name? "; Sname4$
Input "What is the test score for that student? "; score4
```

continues

LISTING 9.2   Continued

```
Print                    ' Prints a blank line
Input "What is the next student's name? "; Sname5$
Input "What is the test score for that student? "; score5
Print                    ' Prints a blank line
' This process continues for 25 more students
```

Anytime you find yourself writing two or more sets of statements and the only differences are the variable names, you are probably not taking advantage of a better programming style. The program in Listing 9.2 begs you to use array variables. Given what you know about programming so far, you won't be able to do anything different if you need to keep all 30 variables in memory for later use (perhaps to calculate an overall class average or some such statistic).

> Another drawback to using a different variable name for each of the 30 variables is that you cannot take advantage of the powerful loop statements you learned in the previous hour. The goal of programming is to make your life simpler, not harder. Whenever you can put repetitive code such as that in Listing 9.2 into a loop, you save wear and tear on your fingers by writing only a single pair of Input statements wrapped inside a For or While loop.

An array is a list of similar variables. Each of the like variables is called an *array element*. Instead of each individual array element having a different name, the entire array has one name. Each element in the list is distinguished by a subscript.

The top of Figure 9.2 shows you what five of the first 30 test score variables look like in memory. Each variable has a different name. The bottom of Figure 9.2 shows you how the same set of variables stored in an array would appear. There are still five variables, and each one is separate and distinct. Unlike the differently named variables, each of the array variables has the same name. They are distinguished not by their names, but by a *subscript,* which is the number inside the parentheses after the array name. Every element in every array has a subscript. This way you know which element in the list to refer to when you want to distinguish one value from another.

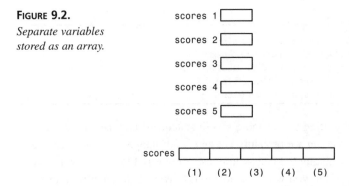

FIGURE 9.2.

Separate variables stored as an array.

Now that the teacher stores the variables in 30 array elements called `scores`, the teacher can use a loop to step through them. The ability to loop through array elements, either initializing or printing them, makes arrays extremely powerful and easy to program. Consider the section of code in Listing 9.3. Notice how the program asks for the student's name and score only once; that request is then repeated inside a loop. You will see that each `Input` statement stores its value in a nonarray variable and immediately assigns that variable to the next element in the array. Liberty BASIC does not allow you to use `Input` to fill an array element directly, although most languages will allow you to do this.

LISTING 9.3   You Can Improve the Grade Program with Arrays.

```
' Filename: Arrays1.bas
' Loop through the questions with array subscripts
For i = 1 To 30
    ' Get input in a non-array variable, then assign to array
    Input "What is the next student's name? "; sn$
    Sname$(i) = sn$
    Input "What is the test score for that student? "; score
    scores(i) = score
    Print                    ' Prints a blank line
Next i
' Rest of program follows
```

Scores is an array of size 30 that initially contains each student's score. The first time through the `For` loop, i is 1. The teacher enters the value for `Sname$(i)` (which is really `Sname$(1)`) and `scores(i)` (which is really `scores(1)`), and then the loop increments i to 2. This continues until the teacher enters all 30 names and scores. The subscript runs through the data and makes the code much cleaner.

Reserving Array Space

Often, you must tell Liberty BASIC beforehand how much array space you will need. Liberty BASIC permits only 10 array elements before requiring you to request more with a Dim statement. Dim stands for *dimension;* it is the statement that reserves array space for your program.

You have to include the appropriate Dim statement at the top of a program that uses array elements to make it work properly. Here are the two statements that dimension 30 student names and scores:

```
Dim Sname$(30)
Dim scores(30)    ' Reserve space for 30 elements each
```

Listing 9.4 shows a complete program for storing student names and scores. It dimensions array memory, asks for all the names and scores, and prints all the values to the printer. Without arrays, there isn't an easy way to duplicate this program, short of having 30 pairs of differently named student variables and inputting them with 30 different sets of statements.

LISTING 9.4   This Grade Program Stores Data in Arrays for Later Printing.

```
' Filename: Arrays2.bas
' Student name and grade listing program
Dim Sname$(30)
Dim scores(30)
'
For i = 1 To 30
   ' Get input in a non-array variable, then assign to array
   Input "What is the next student's name? "; sn$
   Sname$(i) = sn$
   Input "What is the test score for that student? "; score
   scores(i) = sc
   Print                       ' Prints a blank line
Next i
' Now that all the data is entered, print it
Open "Lpt1" For Output As #1
Print #1, "** Grade Listing **"
Print #1, "Name-Score"          ' Column Heading
For i = 1 To 30
   Print #1, Sname$(i); "-"; scores(i)
Next i
Close #1
End
```

> To make the program in Listing 9.4 usable for any situation, you would actu-
> ally make the program dimension all 30 elements (assuming that is the total
> number of students in the class) and then ask the teacher how many stu-
> dents took the test. The For loop can then loop for however many students
> actually took the test. If the entire class took the test, all 30 array elements
> are filled. If fewer took the test, the For loop only loops for as many stu-
> dents as there are test scores.

Parallel Arrays

The student name and grade listing demonstrates a popular use of arrays. The Sname$()
and scores() arrays are known as *parallel arrays*. That is, the arrays each have the same
number of elements, and each element in one corresponds to an element in the other.

With parallel arrays, you can store arrays with any type of data. Although a single array
can hold only one type of data, you can have several parallel arrays that correspond to
each other on a one-to-one basis. Using parallel arrays, you can keep track of an entire
set of names, addresses, phone numbers, and salaries in a payroll program.

Accumulators for Total

An *accumulator* is similar to a counter in that the same variable name appears on both
sides of the equal sign. Unlike counter variables, accumulators usually add something
other than 1 to the variable. Use accumulators for totaling dollar amounts, sales figures,
and so forth. You can use a total to expand on the teacher's grade-printing program and
produce a class average for the bottom of the report.

To compute an average, you must accumulate the test scores, adding one at a time to
an accumulator (the totaling variable). Because an average is based on the total number
entered, you must also count the number of scores entered. After all the scores are entered,
the program must divide the total amount of the scores by the total tests taken. This produces an average. The program in Listing 9.5 shows you how to do this. The counting and
accumulating processes shown in this program are used frequently in data processing,
regardless of the programming language you use.

LISTING 9.5 A Grade-reporting and Averaging Program Can Use an Accumulator
for Score Totals.

```
' Filename: Arrays3.bas
' Student name and grade listing program
' Print an average at the end of the report
```

continues

LISTING 9.5 Continued

```
Dim Sname$(30)
Dim score(30)    ' Assumes no MORE than 30 students
numStds = 0    ' Initialize counter
Total = 0       ' and accumulator
'
' Set ans$ so loop executes at least once
ans$ = "Y"
While (ans$ = "Y") or (ans$ = "y")
    numStds = numStds + 1    ' Increment for number entered
    Input "What is the next student's name? "; sn$
    Sname$(numStds) = sn$
    Input "What is the test score for that student? "; score
    score(numStds) = score
    Total = Total + score(numStds)   ' Must add the latest score
    Input "Another student (Y/N)? "; ans$
    Print                    ' Prints a blank line
Wend
' Now that all the data is entered, print it
Open "Lpt1" For Output As #1
Print #1, "** Grade Listing **"
Print #1, "Name-Score"              ' Column Heading
For i = 1 To numStds
    Print #1, Sname$(i); "-"; score(i)
Next i
Print #1, " "
Print #1, "The average is "; (Total / numStds)
Close #1
End
```

Here is the output from this program:

```
** Grade Listing **
Name-Score
Tim Jones-98
Jane Wells-45
Heath Majors-100
Chris Reed-78

The average is 80.25
```

Swapping Values

The cornerstone of any sorting algorithm is data swapping. As you sort data, you have to rearrange it, swapping higher values for lower values. As Figure 9.3 shows, swapping values simply means replacing one variable's contents with another's and vice versa.

FIGURE 9.3

Swapping the values of two variables.

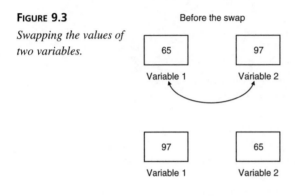

Suppose you assigned two variables named `variable1` and `variable2` with the following statements:

```
variable1 = 65
variable2 = 97
```

The concept of swapping them is simple. How would you do it? If you said the following, you would not quite be correct:

```
variable1 = variable2
variable2 = variable1
```

Can you see why these two assignment statements don't swap the values in the two variables? The first statement assigns `variable2` to `variable1`, which wipes out `variable1`'s original value. The second statement is then redundant because both variables already hold the same value after the first statement.

An accurate approach to swapping variables is to use a third variable, often called a *temporary variable* because you don't use its value once you swap the original variables. Here is the code to perform the swapping accurately:

```
temp = variable1
variable1 = variable2
variable2 = temp
```

Sorting

The following list of numbers isn't sorted:

10
54
34
21
23

Here is the list sorted in *ascending order* (from lowest to highest):

10
21
23
34
54

Here is the list sorted in *descending order* (from highest to lowest):

54
34
23
21
10

You can also sort character string data, such as a list of names. Here is a list of five sorted names (unless otherwise specified, an ascending sort is always used):

Adams, Jim
Fowler, Lisa
Kingston, William
Stephenson, Mike
Williams, Pete

Using the Bubble Sort

There are several ways to sort lists of data. The most popular one for beginning programmers is called the *bubble sort*. The bubble sort isn't the most efficient sorting algorithm. As a matter of fact, it is one of the slowest. However, the bubble sort, unlike other sorting algorithms (such as the heap sort and the quick sort) is easy to understand and to program.

The data that you want to sort is typically stored in an array. Using the array subscripts, you can rearrange the array elements, swapping values until the array is sorted in the order you want.

In the bubble sort, the elements of an array are compared and swapped two at a time. Your program must perform several passes through the array before the list is sorted. During each pass through the array, the bubble sort places the lowest value in the first element of the array. In effect, the smaller values "bubble" their way up the list, hence the name bubble sort.

After the first pass of the bubble sort (controlled by an outer loop in a nested For loop, as you will see in the following program), the lowest value of 10 is still at the top of the array (it happened to be there already). In the second pass the 21 is placed right after the 10 and so on until no more swaps take place. The program in Listing 9.6 shows the bubble sort used on the five values shown earlier.

LISTING 9.6   You Can Sort a List of Values with the Bubble Sort

```
' Filename: Bubble.bas
' Bubble sorting algorithm
Dim Values(5)
'
' Fill the array with an unsorted list of numbers
Values(1) = 10
Values(2) = 54
Values(3) = 34
Values(4) = 21
Values(5) = 23
 ' Sort the array
For pass = 1 To 5        ' Outer loop
   For ctr = 1 To 4        ' Inner loop to form the comparisons each pass
      If (Values(ctr) > Values(ctr + 1)) THEN
         t = Values(ctr) ' Swap the pair currently being looked at
         Values(ctr) = Values(ctr + 1)
         Values(ctr + 1) = t
      End If
   Next ctr
Next pass
' Print the array to show it is sorted
Print "Here is the array after being sorted:"
For i = 1 To 5
   Print Values(i)
Next i
End
```

Here is the output from the program in Listing 9.6:

```
Here is the array after being sorted:
10
21
23
34
54
```

Analyzing the Bubble Sort

To give you a better understanding of the bubble sort routine used in this program, Figure 9.4 shows you a flowchart of the bubble sort process. By using the flowchart and by following the program, you should be able to trace through the bubble sort and better understand how it works. At the heart of any sorting algorithm is a swapping routine, and you can see one in the body of the bubble sort's For loops.

FIGURE 9.4

The flowchart of the bubble sort routine shows the swapping of values.

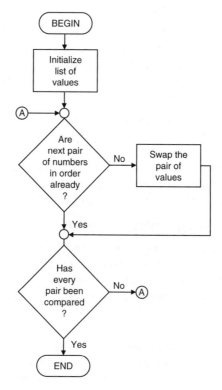

If you want a descending sort, you only have to change one statement in Listing 9.6's program—the first statement inside the For loops. Instead of swapping the values if the second item of the pair is lower, swap them if the second item of the pair is higher. The new line looks like this:

```
If (Values(ctr) < Values(ctr + 1)) Then
```

Searching Arrays

There are many methods for searching arrays for a specific value. Suppose you have several parallel arrays with inventory data. The first array, PartNo$(), holds all your inventory item part numbers. The second array, Desc$(), holds the description of each of those parts. The third array, Price(), contains the price of each corresponding part. You might keep all the inventory data on the disk and then read that data into the parallel arrays when it is time to work with the data.

One use for an inventory program that uses parallel arrays is a look-up routine. A user could type a part number, and the computer program would search the PartNo$() array for a match. When it finds one (for example, at element subscript number 246), you could then print the 246th element in the Desc$() and Price() arrays, which shows the user the description and price of the part number just entered.

There are several ways to search an array for values. The various searching methods each have their own advantages. One of the easiest to program and understand, the *sequential search,* is also one of the least efficient. The search method you decide on depends on how much data you expect to search through and how skilled you are at understanding and writing advanced searching programs. The next few sections walk you through some introductory searching algorithms that you might use someday in the programs you write.

Performing the Sequential Search

The sequential search technique is easy but inefficient. With it, you start at the beginning of the array and look at each value, in sequence, until you find a value in the array that matches the value for which you are searching. (You then can use the subscript of the matching element to look in corresponding parallel arrays for related data.)

The array being searched doesn't have to be sorted for the sequential search to work. The fact that sequential searches work on unsorted arrays makes them more useful than if they required sorted arrays because you don't have to take the processing time (or programming time) to sort the array before each search.

Figure 9.5 shows a flowchart of the sequential search routine (as with most flowcharts in this hour, only the sequential search routine is described, not the now-trivial task of filling the array with data through disk I/O or user input). Study the flowchart and see if you can think of ways to improve the searching technique being used.

FIGURE 9.5

Flowcharting the sequential search technique.

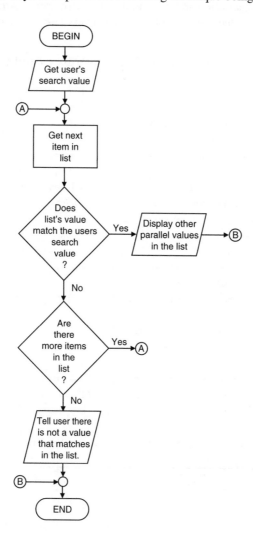

9

The program in Listing 9.7 shows you the sequential search algorithm coded in Liberty BASIC. The inventory arrays described earlier are used in the program. The listing shows only a partial program because the arrays are assumed to have the data already in them. The program asks the user for the part number, and then the sequential search routine finds the matching description and price in the other two arrays. After you study the program, you should find that the sequential search is very easy to understand.

LISTING 9.7   A Sequential Search Can Help an Inventory Application

```
' Filename: Seq.bas
' Sequential search for an item's description and price.
' (This assumes the arrays have been filled elsewhere.)
'
' This code would be part of a larger inventory program.

' ** This program assumes that the variable named TotalNumber
'    contains the total number of items in the inventory,
'    and therefore, in the arrays as well.
' First, get the part number the user wants to look up
  Input "What is the number of the part you want to see? "; searchPart$
  For i = 1 To TotalNumber      ' Look through all inventory items
    If (PartNo$(i) = searchPart$) Then
      Print "Part Number "; searchPart$; "'s description is"
      Print Desc$(i)
      Print "With a price of "; Price(i)
      End    ' Quit the program early once it is found
    End If
  Next i        ' Get the next item since it did not match
' If the program flow gets here (and did not END in the loop),
' the searched part number must not be in the inventory arrays.
  Print
  Print "** Sorry, but that part number is not in the inventory."
End
```

Performing the Binary Search

If your array is already sorted, there is another technique that offers tremendous searching speed advantages over either of the sequential searches shown in the previous sections. This technique is known as the *binary search*. The binary search is more complex to understand and program than the sequential search, but, as with most things in the programming world, it is worth the effort in many cases.

The binary search technique uses a divide-and-conquer approach to searching. One of the primary advantages of the binary search is that with every comparison you make, you can rule out one-half of the remaining array if a match isn't found. In other words, if you are searching for a value in a 100-element array, and the first comparison you make fails to match, you only have at most 50 elements left to search (with the sequential search, you would still have a possible 99 elements left to search). On the second search, assuming there is no match, you rule out one-half of the remaining list, meaning that there are only 25 more items to search through.

The multiplicative advantages of a binary search will surprise you. If you have a friend write down a number from 1 to 1000 and then use the binary search technique to make your guesses (your friend will only have to tell you if you are "too low" or "too high" with each guess), you can often zero in on the number in 5 to 15 tries. This is an amazing feat when there is a pool of 1000 numbers to choose from!

The binary search technique is simple. Your first guess (or the computer's first try at matching a search value to one in the list) should be exactly in the middle of the sorted list. If you guess incorrectly, you only need to know if you were too high or low. If you were too high, your next guess should split the lower half of the list. If you were too low, you should split the higher half of the list. Your new list (one-half the size of the original one) is now the list you split in the middle. Repeat the process until you guess the value.

Suppose your friend thinks of the number 390. Your first guess would be 500 (half of 1000). When your friend says "too high," you would immediately know that your next guess should be between 1 and 499. Splitting that range takes you to your second guess of 250. "Too low," replies your friend, so you know the number is between 251 and 499. Splitting that gives you 375. "Too low" means the number is between 376 and 499. Your next guess might be 430, then 400, then 390 and you've guessed it. One out of 1000 numbers, and it only took six guesses.

Listing 9.8 uses the binary search technique to find the correct inventory value. As you can see from the code, a binary search technique doesn't require a very long program. However, when you first learn the binary search, it takes some getting used to. Therefore, the flowchart in Figure 9.6 will help you understand the binary search technique a little better.

9

LISTING 9.8   A Binary Search Can Speed Searching Tremendously.

```
' Filename: Bin.bas
' Binary search for an item's description and price.
' (This assumes the arrays have been filled
'  and SORTED in PartNum$ order elsewhere.)
'
' This code would be part of a larger inventory program.
' ** This program assumes that the variable named TotalNumber
'    contains the total number of items in the inventory,
'    and therefore, in the arrays as well.
' First, get the part number the user wants to look up
  Input "What is the number of the part you want to see? "; searchPart$
  first = 1     ' Must begin the lower-bound of the search at 1
  last = TotalNumber   ' The upper-bound of the search
  While (first <= last)
    mid = int((first + last) / 2)    ' Note the integer function
    If (searchPart$ = PartNo$(mid)) Then
       Print "Part number "; searchPart$; "'s description is"
       Print Desc$(mid)
       Print "With a price of "; Price(mid)
       End
    If (searchPart$ < PartNo$(mid)) Then    ' Must half array
       last = mid - 1
    Else
       first = mid + 1
    End If
  Wend

' The searched part was not found if the code gets here (the END
' statement above would have been triggered otherwise).
  Print
  Print "** Sorry, but that part number is not in the inventory."
End
```

FIGURE 9.6

Flowcharting the binary search.

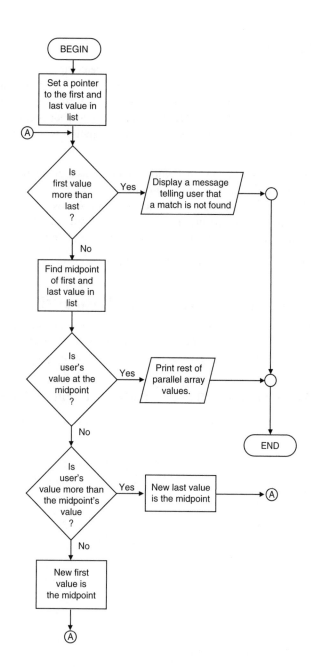

Subroutines

No discussion on programming languages would be complete without talking a little about subroutines. A *subroutine* is a set of code inside a program that you execute from another part of a program. Sometimes subroutines are called *procedures* or *user-defined functions*. A subroutine is like a detour; it is a side trip your program makes for a few statements, and then the program gets back on the path it was executing and continues from there.

The subroutine is a set of code that works as a unit, as a procedure works. Subroutines are available for all languages and aren't difficult to understand. The algorithms presented in this hour make perfect candidates for subroutines. A subroutine turns your program into a collection of modules that you can integrate. Instead of one long program, your program becomes lots of little sets (subroutines) of code.

To call subroutines from Liberty BASIC, use the Gosub statement. Use Return to end the subroutine.

Understanding the Need for Subroutines

Suppose you're writing a program that prints your name and address on the printer several times. Without having subroutines, you would write a program similar to the outline shown in Listing 9.9. The program repeats the same printing code over and over.

LISTING 9.9 A Program Outline That Doesn't Use Subroutines Can Be Hard to Maintain.

```
' Long program that prints name and address throughout
' (The rest of the code is not shown.)
'      :
'  Program statements go here
'      :
Print #1, "Sally Delaney"
Print #1, "304 West Sycamore"
Print #1, "St. Louis, MO  63443"
'      :
'  More program statements go here
'      :
Print #1, "Sally Delaney"
Print #1, "304 West Sycamore"
Print #1, "St. Louis, MO  63443"
'      :
'  More program statements go here
```

continues

LISTING 9.9   Continued

```
'    :
Print #1, "Sally Delaney"
Print #1, "304 West Sycamore"
Print #1, "St. Louis, MO  63443"
'    :
'  More program statements go here
'    :
Print #1, "Sally Delaney"
Print #1, "304 West Sycamore"
Print #1, "St. Louis, MO  63443"
'    :
'  Rest of program finishes up here
'    :
```

Not only is repeating the same code tedious, but by requiring more typing, it lends itself to errors. If you only have to type in the code once, but can still execute that code repeatedly whenever you want (as in a subroutine), your chances of typing errors decrease. Also, if your address ever changes, you only have to change it in one place (inside the subroutine), not everywhere it appears in the program.

If you put the Print #1 statements in a subroutine, you would save yourself some typing. When you're ready to execute the subroutine, issue a Gosub (for *go subroutine*) statement that tells Liberty BASIC exactly which subroutine to execute. You have to label the subroutine and put that label in the Gosub statement because you can have more than one subroutine in any program. Liberty BASIC has to know which one you want to execute.

Listing 9.10 is an improved version of the previous program outline. Notice that a statement that begins [PrNmAddr] precedes the subroutine's name and address printing code. This is a label that you make up that names the subroutine's location.

LISTING 9.10   A Program Outline That Uses Subroutines Is Simple.

```
' Long program that prints name and address throughout
' (The rest of the code is not shown.)
'
'    :
'  Program statements go here
```

continues

LISTING 9.10   Continued

```
'    :
Gosub [PrNmAddr]          ' Executes the subroutine
'    :
'  More program statements go here
'    :
Gosub [PrNmAddr]          ' Executes the subroutine
'    :
'  More program statements go here
'    :
Gosub PrNmAddr            ' Executes the subroutine
'    :
'  More program statements go here
'    :
End             ' Required so subroutine doesn't execute on its
                ' own by the program falling through to it


[PrNmAddr]
    Print #1, "Sally Delaney"
    Print #1, "304 West Sycamore"
    Print #1, "St. Louis, MO  63443"
    Return
```

The End is put before the subroutine so the program doesn't continue through to the subroutine and attempt to execute it one last time before quitting.

The purpose of the subroutine is to execute the same routine more than once. Grouping a routine into a subroutine makes a lot of sense; it helps organize your program. Listing 9.11 shows a complete program with three subroutines. The subroutines perform the following tasks:

1. Ask the user for a list of numbers.

2. Sort the numbers.

3. Print the numbers.

As you can see, the first part of the program is nothing more than a calling procedure that controls the execution of the subroutine. By breaking your program into modules such as this program does, you can help zero in on code later if you want to change something. If you want to change to a different sorting method, you can quickly find the sorting routine without having to trace through a bunch of unrelated code.

LISTING 9.11   A Program That Uses Subroutines for Everything Is Easier to Maintain and Understand.

```
' Filename: Subs.bas
' Program with subroutines
 Dim Values(10)
 '
 Gosub [AskForData]    ' Get user's list of numbers
 Gosub [SortData]      ' Sort the numbers
 Gosub [PrintData]     ' Print the numbers

End
 '
[AskForData]          ' Gets 10 values from the user
   Print "** Number Sorting Program **"
   For i = 1 To 10
       Input "What is a number for the list? "; Value
       Values(i) = Value
   Next i
   Return
[SortData]            ' Sorts the 10 values
   For pass = 1 To 10
      For ctr = 1 To 9
         If (Values(ctr) > Values(ctr + 1)) Then
            t = Values(ctr)
            Values(ctr) = Values(ctr + 1)
            Values(ctr + 1) = t
         End If
      Next ctr
   Next pass
   Return
[PrintData]
   Print
   Print "After the sort:"
   For i = 1 To 10
      Print Values(i); " ";   ' Print list with a space between the
                              ' numbers
   Next i
   Return
End
```

9

By indenting the lines of a subroutine to the right by two or three spaces, you help set apart the subroutine from the rest of the program. Although Liberty BASIC ignores the extra spaces, the spaces make the program easier to maintain.

Nested Loops

As with almost all statements, you can nest two or more loops inside one another. Several listings in this hour have done just that, including Listing 9.11. As a programmer, you must make sure you understand the concept of nested loops. Anytime your program needs to repeat a loop more than once, use a *nested loop*. Figure 9.7 shows an outline of a nested For loop. Think of the inside loop as looping "faster" than the outside loop. The inside loop iterates faster because the variable In goes from 1 to 10 in the inside loop before the outside loop's first iteration has completed. Because the outside loop doesn't repeat until the Next Out statement, the inside For loop has a chance to finish in its entirety. When the outside loop finally does iterate a second time, the inside loop starts all over again.

FIGURE 9.7

The outside loop determines how many times the inside loop executes.

```
** Number Sorting Program **
What is a number for the list? 6
What is a number for the list? 3
What is a number for the list? 4
What is a number for the list? 8
What is a number for the list? 7
What is a number for the list? 1
What is a number for the list? 2
What is a number for the list? 9
What is a number for the list? 5
What is a number for the list? 3

After the sort:
1  2  3  3  4  5  6  7  8  9

Press any key to continue
```

Figure 9.7's inner loop executes a total of 40 times. The outside loop iterates four times, and the inside loop executes 10 times for each of the outer loop's iterations.

Figure 9.8 shows two loops nested within an outer loop. Both loops execute completely before the outside loop finishes its first iteration. When the outside loop starts its second iteration, the two inside loops repeat all over again.

FIGURE 9.8

*Two or more loops
can nest within
another loop.*

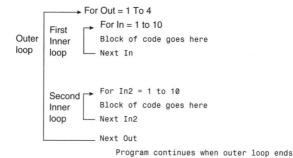

```
                              ┌─► For Out = 1 To 4
                         First │  ┌─► For In = 1 to 10
                 Outer   Inner │  │   Block of code goes here
                 loop    loop  │  └── Next In
                               │
                         Second│  ┌─► For In2 = 1 to 10
                         Inner  │  │   Block of code goes here
                         loop   │  └── Next In2
                               │
                               └──── Next Out
                         Program continues when outer loop ends
```

The blocks of code inside Figure 9.8's innermost loops execute a total of 40 times each. The outside loop iterates four times, and each inner loop executes—first the top and then the bottom—in its entirety each time the outer loop iterates once again.

Be sure that you match `Next` with `For` statements when you nest loops. Each `Next` must go with the most recent `For` before it in the code. Liberty BASIC and Visual Basic both issue errors if you write a program whose inside loop's `Next` statement appears after the outside loop's `Next` statement. If you omit the `Next` variable, Liberty BASIC aligns each `Next` with the most recent `For` for you, but adding the `Next` statement's variable often helps to document the loops and more clearly show where a loop begins and ends.

Summary

The techniques you learned in this hour will be useful throughout your entire programming career. Sorting, searching, and subroutines are needed for useful data processing. The computer, thanks to your programs, can do these mundane tasks while you concentrate on more important things.

The next hour gives you a break from algorithms and shows you how to write some programs that use graphics. Programming can be fun and graphics are quite possibly the most fun part of programming.

Q&A

Q How do subroutines improve a program's accuracy?

A A program is easier to write and maintain when you group routine code together in subroutines. The subroutines help you focus on specific parts of the program that you need to change or fix if bugs exist in the code. When your whole program is comprised of small routines, in subroutines, you make your code more modular and you help ensure that code in one part of the program doesn't affect code in another part of the program.

Workshop

The quiz questions are provided for your further understanding. See Appendix B, "Quiz Answers," for answers.

Quiz

1. What is an accumulator?
2. True or false: The following statement is an accumulator statement:

   ```
   Num = Num - 1
   ```
3. What is the difference between the terms *ascending sort* and *descending sort*?
4. Why is a third variable needed when you want to swap the values of two variables?
5. Which sort is the easiest to write and understand?
6. True or false: A counter statement is a special kind of accumulator statement?
7. What is the simplest kind of search technique?
8. Which is more efficient: the binary search or the sequential search?
9. What is the difference between the Liberty BASIC `Goto` and `Gosub` statements?
10. True or false: Using subroutines saves typing the same code over and over throughout a program?

HOUR 10

Having Fun with Liberty BASIC

Now is the time to sit back and have some fun with Liberty BASIC. Sure, programming is fun in itself, and you already know how easy and enjoyable writing programs with Liberty BASIC can be. Nevertheless, there is more you can do with Liberty BASIC than writing data-processing programs for business and engineering. You can also use Liberty BASIC to generate graphics.

The material you master in this chapter gives you the framework for adding pizzazz to your programs. You will get an idea of how game programmers do their jobs. You will learn some fundamental concepts that you need in order to write programs that capture a user's attention.

Most computer languages that have graphics commands, such as Liberty BASIC, use unique commands that don't work in other languages. For example, a Liberty BASIC graphics command that draws a line won't work in Visual Basic even though many of the commands between the languages are identical. Nevertheless, after learning how Liberty BASIC draws graphics on the screen, you will also have a better idea of the way other languages do the same.

The highlights of this hour include

- Using handles for graphics output
- Coloring your graphics
- Positioning the pen for drawing
- Drawing boxes, lines, and circles
- Working with bitmapped graphics
- Animating with sprites

Introduction to Graphics

Your graphics screen is made up of many columns and rows. A measurement known as *resolution* determines how detailed your screen's graphics can be. If the resolution is higher, your graphics will look better. Similarly, a lower resolution will make your graphics look worse. In its lowest graphics resolution mode, a standard VGA screen can display 640 columns and 480 rows of dots, as Figure 10.1 illustrates. Where every column and row intersects there is a graphics dot on the screen. The dot is called a *picture element*, or *pixel* for short. Because 640 times 480 equals 307,200, there are a total of 307,200 pixels on a low-resolution VGA screen and you can turn those pixels on and off and set them to various colors.

Most monitors and graphics cards support much higher resolution than 640 rows by 480 columns of pixels. The row and column intersection of each pixel forms an address for those pixels. For example, (320, 120) would be the address (or *coordinate pair*) of the pixel at the 320th row from the top of the screen or current window and the 120th column from the left edge of the screen or window.

FIGURE **10.1**

Resolution determines where graphics appear on your screen.

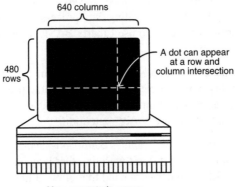

640 columns

480 rows

A dot can appear at a row and column intersection

Your computer's screen

Liberty BASIC calls the center pixel inside a window the *home* position.

Windows Helps to Standardize Graphics

Most computer languages that were designed after Windows became popular, including newer versions of older languages such as Visual C++, support the use of standard Windows graphics routines. Instead of using specific commands, as you're about to learn, to draw lines on your screen, you simply call built-in Windows functions that do the same thing. Windows then takes over the drawing task. By supporting Windows graphics function calls, you can work with graphics in Windows programs without learning language-specific commands.

Therefore, when writing graphics programs for Windows, you'll most likely call standard Windows functions that do the work. Nevertheless, a basic understanding of fundamental graphics commands actually helps you understand what Windows does under the hood when you call Windows graphics functions. Much of the rest of this hour teaches you specific Liberty BASIC graphics commands that are not found in other languages. This enables you to write graphics programs now, with Liberty BASIC, without having to master the rather advanced—and not always forthright—Windows graphics function calls. Later, as your Windows programming skills improve, you can begin to master the Windows graphics function calls.

10

Handles and Graphics Windows

A *handle* is not really a computer device but a program pointer to a device, such as a screen or a window on your screen. When your program writes to a handle connected to a window, that window displays the text that your program writes. Windows programs use handles all the time; instead of writing to a window, you'll write to a handle that represents a window. If your program opens two windows, your program will need to define two handles, one for each window.

These handles give programmers more flexibility than would otherwise be available. This is because you can create arrays of handles and manipulate handle values more easily than you can actual windows and other devices that handles represent, such as printers. If, for example, you defined an array of ten handles to ten different windows, you could easily write to a different window by referring to that window's array subscript.

Liberty BASIC provides an excellent introduction to writing pure Windows programs because when you draw graphics with Liberty BASIC you actually draw to a handle you've opened. The end result is that your drawing appears in a window or inside a *graphics box control*, a Liberty BASIC term for a region on your screen that appears in a window.

Opening Handles

Before you can draw with Liberty BASIC, you must open a graphics handle the same way you open a printer device for printing onto paper. Here is the typical Open statement used:

```
Open "Drawing" For Graphic As #handle
```

#handle is a graphics window that pops up over the Liberty BASIC output window and onto which you can draw lines, circles, and other shapes in various colors.

When Liberty BASIC executes the Open command, a graphics window with the title Drawing appears on your screen, such as the one shown in Figure 10.2.

FIGURE 10.2

A graphics window appears when you open a drawing handle.

Once you open such a window, you can

- Color the window's background
- Draw lines in the window
- Draw squares and rectangles in the window
- Draw circles and ellipses in the window

These are actually tasks you can perform in Windows-based programming as well. You can see that Liberty BASIC provides a good introduction for your future as a programmer.

Once you open a handle to a window, you use Print #handle to send color and graphics to the window. Liberty BASIC actually supports a graphics command set that contains keywords you print inside the Print #handle statement. The following sections show you some of the commands available.

Coloring Windows

You can fill the background of a graphics window with any of the colors in Table 10.1 by issuing the `fill` command, such as the one here:

```
Print #handle, "fill green"
```

TABLE 10.1   Color Values Available in the `fill` Command.

black	blue	brown
cyan	darkblue	darkcyan
darkgray	darkgreen	darkpink
darkred	green	lightgray
palegray	pink	red
yellow	white	

The color that follows `fill` is the color your graphics window's background becomes.

> As soon as you create a graphics window using the `Open` command, fill the window with a background color before beginning to draw on the window.

Erasing the Graphics Window

To erase a graphics window, issue the `cls` command as follows:

```
Print #handle, "cls"
```

Any graphics you've drawn will be erased. In addition, any fill color you used to color the window previously will revert back to the default white.

Putting Down the Pen

Before you can draw any graphics in the graphics window, you must place an imaginary graphics pen down on the graphics window. The default location for the pen is in an up position; therefore, if you draw before placing the pen down, nothing appears in the graphics window because the pen is not touching the window.

To place the pen down, issue the `down` command as follows:

```
Print #handle, "down"
```

You can now draw with the pen. If you want to turn off drawing for subsequent commands, issue the up command as follows:

```
Print #handle, "up"
```

During testing of your graphics programs, you'll almost certainly produce graphics that are incorrect. During the debugging process, you might want to insert an up command before a section that draws shapes. The shapes won't appear because the pen is up and you can see more easily what the drawing commands before the up command produced. Once you're satisfied with the commands that appear before the up command, you can move the up command further down the program to test each drawing section until you locate any problem drawing commands.

The starting location of the pen is usually the window's upper left corner. To place the pen in the center of the graphics window, locate the pen in the home position as follows:

```
Print #handle, "home"
```

Once in the home position, the center of the window, your graphics will be centered until you move the pen to a different location.

Drawing Boxes

To draw a box, you must specify the *x* and *y* *coordinates* of the bottom right corner of the box. The x and y coordinates are simply numbers representing the pixels located at the bottom right edge of the box and the upper left edge of the box; these will be wherever you last left the drawing pen (such as the home position).

The following statement draws a box 100 pixels wide:

```
Print #handle, "box 100, 100"
```

You can see the results of this box by running the program below:

```
' Filename: Box1.bas
Open "Drawing" for graphics as #handle
  Print #handle, "home"
  Print #handle, "down"
  Print #handle, "box 100, 100"
  Wait
Close #handle
End
```

The `Wait` command is useful for studying graphics because it causes the program to halt until you close the graphics window. Without the `Wait` command, the window will appear and close immediately without giving you time to study the output.

Figure 10.3 shows the resulting box that appears in the graphics window.

FIGURE 10.3

The box appears in the center of the window.

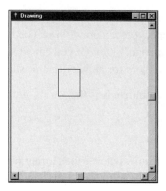

 Liberty BASIC lets you combine multiple graphics commands into one `Print #` statement. The following statement does the same as all the `Print #` commands in the previous program:

```
Print #handle, "home ; down ; box 100, 100"
```

You can color the inside of the box as well as specify a color (other than the default black color) used for the pen that draws the box. The following command draws a green box with a black outline because black is the default color for the outline of your graphics shapes:

```
Print #handle, "backcolor green"
Print #handle, "boxfilled 100, 100"
```

The first `Print #` sets the color that will be used for filling shapes to the color green. The second statement draws a box filled with whatever the background color is currently set to.

To change the pen's color from the default color of black to a different color, use the `color` command as the following statement does:

```
Print #handle, "color red"
```

Any shape you now draw will have a red outline. The following three lines, therefore, draw a green box with a red outline:

```
Print #handle, "color red"
Print #handle, "backcolor green"
Print #handle, "boxfilled 100, 100"
```

Drawing Lines

From the pen's current down position, whether that position is in the home position or elsewhere after drawing another shape, you can draw lines. The lines will be the same color as your most recent color command, although you can always issue a new color command to draw a line and change colors for another line or shape.

One of the most useful line-drawing commands is the goto command, which is issued as follows:

```
Print #handle, "goto 200, 300"
```

This command draws a straight line from whatever the current pen position is to the 200th pixel across and the 300th pixel down in the output window. If you had just drawn a shape such as a box, the pen would be in the lower right corner of the box.

Remember that you can, at any time during a graphics-drawing program, reposition the pen in the center of the output window by issuing another home command.

You can draw a line from any pixel to any other by issuing a line command such as this one:

```
print #handle, "line 10 10 250 300"
```

The first two numbers that follow line are the line's starting pixel column and row, and the second pair of numbers indicates the pixel location (column and row) of the end of the line.

Drawing Circles and Ellipses

Use the circle command to draw a circle on the output window. You must specify the *radius* (the distance from the center of the circle to its outer edge) in pixels.

The following statement draws a circle, colored with the current pen color, that has a radius of 100 pixels, meaning the circle's total width across from one outer edge to the other is 200 pixels:

```
Print #handle, "circle 100"
```

If you want to draw a circle that is filled with the current background, use the `circle-filled` command. The following draws a blue circle with a green outline:

```
Print #handle, "color blue"
Print #handle, "backcolor green"
Print #handle, "circlefilled 100"
```

Perhaps you don't want to draw a perfect circle but an ellipse such as an oval. Use the `ellipse` command to do just that. The `ellipse` command requires a width and height value. The pen's current position determines the center of your ellipse.

The following command draws an ellipse that is twice as wide as it is high:

```
Print #handle, "ellipse 200, 100"
```

Figure 10.4 shows the resulting ellipse.

10

FIGURE 10.4

Draw an ellipse by setting the width and height.

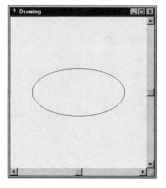

You can fill the ellipse with the current backcolor by using an `ellipsefilled` command, such as this one:

```
Print #handle, "ellipsefilled 300, 150"
```

Placing Bitmaps on your Output

A *bitmap* is a graphic image placed in a file with the filename extension of `.bmp`. Your Windows desktop, if it contains graphics, is the result of a bitmapped image placed on your desktop from the Windows Desktop properties dialog box available when you right-click over your desktop and select Properties.

You can display bitmaps in your Liberty BASIC programs and those bitmapped images will appear in your graphics window. Before you can place a bitmap on the screen, however, you must use the `Loadbmp` command to load the bitmap into memory. Unlike the other graphics commands you've seen so far this hour, the Loadbmp command is not a graphics command that appears inside a Print # statement but is a standalone statement.

The following command loads a bitmap file named logo.bmp into memory and assigns the name winlogo to the image:

```
Loadbmp "winlogo", "c:\logo.bmp"
```

The first string following Loadbmp is a name you assign to this particular bitmap. The second string contains the full path and filename of the bitmap you want to load into memory. Keep in mind that loading the bitmap into memory does not display the bitmap in your graphics window. For that, you need to use the drawbmp command as follows:

```
Print #handle, "drawbmp winlogo 30 40"
```

This command draws the specified bitmap at the pixel coordinates specified. Figure 10.5 shows the resulting graphics window.

FIGURE 10.5

You can place a bitmap in your graphics window.

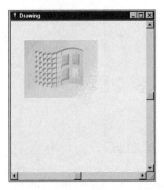

For complicated graphics, you are much better off drawing in a graphics program such as Paint, which comes with Windows; saving the image as a bitmap file; and using the bitmap-related graphics commands to place that image in your graphics window. Trying to draw complicated images with the line, circle, and box commands is virtually impossible.

You can improve your graphics-building skills by loading and running some of these sample files supplied with Liberty BASIC:

```
Boxes.bas
Circles.bas
Clock.bas
Draw_r.bas
Draw1.bas
```

```
Drawx.bas
Ellipses.bas
Graphics.bas
Hanoi.bas
Mandala.bas  (shown in Fig. 10.6)
Pie.bas
Rndtest.bas
Segment.bas
Slotmach.bas
Spaceshp.bas
Turtle.bas
```

FIGURE 10.6

The `Mandala.bas` *program shows the power of line drawing in Liberty BASIC.*

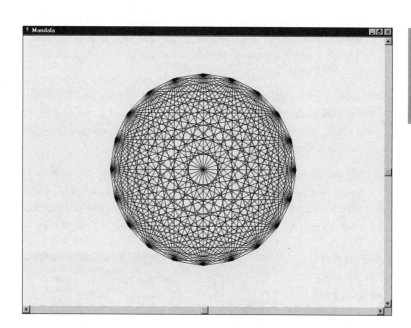

10

 Some of these sample programs explore and demonstrate advanced graphics commands that you haven't learned. You can study Liberty BASIC's online help to learn about commands that are new to you.

Sprite Animation

Liberty BASIC includes an advanced graphics feature called *sprite animation* that enables you to draw figures that respond to events such as player's movements in games. A sprite might be defined as a graphic image of a spaceship, and if a player's graphic bullets touch the spaceship, indicating a hit, the sprite animation informs the program of the sprite's coverage and the program can assume a hit has been made and process accordingly.

This text does not go into depth teaching you sprite animation because Liberty BASIC's implementation is extremely language-dependent and no other language supports Liberty BASIC's use of sprites. In addition, several advanced commands are required to understand their usage. Nevertheless, you should know a little about how sprite animation works in case you have an interest in going to more advanced graphics programming someday. Although other graphics tools are available that far outperform Liberty BASIC's sprite animation toolset, your introduction to Liberty BASIC's sprites should come in handy later.

The use of sprites goes beyond just missile-hitting, moving graphics. With sprites, you can place one image over another so that the two combined appear to be part of the same picture. In other words, the background of the top image becomes transparent instead of having a square background that might look awkward.

Figure 10.7 shows a page from Liberty BASIC's online help demonstrating the use of a sprite to combine two images into one. The frog is a square bitmap graphic image, as saved bitmaps always are. But when saved as a sprite object, your program can place the frog on top of a background and the two appear as though they are the same image.

FIGURE 10.7

Sprite animation helps make the smaller image's background transparent.

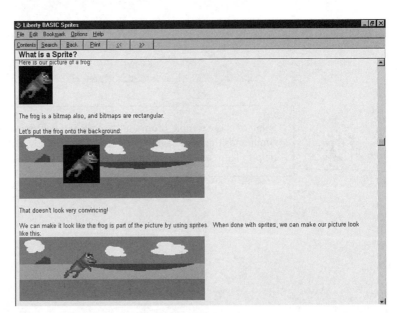

The advantage to the frog's transparent background is not just so that the frog looks better on the background. Once you've masked the frog's square background, your code can move the frog to a different location and it appears as though the frog is moving across the background. You might use two or three sets of frog images, one with the frog's legs in different positions, to portray the frog's leap, flight, and landing. Without the transparency, the dark, square background behind the frog would take away from the image of the frog leaping through the background.

Liberty BASIC provides masking tools that enable you to mask the background. Once you've masked the square background of an image so that you can move that image more naturally across a background, you now can implement *collision detection* using the `spritecollides` graphics command to determine if one graphic sprite (such as a masked missile image) collides with another image (such as a ship) and, if so, then your program can respond accordingly. The `spritecollides` command works automatically and informs you if any collision has taken place.

The sample programs named `Sprittst.bas` and `Sprittim.bas` demonstrate the use of sprites. If you want more information, look in Liberty BASIC's online help under *Sprites and Animation*.

Summary

As you saw here, Liberty BASIC programming is far from boring. By drawing graphics, you can spruce up your programs and really get the user's attention. Graphics are important in today's visual computing environments. Although Liberty BASIC's graphics capabilities are limited, you will learn much about how graphics are reproduced in other languages and environments by first learning Liberty BASIC's way.

The next hour discusses ways you can begin moving toward more of a Windows-type program. You'll learn how to manipulate windows and controls, such as command buttons, inside those windows through Liberty BASIC programming.

Q&A

Q How do I know what screen size my users will have?

A Several ways exist to learn your user's target screen size. As you learn more programming and familiarize yourself with additional graphics commands, you will learn how to adapt to various screen sizes and resolutions. In the meantime, limit your Liberty BASIC programs to an assumption of 640 × 480 resolution, the lowest resolution your users are likely to have.

Q Should I create animated graphics in Liberty BASIC?

A Certainly. Before doing so, you need to learn more about sprite animation. Keep in mind that the sprite tools available in Liberty BASIC are not the standard commands and tools available in other languages. The sprite-related concepts you master will help you learn other graphics commands in other languages but Liberty BASIC serves only as a good introduction to the large realm of graphics animation.

Workshop

The quiz questions are provided for your further understanding. See Appendix B, "Quiz Answers," for answers.

Quiz

1. What is resolution?
2. What is another name for *picture element*?
3. Liberty BASIC uses a special home position for graphics. Where is the home position?
4. What is a handle?
5. How can you erase a graphics window?
6. True or false: You use the `Print` statement to output graphics to your program's graphics output window.
7. What does the `Goto` graphics command do?
8. What is a coordinate pair?
9. How does sprite programming help programmers combine images?
10. What role does masking play in sprite animation?

HOUR 11

Advanced Programming Issues

By adding Windows controls such as command buttons, check boxes, and option buttons to your applications, you improve the way your users interact with your programs. Such controls give your programs a true Windows feel to them, and by providing controls that are already familiar to users of Windows, you decrease the learning curve needed for your users to adapt to and interact with the programs you write.

Liberty BASIC supports several common Windows controls, and in this hour you learn how to place those controls in your program's windows. Once you create and display those controls, you then must retrieve the values selected and entered into those controls by your user and respond accordingly.

The highlights of this hour include:

- Displaying multiple program windows
- Offering command buttons for users
- Working with static text

- Placing text boxes on windows
- Displaying items in lists
- Managing check boxes
- Responding to option buttons

Working with Windows

Everything that happens inside a Liberty BASIC GUI interface happens inside a window.
You've already seen that all Liberty BASIC program output appears in windows, and you
will now be able to place controls, such as command buttons and other Windows elements, in program windows and to let your program's users interact with those controls.

Liberty BASIC views windows as devices. You've already worked with one device, the
printer, and you already know that to work with a printer, you must open the printer in
your program and assign the printer a device number as the following statement does:

```
Open "Lpt1" For Output As #1
```

Subsequent `Print` statements then send output to the printer such as the following:

```
Print #1, "This message appears on the printer"
Print #1, "This is the second line that appears on the printer."
```

A program's window is also a device; you can open one or more windows by using an
`Open` statement and assigning each window that you open a different device number. The
following statement opens a program window:

```
Open "Window" for graphics as #1
```

The following three statements open three program windows:

```
Open "Window 1" for graphics as #1
Open "Window 2" for graphics as #2
Open "Window 3" for graphics as #3
```

Only one program window can be active at any one time. A blue title bar indicates an
active window. (Depending on your Windows setup, your active window might show a
different color in its title bar.) This is shown in Figure 11.1. You'll notice that Liberty
BASIC goes ahead and opens the standard output window you've always seen to this
point. The standard output window displays the title, `Program name`, followed by the
name of the source code file.

FIGURE 11.1

You may open multiple windows, but only one is active at any one time.

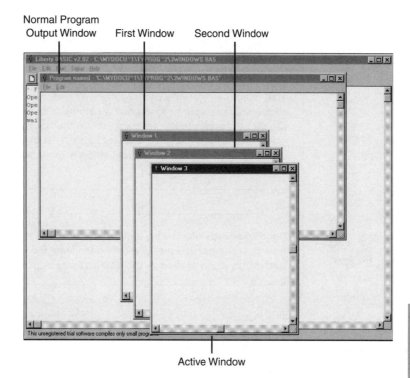

Normal Program Output Window First Window Second Window

Active Window

11

Normally, Liberty BASIC opens the standard output window you've seen throughout these hours. In addition, you can open extra windows, as you now know. You may want all your output to reside inside the window you're opening, and you may not want the standard output window to open at all since you won't be sending output there. If so, Liberty BASIC will suppress the opening of the regular program output window when you issue the NoMainWin command at the top of your program.

```
' Suppress the regular program output window
NoMainWin
Open "Window 1" for graphics as #1
Open "Window 2" for graphics as #2
Open "Window 3" for graphics as #3
```

If you want to try these Open statements, you need to insert a Wait statement after the third Open statement. Liberty BASIC will then wait for you to close the program windows yourself to terminate the program. If you don't issue a Wait command, Liberty BASIC will open the windows and immediately close them because your program will end. You'll learn better ways to temporarily halt your program, such as adding a command button that you can click to terminate the program, later in this hour. If you execute the previous three Open statements, followed by a Wait statement, you may need to drag the third output window from atop the other two to see the windows beneath the third one.

Notice that each window has a different title in the title bar. The title comes from the Open statement that you used to create the window. The Open statement's string appears as the window's title.

As with the Open statement that you use to open a printer device, issue a Close statement to close each window you open. Although many programmers close the windows right before the program's End statement, you don't have to wait until the final statements to close a window. You can issue Close to close a window as soon as you no longer need that window in the program. For example, if you open a window to get the user's input, you might want to close that window after the user enters the input data.

To close the three windows opened by the previous Open statements, you could do this:

```
Close #1
Close #2
Close #3
```

Modifying Open

You can modify the way you open windows. You don't have to open them by using numbers for the handles. You can use names for handles and refer to your devices, such as your program's windows or the printer by the name. For example, you can open the printer device by using a text handle instead of a number:

```
Open "Lpt1" For Output As #printer
```

Subsequent Print statements will then print to the handle:

```
Print #printer, "This message appears on the printer"
Print #printer, "This is the second line that appears on the printer."
```

This has the same effect as printing to a number you've assigned to the printer. By using a handle, you help self-document your code because device handles such as `#printer` are much easier to recognize than `#2`. Therefore, if you've opened several devices, such as a printer and multiple windows, you can more easily refer to them in the program by their device names. Given the following `Open` statements, therefore, subsequent `Print` statements will be directed to the appropriate device. You'll know by the name which of the following `Print` statements prints to the printer and which ones print to windows:

```
Open "Lpt1" For Output As #printer
Open "Window 1" for graphics as #Win1
Open "Window 2" for graphics as #Win2
Open "Window 3" for graphics as #Win3
```

If, instead of such device handles, you used device numbers, you would have to refer back to the program's `Open` statement to remember which number you assigned to which device.

Window Extras

You saw in the previous section that the text in a window's title bar is the same as the text you specify in the `Open` statement. Other ways exist for you to control the way in which your window opens. You can control the window's size and location on the screen.

To control the size, initialize variables named `WindowWidth` and `WindowHeight` to the window's size, in pixels, before you open the window. The following code initializes the next window that is opened to 600 pixels by 800 pixels:

```
WindowHeight = 600   ' Set the next window's height
WindowWidth = 800    ' Set the next window's width
Open "Window 1" for graphics as #Win1
```

You can also determine how far in pixels from the left edge of the screen and from the top edge of the screen the window appears by setting the variables named `UpperLeftX` and `UpperLeftY` to represent the number of pixels from the left and top of the screen, respectively.

The following code opens a new window 100 by 100 pixels from the screen's top left edge. The window will open at 200 pixels wide by 300 pixels tall:

```
UpperLeftX = 100     ' 100 pixels from the left edge
UpperLeftY = 100     ' 100 pixels from the top edge
WindowWidth = 200    ' 200 pixels wide
WindowHeight = 300   ' 300 pixels tall
Open "Window 1" for graphics as #Win1
```

11

If you set the background color variable, named `backgroundColor$`, to one of the colors you saw in Table 10.1 in the previous hour's lesson, the window's background opens in the color you specify. The following code opens a blue window:

```
UpperLeftX = 100     ' 100 pixels from the left edge
UpperLeftY = 100     ' 100 pixels from the top edge
WindowWidth = 200    ' 200 pixels wide
WindowHeight = 300   ' 300 pixels tall
backgroundColor$ = "Blue"
Open "Window 1" for graphics as #Win1
```

Adding Controls to Your Windows

To add a control to your window, you'll need to inform Liberty BASIC of several characteristics of the control, such as the control type (whether or not the control is a command button, text box, or whatever) and other control properties as explained in each of the sections that follow.

> You can get a good idea of what kinds of controls are possible by opening the sample programs that come with Liberty BASIC named `buttons1.bas` (whose output is shown in Figure 11.2), `checkbox.bas`, `combo.bas`, `combobox.bas`, `dialog3.bas`, `popmenu2.bas`, and `radiobtn.bas`.

FIGURE 11.2

The sample program named `buttons1.bas` *shows how to place command buttons in your program windows.*

Command Buttons

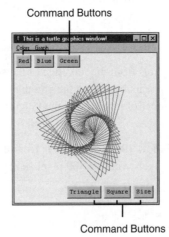

Command Buttons

Adding Command Buttons

To add command buttons to your window, you must use the `Button` command. The `Button` command informs Liberty BASIC of your button's name, location, and size. You must issue the `Button` command before the `Open` statement that will open the window in which the button is to appear.

Study the code shown in Listing 11.1. The output appears in Figure 11.3.

LISTING 11.1   A Button Can Determine When the User Wants to Quit the Program.

```
' Filename: Button.bas
NoMainWin
' First, define the button
Button #Win.but1, "Hello", [Push], UL, 25, 25
Open "Button Up" for graphics as #Win
' Pause to view the window
WAIT

' Following code executes when the user clicks the button
[Push]
Close #Win
End
```

FIGURE 11.3

When the user clicks the button, the program will terminate.

The name of Listing 11.3's button is `but1`, and it will appear in an open window pointed to by the handle `Win`. The string you issue inside a `Button` command determines what text appears on the button. Unless you specify a button's size, Liberty BASIC automatically sizes the button to conform to the text. If you want to specify a larger size, add the width and height pixel values to the end of the `Button` command. To set a wider size for the button in Figure 11.3, the fourth line of Listing 11.1 could have set the button to be a width of 75 and a height of 30 like this:

```
Button #Win.but1, "Hello", [Push], UL, 25, 25, 75, 30
```

The two values to the left of the width and height represent the number of pixels from the edges of the button's orientation inside the window. The orientation is set with the fifth Button value and can be UL (for *upper left*), LL (for *lower left*), UR (for *upper right*), or LR (for *lower right*). So, the orientation simply picks one of the window's four corners for the button and the next two values, in this case 25 and 25, indicate the number of pixels from that corner that the button is to appear.

Of course, you can create and place as many buttons as you need to place in your windows, as long as the buttons' handles differ.

The label you place inside the Button command, in this case [Push], indicates what code is to be executed the moment the user clicks the button. Therefore, you must have a label elsewhere in the program named Push so the program can continue at that point when the user clicks the button.

You can place a bitmap image instead of text on your command buttons by placing a valid filename instead of text inside the Button command's string:

```
Button #Win.but1, "c:\My Pictures\MyFace.bmp", [Push], UL, 25, 25, 75, 30
```

Placing Text in Your Window

You cannot use Print to send text to a window. Instead, you must use the StaticText command. *Static text* is text inside a window that your user will not, and cannot, change, as opposed to text that might appear inside a text box that the user can change. Static text is useful for window messages and labeling areas of the window.

Your program can change static text but your user cannot. Therefore, you can change a message that appears in a window's static text area. You'll use a special Print command that prints directly to the static text area as described in a moment.

The following StaticText command displays the text Liberty BASIC is fun! in the top center of the window.

```
StaticText #Win.text1, "Liberty BASIC is fun!", 100, 20, 200, 200
```

Listing 11.2 contains a program that uses this StaticText command.

LISTING 11.2   Place Static Text Where You Want Text to Appear in the Window.

```
' Filename: Text.bas
NoMainWin
StaticText #Win.text1, "Liberty BASIC is fun!", 100, 20, 200, 200
Open "Text Here" for graphics as #Win

Wait

' Following code executes when the user clicks the button
[Push]
Close #Win
End
```

The static text's handle is `text1`, and if you placed more static text messages in the window, they would have different handles. The different handles are important.

You could easily change the text by printing to `text1`, such as in this statement:

```
Print #Win.text1, "Replacement"
```

The `Print` statement links the static text to the correct window by placing a period between the window handle and the static text handle.

Text Boxes Contain Text the User Can Change

Whereas you used an `Input` statement to grab the user's input earlier in the book, you can use a text box control to enable the user to enter or change data. Text boxes enable you to get user input from a window. A window with several text boxes appears in Figure 11.4.

FIGURE 11.4

Your users will enter data in text boxes.

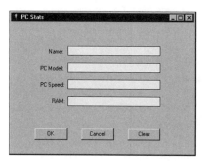

The `TextBox` command produces a text box. Here is a typical `TextBox` statement so that you can see how to form them:

```
Textbox #Win.tbName, 120, 50, 200, 20
```

The window handle in which the text box is to appear must come first, followed by a period and then the name of the text box. The four remaining arguments specify, in pixels,

11

the text box's starting location from the left edge of the window, starting location from the top edge of the window, width, and height. Liberty BASIC is not always consistent. Unlike the button command, you don't specify [UR], [UL], [LR], or [LL] for text boxes.

Listing 11.3 produces the window shown in Figure 11.4. The code is not complete in that all three command buttons send the program to the [Done] label that simply closes the window and terminates the program. But the primary consideration here is that Listing 11.3 demonstrates all the Windows controls you've seen so far.

LISTING 11.3   Use Text Boxes When You Want to Get Input From Your Users.

```
' Filename: TextBox.bas
' Turn off main program window
NoMainWin

' Set the width and height of the window
WindowWidth = 400
WindowHeight = 300

' Build four static text lines
STATICTEXT #Win.Name, "Name:", 80, 55, 40, 20
STATICTEXT #Win.PCM, "PC Model:", 62, 90, 55, 20
STATICTEXT #Win.PCS, "PC Speed:", 62, 124, 55, 20
STATICTEXT #Win.RAM, "RAM:", 87, 158, 40, 20

' Build four text boxes
Textbox #Win.tbName, 120, 50, 200, 20
Textbox #Win.tbPCM, 120, 85, 200, 20
Textbox #Win.tbPCS, 120, 120, 200, 20
Textbox #Win.tbRAM, 120, 155, 200, 20

' Build three buttons
Button #Win.OK, "OK", [Done], LL, 50, 10, 70, 25
Button #Win.Cancel, "Cancel", [Done], LL, 150, 10, 70, 25
Button #Win.Reset, "Clear", [Done], LL, 250, 10, 70, 25

' Create the window
Open "PC Stats" For Window as #Win
' The text boxes appear when you print them
Print #Win.tbName, ""    ' No default Value
Print #Win.tbPCM, ""     ' No default Value
Print #Win.tbPCS, ""     ' No default Value
Print #Win.tbRAM, ""     ' No default Value
wait

[Done]
Close #Win
End
```

As you can see from Listing 11.3, you must use `Print` statements to place the text boxes in their appropriate location.

> Notice that each text box is preceded by static text that tells the user what the program expects the user to enter in the text box. Always label your text boxes so your user knows what to type.

You can fill in text boxes with *default text*, that is, text that appears and remains in the text box unless the user enters a different value. The following `Print` statement fills in the text box with the city `Indianapolis`, and when the window with this text box appears, `Indianapolis` will automatically appear. The user can click inside the text box to change the text.

```
Print #Win.tbCity, "Indianapolis"   ' A default city
```

Text boxes, unlike static text, are input controls. Therefore, once the user enters a value in a text box, your program needs to know how to retrieve that information. Use the `Input` statement to retrieve a text box's value into a string variable. You must place your `Input` statement after the user indicates that all the text boxes are filled—after the user clicks an OK button, for example—to indicate that the text boxes all have values.

The following statement takes the city the user entered in the text box named `tbCity` and stores the city in a variable named `answer$`:

```
Input #1.tbCity, answer$
```

List Box Controls

When your user must select from a large number of items, you should not create a text box for each one. Instead, use a list box control that displays your items in a scrolling list from which your user can select. Figure 11.5 shows a simple list box control.

FIGURE 11.5

List boxes provide lists of options that your users can select from.

You can always change the contents of your list boxes by changing the contents of the array used. A list box will automatically provide scrollbars if the list is longer than what can currently be displayed.

11

Listing 11.4 creates the list box shown in Figure 11.5.

LISTING 11.4   Use List Boxes When You Want to Offer a List of Items That Your
Users Can Select From.

```
' Filename: ListBox.bas
' Turn off main program window
NoMainWin

' Set the width and height of the window
WindowWidth = 140
WindowHeight = 160

' Build four list box values in an array
Dim ary$(4)
ary$(1) = "Robin"
ary$(2) = "Sparrow"
ary$(3) = "Hummingbird"
ary$(4) = "Blue Jay"

ListBox #Win.lbox, ary$(), [Done], 10, 10, 100, 60

' Create the window
Open "List Box" For Window as #Win
' The text boxes appear when you print them
Print #Win.lbox, "singleclickselect"   ' Let user click once
wait

[Done]
Close #Win
End
```

Before you create a list box, initialize a string array that will hold the list box's contents.
You can always change the contents of the array and redisplay the list box to update its
contents, even during the execution of the program. (You learned about arrays in Hour 9,
"Programming Algorithms.")

The ListBox command creates the list box for a specific window that you display with a
Print command when you're ready for the list box to appear. The ListBox command
that builds the list box in Figure 11.5 looks like this:

```
ListBox #Win.lbox, ary$(), [Done], 10, 10, 100, 60
```

After specifying the window and the list box name separated by a period, you must specify the name of the string array that is to hold the list box's contents. Remember that if
the list box is not tall enough to display all items from the array, scroll bars automatically

appear so that the user can scroll through all the items. You must then specify the label to jump to when the user selects an item from the list. The next four arguments for the ListBox command should be the list box's position in pixels from the left and top edges of the window and the list box's width and height.

The Print statement that displayed the list box in Figure 11.5 appears here:

```
Print #Win.lbox, "singleclickselect"   ' Let user click once
```

The string "singleclickselect" informs Liberty BASIC that the user is to be able to select an item from the list, thereby highlighting the item to show its selection, by single-clicking over that list box value. If you used the string "doubleclickselect" then the user would have to double-click a list box entry to select that entry.

To determine which list box entry the user selected, use the Input statement:

```
Input #1.lbox, answer$  ' Store selected list box item
```

Combo Box Controls

The combo box is similar to the list box control but consumes far less screen space because a combo box first appears at a set size, but when the user opens a combo box, by clicking the box's down arrow, the combo box drops down to show several items it contains. When the user selects an item, the combo box returns to its more compact size. Figure 11.6 shows a combo box that's closed, and Figure 11.7 shows the same combo box that has expanded to show its contents due to the user's click.

11

FIGURE 11.6

Combo boxes appear on the form in a compact size.

No Selected Items

FIGURE 11.7

As soon as the user opens the combo box, the list opens to show its contents.

Selection will Appear Here

Select from Here

Listing 11.5 creates the combo box shown in Figures 11.6 and 11.7.

LISTING 11.5   Use List Boxes When You Want to Offer a List of Items That Your Users Can Select From.

```
' Filename: ComboBox.bas
' Turn off main program window
NoMainWin

' Set the width and height of the window
WindowWidth = 140
WindowHeight = 160

' Build several combo box values in an array
Dim ary$(10)
ary$(1) = "Tire"
ary$(2) = "Engine"
ary$(3) = "Door"
ary$(4) = "Wheel"
ary$(5) = "Trunk"
ary$(6) = "Ignition"
ary$(7) = "Lights"
ary$(8) = "Hood"
ary$(9) = "Tank"
ary$(10) = "Radio"

ComboBox #Win.cmbox, ary$(), [Done], 10, 10, 175, 300

' Create the window
Open "Combo Box" For Window as #Win
' The text boxes appear when you print them
Print #Win.cmbox, "selection?"
wait

[Done]
Close #Win
End
```

About the only change that you make from specifying a combo box instead of a list box is in the Print statement. Use "selection?" as your string instead of "singleclickselect" or "doubleclickselect", and as soon as your user selects an item from the combo box's drop-down list, the combo box collapses back to its original size and the selected item appears in the single combo box field.

Check Boxes

A check box offers an option that the user can select or deselect by clicking the check box. A check box might appear by itself or along with several other check boxes. The check box, when clicked, displays a checkmark (meaning the user has selected the check box option) and the checkmark goes away when the user clicks the check box once again.

A single check box offers the true or false value selection. If you just want a yes or no answer to a prompt, don't supply two check box options, but supply only one. Actually, check boxes are better suited for indicating selected options than for answering yes or no questions. Figure 11.8 shows a form with three check box controls. Each of the controls might be checked or unchecked depending on the user and depending on the way the program handles the check box selection.

Figure 11.8

Your users can select an option with check boxes.

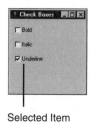

Selected Item

11

Listing 11.6 contains the code that produces the window in Figure 11.8.

Listing 11.6 Use Check Boxes to Offer Your User One or More Options.

```
' Filename: CheckBox.bas
' Turn off main program window
NoMainWin

' Set the width and height of the window
WindowWidth = 170
WindowHeight = 180

' Build several combo box values in an array
CheckBox #Win.Bold, "Bold", [set], [reset], 10, 10, 40, 25
CheckBox #Win.Italic, "Italic", [set], [reset], 10, 40, 40, 25
CheckBox #Win.Under, "Underline", [set], [reset], 10, 70, 80, 25

' Create the window
```

continues

Listing 11.6 Continued

```
Open "Check Boxes" For Window as #Win
wait

[reset]
' Code goes here that handles actions when
' the user unchecks a box

[set]
' Code goes here that handles actions when
' the user checks a box

wait
Close #Win
End
```

Here is the CheckBox statement that produced one of the three check boxes in Figure 11.8:

```
CheckBox #Win.Bold, "Bold", [set], [reset], 10, 10, 40, 25
```

The [set] and [reset] values are labels you use to specify where the program is to branch to if the user checks ([set]) or unchecks ([reset]) the check box. In Listing 11.6, both labels appear in the concluding parts of the program and do nothing active. The remaining four values specify in pixels where the check box is to appear from the left edge of the window, where the check box is to appear from the top edge of the window, the width of the check box, and the height of the check box.

You'll need to code a CheckBox statement for each check box you want to appear in the window. Each check box can have a different pair of labels so that your program can branch to a different location no matter which check box the user checks or unchecks.

Although the label branched to let you know which check box the user checked or unchecked, you can also use the Input statement to determine whether the user checked or unchecked the check box. The value of the Input will either be set or reset representing the [set] or the [reset] label. Here is an Input statement that stores the checked condition of a check box named check1:

```
Input #Win.check1, answer$  ' answer$ contains either set or reset
```

After such an Input statement, you can test whether or not the check box is checked with this If statement:

```
If (answer$ = "set") Then
   ' Code to handle checked conditions
Else
   ' Code to handle unchecked conditions
End If
```

Remember that your window can contain one, two, or more check boxes. Although you can, through tedious coding, ensure that one and only one check box is selected at any time, Liberty BASIC supplies a better way to provide mutually exclusive options. Use check boxes when you want to provide your user with one or more options that the user can select at any one time. Use option buttons to handle situations where the user can select only one option from several options that you provide.

Option Buttons

Option buttons let the user select from one of several choices. Unlike check boxes, however, Liberty BASIC lets the user select one and only one option button at a time. Figure 11.9 shows three option buttons with only one selected. If the user clicks another, Liberty BASIC takes care of unselecting the first option button and selecting the one the user clicked.

FIGURE 11.9

Your users can select one and only one option button at a time.

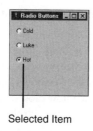

Selected Item

Option buttons are sometimes called *radio buttons* because they mimic the way old car radio pushbuttons used to work. Only one pushbutton could be pushed at a time; as soon as you pushed in another, the first one reset by popping out. Liberty BASIC uses the term *radio button* when defining the command that builds such a button: the `RadioButton` command.

The `RadioButton` command works just as the `CheckBox` button works, and you set both up in the same way. As with the `CheckBox` command, you can retrieve the value of a radio button with an `Input` such as this:

```
Input #Win.RadB, answer$   ' Returns either set or reset
```

Never place just one option button on a form because the user can select that option button but cannot deselect it.

Summary

In this hour, you learned how to turn your Liberty BASIC programs into true Windows programs by adding controls such as option buttons, check boxes, and command buttons. Creating the window with your controls is the first step in working with such a program, but you also must understand how to retrieve the user's selection so your program will know if the user clicked a button, entered text, or clicked in a check box.

The next hour enables you to use your new knowledge of Liberty BASIC to springboard into a new language—Java—and write programs in one of the hottest programming languages in use today.

Q&A

Q Why would I use the NoMainWin command to close my output window if I want my program to display output?

A You should close the primary program output window when you want to create your own window or windows. The output window you've worked with up to this point has been useful, but once you learn how to place Windows controls in your program, you'll want to keep the default output window closed and open only those windows you create that have appropriate Windows controls appearing in them.

Q How do I know whether to use check boxes or option buttons?

A Use check boxes when the user can select zero, one, or more options at any one time. For example, you might list five options that match the user's entertainment interest and if the user likes three of the options, the user can select three options by clicking each check box next to the matching option. Use option buttons, also known as radio buttons, when the user can select one and only one of the options listed. If the user selects one radio button and then selects another, the first one will no longer be selected.

Workshop

The quiz questions are provided for your further understanding. See Appendix B, "Quiz Answers," for answers.

Quiz

1. True or false: Liberty BASIC treats a new window just as another device.

2. How many open windows can be active at any one time?

3. What is the difference between these values: UpperLeftX, UpperLeftY, WindowWidth, and WindowHeight?

4. Which must you do first: build a button or open the window in which the button is to appear?

5. How do you set a button's orientation within a window?

6. What is the difference between a list box and a combo box control?

7. How can you determine which item the user selected from a list box?

8. What option determines whether the user will be able to select a list box item using a single-click or a double-click?

9. Why are two branches needed for check box items?

10. What happens if the user selects a radio button and then selects another one?

11

PART III

Stepping Up to Java

Hour

HOUR 12

Programming with Java

The world of Web pages gained an unexpected boost in capabilities when the Java language was introduced. Originally designed to be used for embedded applications such as those inside computer modules in automobiles, Java quickly became the standard language used to activate Web pages. Java almost single-handedly rescued static Web pages and turned the Web into an interactive medium with which users can interact with changing Web pages.

If you plan to work as a programmer on Web-based applications, you will have to learn Java. Java is simple to learn, however. The inventors of Java used C and C++ as their model language. Java is a small language. Its strength is in its size because small programs can load quickly along with Web pages to present interactive Web pages to users on the Internet. Also, Java works on many different kinds of computers.

The highlights of this hour include

- Seeing what Java is all about
- Receiving Java programs that travel with Web pages

- Understanding the need for small Java programs
- Comparing Java to other languages
- Compiling Java programs
- Extending the built-in Java classes for your Java programs

Introducing Java

Colorful browsers brought the Internet to the world by taking the Internet's original usage out of the exclusive hands of scientific, corporate, and educational researchers. The new Web browsers made the Internet accessible to anybody and everybody with their simple to-and-fro navigational tools and appealing graphical nature. Soon, millions of users all over the world were moving back and forth between Web sites as easily as they moved from page to page in their word processors.

Internet browsers filled their job requirements better than anyone could have imagined. Yet, within two or three years, the browser was stale due to the static nature of its screens. In other words, despite the colorful and cross-linked pages that browsers made available to the world, the pages did not have enough action in them to keep users occupied; more important, the browser technology was too static to make Web sites truly come alive.

 Think about this: As PCs became faster, became more graphical, and began supporting multimedia, viewing only pictures and text, which was at first unique online, became dull quickly. Users needed more interaction to keep their attention when online.

Users seem to want more from the Internet than just a distributed set of interconnected graphical screens. Despite the Web's hypertext nature, those hypertext links simply take you from one page to another without doing any work for you except eliminating the need to type long Web page addresses. Users want real computing power coming at them from the Web sites they visit. For example, instead of reading about the rules of baseball, you might want to see a baseball game in action or get an introductory graphical tutorial on the basics of the game.

Java, developed by Sun Microsystems in the mid-1990s, changed the way that Web sites operate. Java is a programming language with language features similar to C++. Fortunately, Java also contains many language features that are similar to Liberty BASIC, such as the `for` loop, the `if` statement, and the `while` loop.

Sun and Java

In 1995, when Sun Microsystems created Java, Java was designed to be a better C++ than C++. Both C++ and Java are efficient programming languages that you can use to write almost any computer application. Java's initial emphasis, though, was online Internet programming. Java was a small and efficient language with safeguards in place to add security to online programs that C++ simply couldn't handle.

Today, Java works in many environments; some programmers develop large, complex applications in Java, and those applications have nothing to do with the Internet. By making Java a lot like the C++ language already in use, Sun Microsystems helped to ensure a rapid acceptance and usage within the programming world.

Instead of using Web browsers to view data, with Java capabilities browsers now can seamlessly download programs written in Java and execute those programs on the end user's computer as opposed to the remote server serving up the Web page. When you view a Java-enabled Web page, you see not only the usual graphical page, but you'll also be able to interact with Java programs that run on your own computer, brought to your computer via the Web's connection.

Don't make the mistake of thinking that all the sounds and animation you've seen on the Web represent Java technology. For example, when you listen to a Web page's sound file, your own computer's sound-producing software is probably playing the sound data that comes from the Web site to your browser. Java takes computer interaction a step further than that, as you'll see in this part of the book.

12

You can write two kinds of Java programs:

- *Java applets* are small programs that travel with Web page code and execute on the Web user's computer.

- *Java applications* are complete standalone programs that don't require a Web browser to execute.

The first Java programs appeared as Java applets. After all, the original and primary goal of Java was to place executable code on Web pages so that users could gain more interactivity with Web sites. As Java became more popular, programmers began using Java to write standalone programs that executed without the need for Web browsers. For example, if you want to write a rental property management application that runs independently of an Internet connection, you can select Java as the programming language you use to develop the application.

Figure 12.1 shows a Web page in which someone has embedded a Java applet. When the user surfs to the Web page, the Web page appears and a moment or two later the space ship starts traveling across the box. Web page authors create Web pages using a formatting language called *HTML*. HTML alone certainly couldn't move that ship. The applet rides from the server to the end user's computer via the Web page's HTML code. The applet actually executes on the end user's computer and not on the serving computer. By executing on the user's machine, as opposed to the server's machine, the user can interact with the Java applet and the applet can respond to the user in real time.

FIGURE 12.1

It's the Java applet that gives the space-ship the gas needed to move.

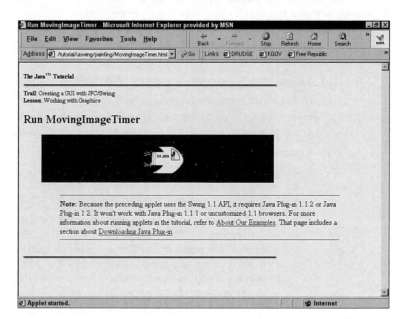

Java Provides Executable Content

When working with Java, you'll often hear and read about *executable content*. Executable content is what Java is really all about. A Web page contains executable content via Web commands in the form of a Java applet. Any Web page's content is executable on the target user's computer. Figure 12.2 shows an overview of a Web document with two embedded Java applets. The language behind Web pages is called *HTML* and you'll learn more about HTML in Hour 18, "Web Pages with HTML."

FIGURE 12.2

HTML serves up Java's executable content.

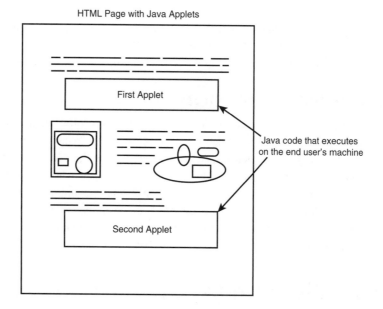

HTML Page with Java Applets

First Applet

Second Applet

Java code that executes on the end user's machine

When the end user enters the URL that displays the page shown in Figure 12.2 (or when the user clicks hypertext links to navigate to the page), the user's Web-browsing software loads the HTML code, formats the page's text according to the HTML commands, displays any graphics images that appear on the page, and loads the executable content (as applets). The executable content executes either immediately or upon a predetermined event, such as a mouse click over a hotspot on the Web page.

The best method of running Java applets is not always obvious to the end user. The user might think he or she is viewing a busy Web page when, in reality, an applet is providing animation. The look of that animation is smooth because the animation software runs on the user's computer. Because of the applet, the speed of the animation is not dependent on the download time or on Internet traffic.

Before Java-enabled Web pages, the user did have some interaction with the remote site. However, that interaction was severely limited. Web page animation was controlled by the user's animation software. If a computer system had no software that could display animation, that feature of the Web page was lost for that system's user. If the user was to interact with the remote site in a question-answer session, such as order-taking, the user would often have to fill in the form completely before error-checking could be done to any of the user's responses. The user would have to trigger any and all interactions with the remote site; the response would then be limited to the remote site's speed and the current traffic flow on the Internet.

12

CGI (*Common Gateway Interface*) programming provides the primitive interaction you often see on non-Java Web sites.

Seamless Execution

Surely you have traveled to a Web site, downloaded software, and then logged off to execute that software. Java makes this process seamless. When you travel to a remote site,
the Java software applet runs without you doing anything at all. In addition, the software
applet automatically downloads itself to your PC, runs when you trigger its execution,
and then goes away when you leave the Web site, without taking up permanent disk
space. Think of the possibilities for software developers; your users will be able to test-
drive your software without running an installation program and without having to
remove the software when the demonstration concludes.

Multi-Platform Executable Content

Now that you've seen how Java-enabled Web sites appear to the user, think about the
requirements of such executable content. When you write a Java-based Web page, you
want the code to work on the end user's computer no matter what kind of computer the
user operates.

Whereas most language compilers, such as Liberty BASIC and Visual C++, turn programs
into machine-dependent executable programs, Java development tools don't go quite that
far. All Java compilers compile your Java code into a special machine-independent module.
The Java compiler first compiles the code into an in-between stage called *bytecode*. Your
Java-enabled Web browsing software then translates this compiled bytecode into instructions that your computer executes.

No computer can really read bytecode, but each computer's Java-enabled browser can. In
other words, given a Java applet's bytecode, a PC can run the applet using a Web
browser, and a UNIX-based minicomputer can run that very same bytecode by using its
own Java-enabled browser such as Netscape. Each Web browser actually interprets the
machine-dependent bytecode and then translates that bytecode into machine-specific
instructions that a particular computer can understand (see Figure 12.2).

Figure 12.3 shows the Java compilation/translation scenario. You'll use the Java language to produce bytecode for a *virtual machine*, not a specific machine, because the bytecode is machine independent. A virtual machine is not a particular kind of computer but is an imaginary computer. Each computer must have a virtual machine interpreter to run Java code. The interpreter translates the compiled bytecode into specific instructions for that computer. Therefore, the Java compiler doesn't have to compile for any one computer, just bytecode for an imaginary computer called the virtual machine. The bytecode is sent to the Web page that is to contain the applet, and when the end user requests that Web page, the user's Web browser reads the bytecode and automatically interprets the bytecode into code readable by the user's computer. The user is unaware that all this took place; the Web page is displayed and the executing applet is seen along with the rest of the Web page's content.

FIGURE 12.3

Your Java session produces compiled bytecode that subsequent computers translate to run the program.

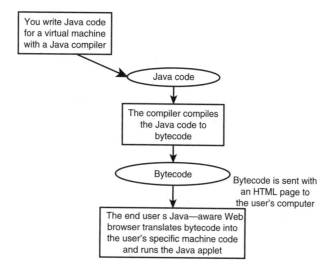

12

The Web browser automatically runs the Java applet. Some applets run automatically, and some run in response to a user event such as a mouse click. It's important that you realize that the user doesn't necessarily know or care that a small program is running. To the user, the Java-based Web page simply does more than one without Java. The page usually responds much more quickly, as fast as the user's computer can translate the Java bytecode into executable content. All traces of the program then go away when the applet ends, or when the user leaves the Web page.

Java enables the fastest response time possible for a user's interaction with a Web page. Although the user still has to wait for the Web page to download, and although the user still has to wait for the bytecode to get to the computer, the applet (comprising the Web page's executable content) executes as quickly as the user's computer can run the applet. The user is no longer bound to download time once the computer gets the executable content. All other forms of Web page interaction, such as Web page interaction written in CGI, are slaves to download response time and current Internet activity.

Java Usage Summary

As a newcomer to Java technology, you might appreciate a summary of the process one goes through when viewing a Java-enabled Web page with a Java-aware Web browser such as Internet Explorer. Here are the steps that occur:

1. You log on to the Internet, using your Web-browsing software.
2. You see your Web browser's default home page.
3. You enter a Java-enabled Web site's URL.
4. The serving computer sends the Web page, in HTML format, to your Web browser.
5. The HTML-based document's commands inform your Web browser of the Web page's Java-based executable content.
6. Your Web browser downloads graphics images from the server if any graphics appear on the Web page.
7. Depending on how the Java applet is to be triggered (either automatically or by a user's event), the server will also send the bytecode to your computer when the time is right.
8. Your computer's Web browser interprets the bytecode and executes the Java executable content.
9. When you leave the Web page, the executable content goes away. (Some Web browsers will keep the Java code in memory for a while in case you return to the page.)

Because the previous steps were based on the user's perspective, this is also a good time to explain what you, the Java programmer, will go through to create Web pages with Java applets. Here are the general steps you'll follow:

1. Start your Java compiler.
2. Write the Java applet.
3. Create the HTML Web page that will contain the Java applet. Use appropriate HTML commands to indicate the applet and its parameters.

4. Compile the Java applet. Your Java development system will place the applet in its appropriate location for the HTML Web page that will contain the applet.

5. If the compiler finds errors, fix them and recompile the file.

6. Test and debug the applet.

7. Store the applet and HTML on your Web server, where they will await an Internet user's request.

You'll Start with Standalone Java

Although Java is still used more for Internet applets than for standalone applications, you won't be learning Java from the applet perspective just yet. You'll find that it's easier to learn Java by mastering the standalone Java language first and then moving to Web applets, which you'll do in Hour 15, "Applets and Web Pages." While learning the Java language, the Web page information would simply sidetrack you from mastering the language commands.

Sun Microsystems never intended the Java language to be a competitor to C++ and the other languages people use to write non-Web, stand-alone applications. Sun just meant for Java to work in the applet environment. But Java has surpassed its authors' hopes and dreams. Java has become a major competitor in the programming language field.

Within a year of its creation, Java magazines began springing up, Java compilers were sold as well as given away free (worth every penny!), and developers quickly learned that Java is a great language in its own right. Standalone Java applications run from a program window and not from a Web browser or applet viewer as Java applets do. A Java application looks and acts just like any application written in any traditional programming language. Java is not just for Web pages anymore.

12

When is Java not Java?

Perhaps you've heard of *JavaScript*. Although the names are similar, and a few commands and operators overlap, JavaScript is very little like Java. Even though both work inside the HTML of Web pages, add interactivity to Web pages, and share some language elements (a few operators overlap), JavaScript is a lightweight compared to Java.

JavaScript is a small language with which you can cause buttons and other Web page elements to move and change as the mouse is clicked and keys are pressed. JavaScript also enables you to create menus and other Web page interactive features. But you cannot write JavaScript applications that stand by themselves without Web pages encompassing them. Java is a far more powerful, complex language that is rich with features. JavaScript is primarily used with Dynamic HTML to spruce up a Web page, but you'll not see full-blown applications or applets written in JavaScript. You'll learn about JavaScript in Hour 19, "Scripting with JavaScript."

Java's Interface

Java's interface elements—items such as check boxes and command buttons—tend to look the same across computer platforms. So, in most cases, they look the same on Macs as they do on Windows computers. That's unique because when other languages are used (such as C++), those interface elements typically take on the parent computer's operating system style. Your Java programs should work on most computers and will look about the same on all of them. If you really want your programs to achieve the specific look of a particular operating system, such as a Microsoft Win32 operating system (*Win32* is the standard name for Windows 9*x*, Windows ME, and so on—Microsoft's operating systems have more names than a hospital birthing ward), you can request that your program take on that operating system's style.

Over time, Java has become even more portable across different kinds of hardware. With each major and minor release, the Java language grows, adding a richer set of supporting routines so you code less and get more done faster. By including many routines that programmers use, programmers can more easily maintain Java applications because less coding means less work when a change must be made to a program. For example, most Java compilers now support a feature called *Swing* that lets you place windows, dialog boxes, and other Windows elements on the screen without much effort. Of course, you could ignore Swing and do it all the hard way and not get any sleep. But by signaling to Java that you want to use Swing, you'll put interactive code together faster.

Just look at some of the standard features found in Java 2 that are often unavailable in other languages:

- Drag and drop: Enables users to move items from one screen location or program to another by dragging those items with the mouse.
- Sound: Adds sound effects to spice up your applications.
- Network support: Allows access to other computers on a user's network after getting proper security clearance from the user.
- Collections: Stores data in advanced data structure repositories such as linked lists.
- 2D and 3D graphics: Dazzles the audience with eye-catching creations.
- Database API: An *API* is an abbreviation for *Applications Programming Interface* (programmers never use easy words when hard ones sound smarter) and Java supports a heavy-duty database API that enables your Java code to access, report, and retrieve from a data source such as a company database.
- Timers: Enables you to drop time-keeping routines into your programs that produce timed input responses, clocks, calendars, and other time-related operations.

Security Issues

Security should always be your concern when writing online applications. In practice, Java-enabled applets can be prone to security problems if the proper precautions aren't in place. After all, when you visit a Java-enabled Web page, you aren't always sure if an applet is running or what exactly an applet is trying to do to your computer's disk or memory.

Fortunately, Sun Microsystems developed Java to be a network-based programming language. Therefore, security is inherent in the language, both for the developer and for the Internet user. What follows are some of the security-related protections built into the Java language:

- A Java applet is not allowed to venture into the end user's memory areas where it doesn't belong.

- A Java applet cannot create, read, rename, copy, or write files on the end user's file system.

- A Java applet cannot connect to additional machines on the end user's network.

- A Java applet cannot call system routines on the end user's system.

> You can locally load and run a Java applet from your own browser by loading an applet from your own disk drive or network. In the case of a locally loaded applet, the applet generally has permission to read and write to the local file system. In addition, some applet viewers do let the end user specify a list of files that a Web applet can access.

12

As you can see, Java developers do understand the need for security, and the most obvious security footholds are barred from an applet's access. As more people write Java applets, additional security concerns are sure to enter into the picture.

Java changes as technology and computers change. Modern Java compilers support all the modern security methods such as *electronic signatures* (signing documents online), *public* and *private* keys (encryption just like spies use), and *site certificates* whereby your Web browser checks to ensure the software is valid and certified to be safe.

Give Java a Spin

Now that you know more about Java, you can take a look at a Java-enabled Web page. Use Internet Explorer 4.0 (or later) or Netscape's Navigator to locate this Web site:
`http://www.msnbc.com.`

When you go to this Web site, it first analyzes your PC to see if you've visited MSNBC before. If not, a short download of a Java-based applet (along with ActiveX controls to sweeten the Web site even more and make it more powerful) occurs. After the download completes, you'll see a colorful newspaper-like Web page control that details current news events of the day. The Java applet controls the news ticker that flashes across the screen. Figure 12.4 shows the resulting page and the location of the Java-based news ticker.

FIGURE 12.4

Java applets can enliven a Web page.

The Java-Enabled News Ticker

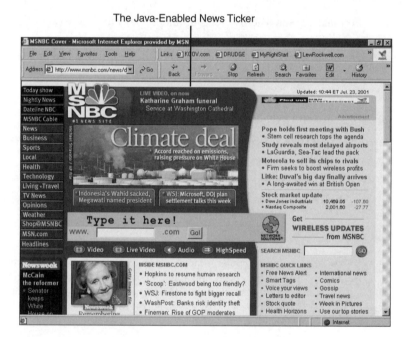

Java Language Specifics

Java is not a difficult language to learn. Java includes several prebuilt procedures that are often used to perform standard operations such as I/O. Java programs are typically small because the smaller the applets are that you write, the faster those applets will load and run on the user's machine. Java is an *OOP (object-oriented programming)* language and is similar to C++ in many ways. Both languages have common keywords, comments, and built-in functions. Java's OOP nature means that you can extend language objects that others write to complete applications faster.

Given Java's C++ roots, once you learn Java, you will already know a lot about C++. However, Java's developers did try to make Java better than C++. For example, Java, unlike C++ (or C) but similar to Liberty BASIC, supports the string data type. Java also supports true arrays, as Liberty BASIC does, whereas C++ does not.

Java Example

Listing 12.1 shows a very simple Java program so that you can familiarize yourself with the format of the language. This particular program bears little resemblance to Liberty BASIC programs, but you'll soon see that your knowledge of Liberty BASIC will speed your mastery of Java.

LISTING 12.1   Your First Java Program May Look Cryptic.

```
//**********************
// A simple Java applet
//**********************
import java.applet.*;   // Required support files
import java.awt.*;

//————————————————
// Main class
//————————————————
public class Simple extends Applet
{
  public void init()
  {
    resize(320, 240);    // Applet's window size
  }
//————————————————
public void paint(Graphics g)
  {
    // Change subsequent text color to red
    g.setColor(Color.red);
    // Write a simple message in the window
    g.drawString("Very simple!", 75, 100);
  }
}
```

When embedded inside a Web page as you'll learn how to do in Hour 15, "Applets and Web Pages," Listing 12.1 is simple and displays the message `Very simple!` in red on the screen's browser, 75 *pixels,* or *picture elements,* which are the dots on the screen as you learned in Hour 10, "Having Fun with Liberty BASIC") from the right edge and 100 pixels from the top of the screen. The screen in this case would be whichever Java-enabled Web browser is used to view the page with the HTML code that contains this applet.

12

Before going into the specifics of Listing 12.1, take a moment to consider these points:

- Java remarks, called *comments*, begin with two forward slashes—//.
- All Java programs are case sensitive. Therefore, if you initially name a variable intSum, don't refer to that variable later as INTSUM because Java will not recognize that both are the same.
- Java is a free-form language. You can indent and include lots of whitespace to make your programs easier to read and maintain.
- A semicolon generally follows each complete executable line. No semicolons follow comments or braces, however. Also, a class or procedure's definition line (the first line in a class or procedure) doesn't end with a semicolon because these statements define classes and procedures but don't execute or produce output.
- A pair of braces encloses a group of lines that Java treats as a single block of code. Generally, a block can appear anywhere that a single statement can appear. The braces also designate start and stop points for procedures.

These Java coding principles apply to small as well as large standalone Java programs.

Analyzing the Code

The details of Listing 12.1 are easy to understand. In Listing 12.1, comments help divide the sections of the applet from one another as well as document some lines in the code.

The import commands in Listing 12.1 appear in almost every Java program that you'll write. The import command is analogous to the C and C++ #include preprocessor directive except that import is a Java command and not a language directive. import inserts classes from special class packages provided by your Java compiler. Remember that in OOP, a class defines an object. A *class package* is a collection of classes that are logically grouped together. For example, graphics routines often appear in a class package. You can use the graphics objects from the class as long as you import that class package.

The import command follows these two formats:

```
import specificPackage.specificClass;
```

```
import specificPackage.*;
```

When you know the name of a class that you want to use, you can specify that name inside the import command. The specificPackage is the name of the class package from which you want to import the class named specificClass. For example, if you want to import a class package file named java.printer.routines, you'd do this:

```
import java.printer.routines;
```

The second format of import uses the * wildcard character to specify that you want
to import *all* classes from a class package. Listing 12.1 uses this import format for its
imported classes. The java.applet class package is a necessary class for you to use
when the applet is to be embedded in a Web page. Therefore, you'll always import
java.applet and all its classes at the top of every applet that you write. The java.awt
class package contains many graphics routines that enable you to send output to a Web
page's applet window. Instead of printing text onscreen, your applet must *draw the text*
pixel by pixel. Listing 12.1 contains a drawString() function that is a class procedure
defined in the java.awt class package.

The following line from Listing 12.1 defines a class named Simple:

```
public class Simple extends Applet
```

The opening brace that follows this public statement makes up the body of the applet's
Simple class and the class doesn't terminate until the closing brace. A statement such as
this public statement must appear in your applet because your applet is actually an
entirely new class, from the predefined Applet class, that you are extending. In this
example, the applet is taking the generic class called Applet (defined in the java.applet
class package) and extending the class by naming the copy Simple; the code in the body
of Simple is the added functionality for this newly extended class. Without the added
code, Simple would be no different from the built-in Applet class and the applet would
appear in the Web page but could do nothing. The new code is what makes the applet
perform.

The next few lines in Listing 12.1 define a new method called init(). (*Methods* act
much like functions except that you apply the methods to objects such as the screen window object.) In reality, the listing is redefining a method that already exists. When the
subclassed Applet became Simple, a method named init() came with the Applet class
but it does nothing except prepare the applet to run. init() is a method that's applied to
the Simple class. Every Java programmer *must* redefine init() and almost every Java
applet includes the resize() function in the body of init() as done here:

```
public void init()
   {
     resize(320, 240);    // Applet's window size
   }
```

The resize() method simply informs your class of your applet's window size in the target Web page. You can also insert any other code inside init() that you want executed
after the initial loading of the applet. resize() requires two arguments: an *x* and a *y*
coordinate. Enter the coordinates in pixels. In Listing 12.1, the resize() function is
defining the Java applet's window size (the window will appear inside the Web page on
the user's machine) as 320 pixels wide by 240 pixels high.

12

The paint() method should appear in every applet that you create and paint() should follow init(). Your applet executes paint() every time your applet window needs redrawing. If the user hides the applet's window with another window and then unhides it later, the hidden portion must reappear and it is paint() that determines what happens every time the window is redrawn. As long as you've supplied a paint() method—and you must—you can be assured that your applet window will reappear properly with the text, colors, and whatever else that paint() puts on the window.

In Listing 12.1, the paint() method looks like this:

```
public void paint(Graphics g)
  {
    // Change subsequent text color to red
    g.setColor(Color.red);
    // Write a simple message in the window
    g.drawString("Very simple!", 75, 100);
  }
```

Unlike init(), paint() requires an argument inside its parentheses. The argument is a value that the paint() method operates on. Although Graphics g is a strange argument, the argument represents your Web page's graphical applet window. Whatever paint() does to the value named g happens to your applet's window.

The setColor() method, therefore, sets the color for all text that will subsequently appear on the output window, g, until another setColor() appears. Although the window's background remains gray (you can change the background color if you want), text that appears will be red. After the applet sets the text color to red, two red words appear in the applet's window due to this line:

```
g.drawString("Very simple!", 75, 100);
```

drawString() is a commonly used Java method that sends text strings to the applet's window. drawString() respects the color set by setColor() so the text, Very simple!, will appear in red. Notice the g before the method name. You could, if you opened several different windows with an applet, send text to different windows by prefacing drawString() with each window's designated context name, such as g used here. The two arguments that end the drawString() method indicate how wide and high, in pixels, the text is to appear.

You now know all there is to know about Listing 12.1's applet. If you're still somewhat confused, don't panic because the next few hours cover the language in more detail. Java programming isn't difficult to understand, but some of the statements can be tricky due to the object and class situations brought on by OOP.

Get Ready to Begin

If you've not yet installed Java Forte, insert this book's CD-ROM and follow the instructions. You will then be ready to write your first Java program in the next hour.

Summary

The goal of this hour was to introduce you to the Java language. Java activates Web pages by sending small active applications, called applets, along with Web pages. Part of this introduction was a language overview. Unlike more traditional programming languages such as Liberty BASIC, a Java program is often part of something else, most notably a Web page. The program travels with the Web page to a user's machine and executes using the user's own computing power.

You may not understand much of the Java language yet, but you can understand a simple Java program better now that you've finished this hour. An applet is actually a subclass— an inherited version of a predefined class—that comes with the Java compiler. You add functionality to the Java `Applet` class to make the program your own.

Q&A

12

Q Do I embed my Java program code directly inside the HTML code on my Web page?

A No. HTML is only for formatting a Web page's appearance and for placing the applet in the correct location, but your compiled applet, in bytecode, travels along with a Web page to the destination computer. HTML always appears and downloads in source code format, whereas a Java program always downloads in bytecode format. Therefore, the two files must travel separately to the end user's computer.

Q Can a user stop my Java program from executing?

A Certain Web-based security features can keep Java applets that arrive with a Web page from executing on the user's machine. Although the Java language includes built-in security controls to keep Java authors from invading a user's machine from the Internet, the user can still keep the applet from executing by setting certain browser options.

Workshop

The quiz questions are provided for your further understanding. For the answers, see Appendix B, "Quiz Answers."

Quiz

1. True or false: The faster the user's computer is, the faster the Java applet that appears with the Web page runs.

2. True or false: The faster the user's computer is, the faster the Java applet downloads on the user's machine.

3. What is the language behind Web page formatting called?

4. What is bytecode?

5. Why is the concept of a virtual machine important?

6. How does the Java language provide security support for the end user who views Java-enabled Web pages?

7. What is the purpose of the `import` command?

8. How do you send text to the screen in a Java applet?

9. Why is the `paint()` method important?

10. What specifies a Java comment in Java programs?

Hour 13

Java's Details

In this hour, you will gain a deeper understanding of the Java programming language. Java has its roots in C and C++. Once you become familiar with Java, you will then be familiar with much of C and C++. Java has become extremely popular and is even taking over C++ in the number of programming projects being written.

Java is actually simpler to learn than C++ because many of the skills of Java programming come from knowing which internal prebuilt Java procedures to run. As you saw in the previous hour's overview, when you want to print a message in color, you don't have to do much more than find the name of the prebuilt procedure that first sets the color, find the name of the procedure that prints in an output window, and then use those procedures in your program.

The highlights of this hour include

- Seeing how Java treats literals
- Declaring variables
- Understanding operators

- Controlling programs with `if` statements
- Validating user input
- Looping with the `for` and `while` statements

Defining Java Data

Liberty BASIC supports numeric and string data types. Most languages, including Java, break data down further into several different types. Data can be either *literals,* constant values that do not change such as your first name or date of birth, and variables, which, as you know already from Liberty BASIC, are named storage locations for data that can change.

Java Literals

A literal is just a number, character, or string of characters. Several kinds of Java literals exist. Java supports *integer* (whole numbers without decimal places) and *floating-point* (numbers with decimal place) literals. Here are some valid integer literals:

```
23   -53819   0
```

Here are sample floating-point literals:

```
90544.5432211    -.0000324    -2.354    67.1
```

Java also supports two *Boolean* literals. These Boolean literals are `true` and `false`. You'll use Boolean literals to test or set Boolean values to `true` or `false` to determine if certain events are to occur.

A character literal is a single character. You must enclose character literals inside single quotation marks. The following are character literals:

```
'J'    '@'    '4'    'p'
```

A character literal doesn't have to be alphabetic. You cannot compute with a number inside a character literal. Therefore, `'4'` is a character literal but `4` is an integer literal. If you need to represent several characters as a single literal, use a string literal as described at the end of this section. Programmers work with literals all the time, such as when printing a corporation's name on a report.

Java supports special character literals called *escape sequences*. Due to the special nature of some character literals, you cannot always represent a character inside single quotation marks. For example, a tab character can appear on a screen to move the cursor forward a few characters to the next tab stop. But to store a tab character in a variable, you cannot assign the tab key directly to a variable—you must use an escape sequence to represent the tab character if you need one. These escape characters do consume more than one position inside the single quotes, such as '\n', but they only take one character's storage location as do all character literals. Table 13.1 lists some Java escape sequences.

TABLE 13.1   Java's Escape Sequence Characters Represent Nontypable Characters.

Escape Sequence	Represents
'\f'	Form feed
'\n'	Newline (linefeed followed by a carriage return)
'\t'	Tab (horizontal)
'\007'	Ring the PC's speaker
'\''	Single quotation mark
'\"'	Quotation mark

Remember that Java came from C and C++. C and C++ support the same data types as Java (except for strings) as well as the same escape sequences. As you learn more about Java's operators and control statements throughout the rest of this hour, virtually all you learn is applicable in C and C++ as well.

You can use an escape character to move the cursor down a line with the newline escape sequence, or you could use one to place a single quotation mark on a window. You could not represent a single quote by placing it inside two single quotes like this: ' ' '.

Specify string literals by enclosing them in quotation marks. All of the following items are string literals:

```
"This is a string."    "12345"     ""    "q"
```

You can place an escape sequence character inside a string. Therefore, the following string literal contains starting and ending quotation marks due to two escape sequences that represent the quote marks: "\"Java\"".

13

Java Variables

As in Liberty BASIC, you're in charge of naming Java variables. Unlike Liberty BASIC, you must inform Java that you need to use a variable by declaring that variable before you use it. When you declare a variable, you tell Java the name and data type of that variable. Java then reserves storage for that variable throughout the variable's lifetime. A variable's life may be for the entire program (as is the case with *global* variables) or may exist only for a few lines of code (as is the case with *local* variables), depending on how and where you declare the variable. Once you declare a variable, Java protects that variable's data type; that is, you cannot store a string in an integer variable.

Integer Variables

Table 13.2 lists the four kinds of integer variables Java supports. The integer variable you use depends on what you're going to store in that variable. For example, if you're going to store a child's age in a variable, you could do so in a `byte` variable. If you are going to store intergalactic distances, you need to use a `long` integer.

TABLE 13.2 Java Variable Sizes Determine Which Integer Variable You Use.

Data Type	Storage Needed	Data Range
byte	1 byte	−127 to +128
short	2 bytes	−32,767 to +32,768
int	4 bytes	−2,147,483,647 to +2,147,483,648
long	8 bytes	−9.2233 times 10 to the 18th power to +9.2233 times 10 to the 18th power

A byte of memory represents a single character of storage. Therefore, you can store approximately 16 million characters, or byte integers, in 16 million bytes of free memory.

Generally, you'll find variable declarations near the beginning of Java programs and procedures. To declare a variable, use Table 13.2's first column to tell Java the kind of variable you require. The following statement declares an integer variable named `numKeys`:

```
int numKeys;   // Defines a 4-byte integer variable
```

Remember to follow your variable declarations, as with all Java statements, with semicolons. The following statements define four variables, one for each type of Java integer:

```
byte a;
short b;
int c;
long d;
```

You can define several variables of the same data type on one line like this:

```
int x, y, z;    // Defines 3 integer variables
```

 Java declares variables but does not initialize variables for you, unlike Liberty BASIC. Therefore, don't assume zero or blanks are in numeric and string variables. Be sure to initialize each variable with a value before you use that variable inside a calculation.

Use the assignment operator, =, to assign values to your variables. You can assign a variable an initial value at the same time you define a variable. The following statements declare four variables and initialize three of them:

```
byte f = 32;
int c, d = 7639;    // Defines but does not initialize c
long highCount = 0;
```

Floating-Point Variables

Table 13.3 lists the two kinds of floating-point variables that Java supports. You'll use the larger floating-point variable to represent extremely large or small values with a high degree of accuracy. Generally, only scientific and mathematically related programs need the `double` data type. For most floating-point calculations, `float` works just fine.

TABLE 13.3 Java Supports Two Floating-Point Variable Data Types.

Data Type	Storage Needed	Decimal Accuracy
float	4 bytes	6 decimal places
double	8 bytes	14 decimal places

The following statements declare and initialize floating-point variables that can hold decimal numbers:

```
float w = -234.4332;
float x = 76545.39;
double y = -0.29384848458, z = 9283.11223344;
```

Boolean Variables

Use the `boolean` keyword to declare Boolean variables. A Boolean variable can hold only `true` or `false`. The following statements declare and initialize three Boolean variables:

```
boolean hasPrinted = false;
boolean gotAnswer = false; keyPressed = true;
```

These conditional values specify whether or not an event took place.

13

Character Variables

Declare character variables with the `char` keyword as the following statements do:

```
char firstInitial;
char lastInitial = 'Z';
```

You may assign any of the character literals you learned about earlier this hour, including escape sequences, to character variables. The following statements store the letter A in a variable and a tab character in another variable:

```
c1 = 'A';
tabChar = '\t';
```

String Variables

Java does not actually support string variables, and neither do C or C++, but Java includes a built-in class that defines string data as variables so you can declare string variables just as you can the other data types. Use the `String` keyword (notice the upper-case S: most programmers use an initial uppercase letter for names of classes) to declare string variables. You cannot directly change a string variable once you declare and initialize the variable but you can use built-in functions to change string variables.

The following statements declare three strings:

```
String s;                          // No initialization
String langName = "Java";          // An initialized string
String warning = "Don't press Enter yet!"; // Initialized
```

Arrays

Java supports arrays, which are lists of zero or more variables of the same data type, as you learned in Hour 9, "Programming Algorithms." All array subscripts begin at 0, so a 10-element array named `ara` utilizes these array elements: `ara[0]` through `ara[9]`. Of course, you don't have to name arrays `ara`, you can assign any name you wish to an array.

To define an array, use the `new` command. The following statements define three arrays:

```
int countList[] = new int[100];   // Declare an array of 100 elements
double temps[] = new double[30];  // Declare 30 double elements\
char initials[] = new char[1000]; // Declare 1,000 characters
```

Although their declarations require more typing than nonarray variables, once you've declared arrays, you can use the array elements just as you use other variables. For example, the following statements work with individual array elements:

```
countList[0] = 10;
countList[50] = 394;
temps[2] = 34334.9298;
initials[1] = 'a';
initials[2] = initials[1];
```

Operators

Java supports several mathematical and conditional operators. You don't have to be a math expert to understand them but Java's operators are somewhat more involved than Liberty BASIC's due to Java's heavier reliance on operators (the same holds for C and C++).

The Primary Math Operators

Table 13.4 contains Java's primary math operators. They are simple and work much the same as Liberty BASIC's.

TABLE 13.4 Java Supports Fundamental Math Operators.

Operator	Name	Sample
+	Addition	`4 + count`
-	Subtraction	`gross - net`
*	Multiplication	`pay * taxRate`
/	Division	`bonus / factor`
%	Modulus	`bonus % factor`

You can use parentheses to group calculations together. Java normally computes division and multiplication in a formula before addition and subtraction, but the following makes sure the addition is computed first so an average can result:

```
average = (sales1 + sales2 + sales3 + sales4) / 4;
```

The modulus operator returns the remainder when you divide one integer into another. The assignment operator evaluates from right to left so you can combine multiple assignments as in this statement:

```
a = b = c = d = e = 0;  // Stores 0 in all five variables
```

13

Increment and Decrement Operators

As you learned in Hour 9, "Programming Algorithms," your programs will often keep track of running totals or count down or up to a value such as a total score. To add one or subtract one from a variable, you can use Java's increment (++) and decrement (–) operators as follows:

```
runningTotal++;  // Adds 1 to variable
countdown--;     // Subtracts 1 from variable
```

You may place increment and decrement operators inside expressions such as this:

```
answer = aVar++ * 4;
```

You can place increment and decrement operators on either side of a variable. If you place them on the left, *prefix* notation occurs and Java computes the increment or decrement before other operators. If you place them on the right, *postfix* notation occurs and Java computes the increment and decrement after other operators.

Assuming x contains a 5 before the next statement, answer receives the value of 12:

```
answer = ++x * 2;  // Evaluate prefix first
```

The next statement performs a different calculation, however, due to the postfix notation. Java does not update x until after x is evaluated in the rest of the expression.

```
answer = x++ * 2;  // Evaluate postfix last
```

In this expression, answer will contain 10 because the multiplication occurs before x increments. As with the prefix version, x always ends up with 6 before the statement completes. The choice of prefix or postfix depends on how you formulate the expression. If, for example, you used the same variable more than once on the right side of the equal sign, you should use postfix notation if you increment the variable so the expression is accurate. In other words, the following assignment statement uses postfix increment because age is incremented after it's used for the assignment:

```
ageFactor = age++ * .45 + age;  // Uses postfix
```

This statement uses the value of age twice in the calculation and then, after assigning the answer to ageFactor, increments the value in age. If prefix had been used, age would first be incremented before being used in the expression.

Arithmetic Assignments

Often, you will update, or change, the value of a variable based on that variable's existing value. For example, suppose you are keeping track of a 10-question polling result. Every time the user answers a polling questionnaire, you'll add ten to a running total.

Any time you want to modify the value of a variable, while using that variable's current value in the expression, put the variable on both sides of the assignment operator. The following statement adds ten to the variable named `totalAnswers`:

```
totalAnswers = totalAnswers + 10;  // Adds 10
```

You can divide a variable by two, as done with `aVar` here:

```
aVar = aVar / 2.0;
```

This updating of variables occurs so frequently that the Java language borrowed common C and C++ operators called *arithmetic assignment* operators. Table 13.5 explains these.

TABLE 13.5   Java's Arithmetic Operators Shortcut the Updating of Variables.

Operator	Sample	Description
+=	n += 2	Adds to a variable
-=	NetPay -= 10.0	Subtracts from a variable
*=	pay *= .7	Multiplies a variable's contents
/=	bonus /= scale	Divides a variable's contents
%=	Num %= 1	Computes the remainder based on a variable's current contents

Given Table 13.5's operator listing, the following statements use the arithmetic assignments to produce the same results described before the table:

```
totalAnswers += 10;   // Same as totalAnswers = totalAnswers + 10;
aVar /= 2.0;          // Same as aVar = aVar / 2.0;
```

Comparison Operators

Table 13.6 describes Java's conditional operators. These operators do not perform mathematical operations but return a Boolean `true` or `false` result that indicates how one data value relates to another. You should have little trouble understanding these operators, as they are similar to Liberty BASIC's comparison operators.

13

TABLE 13.6   Java's Comparison Operators Compare How Data Values Relate to One Another.

Operator	Sample	Description
==	sales == max	Tests for equality
!=	profit != goal	Tests for inequality
<	n < m	Tests for less than
>	amt > 0	Tests for greater than
<=	top <= bottom	Tests for less than or equal to
>=	age >= 21	Tests for greater than or equal to

> Don't confuse the equality operator, ==, with the assignment, =. Liberty BASIC uses = for both purposes, but Java, C, and C++ use = for assignment and == to test for equality.

The Conditional Operator

The *conditional operator* is the only Java operator that requires three values. The conditional operator actually combines *if-then-else* logic into a simple, clear operation. The conditional operator returns one of two values depending on the result of a comparison operator.

Here is the general format of the conditional operator:

```
(comparison) ? true result : false result;
```

Often, you'll assign a conditional to a variable as in the following statement:

```
minVal = (a < b) ? a: b;   // Stores the lesser of a or b
```

If the comparison of (a < b) results in true, a is assigned to minVal. Otherwise, if (a < b) is false, the conditional assigns b to minVal. Although you'll learn about Java's if statement in the section *The if and if-else Statements* later this hour, Java's if statement is close enough to Liberty BASIC's if statement that you can understand much of it now. As a comparison, and to help strengthen your understanding of the conditional operator, here is the identical logic using if-else statements:

```
if (a < b)
  minVal = a;
else
  minVal = b;
```

Use a conditional when you must make a fairly simple calculation based on the result of a comparison, such as `(a < b)` here. In most instances, a multi-statement `if-else` is easier to maintain than a conditional statement that tries to do too much.

Programming Control

Now that you know how to define Java data and work with its operators, you need to know how to manipulate that data through program control. Java programmers group statements together in *blocks* of code. A block of code is one or more statements enclosed within a pair of braces such as this:

```
{
    count++;
    System.out.println("The count is now higher");
}
```

Blocks can contain other blocks so you can *nest* one block inside another. The indention of a block's body helps to show where the block begins and ends in long programs.

Learn the Format

As you learn programming languages, you'll see how statements are formatted or put together. A general notation is often used to show you how to code a programming language statement.

Italicized words are placeholders that you fill in with your own values. The nonitalicized words, such as `if`, are required. If any part of the format appears inside square brackets, with the exception of array brackets, that part of the statement is optional.

The following format shows that `if` is required but the `else` portion is optional. You fill in the italicized placeholder code with other programming statements:

```
if (condition)
    { Block of one or more Java statements; }
[ else
    { Block of one or more Java statements; } ]
```

13

The `if` and `if-else` Statements

Here is the general format of the `if` statement:

```
if (condition)
    { Block of one or more Java statements; }
```

> Never put a semicolon at the end of the *condition*'s parentheses! Semicolons
> go only at the end of the executable statements. The *condition* does not ter-
> minate the `if` statement but only introduces the `if`. If you placed a semi-
> colon after the condition then a *null statement* would execute, meaning
> nothing would happen no matter how the condition tested and the block
> would always execute.

Consider the following `if` statement:

```
if (age >= 21)
  { g.drawString("You have authorization for the payment", 25, 50);
    makePmt(pmt);
  }
// Rest of program goes here
```

The two statements in the body of the `if` execute only if `age` contains a value of 21 or
more. If `age` is less than 21, the block of code does *not* execute. Whether or not the block
executes does not keep the subsequent statements in the program from continuing.

A great use for `if` is *input verification*. When you ask the user for a value, you should
check the value to make sure the user entered a reasonable answer. For example, the following code asks the user for his or her age. If the user enters zero or a negative value,
the program's `if` statement displays an error message and prompts the user again.

```
getAge(age);  // Calls a procedure to get the user's age
if (age <= 0)
  {  // The following lines output to the user's screen
    System.out.println('\007');  // This escape code rings the speaker
    System.out.println("You entered a bad age value.");
    System.out.println("Try again please.");
    getAge(age);
  }
// Code goes here to process the age
```

The `if-else` adds an `else` block to the `if` statement. Here is the format of the `if-else`
statement:

```
if (condition)
  { Block of one or more Java statements; }
else
  { Block of one or more Java statements; }
```

If the `condition` evaluates to true, the first block of Java statements executes. If, however, the `condition` evaluates to false, the second block of Java statements executes.

The section of Java code in Listing 13.1 computes a payroll amount based on the following general rules:

- If the employee works 40 or fewer hours, the employee gets paid an hourly rate times the number of hours worked.

- If the employee works from 40 to 50 hours, the employee gets paid one-and-one-half times the hourly pay for all hours over 40.

- If the employee works more than 50 hours, the employee gets paid twice the hourly rate for those hours over 50.

LISTING 13.1   Using `if-else` to Compute an Employee's Overtime

```
// Assume all variables are declared and initialized
// to zero in earlier code
//
// Check for double-time first
if (hours > 50)
  { dbleTime = 2.0 * payRate * (hours - 50);
    // 1.5 pay for middle 10 hours
    halftime = 1.5 * payRate * 10.0;
else
  // No double because no hours over 50
  { dbleTime = 0.0; }
//
// Check for time-and-a-half
if ((hours > 40) && (hours <= 50))
  { halftime = 1.5 * payRate * (hours - 40); }
//
// Compute regular pay for everybody
if (hours <= 40)
  { regPay = hours * payRate; }
else
  { regPay = 40 * payRate; }
//
// Add the parts to get total gross pay
totalPay = regPay + halftime + dbleTime;
```

13

You'll notice a new operator in Listing 13.1, the *And* operator, `&&`. `&&` combines two conditions. Both conditions must be true for the entire `if` to be true. Therefore, `if ((hours > 40) && (hours <= 50))` means the hours must be over 40 and less than or equal to 50 for the `if` to be true.

The `while` Loop

Java supports several kinds of loops. The `while` loop continues as long as a condition is true. Here is the format of the `while` loop:

```
while (condition)
  { Block of one or more Java statements; }
```

While the `condition` remains true, the block repeats, but as soon as the `condition` becomes false, the loop body stops executing. It's incumbent upon you to modify the `condition` inside the loop's body or the loop will never stop.

In some cases, the body of the `while` loop will never execute. If the `condition` is false upon entering the loop, Java skips the loop's body and continues with the rest of the program. Earlier, you saw how an `if` statement can inform a user if the user enters invalid data. With looping, you can take the user's input validation a step further: you can keep asking the user for an answer until the user enters a value that falls within your program's expected range.

The following code uses a `while` loop to keep asking the user for an age value until the user enters a value greater than zero:

```
getAge(age);   // Calls a procedure to get the user's age
while (age <= 0)
  {  // User didn't enter proper age
     System.out.println('\007');   // Rings the PC's speaker
     System.out.println("\nYou entered a bad age value.");
     System.out.println("Try again please.");
     getAge(age);
  }
System.out.println("\nThank you");
// When execution gets here, age contains a positive value
```

Here is an example of the output:

```
How old are you? -16
<beep>

You entered a bad age value.
Try again please.
How old are you? 0
<beep>

You entered a bad age value.
Try again please.
How old are you? 22

Thank you
```

The `for` Loop

The `for` loop works very much like Liberty BASIC's except the Java `for` loop is more compact than Liberty BASIC's. Here is the general format of the `for` loop:

```
for (startExpression; testExpression; countExpression)
  { Block of one or more Java statements; }
```

Java evaluates the *startExpression* before the loop begins. Typically, the *startExpression* is an assignment statement (such as `ctr = 1;`), but the *startExpression* can be any legal expression you specify. Java evaluates the *startExpression* only once, at the top of the loop, just before the loop begins.

> Although semicolons appear twice in the `for`'s parenthetical control statement, you should never put a semicolon after the `for`'s closing parentheses or the `for` loop will never repeat its body of code.

The `for` statement tests its condition at the top of the loop. Here's the way the test works:

- If the *testExpression* is true when the loop begins, the body of the loop executes
- If the *testExpression* is false when the loop begins, the body of the loop never executes.

A count is one of the quickest ways to see how the `for` loop operates. Consider the following `for` loop:

```
for (ctr = 1; ctr <= 10; ctr++)
  { System.out.println(ctr); }
```

When the code runs, here is what the user sees:

```
1
2
3
4
5
6
7
8
9
10
```

An equivalent Liberty BASIC `For` loop would look like this:

```
For ctr = 1 To 10
  Print ctr
Next ctr
```

13

You don't have to increment the *countExpression*. You can increment or decrement the variable by any value each time the loop executes. The following code prints all even numbers below 20:

```
System.out.println("Even numbers below 20:");
for (num = 2; num <= 20; num+= 2)   // Adds 2 each loop iteration
  { System.out.println(num); }
```

From Details to High-Level

Throughout this hour, you've been studying the details of the Java language. If you've made it through without too many scars, you will be surprised at how much you also know of C and C++ when you look at a program written in one of those two languages.

Two areas of Java programming that this hour did not concentrate on are

- Input and output
- Object-oriented programming (OOP) concepts

It was important to focus on the language specifics in this hour. Now that you have done that, you are ready to tackle the other side of Java. Fortunately, input and output are rather simple in Java because the built-in library routines that come with Java enable you to get the user's input and display output relatively easily. As you learn about Java input and output in the next hour, you'll also learn about how Java supports OOP.

Summary

The goal of this hour was to teach you about Java operators and the language's fundamental commands. You now understand how to control Java programs and how to form mathematical expressions in Java. You saw how knowledge of Liberty BASIC helped you master Java more quickly due to the similarities between the programming languages.

When you finish the next hour, you will put everything together and begin using the Forte Java compiler to enter and test the programs you write.

Q&A

Q Why should I use escape characters?

A Escape characters were more important before windows-type environments due to the row and column textual nature of older computer screens, but you'll still use escape characters in modern-day Java (and C and C++) programs to represent characters that you cannot type directly from your keyboard, such as a carriage return character.

Q Which should I use, the conditional operator or the `if` statement?

A Although you saw both the conditional operator and an equivalent `if` statement for comparison in this hour, the two are for different purposes. The `if` statement can be much more complex than the conditional statement because you can use the `else` and blocks to execute many statements depending on the complexity of the problem you're coding. Use the conditional for short, one-statement conditional bodies that produce results that you'll assign to other variables. Most of the time, a multiline `if-else` statement is easier to maintain than a complex conditional statement.

Workshop

The quiz questions are provided for your further understanding. For the answers, see Appendix B, "Quiz Answers."

Quiz

1. True or false: You can change a Java literal just as you can change the value of a variable.

2. How would you store a quotation mark in a character variable named `aQuote`?

3. How many integer data types does Java support?

4. What is the lowest subscript in a Java array?

5. How many different values can a Boolean variable hold?

6. Describe what the modulus operator does.

7. Rewrite the following code in Java using only one variable and one operator:

   ```
   sum = sum * 18;
   ```

8. What is in the value of `y` when the following code completes?

   ```
   x = 4;
   y = ++x + 3 * 2;
   ```

9. What is wrong with the following `for` loop?

   ```
   for (num = 1; num > 20; num++);
      { System.out.println("Hello!"); }
   ```

10. True or false: You must increment the `for` loop's variable by one each time through the loop.

13

HOUR 14

Java Has Class

In this hour you will learn all about Java classes after performing some hands-on programming with the Forte for Java development system. This, perhaps, is one of the heaviest hours in this 24-hour tutorial due to the nature of object-oriented programming (OOP).

Most Java programming revolves around an object's class data and method. Java contains all kinds of rules and conventions for specifying class data and methods. In this hour, you'll learn how methods perform their work and you'll see how to set up data that responds to those methods.

The highlights of this hour include

- Working inside the Forte for Java IDE (Integrated Development Environment)
- Displaying Java output in windows
- Using classes to define objects
- Understanding how methods behave
- Passing and returning arguments
- Overloading methods to ease programming duties

Using Forte to Run Java Programs

You probably don't want to wait any longer to begin coding in Java. You've now got enough of the language's background to begin with some hands-on work.

Listing 14.1 contains a Java source program that asks for two numbers and displays the sum of them. Considering that a pocket calculator could do this in four button presses, the Java source code might seem rather long for such a simple calculation. Some overhead is required for Java applications, and the OOP mechanisms, such as private data members, add some code, as you'll see throughout the last half of this hour. (Hence the apparent wordiness of the code.) Fortunately, the wordiness does not increase in direct proportion to an application's requirements.

This program is a standalone application and is not a Java applet that appears inside a Web page. Java applets use the same Java language as standalone Java applications but require some extra code to make the applet work inside a Web page, as you'll learn about in the next hour, "Applets and Web Pages."

LISTING 14.1   This Simple Java Program Adds Two Numbers Together.

```
public class Main_1 extends java.lang.Object {

  public Main_1() {
  }

  public static void main (String args[]) {
    int intSum;              // Holds the sum

    // Compute sum
    intSum = 14 + 35;

    // Show user the sum
    System.out.println("The total is " +  intSum);

    System.exit(0);          // Stops the execution
  }
}
```

To run Listing 14.1's program, just follow these steps:

1. Start your Forte for Java compiler. When you start Forte, a startup screen appears for a few moments and then the Welcome window, shown in Figure 14.1, allows you to open a new file, to type in new code, or to load an existing Java program.

Figure 14.1.

You must tell Java to create a new file for your program.

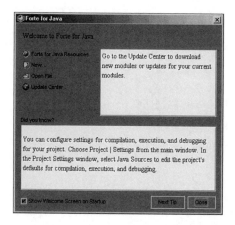

2. Select New. Forte for Java opens a New Template window in which you tell Forte what kind of Java program you want to create. Java comes with several object-oriented tools that help you build programs faster, some of which you'll learn about throughout the rest of this hour.

3. Click the icon to the left of Classes to open the Classes list.

4. Select Main and click Next. You are telling Forte that you want to create a stand-alone Java application. All Java programs use main as the starting point of the program's execution. main is the name of a procedure, or routine, and some small Java programs contain only a main procedure. The Forte for Java system will actually build part of the main procedure for you so that you don't have to type the entire program in Listing 14.1.

5. The Customize window you now see is where you can request that Forte customize the classes or procedures you write. You will not enter anything in this or subsequent windows, so click Finish to build your initial program file. Forte will ask if you want to add the current file to the *project*. A project is a collection of files that comprise a Java application. Your program will have only one file in the project, Listing 14.1's source code, so click Yes to add the current file to the project. All programs compiled and executed from within Forte must be project files even if the project contains only a single source code file. Forte builds the outline of your program shown in Listing 14.2.

14

LISTING 14.2   The Forte for Java System Builds an Outline of Your Code So You Have Less to Type.

```
/*
 * Main_1.java
 *
 * Created on August 2, 2004, 1:54 PM
 */

/**
 *
 * @author Greg Perry
 * @version
 */
public class Main_1 extends java.lang.Object {

/** Creates new Main_1 */
  public Main_1() {
  }

  /**
   * @param args the command line arguments
   */
  public static void main (String args[]) {
  }

}
```

Forte for Java adds several comments and uses the same syntax as C uses, which is still supported by the Java language. All text between an opening /* and a closing */ pair of characters, even if the words span multiple lines, is considered by the compiler to be a comment. Forte adds several comments to your code that begin with asterisks just to help separate the comments from actual executable program code. You can also use the newer-style comments that begin with //. The advantage of the old style is that each comment line doesn't have to begin with //, only the first one in multiple lines of comments.

Commented items that begin with an ampersand, @, are special commented lines supplied by Forte that you should replace with something other than values, such as your name. Of course, because they're inside comments you can put anything you want there. But as Hour 3, "Designing a Program," explained, maintenance is vital when working in a group of programmers, and each programmer should put his or her name in the source code along with a version number of the code to show what was worked on. For now, you can remove these comment lines preceded by the ampersand by selecting and deleting them as you would do in a word processor.

Unless you specify another filename (which you did not do in the previous steps), Forte uses a default filename for your Java project. If you've never created a Java project before, Forte uses `Main.java` for the filename. Subsequently, Forte will use the names `Main_1.java`, `Main_2.java`, and so on as you create additional files over the life of your Java development. In reality, you'll assign better filenames to the projects you create. Therefore, if you were creating a Java application that managed an inventory, you might save that application under the name `Inv.java`. All java source code ends in the `.java` filename extension.

Within the file, Forte creates two procedures for you, one with the name of your program, which in this example will be `Main.java`, and one that is the regular `main` procedure. You won't be using the `Main` procedure in this example, but go ahead and leave it there for this hour.

The `main` procedure has the words `public static void` before the name to define how this procedure is to be viewed. These keywords basically tell the compiler that `main` is a public procedure that can be seen from the rest of the files in the project, if the project has additional files and the `main` procedure returns no values.

Values, called *arguments,* are placed inside `main`'s parentheses in order to be passed to `main` from other places. When your programs have multiple procedures, each procedure can transfer values back and forth through this argument list. `main`'s argument list is there in case you want to send values from the operating system to the program when the program first starts. In most cases you won't do this but a string array exists in most Java `main` procedures just in case.

Java created this program shell for you so that your only job is to fill in the source code with the rest of Listing 14.1's code, compile the program, and see the results. To finish the program, follow these steps:

1. Place your cursor before the closing brace,}, of the `main` procedure (the line right beneath `public static void main (String args[]) {`) and type `main`'s body of code as shown in Listing 14.3.

LISTING 14.3 Type This to Complete the `main` Procedure That Forte Began for You.

```
int intSum;          // Holds the sum

// Compute sum
intSum = 14 + 35;

// Show user the sum
System.out.println("The total is " +  intSum);

System.exit(0);       // Stops the execution
```

14

2. Your program should now look like the one in Listing 14.4. Although you may have changed, added, or deleted some comments, your noncomment code should exactly match that of the listing.

LISTING 14.4

```
/*
 * Main_1.java
 *
 * Created on August 2, 2004, 1:54 PM
 */

/**
 * @author Greg Perry
 */
public class Main_1 extends java.lang.Object {

/** Creates new Main_1 */
  public Main_1() {
  }

  public static void main (String args[]) {
    int intSum;            // Holds the sum

    // Compute sum
    intSum = 14 + 35;

    // Show user the sum
    System.out.println("The total is " +  intSum);
    System.exit(0);        // Stops the execution
  }

}
```

3. You can now compile and run the program. Forte for Java does both in one step when you press F6. If you don't see the Output window, click the Output tab at the bottom of your screen and the output window shows the following program result:

```
The total is 49
```

Going GUI

You've successfully run your first Java program, but the output is text based and does not take advantage of the Windows environment very well. Listing 14.5 contains the same program as the previous one except the code takes advantage of *Swing*. Swing is a set of Java library routines that enable you to add message boxes, get input from input boxes, and add window-like features to your program. You can make the changes to Main_1.java, load the Main_2.java program from this tutorial's CD-ROM, or start a new project from scratch. The easiest thing to do is just make the changes needed so your program now matches Listing 14.5. By the way, be sure to change the name of your program (it's probably either Main or Main_1 if you've been following to now) to Main_2 and save your file with File, Save after making the changes in Listing 14.5.

LISTING 14.5   Move Away from the Text Mode into Windowed Features

```java
/*
 * Main_2.java
 *
 * Created on August 2, 2004, 2:34 PM
 */
import javax.swing;
public class Main_1 extends java.lang.Object {

/** Creates new Main_2 */
  public Main_2() {
  }

  public static void main (String args[]) {
    int intSum;            // Holds the sum

    // Compute sum
    intSum = 14 + 35;

    // Show user the sum in a message window
    JOptionPane.showMessageDialog(null, "The total is " + intSum);
    System.exit(0);        // Stops the execution
  }

}
```

When you execute your program, the message box shown in Figure 14.2 appears. That's better and more modern than outputting straight text, isn't it? Click the message box's button to close the message box window when you're done.

14

Figure **14.2.**

*Swing makes your out-
put look better.*

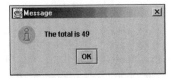

The Java libraries, such as Swing, are full of objects you can bring into your own code and use. Part of the fun of getting to know Java is figuring out what all the language can do for you through the use of these object-oriented library routines. Need to add a command button or other feature to your program? Look for an object library that supplies that feature and just plug the object into your program! That's one of the beauties of Java and OOP.

> The Swing object library can be used by this program because of the `import` command that imports, or brings into your program, all the window-like objects from the library named `javax.swing`. One of the many features of this library is the `JOptionPane` routine that enables you to send output to a windowed message box instead of as text in a window as you did in the previous section using `System.out.println`. `System` is actually an object, your computer, and `out` is a subobject, or a *derived* object, that represents a text window.

Java and OOP

Java is an OOP (*object-oriented programming*) language, and just about everything you do works with an object of some kind. An object is little more than a place where more than one variable resides. Objects give their variables special treatment such as protecting the variables' details from the rest of the code, but still, an object is a place where two or more variables often appear together in a group.

Consider this object declaration:

```
public class Employee {
   protected String firstName[15] = new String
   protected String lastName[15] = new String;
   protected float salary;
   protected int age;
   // Rest of object's declaration follows
}
```

Although several variables are declared here, two as arrays, they are collected together into the class called `Employee`. Just as the integer data type is not a variable but defines data, neither is `Employee` a variable; it is a class that declares what subsequent variables will look like. The class simply defines the format of an object that you generate from that class just as the integer data type defines the format of a variable that you generate from the integer data type. The `protected` keyword tells Java that those members are not accessible from outside the class; that is, only code that you subsequently place inside the class can use the protected data.

Figure 14.3 shows how the `Employee` object's data values appear in memory. Variables inside objects are called *members* but they're really just variables. After the variable members are defined in the object, the rest of the declaration often contains procedures called *methods*, which are routines that act upon the object's data.

FIGURE 14.3.
Objects can contain lots of variables and their data types don't have to match.

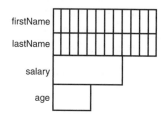

Overview of Classes

All Java programs are actually objects themselves. The entire Java program you write is an object. There exists a special highest-level object called the `java.lang.Object`. Your program is a derivation from that object. When you *derive* one object from another, or inherit an object from another, the derived object takes on all the properties of its parent object, the higher-level object.

Here is the line that derived from this special Java application object in this hour's earlier programs:

```
public class Main_1 extends java.lang.Object {
```

In other words, you created a Java application, an object, from the `java.lang.Object` object. More specifically, you created a new class by inheriting from the `java.lang.Object` class. You extended a new object from an existing one that represented a generic Java application.

Why Inherit?

You inherit to eliminate redundant coding. When you inherit from a class, your derived class (sometimes called the subclass) inherits all methods and data values from the parent class. Therefore, with the simple `extends` keyword, your new class that you inherit from a parent class gains all the parent's power, behaviors, and data.

When you define methods and data members in the inherited class, that class becomes stronger than its parent class because the inherited class now has extended abilities.

14

An object is more than a variable. An object is an active variable that, with its data and methods, not only has characteristics from the data values but also can perform operations on that data with its member code. As you pursue your programming career and learn more about objects, you will learn how languages such as Java specifically activate objects so that you can use those objects in other programs you write. You can reuse objects in a second program that you previously wrote simply by copying the object's class definition to your new program.

Unlike the built-in data types, such as int, if you perform a math operation on one of your objects, you'll have to teach Java how to do the math by writing a method that performs the work. Once you supply the code, however, calculating with the objects is basically as easy to do as calculating with the built-in types.

Listing 14.6 demonstrates a class with data values (often called *data members* or just *members*) and methods (procedures inside the class).

LISTING 14.6   A Class Can Have Both Data Members and Procedure Methods.

```
//******
// The Box Class
//******
class Box        // A new class, so there is no
  // extension or inheritance from another class
{
    float area;      // A class data member
    int colorCode;  // A class data member

    void calcArea (float width, float length)
      {
        // Computes a value from data passed to the object
        area = width * length;
      }
    void setColor
      {
        // Sets a color for the object
        colorCode = colorValue;
      }
}
```

Box is a class with four members: two of Box's members are data members (area and colorCode) and two are methods (calcArea() and setColor()). Box is not an object, just a definition of the object (the class). You can, however, instantiate objects from the Box class, meaning you can define object variables.

Box is not a fully working, complete class. You would need to add additional members before Box to effectively define a full class with ample data and methods.

Java does not normally know what a Box is. Only after you declare the Box class, as in Listing 14.5, can you then define (instantiate) an object like this:

```
Box hatHolder;    // This instantiates a new object
```

The new variable named hatHolder is an object variable. Can you see that, loosely speaking, an object is a lot like a variable? You first have to tell Java about the object's type by defining the object's class, and you then have to define one or more objects just as you can define one or more variables. Unlike a variable, however, the hatHolder objects contain more than a single data type; hatHolder is a combination int and float value along with two methods that manipulate those data values.

If you want to execute one of the object's methods, you only need to use the dot operator. Suppose you wanted to calculate the area of the hatHolder object. The following statement executes hatHolder's calcArea() method:

```
hatHolder.calcArea(4.3, 10.244);  // Executes the calcArea method
```

In the previous hour, you learned how to use the new keyword to declare an array. new also defines objects. You may use new instead of defining them with the simpler *className objectName;* format. Here is how you would instantiate a Box object using new:

```
Box hatHolder = new Box();  // Instantiates a new Box object
```

Always use the parentheses when you use new with object instantiation. You can instantiate two Box objects as follows:

```
Box slot1 = new Box();
Box slot2 = new Box();
```

You now can calculate the area for the second Box object:

```
slot2.calcArea(1.0, 5.0);  // Sets the second object's area
```

You can specify the color for the first box as follows:

```
slot1.setColor(4);  // Sets the first object's color
```

14

Do You Understand OOP?

The nature of objects and OOP sneaks up on you. Relax if you don't feel as though you're mastering objects as quickly as you learned the non-OOP Java language, such as `for` loops. This is your first book of programming! Complete books much thicker than this are devoted to the explanation of OOP concepts and many of them fail miserably despite their length.

OOP requires a special kind of thinking that does not always come quickly. Throughout this hour, you'll familiarize yourself with OOP. When you're ready to return to OOP with Java or another OOP-based language such as C++, this introduction will pay dividends.

Methods Do the Work in Classes

Although you've seen methods in action, and although you know a little about what methods are all about (detours from code you call or class procedures you write that activate class objects), this section explains methods in a little more detail and fills in a few more pieces of the method puzzle.

A Method's Execution

Methods perform work. Methods operate on class data by using the controlling statements you learned about in the previous hour and also by utilizing variables to hold data. A method's argument list inside the method's parentheses may contain values or the list may be empty. If arguments exist, the code that calls the method must initialize those values and send the expected arguments and types.

> Think of an argument as a variable that's passed from one statement to a method. Arguments act like variables.

Figure 14.4 shows how the code in one method calls another method and sends that called method two arguments. Java sends a copy of the argument but does not really send the argument variables themselves. Therefore, if the called method changes an argument in any way, the change is not noticed when the calling code regains control.

> Java is known as a *call-by-value* language because a called method can never change the calling method's argument data. The called method can use and modify the arguments within the called method's statements, but when control returns to the calling code, the variables sent as arguments to the methods are unmodified in the calling method.

FIGURE 14.4.

The calling code sends two expected arguments to the called code.

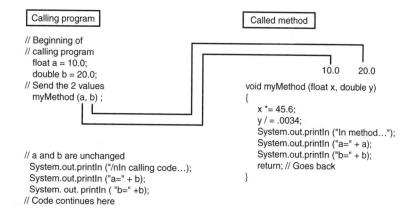

Figure 14.4's receiving method takes two values, computes with them, prints their newly computed values, and then returns control to the calling class.

Here is the output from Figure 14.4's code:

```
In method...
a=456.000
b=4608.294930876

In calling class...
a=10.0
b=20.0
```

As you can see, the called method receives two values and changes those values but the changes last only inside the method. The calling class code's variables are not, and cannot be, changed by the method.

The method arguments in Figure 14.4 are named x and y even though the calling program names those variables a and b. The received names might or might not match those in the calling code because only values are passed and not variables. The biggest concern you must have when passing data to methods is to get the number of arguments and data types correct. The method is expecting a float followed by a double, as you can see from this method's declaration line:

```
void myMethod(float x, double y)
```

The calling code must provide two variables that match this pattern. The first definition line of a called method must always declare the arguments and their data types.

The passing of data between code and methods is not strictly one-way. A method can return a value to the calling code. Although you can send zero, one, or multiple arguments to a method, a method can only return one value. Figure 14.5 illustrates the return nature of methods.

14

Here is the output from Figure 14.5's program:

```
In calling class...
a=10.0
b=20.0
```

The `doubleIt()` method is a two-way method in that the calling code passes an argument and the method also returns a value back to the calling code. The called method does not change any value and returns the doubled value back to the calling code. The calling code captures the return value in the variable named `doub`.

If a method requires no arguments, leave the argument list empty.

FIGURE 14.5.

A called method can return only a single value.

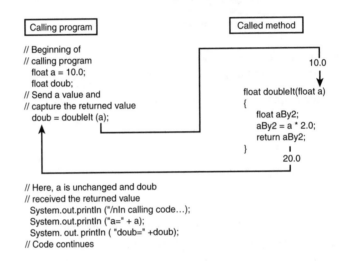

Summary

You now have the basics of object-oriented programming. You should have a better idea what classes, methods, and data are all about. The `new` operator creates the class objects that your program can use. The object is much more than just a variable that holds data; objects contain methods so objects are more active than variables.

The next hour takes a quick tour of Java-based Web page applets. You'll see exactly how to embed a Java program inside a Web page and how to set up the program to run when the user loads the Web page inside a Web browser.

Q&A

Q Forte for Java has many options. How can learn more about it?

A Forte for Java certainly is a comprehensive package with which you can develop many different kinds of Java applications and applets within. The online help system is complete and Sun Microsystems' Web site at http://www.sun.com/ contains information about Forte for Java and about all aspects of the Java language from both the programmer's as well as the user's perspective.

Q If I wanted to pass arguments to `main()` from my operating system, how would I do that?

A Suppose you wrote a Java program that calculated the sales commission for any salesperson in your company. You could pass the salesperson's employee number to `main()` and the program would then calculate the appropriate commission after looking up that salesperson's sales data in the company files. Several ways exist to pass such an employee number. One way would be to place the program in your Windows Start menu, right-click on the compiled program's filename, select Properties, and type the number to the right of the filename. All arguments passed to the program appear to the right of the filename when you execute the file in such a way.

Of course, changing the program's properties is certainly a tedious way to execute the program for all salespeople for whom you want to calculate commission. These command-line arguments actually were more important in the pre-Windows DOS operating system where typed filenames to execute programs were more common. In such an application today, you would make your program more usable if you forgo the command-line arguments in favor of prompting the user for the salesperson's employee number inside the program once the program starts.

Workshop

The quiz questions are provided for your further understanding. For the answers, see Appendix B, "Quiz Answers."

Quiz

1. What alternative to the Java comment `//` can you use for commenting code?
2. What are arguments?
3. Where does the argument list reside in the `main()` procedure?
4. What does Swing add to Java programs?
5. What command brings Java object libraries into Java programs?

14

6. How does a class differ from an object?

7. True or false: All Java programs derive from a single Java object named `java.lang.Object`.

8. What takes place when you instantiate an object?

9. What happens when you extend an object from another?

10. True or false: If an argument list requires no arguments, you should keep the argument list empty.

HOUR 15

Applets and Web Pages

In this hour you will learn how to embed Java applets inside Web pages. As explained first in Hour 12, Java applets are small programs that travel with Web page code and execute on the end-user's computer. Generally, you'll want to keep your applets small because they load with the user's Web page. Unlike standalone Java applications, which can be much larger, the more efficient your applets are, the faster they load with a Web page and the more likely your users are to return to your site.

As you'll see, the Java language does not change whether you're programming for an application or an applet. The way you set up a Java applet is different from the way you set up a standalone application but once you've set up the applet's outline, the code that does the work is straight Java.

The highlights of this hour include

- Using an appletviewer and Web page for applets
- Generating the Java outline, or skeleton, for an applet
- Generating a Java applet skeleton that utilizes Swing
- Using HTML code to carry your applet to your users

About Writing Java Applets

When you write a Java program that you want transmitted over the Internet, remember that the program embeds itself in the Web page. The language behind all Web pages is HTML and you'll learn all about HTML—if you're not already familiar with HTML—in Hour 18, "Web Pages with HTML." If you're not yet familiar with HTML, you don't need to understand much HTML to make Java applets work. This hour explains only the HTML commands needed to embed a Java applet because the focus for this section is primarily Java.

Although the Java language does not differ when you write Java applets and when you write standalone Java programs, you will need to set up your program differently when your program is an applet as opposed to a standalone program.

Many Java developers use an *appletviewer* to test the applets they run. Instead of compiling their Java applet and transporting the applet to a Web browser to test the applet, an appletviewer enables the Java programmer to test their applets without using a browser. Fortunately, you don't even need to use an appletviewer to test the Java applets that you write because Forte for Java enables you to test both applets and standalone Java programs from within the development system.

Creating a Java Applet

One of the best ways to learn how to create, test, and run Java applets is to create one yourself and go through the process of testing and running the applet. This hour spends some time walking you through the creation of a Java applet as well as testing the applet and viewing the applet inside a Web browser.

The Java Applet Skeleton

Many Java applets follow the same pattern to set up the initial procedure and to work within a Web page. If you want to create a Swing-enabled applet to take advantage of windows and dialog boxes, you will use the applet outline shown in Listing 15.1. Be warned, however, that programming with Swing requires that you learn some extra non-Java fundamentals. Swing makes it easier for you to place Windows controls on your applet but you must learn how Swing generates those controls. You can glean some information about Swing from Forte for Java's online help.

If you use Forte for Java's New command to create a Swing-based Java applet, it creates this applet skeleton for you. The name of the applet, JApplet.java, will change if you have Forte create several applets over time because Forte will not overwrite existing files.

A second Java applet's file and class name will be JApplet1.java, the next would be JApplet2.java, and so on.

LISTING 15.1   A Swing-based Java Applet Uses This Program Outline.

```
/*
 * JApplet.java
 */
public class JApplet extends javax.swing.JApplet {

  /* Creates a new applet */
  public JApplet () {
    /* Applet code goes here */
  }
}
```

Listing 15.1 simply creates a Java applet using the Swing library so that subsequent statements that you add to the code, inside the `JApplet()` function, will be able to access the Swing library. You may see other comments that the Forte system adds to the code if you generate this yourself; some comments have been removed from Listing 15.1 so you can focus on what's important for this section of the chapter. To create this applet's outline, select the JApplet from the Classes entry when you create a new applet from Forte for Java.

Inheriting from the `javax.swing.JApplet` brings the Swing object libraries into your program. Loading these Swing classes causes your applet to load a little slower than it otherwise would and consumes more Web page downloading bandwidth. Of course, the Windows elements such as message boxes that you gain with the Swing class often outweigh the slight extra load times needed for Swing applets. But if you want to create a simple Java applet that is text-based, the skeleton, or outline, of your Java program will look like the one in Listing 15.2.

LISTING 15.2   A Text-based Java Applet Uses This Program Outline.

```
/*
 * JApplet.java
 */
import java.applet.*;   // Required for applet
import java.awt.*;      // For graphics support

public class JApplet extends java.applet.Applet {

  /* Creates a new applet */
  public void init()
    { resize(320, 240);  //  applet's window size
    }
  /* More applet code goes here */
}
```

You can enter this program in Forte by following these steps:

1. Select File, New to open the Template Chooser window.

2. Click to open the Classes folder.

3. Select the Applet entry.

4. Click Finish to create the code.

5. Click Yes to add the new file to the current project.

6. Edit the init() routine's code so it matches that of Listing 15.2. This is the only code in the applet that does work. init() creates a window of 320 pixels tall by 240 pixels wide. Nothing appears in the window because no text is being written in Listing 15.2.

7. You can now click the Run toolbar button to see what the applet produces. The applet only produces a small window and nothing else. You can add to the applet as you learn more about Java and place that applet code inside a Web page.

Finishing an Applet

As you gain familiarity with Java, you'll soon learn which object library or libraries you need to include. For example, to use graphics in your Java applet, you'll need to include the java.awt.* that includes all libraries including the Graphics library you need for drawing text onto a window. Use the following command to bring in these libraries:

```
import java.awt.*;  // Bring in the graphics library
```

Importing a graphics library doesn't necessarily mean that you are writing a graphics applet. Many routines in the java.awt.Graphics library use graphics to produce nongraphic output, such as text. To place text in a window, for example, is easily achieved when you use the drawString() method found in the java.awt.Graphics library.

You'll notice that the non-Swing applet defines a method named init(). The init() method is a method you'll want to put into your non-Swing applets. When you inherit from the Applet class, you inherit all methods from that class including one called the init() method; but the init() method that you inherit does nothing. You must redefine the method for your specific applet. Therefore, when you write an applet by extending the Applet class, you will have to supply an init() method of your own.

15

> `resize()` is always the first method executed in your applet. Put all initial-
> ization code inside `init()`.

Almost every `init()` that you write will call the `resize()` method, just as the skeleton did and just as the complete applet in Listing 15.3 does. Notice the name, `JANoSwng.java` indicating that the code contains no Swing routines. The `resize()` method simply informs your class of your applet's window size in the target Web page. You can also insert other code inside `init()` that you want executed right after the initial loading of your applet. `resize()` requires two arguments: an x coordinate and a y coordinate. Enter the x and y coordinate values in screen pixels. As Figure 15.1 illustrates, the x coordinate determines the width, in pixels, of your applet's window, and the y coordinate determines the height of your applet's window.

LISTING 15.3   Completing the Text-based Java Applet.

```
/*
 * JANoSwng.java
 */
import java.applet.*;   // Required for applet
import java.awt.*;      // Required to draw text onto window
public class JANoSwng extends JApplet {

  /* Creates a new applet */
  public void init()
    { resize(320, 240);  //  applet's window size
    }
  public void paint(Graphics g)
  {
    // Change subsequent text color to red
    g.setColor(Color.red);
    // Write a simple message in the window
    g.drawString("Very simple!", 75, 100);
    }
}
```

FIGURE 15.1

resize() determines the size of your applet's window.

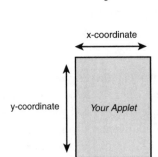

Your Web Page

x-coordinate

y-coordinate

Your Applet

Whenever your applet includes a method that also appears in the class method from which you extended your applet, as does init() in this case, your extended applet's method will always override the original class method. You can be assured that your init() will execute in place of the original Applet class's init().

The paint() method should also appear in applets you create, at least those that do not use the Swing class, and paint() should follow init(). Your applet executes paint() every time your applet window needs redrawing. In a Windows environment, parts of your screen have to be redrawn quite often. For example, you might hide a window and, when you unhide the window, the hidden portion must reappear. Perhaps your end-user minimizes the Web page down to a taskbar icon and then maximizes the window or resizes the window. As long as you've supplied a paint() method—and you must—you can be assured that your applet window will reappear properly with the text, colors, and whatever else appears there.

Look more closely at Listing 15.3's paint() lines:

```
public void paint(Graphics g)
{
  // Change subsequent text color to red
  g.setColor(Color.red);
  // Write a simple message in the window
  g.drawString("Very simple!", 75, 100);
}
```

Unlike init(), paint() requires a parameter inside its parentheses. The parameter is a value that the paint() method operates on. Although Graphics g is a strange parameter, the parameter represents your applet's Web page graphical window. The Graphics g designation is a Java standard designation for your applet's window.

Whatever `paint()` does to the value named `g` happens to your applet's window. The `g` is known as a *graphics device context*. A Windows application does not actually write to your screen; instead, a Windows application writes to windows. The `Graphics g` parameter tells your applet where to write, namely, the window inside the applet's enclosing Web page.

The next line makes a lot of sense despite its wordiness:

```
g.setColor(Color.red);
```

Remember that the `g` represents your Web page applet's window. If you discern that this statement sets your applet window to red, you are almost correct. Actually, the statement sets all subsequent colors to red. Executing multiple `setcolor()` methods between each line of output, you are able to send different colors to the same window.

When you see a period following an object (the object, `g`, represents your applet's window), the value to the right of the period will always be a method or a value. You know that `setColor()` is a method because of the parentheses that follow its name. The `setColor()` method is an internal `java.awt` class method that sets all subsequent output to a specific color. The color must appear inside the parentheses. The color inside the parentheses is the `setColor()` parameter.

Windows is capable of displaying several million colors. As with the *Windows Application Programming Interface* (*Windows API*), a set of routines that C++ programmers use when writing Windows programs, there are several ways to represent all the shades of colors that can appear on your screen. You can specify some standard colors easily. If you don't get too picky on just that right shade of monkey blue you've always loved on your bedroom ceiling, you can specify one of the colors from Table 15.1 for the parameter inside `setColor()`. Notice that you must precede the color name with the `Color` object. The `Color` object is a symbolic object, defined inside the `hava.awt` class package, which represents coloring. You can specify a named value by following the `Color` and separating period with one of the named color values in Table 15.1.

TABLE 15.1   Use These Color Values to Put Colored Text on the Screen.

black	blue	cyan
darkgray	gray	green
lightgray	magenta	orange
pink	red	white
yellow		

As you can see, the syntax is a little tricky but `setColor()` is not necessarily hard to understand. For example, you could later print some green text on your applet's window by placing the following statement before you print the text:

```
g.setColor(Color.green);
```

After printing green text, you then could call `setColor()` once more to set the color back to red like this:

```
g.setColor(Color.red);
```

Referring back to Listing 15.3, once the applet sets the color red, the applet sends two words to the applet window with the following line:

```
g.drawString("Very Simple!", 75, 100);
```

The `drawString()` method is commonly used to send strings to the applet's window. Because `drawString()` respects the color set by `setColor()`, the text, `Very Simple!`, will appear in red. Notice the `g` before the method name. The g happens to be the name of this window, passed to the `paint()` routine like this:

```
public void paint(Graphics g)
```

The `g` refers to the graphics context which is the applet's window. Any name could be used. You could use any variable in place of `g` and then preface the methods inside `paint()` with that variable name.

The second and third parameters of `drawString()` represent the starting x and y coordinates of where you want the text to appear. In other words, `init()` creates an applet window that runs 320 pixels across by 240 pixels down. Then `drawString()` starts drawing its text, `Very Simple!`, exactly 75 pixels down and 100 pixels across the applet window.

OOP-Based Coding

This applet's `setColor()` method demonstrates part of the object-based nature of OOP code. For example, in non-OOP languages, the procedures are more important than the data. In OOP languages, the data, or more accurately, the objects, has the primary focus. When you want to set the applet window's printing color, what is the object? The color, the `setColor()` method, or your applet's window? The applet's window is the object. The window is the target of the color-setting procedure.

The very first item in this applet's `setColor()` line is g, which represents your applet's graphical drawing window as described earlier in this section. Everything else on the line does something to that object. The object g, referring to your applet window, gets its color set with the `setColor()` procedure. Inside `setColor()`, another less-obvious object appears named `Color`. In other words, you want to set a particular color object to a particular color. The phrase `Color.red` does just that, it sets the object in question, `Color`, to red. That object, the red color, is then passed through the `setColor()` procedure to the graphic applet window named g.

Placing the Applet Inside the Web Page

Remember that the primary purpose of an applet is to appear on an Internet end-user's computer when that end-user loads the Web page that contains the applet. Listing 15.4 contains a sample HTML file that forms the skeleton of many HTML files that embed Java applets.

LISTING 15.4   An HTML File That Carries a Java Applet.

```
<HTML>
  <HEAD>
    <TITLE>First Java Applet</TITLE>
  </HEAD>

<BODY>
  <HR>
  <OBJECT
    CODE = JANoSwng.class
    WIDTH=320
    HEIGHT=240 >
  </OBJECT>
  <HR>
  <A HREF="JANoSwng.java">The Java source.</A>
</BODY>
</HTML>
```

Don't get too caught up with the HTML at this time because in Hour 18, "Web Pages with HTML," you'll learn what all the HTML code means. For now, just know that the <OBJECT> command (called a *tag* in HTML terminology) tells the Web page the name of the compiled Java class that is to be embedded and the width and height of the applet's window, which, not coincidentally, are the same width and height values that the applet's init() method prepares for.

HTML supports the <OBJECT> tag that indicates a Java applet. Earlier versions of HTML supported the <APPLET> tag that did the same thing but current standards dictate the use of <OBJECT>.

The <HTML> and </HTML> tags always mark the beginning and end of an HTML file. The <HEAD> and </HEAD> tags mark the beginning and end of the Web page's primary heading, which appears at the top of the Web page and usually contains a title. You can see that this header has a title, delimited with <TITLE> and </TITLE>, that simply contains the name of the Java applet. The <BODY> and </BODY> tags delimit the body of the Web page and generally comprise the largest portion of the Web page, including the Web page document's contents.

The `<HR>` tags do not contain matching `</HR>` tags because `<HR>` is the horizontal rule tag that draws a horizontal line across the screen to separate parts of the Web page. A horizontal line appears every place that `<HR>` appears. Obviously, the lines that follow the first `<HR>` tag specify the applet information. They are

```
<OBJECT
  CODE = JANoSwng.class
  WIDTH=320
  HEIGHT=240 >
</OBJECT>
```

The `<OBJECT>` tag requires extra parameters that many of the other tag commands do not require. The `<OBJECT>` tag indicates that the Web page is to load an applet at that particular page location, thus the `<OBJECT>` tag must contain the applet information, such as the applet name. The Web page must have this correct information so that the Web page can properly locate the applet and display the applet in an appropriate window. The `<OBJECT>` tag is free form, so you can make it span several lines for readability as done here.

The `CODE` parameter (actually, HTML values are called *attributes*) names the class of the applet that is to execute. For now, remember that a class is generally the same as an applet program because most applets contain a single class and the class contains all the functioning applet code. Therefore, the class will generally be your Java file name (with the `java` extension).

The `WIDTH` and `HEIGHT` attributes are always required for all applets that you embed in a Web page. The Web page browser must be told the size of your applet's window (the applet will appear on the page in a window). Finally, the `</OBJECT>` ending tag indicates that the applet parameter information is complete.

> The applet must reside in the same directory as the HTML file unless you preface the name with its location, as the following `CODE` attribute does:
> `CODE="http://www.mySite.com/JavaApps/JANoSwng.class"`

The following line looks as though it references the applet as well:

```
<A HREF="JANoSwng.java">The Java source.</A>
```

The `<A HREF>` tag is not associated with the `<OBJECT>` tag command. This tag provides a hyperlink to a specific location, as you'll learn more about in Hour 18. The location is the applet's source code. Note that the ending `</A>` tag follows the words "`The Java source`." Therefore, the text "`The Java source`" will appear as a hypertext link that the end-user can click on to see the source code of the applet that runs above in the window.

To create an HTML file, you need a text editor. The text editor enables you to create a text file, similar to the way that a word processor enables you to create a document. Create the HTML file using any text editor, such as the Windows Notepad program, and store the file with the .html filename extension.

Viewing the Applet Inside the Web Page

Once you've compiled the Java applet, you may have to use Windows Explorer to copy the compiled applet, called JANoSwng.class, to the same folder in which you've created your HTML source code. You now have, in the same folder, the HTML source code (you never compile HTML source code) and the compiled Java class file. Follow these steps to see your applet run in your Web browser:

1. Start your Web browser, such as Internet Explorer.

2. Select File, Open and browse to the folder that contains the Java class and HTML file.

3. Select the HTML file and click OK. Your applet should appear in its own window, such as the one in Figure 15.2.

FIGURE 15.2

Your applet appears inside the browser window.

The running applet

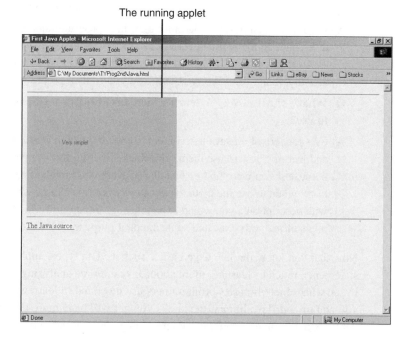

Summary

This hour provided a quick overview of how to work with Java applets. You understand how standalone Java applications work and you know how embedded Java applets work. You may not yet be a Java expert but you do know your way around the language and you are on your way to understanding object libraries.

You now have an idea of how applet authors create their applets and place those applets inside Web pages using HTML code tags. The applets should be much smaller than regular, standalone Java applications because the Java applet must download to the end-user's computer with the Web page and download times can be slow.

The next hour moves on to different programming languages. Although Visual Basic, which you'll learn about in the next hour, is not a true object-oriented language as Java is, you will see how parts of Visual Basic work with objects such as command buttons that you drag with your mouse onto the Windows screen.

Q&A

Q How much of an HTML expert must I be to use Java applets effectively?

A In some companies, people other than Java programmers write HTML code, so you don't have to know much HTML at all. Nevertheless, as you'll see in Hour 18, "Web Pages with HTML," HTML is an extremely simple language, far simpler, actually, than even Liberty BASIC. So, many Java programmers learn HTML.

Q What's the best way to learn which Java library routines are available for me to use?

A One concern of all Java newcomers is knowing which class packages are available and learning how to use them. The chicken-before-the-egg paradox appears here because if you were first given a list of every class method name, how would you know when to use the methods and how would you know what each one did? Even with descriptions, you would experience information overload because many hundreds of methods exist and some are dual-purpose and overlap others in functionality.

Now that you know the language basics, such as data types, applet insertion, and control statements, much of learning more about Java requires analyzing other Java applications to see what object libraries programmers use most and to learn what those libraries do. If you add to your Java library, the books you get will have more time to go into library depth than a 24-hour tutorial on programming could possibly do. If you decide to learn more about Java, an excellent Java text is *Sams Teach Yourself Java 2 in 21 Days, Second Edition* (0672319586).

Workshop

The quiz questions are provided for your further understanding. For the answers, see Appendix B, "Quiz Answers."

15

Quiz

1. Why do you want to keep your Java applets small?

2. What is the purpose of the appletviewer?

3. What features can the Swing library add to a Java applet?

4. What drawback, albeit a small one, does the Swing library sometimes give Java applets?

5. What does the `resize()` method do?

6. What does the `init()` method do?

7. What filename extension does a Java source applet use?

8. What filename extension does a compiled Java applet use?

9. What HTML command embeds a Java applet into the surrounding Web page?

10. What do the HTML `WIDTH` and `HEIGHT` commands specify?

PART IV

Other Programming Languages

Hour

HOUR 16

Programming with Visual Basic

You now have two advantages that most newcomers to Visual Basic don't have: You understand Liberty BASIC, a similar language to Visual Basic; and you understand how controls, properties, and events work within the Windows environment. Therefore, even in this one-hour lesson, you can learn and understand quite a lot about programming with Visual Basic.

Unlike Liberty BASIC, much of the work of a Visual Basic programmer doesn't lie in code but in the design of the application's visual elements, such as the controls that the programmer places on forms at design time. These controls allow interaction to and from the user. The code that the programmer places behind the controls handles the events as well as data calculations and manipulations that produce the information required by the program.

The highlights of this hour include

- When to use the Application Wizard to create an application's shell
- What the programmer must do to make the Wizard's generated application a more specific application
- How to set control property values
- How to embed code within a Visual Basic application
- How to place and size controls so they look correct on the form
- What kind of code appears in a Visual Basic application

Reviewing the Visual Basic Screen

Unlike most programming languages, Visual Basic is and always has been a Windows programming language. When you learn to write programs with Visual Basic, you learn not only the language but also its environment. Before you can do anything in Visual Basic you must understand the Visual Basic screen.

Figure 16.1 shows the Visual Basic 6 screen with its most important screen elements called out. The toolbox contains Windows controls, such as command buttons and check boxes that you can place on your application window. The Properties window determines how those controls look and behave, including colors and default characteristics. You can add new controls to the toolbox. The Form window works as your application's background, holding the various controls that you place on the application. If the application contains only a single window, you'll design and create only one Form window and that window becomes the program window when the user eventually runs the program.

A Windows application is often comprised of several files, including the following:

- Form files that contain the form and its description, controls, and related event procedure code
- Code modules that hold general-purpose code
- Other files that contain elements needed by the application

The Project window keeps track of all items within an application.

The term *project* is used to describe the collection of all files that compose a single Windows application. (The Project window is often called the Project Explorer window because of its tree-structured nature that mimics the Windows Explorer program.) The Form Layout window lets you determine, by dragging with your mouse, the location of the current form on the user's screen when the user runs the program.

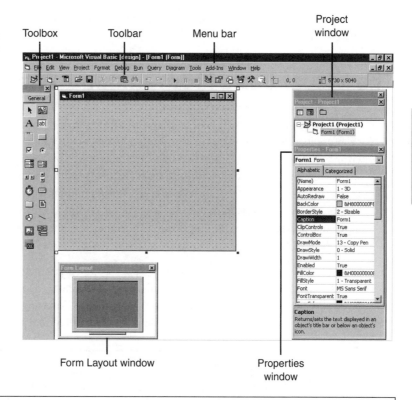

FIGURE 16.1

Visual Basic's screen includes several windows and options.

Toolbox   Toolbar   Menu bar   Project window

Form Layout window   Properties window

If you have access to a copy of Visual Basic, you will not see the same screen as Figure 16.1 shows when you first start Visual Basic. Instead, a dialog box appears that offers several options. The next section explains how to use this dialog box and make a selection from it.

The latest versions of Visual Basic include tools that go far beyond those found in most other languages. However, creating a Visual Basic application from scratch involves little more than these steps:

1. Design the application by stating its goals and detailing its requirements.

2. Place graphics controls on the application's Form window (this is the output definition design stage). As you place the controls, you'll assign many of the initial properties to the controls.

3. Add event procedures that handle control events.

4. Add any other code needed to tie the controls together and process data as required by the application.

5. Test and distribute the application to users.

As you'll see in the next section, Visual Basic can greatly help reduce the time it takes between steps 1 and 5.

The Visual Basic Programming Wizard

If you are familiar with other Windows products, such as Microsoft Publisher, you've seen wizards that work with you, helping you create the documents you require. A *wizard* presents step-by-step questions and prompts that you respond to. As you respond, the wizard generates an application that matches the criteria you specify. Visual Basic offers several wizards, but the one you'll use most frequently with Visual Basic is called the *Application Wizard*. When you write a Visual Basic program, you have a choice to create an application from scratch or use the Application Wizard to create an application's shell or general structure. After the Application Wizard creates the application's shell, you can fill in the details.

This hour will not walk you through the step-by-step process that you'll go through when you use the Application Wizard because the goal of this hour is to give you insight into the requirements of Visual Basic language. Nevertheless, knowing something about the Application Wizard is vital to understanding the nature of Visual Basic.

> It is perhaps surprising to learn that you'll probably create more applications from scratch or by modifying a copy of a similar application than you will by using the Application Wizard. Although the Application Wizard creates a fully functioning program skeleton, you'll develop your own style of programming over time, and you'll probably find it easier to modify a copy of an existing application.

Introducing the Application Wizard

Although the resulting application that the Wizard creates will not do much (the application is only a program outline, after all), you will see how much Visual Basic can automatically create when you use the Application Wizard. As soon as you start Visual Basic, the Application Wizard is there to help. The New Project dialog box, shown in Figure 16.2, appears when you start Visual Basic from the Windows Start menu. The tabs on the New Project dialog box offer these choices:

- New lets you create new applications by using various wizards or starting from scratch.
- Existing lets you select and open an existing Visual Basic project.
- Recent displays a list of Visual Basic projects you've recently opened or created.

FIGURE 16.2

You can select the Application Wizard from the New Project dialog box.

16

Even if you don't have Visual Basic, you can still get an idea of the Application Wizard's power by studying some of these options that the Application Wizard can add to the application. Your only job as the programmer is to answer a few of the Application Wizard's prompts:

- Application style—Creates an application that produces *Single Document Interface (SDI) Style* where only one data file window can be open at once, a *Multiple Document Interface (MDI) Style* where more than one data file window can be open at once, and *Explorer Style* that produces a tree-structured view of data with a data summary window pane at the right of the screen and the detailed data in the right window pane.

- Menu options—As Figure 16.3 shows, you can select from a series of menu bar options and pull-down menu options that appear in the created application.

FIGURE 16.3

You can select from a comprehensive list of menu options to add to your application.

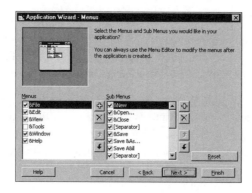

- Toolbar selection—Select from a list of toolbar buttons that you want the created application to include.

- Internet connectivity—Specify whether the application is to have Internet access by providing an embedded browser (available from a menu option in the application) that points to an initial start page when the user activates the browser.

- Special screens—As Figure 16.4 shows, you can add one or more special windows to the application, such as an About dialog box that appears in most standard Windows applications when the user selects Help, About.

FIGURE 16.4

Add one or more spe-cial windows to your application.

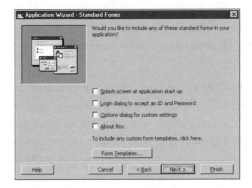

- Database access—Request embedded database technology so that the application created by the Application Wizard has access to special database files you've cre-ated or that you use from other sources.

Along the way, you can terminate the Application Wizard early if you want to quit running it. Click Cancel to stop the Application Wizard and discard the application built to that point. You can rerun the Application Wizard again later to create the program once more.

After running the Application Wizard, you will have created your first Visual Basic appli-cation even if you knew nothing about Visual Basic and without knowing *any* of the Visual Basic programming language! After a few gyrations on the screen, Visual Basic completes the application and you can run the application just as you run any Visual Basic application that you create—by pressing the F5 key, by clicking the Run toolbar button, or by selecting Run, Start from the menu.

You can run a Visual Basic application from Visual Basic's own environment or from Windows itself. Hour 23, "Distributing Applications," explains more about how you can distribute applications and connect the applications to the Windows interface, such as the Start menu.

After the Wizard Completes

After running the Application Wizard, you will have created a fully working program just by answering the Wizard's screen prompts. Depending on your responses to the Wizard, you quickly create a working Visual Basic application that produces the following:

- A standard program window appears that the user can resize and move. The name of the project appears in the window's toolbar.

- A status bar appears that displays the date and time at the bottom of the program window.

- A working menu appears with several options. Only the Help, About menu option works (it produces the About dialog box), but the usual menu options, such as File, Open and Edit, Cut, are all there ready for you to insert active code behind them.

- An Internet browser appears from which the user can sign on and browse the Internet.

- A standard toolbar appears that you can add functionality to and turn on and off from the View menu.

The application doesn't do much yet, but it's ready for you, as the programmer, to complete. You can easily change and add to the application, its menus, and its windows. You'll find in next hour's lesson that you can create working projects quite easily, but the Application Wizard adds functionality that applications often require.

If you happen to have Visual Basic and want to create an application with the Application Wizard, you can stop running the application by clicking the Close window button in the application's upper right corner.

Creating a Simple Application from Scratch

Now that you've seen how easy the Application Wizard is to use, you are ready to take the plunge into the creation of a program from scratch. Again, if you don't have access to a Visual Basic programming environment, you can read through the following task list to get an idea of what Visual Basic requires when you create applications.

This first application displays a picture and a command button. The program will change the picture when you click the command button. You would follow these steps to create this simple application:

1. After starting Visual Basic, select File, New Project to display the New Project dialog box.

2. Select the Standard EXE icon. Your Visual Basic environment will hold only a single form named Form1 (as the title bar shows). The form appears on the background of the Form window editing area, which is white. By selecting the Standard EXE icon, you forgo the use of the Application Wizard to create an application shell.

3. Click the Maximize window button to expand the Form window editing area (the white background, *not* the gray form itself) to its maximum size. This action gives you room to expand the form.

Sizing handles appear around the form because the form is the only object inside the Form window editing area. Notice that the Properties window displays properties about the form.

4. Drag the form's lower right sizing handle down and to the right. As you drag the form, notice the width and height measurements at the right of the toolbar as they change. Size the form so that it measures about 7,400 by 5,200 *twips*. This step produces a sized background for your program. Figure 16.5 shows your screen. (Your Form Layout window may appear beneath your Properties window.)

Twips are screen units used commonly during programming screen controls. The number of twips is somewhat dependent on hardware, however, the general calculation of a twip is approximately 1/1440th of an inch. That is, there are 1440 twips to an inch.

FIGURE 16.5

When you resize the Form window, you are resizing your application's program window.

Form-location coordinates

Size coordinates

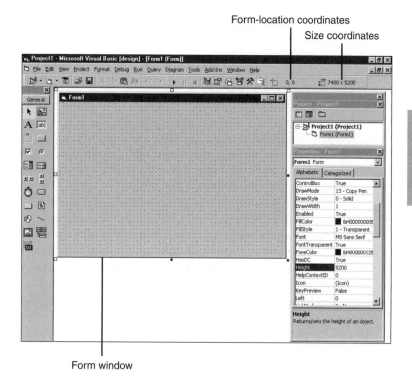

Form window

As you locate and size Form windows, pay attention to the form-location coordinates and the size coordinates at the right of the toolbar. These values always appear in pairs. The first value in the form-location pair represents the number of twips from the left edge of the screen where the window begins. The second value represents the number of twips from the top edge of the screen where the window will appear. The second pair of values, the size coordinates, represents the number of twips wide and high that the window consumes. The form properties for the form-location coordinates are named Left and Top to represent the number of twips from the left and top of the screen. The form properties for the size coordinates are named Width and Height and represent the width and height of the Form window. Visual Basic automatically updates these values in the Properties window when you move and resize the form in the Form window editing area. In addition, you can enter these coordinates directly in the Properties window for the form's attributes.

5. You can display the Form Layout window from the Window menu and then move the thumbnail screen inside the Form Layout window so that your application window is better centered.

6. Close the Form Layout window to allow more room for the other windows.

> The dots that appear inside the Form window make up the *grid*. You can turn the grid on and off by selecting Tools, Options, clicking the General page, and checking or unchecking the Show Grid option. The grid won't appear when you run the application; it appears solely to help you place and size controls on the form.

7. Assign a better name than `Form1` to the form. To do so, you'll see how to work with the Properties window. A property called `(Name)` (enclosed in parentheses to keep the name at the top of the alphabetical property list) holds the selected form's name. (In the future, this tutorial will omit the parentheses from around the `Name` property.) Scroll up the Properties window if necessary until you see the `Name` value, and notice that the `Name` value is currently assigned `Form1`.

8. Click the form's `Name` property and type **frmMyFirst** for the form name. As you type, the name appears to the right of the property called `Name` as well as Visual Basic's title bar.

> You'll change and assign all properties inside the Properties window the same way you just changed the form's name. Scroll to the property, click the property, and enter (or select for those properties with drop-down list boxes) a new property value. Notice that the name `frmMyFirst` is more descriptive than Visual Basic's default form name of `Form1`. Get in the habit of changing the default object names to make them more representative of what they label. It makes your program easier to maintain.

9. Change the form's title bar from its original value to Hat Picture Application by selecting the `Caption` property and typing **Happy Picture Application**. The `Caption` property determines what appears in the form's title bar when the user runs the program. The new name appears in both the Properties window and the form's title bar and helps describe the picture this application will produce.

10. Save the form to disk for safety. Select File, Save Project. The Save Project option saves every file inside your project (your project currently holds only a single form file) as well as a project description file with the filename extension .VBP. Visual Basic asks first for the filename you want to assign to your form. Visual Basic uses the form's Name property as the default filename. If you accept that default name, as you should now do, Visual Basic also adds the extension .FRM to the form's filename. (If your project contained more forms or modules or other objects stored in files, Visual Basic would ask you to name the remaining items as well.) Visual Basic then asks for a project name for the project description file. Name the project **HatApp** before saving the project. Answer No if Visual Basic asks to add the project to the SourceSafe library.

Now that the application's background is complete, you are ready to add the details by putting controls on the form.

Adding the Details

Adding controls to a form typically involves one or more of these steps:

1. Select the control from the toolbox.
2. Place the control in its proper location.
3. Size the control.
4. Set the control's properties.
5. Activate the control with Visual Basic code if needed.

In the steps that follow, you'll quickly learn how to place controls on the form. Generally, you'll perform these steps in one of two ways:

- Double-click the control's icon on the toolbox. Visual Basic then places that control in the center of the form. You can then drag the control to its proper location and size the control by dragging the control's sizing handles in or out.

- Click the control's icon on the toolbox and move the resulting crosshair mouse cursor to the form where the control is to be placed. Click and hold your mouse button where the control is to start. As you drag the mouse, Visual Basic draws the control's outline on your form. When you've drawn the control at its proper location and size, release the mouse button to place the control.

The following steps spruce up the application you began in the previous section:

1. Double-click the Label control so that Visual Basic places the label in the center of your form. The label control contains the letter *A*. (Remember that ToolTips pop up to let you know what a toolbox icon is for.) The label is now the selected tool on your Form window editing area so the sizing handles appear around the label. In addition, the Properties window changes to show the label's properties, and the toolbar's location and size coordinate pairs now reflect the label's measurements. A label displays text on a form. This new label will hold a title banner for your application.

2. Drag the label up the form until it rests approximately 1,320 twips from the left edge of the form window and 120 twips from the top of the form. The toolbar's location coordinates will let you know the location.

3. Double-click the toolbox's Command Button control to place a command button in the center of your form. The icon on each button should illustrate the purpose of the button. You can also point to any button to see a ToolTip pop up at the mouse pointer that shows the name of the button.

4. Locate the toolbox's Image control. Instead of double-clicking to place the control as you did with the label, click the control's icon once. Move your mouse to the Form window and draw the Image control, trying to first anchor the image at 2,520 twips from the form's left edge and 2,880 from the form's top edge. Size the image at approximately 2,175 twips wide and 1,825 twips high. As you size the image, drag the image's sizing handles slowly so that Visual Basic's ScreenTips pop up showing you the coordinates of the image. When the coordinates appear at their proper size, release your mouse button to place the image at that size. Figure 16.6 shows your screen at this point. The Image control displays a graphics image when you run the program.

You can match the location and size twip measurements exactly by filling in the following properties with the measurement values described in the previous step: `Left: 2520`, `Top: 2880`, `Width: 2175`, and `Height: 1825`.

Location twip coordinates and size twip coordinates are always specified in pairs. Often, you'll see such coordinate pairs specified inside parentheses, as in a location value of `(2520, 2880)`. For the coordinates, such a pair of values would signify that the width is 2,520 twips and the height is 2,880 twips.

FIGURE 16.6

*Your application is
taking shape.*

Label control   Command button

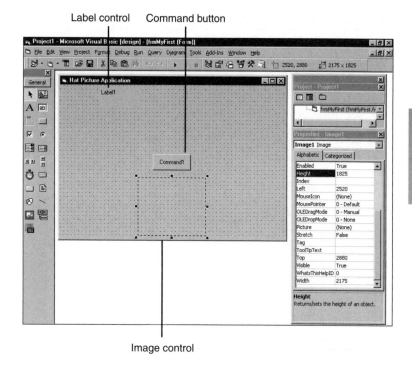

Image control

5. Now that you're more familiar with setting property values for controls, even though you may not understand many of the properties yet, you are now equipped to set additional properties for the form and controls to finalize the look of the application. After you set appropriate property values, you will then add code to connect the controls and make them work together.

Table 16.1 contains a list of properties that you now need to set for the form and the three controls. Remember that you must select the form or specific control before you can change property values for that form or control. To select the form, click anywhere inside the form or title bar but not over any of the controls. The Properties window will change to display the form's properties. Click either the label, command button, or image to select the control, and then you can change one of that control's properties by clicking the property name and typing the new value.

TABLE 16.1 Property Values to Set for the Application's Form and Controls.

Control	Property	Property Value
Form	Max Button	False (open the drop-down list box to see values)
Label	Alignment	Center (open the drop-down list box to see values)
Label	Name	lblHat
Label	Caption	Thinking Caps On!
Label	Font	Courier New
Label	Font style	Bold
Label	Size	36
Label	Left	1320
Label	Height	1695
Label	Top	120
Label	Width	4695
Image	Name	imgHat
Image	Stretch	True
Command Button	Name	cmdHat
Command Button	Caption	Click Here

> At first, setting a control's font information is confusing. When you select the Font property for a control, an ellipsis appears after the property value. The ellipsis indicates that you can set more than one value for the Font property, and clicking the ellipsis displays a Font dialog box. After setting the Font dialog box values and clicking OK, several property values related to the font used on the control's caption will change to reflect your new values.

Finalizing with Code

Adding Visual Basic programming statements will turn your creation into a working, although simple, application. Visual Basic automatically adds the opening and closing statements needed when you write a subroutine as you'll see in the following steps.

1. Double-click the command button to open the Code window. A set of beginning and ending statements will appear for a new procedure related to the command button that look like this:

```
Private Sub cmdHat_Click()

End Sub
```

These lines are two of the three lines needed for code required by the command button. The Code window works like a miniature word processor in which you can add, delete, and change statements that appear in your program code.

> All code appears in procedures and every procedure requires beginning and ending lines of code that define the procedure's start and stop locations. Visual Basic automatically adds the first and final line of many procedures.

16

2. Press the Spacebar three times and type the following line between the two that are there:

```
imgHat.Picture = LoadPicture("\Program Files\Microsoft
Visual Studio\Common\Graphics\Bitmaps\Assorted\Beany.bmp")
```

As soon as you type the LoadPicture's opening parenthesis, Visual Basic offers pop-up help with the statement's format. Some Visual Basic statements, especially those with parentheses, such as the ones you see in this statement, require that you type one or more values. Visual Basic pops up the format of these required values, so you'll know how many to enter. You'll learn more about why these values are required if you decide to pursue the language in more depth. Visual Basic is a large language, so this help comes in handy. By the way, depending on the location where you installed Visual Basic, your pathname to the graphics file may differ from the pathname specified here. You may have to use the Windows Start menu's Find option to locate the Beany.bmp file on your hard disk or on the Visual Basic installation CD-ROM and then change the path accordingly.

3. Run your program and click the command button. A figure appears as shown in Figure 16.7. You have successfully completed your new application without resorting to the Application Wizard. You've created an application that displays a picture when you click the command button. The application contains code, and its controls all have property values that you've set.

4. Click the Close window button to terminate the program. Be sure to save your project before you exit Visual Basic.

FIGURE 16.7

*Your application pro-
duces a graphics
image from the click of
your mouse.*

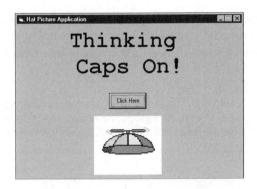

Other Visual Basic Programming Considerations

This hour approaches the Visual Basic language differently from most other languages discussed in these 24 hours. Instead of walking you through specific programming language commands, this hour walked you through the steps required to create a sample application from start to finish. If you look back through the previous sections, you'll notice that very little of the discussion included actual programming language statements. Visual Basic does so much just from its visual environment that adding code sometimes seems like an afterthought.

Even adding menus to the Visual Basic applications that you create from scratch is relatively simple because of another tool called the Menu Editor (see Figure 16.8). The *Menu Editor* lets you build a menu bar and the pull-down options from that menu bar by selecting and specifying options inside the Menu Editor. No code is required as you add the menu options to your application but once you use the Menu Editor to add the options, you'll have to specify event code procedures for each menu option. When the user selects a menu option, a Click event for that menu option occurs and each event procedure that you write will tell Visual Basic how to respond to that event.

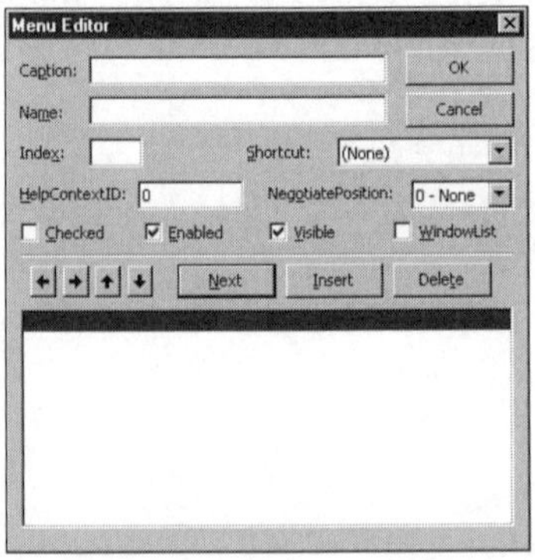

FIGURE 16.8

*Use the Menu Editor
to add menu options to
your Visual Basic
application.*

Understanding Procedures

Consider the following event procedure for the File, Exit menu option:

```
Private Sub mnuFileExit_Click()
   ' Terminate the application
   End
End Sub
```

By studying this simple procedure, you can learn quite a bit about all event procedures. The `Private` keyword indicates that the procedure is *local* to the current form and cannot be called by other form modules. Therefore, if several forms exist in the current Windows application, selecting File, Exit from this form will execute this specific event procedure and not one outside the scope of this form. The opposite of `Private` is `Public` and public procedures are available to any code in the entire application. Such public procedures are known as *global* procedures because any procedure in the application can call them.

The keyword `Sub` or `Function` always follows the `Private` (or `Public`) keyword and indicates the type of the procedure. A subroutine is a procedure that always performs work and then returns control to whatever code was executing before the event took place. A function is a procedure that always performs its job when the event takes place and then returns a value to another place in the program that might need that value. Hour 9, "Programming Algorithms," explains more about the use of subroutines.

The name of the event procedure specifies exactly which control and event this procedure responds to. The body of the procedure may consist of several lines but this one happens to include only two lines, a remark and the `End` statement that stops the running program. All procedures end with an `End Sub` or `End Function` statement. The parentheses that follow the procedure name indicate that the code begins a new procedure; sometimes, when one procedure must pass data values to another, you'll list one or more values separated by commas inside the parentheses. Even if you don't pass data, you must type the parentheses after every procedure declaration.

Some applications include many event procedures when something is to happen in response to an event. Figure 16.9 shows a Code window with several event procedures inside. Visual Basic automatically adds the separating lines between event procedures so you can locate a specific procedure quickly. In addition, the two drop-down list boxes at the top of the Code window enable you to locate specific event procedures related to specific controls by selecting from the lists.

16

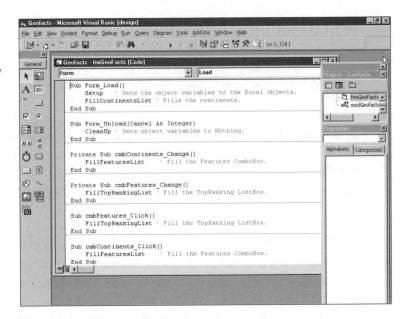

FIGURE 16.9

Visual Basic organizes your application's event procedures in the Code window.

Understanding the Language Behind Visual Basic

The language behind Visual Basic is virtually identical to Liberty BASIC, with the exception of some format differences and differences related to the separation of event procedures I just discussed. Visual Basic includes several statements that are unique to the Windows environment, but for the most part, the languages are the same.

One of the ways that Visual Basic is unique, however, is in its distribution of procedures across different areas of an application. You now know that several small event procedures reside in a form's Code window to handle any events that occur on that form. Other forms can exist as well and code appears in them to handle events that occur there. In addition, other files might be part of a complex application. A *code module* is a file, separate from any form and the form's associated code, which holds code that you might use in more than one application. Suppose that you write a procedure that prints your company logo at the top of a page. Such a logo would appear before any report that you produce, before any accounting statement, and before anything you print. Therefore, you'll use this procedure in many different applications.

Instead of typing the procedure in every application that needs it, you can put the code in a general-purpose code module that you then can copy into a new code module for all applications that need to produce the logo. You can, from anywhere else in the application, call a `Public` general procedure with a `Call` statement such as this:

```
Call logoPrint    ' Detour to the procedure
```

When the `Call` finishes, execution returns to the statement that follows the `Call`.

Your Next Step

This hour offers only a walkthrough of the steps that you take to create a Visual Basic application and it provides some insight into the nature of Visual Basic programming. Although Visual Basic is probably the easiest programming tool available for creating Windows applications, Visual Basic is vast compared to a simpler language such as Liberty BASIC. Therefore, an hour's lesson could not hope to cover more than what is included here. Nevertheless, you now have a firm grasp of what it takes to write Windows applications in Visual Basic.

> If you want more in-depth Visual Basic programming coverage, pick up a copy of *Sams Teach Yourself Visual Basic 6 in 21 Days*, from Sams Publishing, a tutorial that explores Visual Basic programming and takes the beginning Visual Basic programmer to advanced levels in 21 daily lessons.

Summary

Visual Basic is more than a language; it is part of a complete Microsoft programming environment called *Visual Studio*. Other languages are available for Visual Studio, such as Visual C++. Visual Basic was the first language to use the Visual Studio environment. When you create a Visual Basic application, you first create the visual elements of the program by placing the controls from the Toolbox window onto the form. As you place the controls, you set the properties and then write event procedure code to activate the controls when certain events take place.

Of course, you can forego the initial application creation and let Visual Basic create the initial application shell for you. The Visual Basic Application Wizard creates an application that contains menu options, a toolbar, Internet access, and database access. After the Wizard creates the application shell, you then can fill in the details and add controls to complete the form and code to process data properly.

The next hour describes the C and C++ programming languages. In addition to Java and Visual Basic, C++ is one of the most popular languages in wide use today.

Q&A

Q **Can the Application Wizard write my program's code for me?**

A The Application Wizard cannot write code for specific data processing requirements such as payroll calculations or the printing of accounting statements. The
Application Wizard is far too general to generate code that does anything more
than support the Application Wizard's options, such as the About box, the Internet
browser, and the database access. The code that the Application Wizard generates
ensures that these features work in a general way, but you must add your own code
to the application after the Application Wizard generates the program to make the
program perform specific work.

Q **Do all Visual Basic applications contain code in addition to event procedures?**

A Some Visual Basic applications contain code that forms event procedures only but
most other Visual Basic applications contain other kinds of code. More goes on
in most applications than events. Data must be processed, calculations must be performed, reports must be printed, and files must be read and written. The code
behind these specific tasks often appears in a code module separate from the form
module.

Workshop

The quiz questions and exercises are provided for your further understanding. See
Appendix B, "Quiz Answers," for answers.

Quiz

1. How much code do you have to write to add Internet access to a Visual Basic
   application?

2. True or false: The programmer's job is only just beginning when the Application
   Wizard completes its work.

3. Why is it a good practice to change the names of controls from their default names
   that Visual Basic assigns?

4. What happens when you double-click a Toolbox control?

5. What tool do you use to help you create menus for Visual Basic applications?

6. How does Visual Basic determine which control properties appear in the Properties
   window?

7. Name one advantage to running a Visual Basic application inside of Visual Basic's
   environment as opposed to running a compiled application from Windows.

8. Which runs faster: a Visual Basic application running inside Visual Basic's environment or a compiled Visual Basic application running outside Visual Basic's environment?

9. What information can you gather from the following Visual Basic procedure's declaration line?

```
Private Sub scrMeter_Change()
```

10. True or false: All Visual Basic procedures reside in the application's form module.

16

HOUR 17

Programming with C and C++

C is one of those programming languages that most programmers never predicted would take off. Designed as a highly efficient, somewhat cryptic language used to write an operating system named *UNIX*, C is a language designed by systems programmers. In the late 1980s, the same decade after its primary release, virtually every program on the store shelves was written in C. C, followed by its successor C++, quickly replaced the popular Pascal language in the 1980s and only recently have Visual Basic and Java made a dent in C and C++'s massive usage. C's impact on the programming world cannot be stressed enough.

C++ is considered by many to be a better language than C. C++ offers full support for object-oriented programming (OOP). Whereas you work with objects in Visual Basic, the Visual Basic language is not a true OOP language. You'll learn in this hour how and why C++ provides strong OOP support and how the mechanics of C++ provide for more flexible, maintainable, and efficient programming than its predecessor, C.

The highlights of this hour include:

- Understanding why C is so efficient
- Recognizing C commands and operators
- Outputting with C's `printf()` function
- Using C++ to build on C programming skills
- Using C++ classes
- Using Inheritance to decrease programming time

Introducing C

C is highly efficient and C's developers required that efficiency because until C, programmers used *assembly language*, a language just above the machine language level, to write operating systems. Only assembly language had the efficiency needed for systems programs. C brought the advantage of a higher-level language to the table when developers used C for operating systems. Along with the efficiency of a low-level language, C has the high-level-language advantage of being more maintainable and programmers were more easily able to update the operating system and produce accurate code. Assembly language doesn't lend itself very well to proper program maintenance.

To achieve its efficiency, C does have one drawback that other high-level languages don't: C is more cryptic than most other programming languages. Its cryptic nature comes in the form of a huge collection of operators and a small number of keywords. Table 17.1 lists C's keywords. In the standard C language, there are only 32 keywords, which is an extremely small number compared to other languages, such as Visual Basic and COBOL.

TABLE 17.1 32 Supported C Command Keywords

auto	double	int	struct
break	else	long	switch
case	enum	register	typedef
char	extern	return	union
const	float	short	unsigned
continue	for	signed	void
default	goto	sizeof	volatile
do	if	static	while

> Notice that C's keywords all appear in lowercase. C's built-in functions also require lowercase names. C is *case sensitive*, so if you use an uppercase letter anywhere inside a keyword or function, your program will not compile properly.

You should recognize many of C's commands because the Java language that you learned about in Part III of this tutorial borrows heavily from C and C++. As a matter of fact, you already will understand many C and C++ programs that you study if you adapted to Java quickly.

C has more operators than any other programming language, with the exception of the scientific APL language that is rarely, if ever, used anymore. Of course, languages derived from C, such as Java and C++ often have as many or more operators than C. Because you have already studied Java, you understand many of C's operators. For a refresher, you might want to reread Hour 13, "Java's Details."

17

What You Need for C and C++ Programming

To program in C, you need a C compiler. Today, when you obtain a C compiler, you almost always get a C++ compiler as well. Therefore, you get two languages for one, although C++ is really just an extension of the C language. One of the most popular C compilers sold today is the Windows-based Visual C++. Fortunately, Visual C++'s interface is virtually identical to that of Visual Basic's interface, so you'll already feel at home using the Visual C++ environment after the previous hour.

Creating a Windows application in C (or C++) is not as simple as creating one in Visual Basic. Remember that developers created Visual Basic from the beginning to be a Windows programming system. C, on the other hand, began in the world of text-based computers. Therefore, nothing is embedded in the C or C++ programming languages to support a graphical interface.

Looking at C

Listing 17.1 contains a short but complete C program.

LISTING 17.1 C is Cryptic and Requires Several Elements That Other Languages Do Not.

```
/* Prints a message on the screen */
#include <stdio.h>
main()
```

continues

LISTING 17.1   Continued

```
{
    printf("C is efficient.\n");
    return 0;
}
```

If you were to enter the program in Listing 17.1 in your C compiler's editor, compile the program, and run it, you would see this message on the screen:

```
C is efficient.
```

You can test this program using Visual C++ or any of the many shareware C and C++ compilers available on the market or from the Internet.

The program required seven lines to output one simple sentence. Liberty BASIC could have done it in *one* statement using `Print`, and they say C is more efficient! Actually, C is *vastly* more efficient than Liberty BASIC, but the C programmer's job is greater. Remember that BASIC was developed as an interpreted language for beginners. C requires more effort and was written by programmers for programmers. With C's compiled efficiency and power comes the responsibility to master the language and all its nuances.

Listing 17.1 contains three sets of grouping symbols: angled brackets, <>, braces, {}, and parentheses, (). As in Java, be extremely careful when typing a C program because the correct and exact symbol is important. C doesn't handle ambiguity very well, so if you type the wrong symbol, C won't work properly.

Using the `main()` Function's Format

The cornerstone of every C program is the `main()` function just as it is in Java. Because `main()` is a function and not a command, the parentheses after are required. A C function, just like a Java or Visual Basic procedure, is a section of code that does something. The `main()` function is required because execution of a C program always begins in its `main()` function. Programmers use `main()` to control the rest of the program. The `main()` function often includes a series of procedure calls.

The actual code for `main()`, as with all C functions (except the built-in functions whose code you never see), begins after the opening brace, {, and `main()` continues until the closing brace, }, where `main()` terminates and other functions often begin. Other sets of braces, always in pairs, may appear within a function such as `main()` as well.

As in Java, many of C's (and C++'s) statements end with a semicolon (;). The more you work with C, the better you'll learn which statements require the semicolon and which don't. Full statements require the semicolon. In Listing 17.1, the line with `main()` doesn't require a semicolon because `main()` doesn't terminate until the final closing brace in the last line. The brace requires no semicolon because it is a grouping character and does nothing on its own.

The next few sections concentrate on the fundamental C language but the material is applicable to C++ also. C++'s strength over C is its ability for OOP as you'll see later in this hour.

Using the `#include` Statement

You'll never see `#include` in a list of C commands because `#include` is *not* a C *command*. Statements in a C program that begin with the pound sign are called *preprocessor directives*. The compiler analyzes the directive and, instead of compiling the statement, acts upon the statement immediately during compilation.

The `#include` preprocessor directive tells the compiler to insert another file that resides in source code form at the location in the program where the directive resides. Therefore, before the program is actually compiled, more code is inserted, at the programmer's request, at the place where `#include` occurs. That code is compiled along with the programmer's code.

The `stdio.h` file is a source code auxiliary file that helps a C program perform I/O properly. C files that end with the .H extension are called *header files* as opposed to C program source code files that end with the .c filename extension. All C programs perform some kind of I/O, and the most common header file used to help C with its I/O is `stdio.h`. As you learn more about C, you'll learn additional header files that can be helpful, such as the `time.h` header file that includes definitions that help with time and date conversions.

C Data

C supports data formats that work much like Java's data formats. For example, C supports the following kinds of data:

- Character
- Integer
- Floating point (decimal numbers)

C supports several types of integers and floating-point data such as long and short integers as well as single-precision and double-precision floating-point decimal data.

Unlike Java and Liberty BASIC, C does *not* support a string data type. Although C has some built-in functionality to handle strings in some situations, generally the C language leaves it to the programmer and functions to handle strings. C doesn't support an intrinsic string data type. Therefore, the only text-based data type that C supports is a single character.

The fact that C doesn't include support for a built-in string data type isn't a huge problem because ample built-in functions are available in the language to work with string data. Also, C does allow for string *literals*, such as strings that you type directly in the code, just not string variables. Unlike Java and Liberty BASIC, however, string data is not inherently supported in the fundamental language, which sometimes makes for some interesting programming.

Listing 17.1 included a string literal as well. String literals (remember there is no string variable) are always enclosed in quotation marks. Therefore, the following are string literals:

```
"C is efficient. "

"3"

"443-55-9999"
```

Given the cryptic nature of C, you should add comments to your code as much as possible. You will need the comments when you later make changes to the program. Enclose comments between /* and */ or preceded by // as shown in the statements below:

```
/* Ask how old the user is */
   printf("How old are you? "); // Ask for the age
   scanf(" %d", &age);     /* Ampersand required */
```

Declaring Variables

Declaring variables in C is identical to doing so in Java. Consider the following section of a `main()` function:

```
main()
{
   char initial;
   int age;
   float amount;
```

This code declares three variables, initial, age, and amount. They hold three different types of data: a character, an integer, and a floating-point value. These variables are local to the function and cannot be used outside main(). (You can declare variables before main() and those variables would be global to the whole program, but global variables are not recommended, as you already know.)

The assignment statement works just as it does in Visual Basic. You can initialize variables like this:

```
initial = 'G';
age = 21;
amount = 6.75;
```

C Functions

C is built on a foundation of functions—both those functions that you write and the functions supplied by C. The next two sections should help you understand the nature of C functions.

17

Using Built-In Functions

Unlike just about every other programming language in the world, C has *no* input or output statements. Look through Table 17.1 once more. You don't see a print statement or anything else that might be considered an I/O statement.

C performs all its I/O through functions that your C compiler provides. By letting the compiler makers implement I/O in functions, the C language is highly *portable*, meaning that a C program that runs on one kind of computer should run on any other computer that is capable of running C programs. A C program written for a Macintosh will work on a PC without change, assuming that you compile the program using each computer's own C compiler.

The printf() Output Function

The most common I/O function is the printf() function. printf() outputs data to the screen in most cases (although the programmer can route the output to other devices, if needed, through operating system options). Here is the format for printf():

```
printf(controlString [, data]);
```

The *controlString* determines how the output will look. The *controlString* will format any data values that you specify (separated by commas if more than one value is output) in the *data* area. Consider the following printf():

```
printf("Read a lot");
```

This printf() doesn't include a *data* list of any kind. The *controlString* is the only argument to this printf(). When you use a string of text for the *controlString* value, C outputs the text directly to the screen. Therefore, the printf() produces this onscreen when the user runs the program:

```
Read a lot
```

> Remember to use the \n character if you want output to force the cursor to the next line. If the previous printf() was followed by this printf():
>
> ```
> printf("Keep learning");
> ```
>
> the output would look like this:
>
> ```
> Read a lotKeep learning
> ```
>
> Obviously, the second printf() should have used the \n character like this:
>
> ```
> printf("Keep learning\n");
> ```
>
> With \n, subsequent printf() output would appear on the next line.

When you print numbers and characters, you must tell C exactly how to print them. You indicate the format of numbers with *conversion characters* that format data. The conversion characters format data in functions such as printf() (see Table 17.2).

TABLE 17.2 C's Most-Used Conversion Characters

Control Character	Description
%d	Integer
%f	Floating point
%c	Character
%s	String

When you want to print a value inside a string, insert the appropriate conversion characters in the *controlString*. Then, to the right of the *controlString*, list the value you want printed. Figure 17.1 shows how a printf() can print three numbers—an integer, a floating-point value, and another integer.

FIGURE 17.1

Conversion characters determine how and where the output appears.

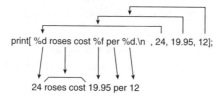

```
print[ %d roses cost %f per %d.\n , 24, 19.95, 12];
```

```
24 roses cost 19.95 per 12
```

Strings and characters have their own conversion characters as well. You don't need %s to print strings by themselves because strings included inside the *controlString* that don't have the formatting percent sign before them print exactly as you type them. Nevertheless, you might need to use %s when combining strings with other data.

The next printf() prints a different type of data value using each of the conversion characters from Table 17.2:

```
print("%s %d %f %c\n", "Sams", 14, -8.76, 'X');
```

This printf() produces this:

```
Sams 14 -8.760000 X
```

The string Sams needs quotation marks, as do all string literals, and the character X needs single quote marks, as do all characters. C formats the floating-point numbers with full precision, hence the four zeros at the end of the value. You can limit the number of places printed by using format specifiers. If the printf()'s conversion characters for the floating-point number had been %5.2, the -8.76 would have been output in five spaces, with two of those five spaces used for the decimal portion. Therefore, the following printf()

```
print("%s %d %f %c\n", "Sams", 14, -8.76, 'X');
```

would yield this output:

```
Sams 14 -8.76 X
```

Working with Strings

Although C doesn't support string variables, there is a way to store strings. C represents all strings with a *null zero* character at the end of the string. This null zero has an ASCII value of zero. When C encounters the null zero, the end of the string is reached. You never see this null zero on a string, but it is there, internally, at the closing quotation mark. You never add the null zero; C adds it.

If a string includes a 0 as part of its text, such as the following address: `"190 S. Oak Road"`, the embedded zero is not the null zero because the embedded zero is a regular ASCII character for zero (ASCII number 48).

Figure 17.2 shows how the string `"Sams"` is stored in memory as a string. The `\0` character is C's representation for the null string. The length of a string includes the characters within the string but never includes the null zero.

C uses a character array to hold strings, including the string's null zero. All of C's data types can appear in their own arrays, but when a character array appears and a null zero is included at the end of the data, C treats that character array just like a string. C uses brackets instead of parentheses for array subscripts. To define a character array that will hold a ten-character string, you could declare the following array:

```
char month[10];   /* Defines a character array */
```

The `month` array can hold ten individual characters or a string if the string includes the null zero. Always leave room for the null zero in the array. C uses zero-based arrays, so `month` can hold a ten-character string in elements 0 through 9 and the null zero in element 10. You can initialize a string when you define the array like this:

```
char month[10] = "September"; /* Declare and initialize the string */
```

You can also assign the array at runtime using a special `strcpy()` function like this:

```
strcpy(month, "September");   /* Assigns September to the month array */
```

To use `strcpy()`, you must include the header file named `string.h` in the same area of the program where you include `stdio.h`.

FIGURE 17.2

Strings always terminate with a null zero character.

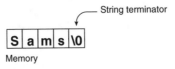

Memory

The only data `printf()` doesn't format is string data. Therefore, if you use `printf()` to print anything other than a single string, you must supply a conversion code.

The `scanf()` Input Function

Getting keyboard input is much more difficult than producing output on the screen. Use `scanf()` to accept keyboard input. `scanf()` is fairly simple now that you understand `printf()` but `scanf()` does behave strangely at times. Here is the format for `scanf()`:

```
scanf(controlString [, data]);
```

Understand the following rule and `scanf()` should work for you every time:

> Prefix each variable inside the `scanf()` with an ampersand unless that variable is an array.

Therefore, the following `scanf()` gets an age value entered by the user:

```
scanf(" %d", &Age);
```

Do you see the blank before the `%d` in `scanf()`'s *controlString*? Always include the blank because the input of values works better with the blank.

The following `scanf()` gets the user's first name into a character array as a result of the user following the prompting `printf()`:

```
printf("What is your first name? ");
scanf(" %s", name);   /* Get the name */
```

The `scanf()` function is a mirror-image function to `printf()`. Often, you will write programs that ask the user for values with a `printf()` and get those values with `scanf()`. When your program gets to `scanf()`, C stops and waits for the user to type values. The variables listed inside `scanf()` (following the *controlString* argument) will accept whatever the user types and `scanf()` quits receiving input when the user presses Enter.

When the user types a space, `scanf()` also stops getting input! Therefore, `scanf()` is good for getting only one word at a time in a string.

Despite its problems, `scanf()` is useful to learn early in your C tutorial so you can practice getting user input. There are many other ways to get user input in C and C++, and often they work better than `scanf()`, but `scanf()`'s similarity to the simpler `printf()` makes `scanf()` an acceptable keyboard-input function for beginners.

The program in Listing 17.2 shows a complete program that prompts for user input and gets output. You can study the program to gain a better understanding of the material you've covered so far in this lesson.

LISTING 17.2 Use `scanf()` and `printf()` for Input and Output.

```c
#include <stdio.h>
main()
{
  int age;
  float weight;
  char first[15], last[15];  /* 2 char arrays */

  printf("\nWhat is your first name? ");
  scanf(" %s", first);  /* No ampersand on char arrays */
  printf("What is your last name? ");
  scanf(" %s", last);

  printf("How old are you? ");
  scanf(" %d", &age);     /* Ampersand required */
  printf("How much do you weigh? ");
  scanf(" %f", &weight); /* Ampersand required */

  printf("\nHere is the information you entered:\n");
  printf("Name: %s %s\n", first, last);
  printf("Weight: %3.0f\n", weight);
  printf("Age: %d", age);
  return 0;  /* Always best to do this */
}
```

Here is a sample execution of Listing 17.2:

```
What is your first name? Joe
What is your last name? Harrison
How old are you? 41
How much do you weigh? 205

Here is the information you entered:
Name: Joe Harrison
Weight: 205
Age: 41
```

Writing General Program Functions

As with a Visual Basic program's collection of event procedures, C programs are modular and are comprised of many functions. Although you *can* put all of a C program's code in the main() function, main() was intended to be used as a controlling function for the rest of the program. Listing 17.3 illustrates the outline of a C program that has proper form.

LISTING 17.3 Use main() to Control the Rest of the Program.

```
#include <stdio.h>
main()
{
  getNums();    /* Get a list of numbers */
  sortNums();   /* Sort the numbers */
  printNums(); /* Print the list */
  return 0;     /* End the program */
}
getNums()
{
  /* Body of function goes here
     that gets a list of values
     from the user */
}
sortNums()
{
  /* Body of function goes here
     that sorts the values */
}
printNums()
{
  /* Body of function goes here
     that prints the values */
}
```

The main() function is composed of a series of function calls to three separate procedures. (The code bodies of the procedures are not included in this example.) The main() function, and hence the entire running program, terminates when the return 0; statement is reached. The return often appears at the end of a function when the function is returning a value to the calling function. The main() function is returning a 0 to the operating system. Zero is a standard return value that the operating system can check.

C Operators

C's collection of operators matches those you learned in Java. For example, the plus sign works exactly as it does in Java. In addition, C supports the increment and decrement operators, ++ and --, that add and subtract one from whatever variable you apply them to. The following statements each add one to the variables a, b, and c:

```
a++;
b++;
c++;
```

The following statements decrease a, b, and c by one:

```
a--;
b--;
c--;
```

C Control Statements Mimic Java's

Actually, Java was patterned after C, so it's accurate to state that Java's control statements mimic those of C (and C++). For example, C supports an if...else statement such as this:

```
if (age < 18)
  { printf("You cannot vote yet\n");
    yrs = 18 - age;
    printf("You can vote in %d years.\n", yrs);
  }
else
  {
    printf("You can vote.\n");
  }
```

C also supports several kinds of looping statements that use the relational operators. For example, the following code shows a while loop that continues as long as the relational expression evaluates to true:

```
while (amount < 25)
  {
    printf("Amount is too small.\n");
    wrongVal++;   /* Keep track of number of problems */
    printf("Try again... What is the new amount? ");
    scanf(" %d", &amount);
  }
```

Learning C++

Much of a C++ program looks like pure C code, which it is. The C++ language introduces some new language elements, but the keywords and structure are similar to C. Most of C++'s change over C is a result of injecting OOP technology into C. The primary differences between C and C++ don't lie in commands and keyword differences but rather in how the language supports the use of objects.

C programs use the .c filename extension, and C++ programs use the .CPP filename extension. Not all C++ compilers support programming in the Windows environment, but most PC-based C++ compilers sold today do provide full Windows programming support, including the support for a visual interface, such as a toolbox with controls, just as Visual Basic provides.

17

Object Terminology

You learned some about OOP in the Java hours earlier in this tutorial. OOP is laden with terminology that might seem daunting at first. The actual implementation of OOP is fairly easy to understand and with your quick Java introduction, you will already be somewhat acquainted with terms such as these:

- Abstraction—The internals of an object do not always have to be known by the programmer to use an object.
- Class—The definition of a related group of objects.
- Inheritance—The ability to create a new class of objects from an existing class. By inheriting a new class of objects, you can create new objects with new behaviors and characteristics based on existing objects and classes.
- Message—A command that acts on specific objects as opposed to the other language commands that are not tied to specific objects.
- Object—A collection of characteristics and behaviors, perhaps even two or more variables treated as a single unit, that appears in OOP programs.
- Polymorphism—A name given to the ability of different objects to respond differently to the same commands (called *messages*).
- Reuse—The ability of the language to utilize objects defined in other programs.

Fundamental Differences Between C and C++

Some of the new language features that C++ provides over C have nothing directly to do with OOP. The following sections preview some of the non-OOP language differences that you'll find between C and C++.

Name Differences

Some differences between C and C++ are simple changes. For example, instead of C's
`#include <stdio.h>` directive, C++ programs almost always include the following
directive:

```
#include <iostream.h>
```

As with the C header files, C++ programmers will include many other header files in
addition to `iostream.h`, but `iostream.h` is the most commonly included file.
`iostream.h` is the header file that defines basic input and output.

I/O Differences

C++ includes several new operators. The two most common C++ operators are >> for
output (the *insertion* operator) and << for input (the *extraction* operator). These operators
are usually combined with the two *stream objects,* cout and cin. cout always represents
an output device and defaults to the screen. cin always represents an input device and
defaults to the keyboard. You can redirect cout and cin to other devices through the
operating system and through compilers such as Visual C++ if you ever have the need.
Your program considers these stream objects to be nothing more than a series of data values that are being input or output.

A few examples will quickly show you how to combine the insertion and the extraction
operators with stream objects. The following statement sends a string and a number to
the screen (typically the output stream goes to the screen although you can change that
destination to a different device):

```
cout << "Here is the total: " << 1000.00;
```

If you want to write several lines of output, you can by embedding the newline character
in the output stream. The following line

```
cout << "Line 1" << '\n' << "Line 2" << '\n' << "Line 3" << '\n';
```

produces this output:

```
[ic:output]Line 1
Line 2
Line 3
```

> Generally, C++ programmers don't use the newline character, \n, at the end of a statement with cout. They use a special object called endl, which not only produces a newline character but also empties the output buffer if you send data to a device that buffers output, such as a printer. Therefore, the following statement would be more likely than the one shown before this tip:
>
> ```
> cout << "Line 1" << '\n' << "Line 2" << '\n' << "Line 3" << endl;
> ```

C++ combines the cin input stream with the >> extraction object to support keyboard input. As with scanf(), keyboard-based input with C++ is fairly simple to understand and implement, but C++'s input capabilities are limited when you use cin > just to start with a way to get keyboard input quickly. However, keep in mind that more advanced and better input methods exist that you will master if you pursue the C++ language.

To get a keyboard value into an integer variable named intAge, you could use the following:

```
cin >> intAge;
```

Of course, you would probably prompt the user first with a cout so the I/O would more likely look like this:

```
cout << "How old are you? ";
cin >> intAge;     // Get the age
```

Introducing C++ Objects

As with Java, to declare a C++ object you first must declare a class. A class is not an object but rather a description of an object. The C++ language includes the class keyword that you use to define a class.

Consider the following class declaration:

```
class Person {
  char strLastName[25];
  int  intAge;
  float flSalary;
};
```

The class name is Person. The class is said to have three *members*. The member names are strLastName, intAge, and flSalary. This class, therefore, describes objects that contain three members. Individually, each member could be considered a separate variable, but taken together (and C++ will *always* consider the members to be part of the class) the members form the class. The members are not objects but parts of objects that you can define with this class.

Remember, a class is a description of an object but not the object itself. In a way, `int` is a keyword that defines a class; `int` is a data type that describes a type of numeric value or variable. Only after you define integer variables do you have an integer object.

Declaring Object Variables

C++, without your help, would have no idea what the `Person` class would be because `Person` is not some internal class native to C++. Therefore, the multilined `class` statement shown earlier tells C++ exactly what the class's characteristics are like. After you define the class, you then can declare variables, or, more accurately, objects of the class. The following statement declares a `Person` object called `Mike`:

```
Person Mike;    // Declares an instance of the Person class
```

Figure 17.3 shows what the object (or variable or instance of the class) looks like. The object named `Mike` is a three-part object. The characteristics are as follows: `Mike` is an object that begins with a 25-character array, followed by an integer, followed by a floating-point value.

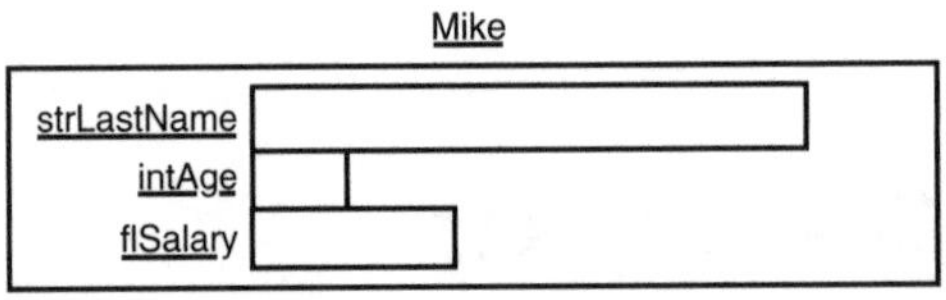

FIGURE 17.3

The object named `Mike` *internally contains three members.*

Mike

strLastName

intAge

flSalary

All `Person` objects that you declare from the `Person` class will look like `Mike`, but they will have different names just as integer variables in a program have different names. In addition, the objects will have local or global scope depending on where you declare them.

Generally, programmers place the `class` definition globally or even stored in a header file that they include in subsequent programs. After the `class` definition appears globally (such as before the `main()` procedure), any place in the rest of the program can declare object variables from the class. The variables might be global, but they will probably be local if the programmer follows the suggested standards and maintains only local variables to a procedure. As with any variables, you can pass object variables between procedures as needed.

Any place in the program can declare additional object variables. The following statement would declare three additional objects that take on the characteristics of the `Person` class:

```
Person Judy, Paul, Terry;
```

Accessing Members

You'll use the dot operator (a period) to access members in an object. For example, the following assignment stores a value in the `Mike` object's `intAge` member:

```
Mike.intAge = 32;   // Initialize the member named age
```

As long as you qualify the member name with the object name, C++ knows which object to assign to. Therefore, if several `Person` objects are declared in the program, the object name before the member informs the program exactly which object member you want to initialize. Anywhere you can use a variable, you can use a member name as long as you qualify the name with the object. For example, you cannot directly assign a string literal to a character array in C++ (or in C), but you can use the `strcpy()` function like this:

```
strcpy(Mike.strLastName, "Johnson");   // Assign the name
```

You could print one of the members like this:

```
cout << Mike.intAge;   // Display the age
```

If you wanted to print the three members, you might do so like this:

```
cout << Mike.strLastName << ", " << Mike.intAge << ", " << Mike.flSalary << endl;
```

Adding Behavior to Objects

Until now, you've only seen how to add characteristics to a class by defining the class members. You can also define the class behaviors. The behaviors describe what objects in the class can do. Adding behaviors to a class requires much more time to cover than the rest of this hour will allow. Nevertheless, by seeing an example or two of a class with defined behavior, you will begin to see how objects begin to take on a life of their own, something that simple variables cannot do.

The following `Person` class definition is more complete than the previous one because it defines not only the characteristics (the members and their data types) but also the behaviors (called *member functions*):

```
class Person {
  char strLastName[25];
  int  intAge;
  float flSalary;
```

```
  // Member functions appear next
  void dispName( void )
    { cout << "The last name is ";
      cout << strLastName << endl;
    }
  void compTaxes(float taxRate)
    {  float taxes;
       taxes = taxRate * flSalary;
       cout << "The taxes are ";
       cout << taxes << endl;
    }
  char [] getName( void )
    { return strLastName; }
  int getAge ( void )
    { return intAge; }
  float getSalary ( void )
    { return flSalary; }
};
```

Just as a member can be an instance of a variable, a member can also be a function. The embedded function, the member function, applies only to objects declared from this class. In other words, only Person objects behave exactly this way but those Person objects can perform the operations defined by the member functions. In a way, the objects are smart; they know how to behave, and the more member functions you supply, the more the objects know how to do.

Many programmers elect to use function declarations (the declaration, or first line of a function, is called the function's *prototype*) in the class statement, but then define the actual function code later. By placing function prototypes after the class itself, you keep the class cleaner like this:

```
class Person {
  char strLastName[25];
  int  intAge;
  float flSalary;
  // Member functions appear next
  void dispName( void );
  void compTaxes(float taxRate);
  char [] getName( void );
  int getAge ( void );
  float getSalary ( void );
};

void Person::dispName( void )
  { cout << "The last name is ";
    cout << strLastName << endl;
  }
```

```
void Person::compTaxes(float taxRate)
  {  float taxes;
     taxes = taxRate * flSalary;
     cout << "The taxes are ";
     cout << taxes << endl;
  }
char [] Person::getName( void )
  { return strLastName; }
int Person::getAge ( void )
  { return intAge; }
float Person::getSalary ( void )
  { return flSalary; }
```

The `class` statement is more compact because only prototypes appear in the definition and not member function code. The member function code could appear elsewhere in the program or, more likely, would be included from a file you or another programmer created that contains the member functions you need to call. Notice that if you place the function's definition later in the program, you must preface the definition with the class name followed by the `::` operator. The class name qualifies the function because different classes may have member functions with the same name as other classes in the program.

Before explaining how to apply the member functions to objects, you need to understand how scope affects objects and their member functions.

Working with Class Scope

As you know, the `class` statement defines a class and its members and member functions. However, special consideration must be given to the scope of individual data and function members. In the previous class definition, all members were *private,* meaning no code outside the class could access the data members. You can override the default privatization of members by using special `public` and `private` qualifiers to make the class available to code.

Consider this modified `Person` class definition (the member function code is omitted for brevity):

```
class Person {
  char strLastName[25];
  int  intAge;
  float flSalary;
  // Member functions appear next
public:
  void dispName( void );
  void compTaxes(float taxRate);
  char [] getName( void );
  int getAge ( void );
  float getSalary ( void );
};
```

17

All members are considered to be private unless you precede them with the `public` key-word. All members before `public` are private but you can optionally place `private:` before the first member so other programmers know your intention is that the class members up to the next `public` keyword remain private. All members (both data members and function members) that follow `public:` are public.

Being private means that any program that uses the class can *never access private members*. This is critical for data protection that the class provides. Earlier in this lesson, you saw the following statement:

```
cout << Mike.intAge;   // Display the age
```

Actually, this statement will not work in the program because the program does *not* have access to the `intAge` data member. The `intAge` data member is private so no code outside the class can access `intAge`. By protecting the data members, you keep the object intact and ensure that only predefined functions available in the class can access the age. That's why you often see member functions that begin with `get` as in the `getAge()` function shown previously. Because `getAge()` is in the public section of the class, any program that defines `Person` objects *can* use the `getAge()` function. Therefore, you cannot display `intAge` directly, but you can call the `getAge()` function like this:

```
cout << Mike.getAge();   // Display the age
```

Notice that when you apply the member function to the object, you use the dot operator just as you do for data members. Other class objects may be defined and also have functions named `getAge()`, so you must qualify the member function by letting the program know you want the `getAge()` function applied to one specific object variable in the program named `Mike`.

Keep in mind that complete college courses and huge texts exist that teach object-oriented programming in C++. You're getting only an overview here, although the overview is actually rather complete. After mastering this introductory hour, you should be able to understand the early portions of a course or text on C++ much more easily.

Things to Come

Given the introduction to C++ that you've now had, you can better understand the advantages that C++ provides over more traditional, non-OOP languages. One of the benefits of OOP is that you can create your own operators. More accurately, you can change the way an operator works when the program uses that operator with one of your objects.

By writing special *operator overloading* member functions, you can make any C++ operator work on your own objects. For example, a plus sign is the addition operator that automatically works on all numeric values. The plus sign, however, cannot work on a Person object such as Mike. Therefore, if you wanted to add two Person objects together to get a total of the salaries, you could write a function that added the salaries of two or more flSalary data members. When you apply the totaling function members to objects, you can produce the total of the salaries, but you can also overload the plus sign operator so that plus works not only for two numbers but also for two Person objects like this:

```
totalSals = Mike + Terry;   // Possible by overloading the +
```

You could never ordinarily use a plus sign between two Person objects such as Mike and Terry because they are objects you created and they contain three data members of different data types. But once you overload the plus operator to add the appropriate values inside Person objects, you can add their values easily.

Such operator overloading means that you can simplify a program's code. Instead of using a function to simulate a common operation, you can actually use the operator itself, applied to your own objects. The member function that describes the operator overloading determines exactly which data members are affected and used by the operation.

 The overloading of operators is how you can use the << and >> to input and output complete classes of objects with multiple members and even use Windows-based controls such as text boxes to receive or initiate the special I/O.

The concept of polymorphism makes the overloading of operators possible. For example, the same operator applied to an integer variable behaves much differently if you apply that operator to a class object that you define.

In addition to overloading operators, you can create your own data types. Keep in mind that a class simply defines a collection of data that is composed of data members that conform to an ordinary data type. You could, for example, create a String class whose only data member is a character array. By overloading the appropriate operators, you can make C++ behave like QBasic and support string-like variables.

The String class is just one example of the many classes you and others can write to support object reuse later down the road. Over time, you will build a large library of classes that you can use for future programs. As you build classes, the amount of code that you have to write should lessen and you should complete applications more quickly. In addition, as you build and debug object class libraries, your programs should become more maintainable.

Using operator overloading and other OOP advantages means that your code will be less bulky. When you need an object, you will simply create one from one of your class libraries just as you add new stereo components when you want to expand your music system.

One of C++'s most productive features is inheritance. When you or someone else writes a class that you use, you are not limited to objects of that class. The C++ language supports inheritance so that you can derive new classes and create new objects that have all the benefits and features of their parent classes but with additional features as well.

Summary

Are you a C or C++ expert after one hour's lesson? No way. Do you understand the fundamentals of C and C++? You'd be surprised at how well you now already understand the language, especially with your Java introduction earlier. You could not master OOP with C++ in one hour either, but you've already learned the fundamentals of how C++ works. At its most basic level, the C++ language offers language improvements over C even if you don't use OOP. Nevertheless, when you begin to use OOP, you will learn to create classes that define objects that seem to take on a life of their own. The objects understand how to perform some duties based on their member functions and you can extend the objects through inheritance to derive new classes that you can use later.

Q&A

Q Why is `#include` not a C command?

A `#include` is a preprocessor directive and is not part of the C language. `#include`, and all other lines that begin with `#`, such as `#define`, control how C compiles a program instead of controlling the way that the C program executes.

Q Can the programmer extend the class by adding functionality if a class does not quite contain enough power?

A Certainly. That's where the power of class inheritance comes into play. The programmer can include the class and then inherit a new class from the existing class. The inherited class contains all the data members and member functions of the parent class without the programmer doing anything special. Then, the programmer can add additional data members and member functions (both private and public) to the class to make the class operate as needed. Such inheritance makes the reuse and extension of objects extremely easy and should improve the efficiency of programmers as more object libraries are written and distributed.

Workshop

The quiz questions and exercises are provided for your further understanding. See Appendix B, "Quiz Answers," for answers.

Quiz

1. How is C more efficient than Liberty BASIC?
2. What is a header file?
3. What function do all C programs begin with?
4. True or false: C supports string literals.
5. What is wrong with the following statement?

```
if (sales < 2500.00);
  {
    printf("You need to work harder.\n");
  }
```

6. What included header file defines I/O in most C++ programs?
7. Where do you define an object's data members and member functions?
8. What two operators and system objects do C++ programmers often use for input and output?
9. What OOP term allows for operator overloading?
10. How does inheritance improve a C++ programmer's efficiency?

17

HOUR 18

Web Pages with HTML

Hypertext Markup Language (HTML) is the code behind Web pages. Using HTML, you place text, graphics, Java and other active content, and hyperlinks throughout Web pages to give those pages the look you desire. Unlike traditional programming languages, HTML is interpreted as your Web page loads. Your Web page, formatted with HTML code, goes across the Internet to any user who requests it. That user's browser then interprets your HTML commands to format the page properly.

This hour introduces you to the world of HTML coding. You will learn how HTML formats text, graphics, and other Web page elements. HTML is a fairly simple language because, instead of issuing commands to process data as you do with procedural languages such as C++, most HTML includes simple formatting instructions to adjust the appearance of the Web page.

The highlights of this hour include

- Understanding how HTML formats Web pages
- Recognizing HTML tags
- Working with HTML text

- Placing graphics on a Web page
- Generating Web page hyperlinks

HTML Programming

A Web page might contain text, graphics, icons and text containing links (also known as *hyperlinks* or *hot spots*), Java applets, and multimedia content. One of the goals of Web page designers is to make Web pages appear uniform no matter what kind of computer the user uses (or, more accurately, which *platform* the user uses, which might be a PC or a mainframe with one of a number of operating systems). Although the same Web page still looks different on different computers and different browser versions, a steady progression is being made to a truly universal browser standard that will show all Web pages uniformly (see the sidebar entitled, "W3C Attempts to Standardize HTML.") The *HTML* is a machine-independent language that Web developers use to design Web pages. A page's HTML listing is actually a set of text commands that, when viewed with a Web browser, produces a Web page that conforms to the look the author intended.

> No matter what programming language you decide to master next, whether it is advanced Java, C++, or another, you should learn the fundamentals of HTML. The Internet plays a huge role in computers today, and you'll almost certainly be connecting your programming efforts to the Web eventually in some way. HTML is the primary Web page language. All the other Web page languages use HTML in some way. Fortunately, HTML is primarily a formatting and hyperlinking language that is rather simple to master, especially now that you understand the way procedural languages such as Liberty BASIC and Java work.

Not only can simple HTML commands produce visually appealing Web pages, many times you don't even have to use HTML to produce a Web page today because many HTML page designers exist that buffer the HTML text from the page that you produce. For example, FrontPage is a product with which you drag items onto a screen from a toolbox and type text in text boxes to create your Web pages visually. FrontPage then translates the page you laid out into HTML commands for you. Microsoft Word and other word processors can often save documents (with formatted text as well as embedded tables, graphics, and multimedia) as HTML pages that Word translates to HTML code.

W3C Attempts to Standardize HTML

The *World Wide Web Consortium*, known as *W3C*, is a standards committee supported and staffed by the computer industry. The goal of W3C is to define standards for HTML and HTML-based languages and Web browsers.

Although Web browsers and HTML language systems don't have to follow the W3C's suggestions for HTML coding, those that do will help to ensure that their Web site will have more of a chance of being seen properly in all Web browsers. The committee makes many coding suggestions, such as using all uppercase letters for HTML command tags. The W3C also defines new HTML commands that browser makers can adopt to make HTML coding easier and to make Web pages richer with content.

You can visit their Web site at www.w3.org and learn more about the consortium.

Following an HTML Example

Figure 18.1 shows a Web page. The page looks rather simple and is free of clutter.

FIGURE 18.1

A Web page created with HTML code.

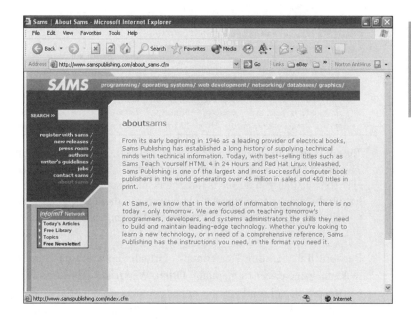

18

Listing 18.1 contains some of the HTML commands that produced Figure 18.1's Web page.

LISTING 18.1   Part of the HTML Commands That Produced the Web Page

```
<html>
<head> <title>Sams | About Sams</title> <body bgcolor="#FFFFFF" text="#666666"
background="images/basics/greygrid.gif" leftmargin="5" topmargin="0"
marginwidth="0" marginheight="0" link="#336699" vlink="#0099CC"alink="#336699">
<table width="720" border="0" cellspacing="0" cellpadding="0">
<tr>
<a href="new_releases_sams.cfm" class="navtop">new releases</a> /<br>
<a href="press/press.cfm" class="navtop">press room</a> /<br>
<a href="authors_sams.cfm" class="navtop">authors</a> /<br>
<a href="write.cfm" class="navtop">writer's guidelines
</a> /<br>
<a href="current_jobs.cfm" class="navtop">jobs</a> /<br>
<a href="contact_sams.cfm" class="navtop">contact sams</a> /<br>
<a href="about_sams.cfm" class="navtopselect">about sams</a> /</font></b><br>
 <tr> <td valign="top">
   <p><b><font color="336699">about</font><font
color="#0099CC">sams</font></b></p>
   <p><font size="-1"> From its early beginning in 1946 as a leading
   provider of electrical books, Sams Publishing has established a
   long history of supplying technical minds with technical information.
   Today, with best-selling titles such as Sams Teach Yourself HTML
   4 in 24 Hours and Red Hat Linux Unleashed, Sams Publishing is one
   of the largest and most successful computer book publishers in the
   world generating over 45 million in sales and 450 titles in print.
```

Take a moment to compare Listing 18.1's HTML commands to Figure 18.1's Web page. The full HTML code required to display Figure 18.1 is much longer than Listing 18.1. The HTML code that you do see is rather advanced so the excerpt of this HTML listing looks a little forbidding. Nevertheless, as you keep comparing the HTML code to the Web page, you'll begin to see some ways that the HTML language formatted and placed text on parts of the Web page.

Be warned that Listing 18.1 contains virtually no whitespace and alignment that would make the page easier to maintain. Often, Web pages generated with Web page design software such as FrontPage are rather compact, as opposed to Web pages that an HTML programmer designs from scratch. Before this hour is over, you will see simpler HTML code written by a programmer that demonstrates more readability. You'll inevitably find both kinds of HTML-based pages because many of the Web pages you use today are generated by Web page design programs instead of coded by hand in HTML. Actually, many Web page programmers use a Web page designing program to produce the initial HTML code, and then they modify the generated HTML code, often cleaning up the code's spacing to make the code more maintainable.

You will notice that the HTML code snippet from the Web site used in Figure 18.1 uses lowercase for the tags (the HTML commands between angled brackets, < and >) and attributes (the words that specify how some of the tags look and behave, such as color). As mentioned in the previous sidebar, one of the W3C's standards is the recommendation for all uppercase tags and attributes. As you can see, that standard is not always followed. Actually, it is safe to say that most Web pages use lowercase, or a mixture of both lowercase and uppercase HTML tags and attributes. Although the browser ignores case and doesn't care which you use, for all new Web development, it's probably best to adopt an all-uppercase approach.

Displaying a Web Page

When you navigate to view a Web page, the remote server sends to your browser only the HTML text, and the browser responds to the commands by formatting text appropriately and placing links and graphics images where the HTML code dictates they should appear. Your browser first receives the full HTML page and then receives whatever graphics images and multimedia content are needed to complete the page.

Browsers provide a Stop button that you can click, or you can press Esc, to keep from receiving graphics and multimedia images for those times when you don't want to wait on them but want to read the text that has already been sent to your browser. In place of the images and multimedia content, most browsers display an icon in place of the image that shows where the image would have appeared if you had let the image load to your computer.

18

Command Tags

The terms within angled brackets (< and >) are called *tag references* (or *tag commands*). Tag commands are central to the HTML program. Many commands contain a beginning and ending tag (a forward slash, /, always precedes an ending tag). A nonbracketed text item is a *literal* (a value that does not change), such as a title that is to appear on the Web page. The tags primarily determine the placement of figures, the format of text, links to other Web sites, and table information when different sets of data are to appear on the same page. For example, `<TITLE>` marks the beginning of a title and `</TITLE>` marks the end.

Many of the tags in Listing 18.1 are formatting tag codes that specify font style and size instructions for the Web browser. Other tags format table cells so that the Web page takes on a table like structure for the HTML programmer.

Tags don't contain formatted text; they offer formatting instructions that your Web browser is to follow. Therefore, when your Web browser sees the `<CENTER>` tag, your Web browser knows to center the text that runs up to the subsequent `</CENTER>` ending tag as the following HTML code would do:

```
<center>
Our Family's Web Page
</center>
```

The HTML code completely determines how text appears. Therefore, except for keeping your HTML code readable, no advantage exists for adding spacing. HTML ignores extra spaces that come before your Web page's text. The following code produces the same, centered title that the previous code did even though the text itself has some extra spaces at the beginning:

```
<CENTER>
     Our Family's Web Page
</CENTER>   .
```

The W3C recommends quotations around non-tag values such as the title. Web browsers do not require the quotation marks but you can use them as follows if you wish:

```
<CENTER>
     "Our Family's Web Page"
</CENTER>
```

You can document HTML code with the following comment tag:

```
<!-- This is an HTML comment -->
```

Everything between `<!--` and `-->` is treated as an HTML comment, even if the comment spans multiple lines.

A Simpler Example

Many Web sites are a good deal simpler than the one previously shown. Don't get bogged down in advanced HTML commands when you first begin studying HTML because even simple HTML commands can produce quite attractive and complete Web pages. For example, consider how simple Listing 18.2's HTML code appears. You should have little trouble following the HTML commands even if HTML is new to you. Notice that some command tags contain quotation marks around their literals while others do not. Web browsers do not require the quotation marks but the W3C suggests that they be used. You will find that most Web pages use a combination even though it's not consistent.

LISTING 18.2   Simple HTML Commands Can Produce Attractive Web Pages.

```
<HTML>
 <HEAD>
   <TITLE>Simple Web Page</TITLE>
 </HEAD>
 <BODY>
```

continues

LISTING 18.2 Continued

```
<CENTER>
  <H1>"Fancy, yet simple!"</H1><P>
</CENTER>
<HR NOSHADE>
<CENTER>
  HTML is the key to attractive Web pages. Your Web pages will
  carry with them text, images, and multimedia content that the
  HTML code formats into the resulting Web pages.
  <IMG SRC="Beany.gif" ALT="Beany Cap">
</CENTER>
<H1><I><A HREF=www.microsoft.com>Click here to see Microsoft's Web site
    </A></I>
  </H1><MARQUEE>This text scrolls across the screen</MARQUEE><P>
 </BODY>
</HTML>
```

Figure 18.2 shows the resulting Web page that Listing 18.2's HTML commands produce. The <MARQUEE> command tag works only in Internet Explorer browsers, although other Web browsers might adopt the tag some day. As you can see, the Web page is attractive and fairly complex despite the simple HTML code that created it. To reproduce this Web page, you would need to have the graphic named Beany.gif in the same folder as the HTML code. You can substitute another GIF image, if you have one, for Beany.gif if you want to create a Web page similar to this one.

18

FIGURE 18.2

A nice Web page that requires only simple HTML code.

Developers add to the HTML language constantly. As the Web becomes more complex, the needs of the HTML language expand. For example, HTML did not originally support tables of information but tables are now standard. One of the most important additions to the HTML language was the ability of a Web page to become active using an embedded program. You've seen that already in Hour 15, "Applets and Web Pages." The W3C wants to extend the next version of HTML into a conglomerate Web programming language called XHTML that includes both HTML and XML. You'll learn about XML in Hour 20, "Dynamic HTML and XML."

> The next time that you log on to the Internet, locate the menu option that lets you view the HTML source code. If you use Internet Explorer, the source display command is View, Source, and if you use Netscape Navigator, the command is View, Document Source.

Transferring a packet of HTML code, such as that in Listing 18.2, is much less time-consuming than transferring a graphics image of the Web page. Your Web browser reads the HTML commands and then formats the text or graphics images according to their instructions. Although your browser must be more capable than a simple graphics viewer, your CPU's time is much less precious than modem downloading time.

As stated earlier, several powerful Web-design tools exist to create Web pages using modern graphical cut-and-paste methods; you can create a fancy Web page simply by using a text editor and knowing the HTML language. Often, programmers use graphical tools to lay out the overall Web page and then use a text editor to hone the HTML source code to finalize the page.

A Quick HTML Primer

All Web pages require a fundamental set of HTML codes. Listing 18.3 shows the minimal HTML code needed to display a Web page.

LISTING 18.3 The General Format for All HTML Web Pages

```
<HTML>
  <!-- This is a comment -->
  <HEAD>
    <TITLE>The window's title bar text goes here</TITLE>
  </HEAD>
  <BODY>
    <!-- The bulk of the Web page text, graphics, and HTML
         code goes here -->
  </BODY>
</HTML>
```

The angled bracket commands are the HTML command tags that format the page's data and instruct the browser on how to display the page. Most HTML tags appear in pairs, such as `<BODY>` and `</BODY>`. The closing tag, indicated with a slash (/), tells the browser where the tag command ends.

Notice that the first tag in all Web pages should be `<HTML>`, indicating the beginning of the HTML code. The end tag is `</HTML>`, indicating that the Web page is through.

The heading section, enclosed with `<HEAD>` and `</HEAD>`, contains title bar information using the `<TITLE>` and `</TITLE>` tags and other preliminary Web page data such as *metatags,* advanced HTML code that programmers can place inside Web pages to get noticed by search engines. Often, the title bar is the only text that appears in the heading section.

The body section, enclosed with `<BODY>` and `</BODY>`, includes the bulk of the Web page content. The user is most interested in the data between these two tags.

HTML Text Formatting

To make text appear on the browser's screen, simply type the text inside the HTML code. Your Web page body could include lines of text like this:

```
<BODY>
This text will appear
on whatever Web browser screen
opens this HTML code.
</BODY>
```

The text may or may not be enclosed in quotation marks. Web browsers do not automatically format text. These three lines of text all appear on one line inside the browser, like this:

```
This text will appear on whatever Web browser screen opens this HTML code.
```

If you want to add line breaks, you must include the `<BR>` tag (no ending `<BR>` tag exists). `<BR>` tells the Web browser to break the line at that point and move to the next line. The following `<BODY>` section displays three lines of text:

```
<BODY>
This text will appear<BR>
on whatever Web browser screen<BR>
opens this HTML code.
</BODY>
```

Again, the text breaks onto three lines only because of the `<BR>` tags and not because the lines happen to end there.

18

Text automatically appears right justified on the browser's window. You can change the alignment to centered, right aligned, or left aligned by placing text between these tags:

`<P ALIGN=CENTER>` and `</P>`

`<P ALIGN=RIGHT>` and `</P>`

`<P ALIGN=LEFT>` and `</P>`

> The `<CENTER>` tag does the same thing as `<P ALIGN=CENTER>`, with the added benefit of centering pictures as well as text.

The ALIGN=*VALUE* is known as an *attribute*. The command tag, `<P>`, requires more information to work and the attribute for `<P>` describes how ALIGN is to work. You can add italics, boldfacing, and underlining to your text. The following HTML code contains such formatting:

```
This line contains <U>two underlined</U> words.
This line contains <I>two italicized</I> words.
This line contains <B>two boldfaced</B> words.
```

> Generally, Web page designers refrain from using underlining on Web pages because most hyperlinks appear as underlined text. Therefore, if you include underlined text that does not serve as a link to another Web page, users may waste time trying to click on those underlined words to see what happens

The `<H>` tag controls the size of headlines that you use as titles on your page. You can use `<H1>` (the largest) through `<h6>` (the smallest) to display headlines. Figure 18.4 shows the Web page created by the HTML code in Listing 18.4.

FIGURE 18.3

HTML supports up to seven headline sizes.

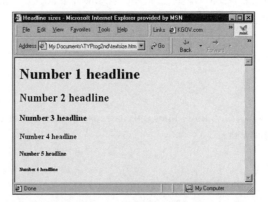

LISTING 18.4   Examples of the `<H>` Tag Show How to Change Headline Text Size.

```
<HTML>
  <HEAD>
    <TITLE>Headline sizes</TITLE>
  </HEAD>
  <BODY>
    <!-- An automatic line break
         occurs after each headline -->
    <H1>Number 1 headline </H1>
    <H2>Number 2 headline </H2>
    <H3>Number 3 headline </H3>
    <H4>Number 4 headline </H4>
    <H5>Number 5 headline </H5>
    <H6>Number 6 headline </H6>
  </BODY>
</HTML>
```

Using a method similar to the headline tag, you can control the size of your text using the `<FONT SIZE>` tag. You can specify a font size from 1 (the smallest, which is exactly the opposite of the `<H>` tag's numbering system) to 7, as Listing 18.5 demonstrates. Figure 18.4 shows the results.

18

LISTING 18.5   Examples of the `<FONT SIZE>` Tag Illustrate How to Change Text Size.

```
<HTML>
  <HEAD>
    <TITLE>Text sizes</TITLE>
  </HEAD>
  <BODY>
    <FONT SIZE=1>Smallest text size</FONT> <BR>
    <FONT SIZE=2>Growing...</FONT> <BR>
    <FONT SIZE=3>Growing...</FONT> <BR>
    <FONT SIZE=4>Growing...</FONT> <BR>
    <FONT SIZE=5>Growing...</FONT> <BR>
    <FONT SIZE=6>Growing...</FONT> <BR>
    <FONT SIZE=7>Largest text size</FONT>
  </BODY>
</HTML>
```

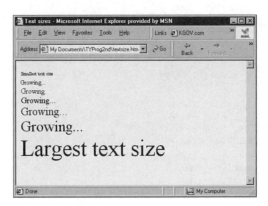

Simple HTML Graphics

The `<IMG>` tag places images on your Web pages when you use the `ARC=` attribute with the tag. After you designate an image's location and filename, the image appears. Graphics are simple to display and, unless you want to apply advanced formatting techniques to your Web page images, the `<IMG>` tag is all you'll need for many of your Web page graphics.

Here is a simple Web page command that displays an image on the screen:

```
<IMG SRC="images/myphoto.jpg">
```

The image appears wherever this `<IMG>` tag appears inside the HTML code. It's up to you to ensure that the image is formatted in a type of file that browsers can display. The common image formats are gif, JPEG, and PNG, and most graphics programs produce images in these three formats.

You can easily place a border around a graphic, in effect adding a framed image to your Web page. The `<BORDER>` tag is an extension of the `<IMG>` tag. In addition, you can align your graphic image to the left, center, or right edge of the screen by placing the `ALIGN=` attribute inside the `<IMG>` tag. Consider the following complex image tag:

```
<IMG SRC="/images/Dogs.gif" ALIGN=LEFT BORDER=10 ALT="My Dogs">
```

The image comes from a Web folder named `images` where all the site's images are located. The `ALIGN` attribute instructs the browser to left-align the image to the left browser window. The `BORDER=10` attribute instructs the browser to place a border around the picture and to make the border 10 points wide. Given that a point is approximately 1/72nd of an inch, the border will be about 1/7th of an inch thick.

The ALT= attribute, the *alternate* attribute, is important if you want pop-up text to appear when your user points to your Web page's picture. Sometimes, Web users have slow connections and they turn off the display of Web page pictures to speed their surfing experience. These users will see the alternate text in place of the picture so they know what the picture intended to show.

Using Hyperlinks

An *anchor* tag, indicated by `<A>` and `</A>`, creates a hyperlink to another page location. The browser that displays your Web page creates an underlined link at the point of your HTML's `<A>` tag.

The following lines send the user to the Pearson Education Web site when the user clicks the hyperlink:

```
<A HREF="http://www.pearsoned.com">
Click for great learning
</A>
```

Everything between the `<A>` tag and the closing `</A>` tag comprises the anchor, and the HREF attribute forces the hyperlink. The four words, `Click for great learning`, will be underlined on the screen, and the user can click anywhere in that text to access the corresponding Web site.

You can even specify graphics and multiline text as hyperlinks. When the user clicks the hyperlink, the browser accesses the linked Web page. The user can click the browser's Back button to access the current page.

The HTML statement that follows shows you how to use an image as a hyperlink. Remember that everything you place between the initial `<A HREF>` tag and attribute, along with the `</A>` ending tag is a hyperlink, whether you place graphics, text, or both there.

```
<A HREF="http://www.MinskeyFamilyPics.com">
  <IMG SRC="images/Flag.gif">
</A>
```

When the Web page appears that includes this statement, the user's mouse pointer will change to a hand when the user points to the image on the screen that is named `Flag.gif`. If the user then clicks the image, the browser opens the page located at `http://www.MinskeyFamilyPics.com`.

18

Summary

By now, you have a preliminary understanding of how to use HTML to code and format Web pages. Once you understand the general nature of HTML code, creating and formatting Web pages becomes a simple matter. When you are ready to add tables, frames, and other advanced elements to your page, you'll need to master more advanced command tags, but you should have little trouble doing so as long as you build gradually on the knowledge you have already acquired. Using only the tags discussed in this hour, you can create nice-looking, although simple, Web pages that contain text, graphics, and links to other sites.

Q&A

Q Why do some HTML tags require both opening and ending tags while others do not use ending tags?

A A command tag requires a beginning and ending tag when you are about to format a specific element on the Web page. For example, when italicizing text, you must begin the italics with the `<I>` tag and the italicized text follows. Without the ending tag, `</I>`, all text on the rest of the Web page would be italicized. Command tags such as line breaks, `<BR>`, do not format specific text or graphics and can stand alone because they cause a single action, a line break.

Q If I don't have Web page designer software, how can I use a text editor such as Notepad to practice learning HTML?

A Start Notepad and enter your HTML commands. Save your text with any of the following filename extensions: .htm, .html, .HTM, or .HTML, the case doesn't matter. If you don't specify the extension, Notepad will save your file as a text file with the .TXT extension. Web pages should always use one of the extensions just listed. You then can start your Web browser, such as Internet Explorer, and select File, Open and locate the file you just created. When you click OK, your HTML-based Web page will appear. If you did not code something properly, you will not get an error, but the page will not look right.

Workshop

The quiz questions and exercises are provided for your further understanding. See Appendix B, "Quiz Answers," for answers.

Quiz

1. Why is a working knowledge of HTML so important for all programmers today?
2. What does a Web page design program such as FrontPage do?
3. What is a command tag?
4. How do you code an HTML comment?
5. What do the `<title>` and `</title>` command tags control?
6. How do you increase the size of headline text?
7. How do you increase the size of regular Web page text?
8. Why would you specify alternate text for Web page graphics?
9. True or false: You can turn both graphics and text into hyperlinks on a Web page.
10. Why is it generally a bad practice to underline text on a Web page?

18

HOUR 19

Scripting with JavaScript

You know Java, but that means little when it comes to JavaScript. The names are similar but their features and goals differ. JavaScript enables you to add multimedia capabilities to your Web site. JavaScript is linked to DHTML (*dynamic HTML*). You will learn about DHTML in Hour 20, "Dynamic HTML and XML," and this hour's JavaScript discussion provides a good introduction to Hour 20's concepts.

By itself, JavaScript is a script-based programming environment that you use to spruce up Web sites and make those sites more interactive. You embed JavaScript source code directly inside your HTML code, unlike compiled Java applets, which are pulled along with the Web page to run on the user's computers.

The highlights of this hour include the following:

- Understanding the origins of the JavaScript language
- Learning where a scriptlet executes
- Executing a JavaScript scriptlet in response to a user's actions

JavaScript's Actions

JavaScript activates various Web page elements, such as command button *rollover effects*. A rollover effect occurs when the user points to a button and the button changes—perhaps the color or the text changes in some way as the mouse pointer moves over the button. If the user removes the mouse pointer from the button, the button returns to normal. In this way, as the mouse pointer rolls over the button, the button reacts.

JavaScript code can also verify user entries on a Web page. In addition, it works with other Web technologies to build effective and intelligent Web pages.

Netscape, the company that authored Netscape Navigator, created JavaScript several years ago. All major browsers of version 3.0 and later support the use of JavaScript (so Internet Explorer 5, for example, has no trouble with JavaScript code that appears on a Web page). Subsequent versions of Internet Explorer may or may not support JavaScript directly but you can always download add-in programs for Internet Explorer from Microsoft's Web site and other Web sites that enable Internet Explorer's support for JavaScript code.

JavaScript is not the same language as Java. Java is a programming language based on C++, and it includes industrial-strength language elements; JavaScript is somewhat simpler than Java. JavaScript is a scripting language that requires less learning than a full-fledged, compiled programming language. In addition, unlike most programming languages, JavaScript is interpreted, meaning that you won't have to recompile your JavaScript code every time you make a change. A JavaScript program is called a *scriptlet*.

Many people think of JavaScript when they think of rollover effects but JavaScript also ties in well with Web page forms such as the one in Figure 19.1. JavaScript controls the text boxes, lists, and list boxes on forms. One of the great things about a JavaScript scriptlet is its speed; all the script code loads and then executes on the user's computer (the *client*, as opposed to the *server* computer that hosts the Web site). JavaScript can interact with the mouse and keyboard to respond immediately when the user makes a movement.

FIGURE 19.1

*JavaScript works
behind the scenes with
Web forms.*

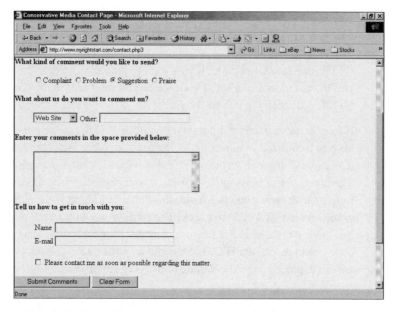

The designers of HTML don't intend to make HTML a complete language that will perform all Web page activity, formatting, and control. The designers of HTML added the
`<script>` tag (and a corresponding `</script>` tag) to enclose extensions to HTML, such
as JavaScript code.

The Web browser does not interpret code between `<script>` and `</script>`. This allows
the Web page designer to put whatever he or she wants inside the extensible script area.
It's up to the browser to support whatever the Web designer puts between the scripting
tags. As a further precaution to protect JavaScript code from HTML formatting attempts,
you'll add all your JavaScript code inside HTML, not only between `<script>` and
`</script>` tags but also between comments.

The following section of HTML code demonstrates how a one-line JavaScript statement,
hidden by a comment with the `<script>` tags, appears inside the HTML code:

```
<html>
  <script language="JavaScript">
  <!—
    document.form1.CoTitle.Text="King Chemicals, Inc."
  // —>
```

You can store JavaScript scriptlet code outside an HTML file. The `<script>`
tag supports the loading of a scriptlet from an external file. All JavaScript
code that you place in a single scriptlet file must end in the `.JavaScript`
filename extension.

You can always view the source code of any JavaScript scriptlet. JavaScript source code travels with HTML, embedded within the HTML code. If you view a Web page with JavaScript code, you can select View, Source from the browser's menu to see both the HTML and JavaScript code. If you want to pursue a career in JavaScript programming, you'll want to look at a lot of code—and you can because the code appears inside the HTML code that you can easily view.

If JavaScript scriptlets did not travel with the HTML, the server computer's power would have to be utilized to interact with the user. An older Web technology named CGI (Common Gateway Interface) utilized server-side computing power primarily for forms. Therefore, if you filled out a form on a Web page that used CGI, you would fill in the form's blank areas and click a button, such as a Submit button, that sent that information to the server's CGI code to check. The transfer would take a few moments, and if you had made a mistake in the form, such as entering an invalid state abbreviation, the CGI code would resend the HTML page and an error message back to you. This slow back-and-forth process would continue until you gave up on the form or got it correct.

With JavaScript, the JavaScript code comes as a part of the HTML code. The code runs on the user's (client's) computer and not on the Web server. Therefore, if you make a mistake on the form's state abbreviation blank, the JavaScript code will immediately warn you of the problem so you can easily back up to the previous blank and correct the problem before submitting the form.

Reviewing JavaScript's Objects

Every element on your Web page is an object to JavaScript. By naming each element, you can manipulate those elements through JavaScript code. You might be surprised at the plethora of objects JavaScript recognizes. JavaScript even recognizes your browser's history list as an object. Table 19.1 lists a few of the Web page–based objects that JavaScript can view.

TABLE 19.1 JavaScript Recognizes Many Kinds of Objects.

window	document	form
applet	anchor	area
button	checkbox	fileUpload
image	password	radio
reset	select	submit
text	textarea	ids

continues

TABLE 19.1   Continued

link	plugin	tags
frame	history	location
menubar	scrollbar	statusbar

As with the Visual Basic controls, the JavaScript objects all support characteristics that your JavaScript code can modify to change the behavior of those objects. For example, the `checkbox` object supports the `Checked` property. When `Checked` is `True`, the check box is selected on the screen; `False` means that the user has not selected the check box.

In addition to properties you can set and test for, JavaScript objects support methods. A JavaScript method is a built-in routine designed to do something with that object. For example, a `document` object is the Web page itself. When you want your JavaScript scriptlet to write text to the screen, you'll apply the `write` method to the `document` object like this:

```
document.write("This appears on the screen.")
```

This is only an overview. If you later study JavaScript in more depth, you will learn the common methods that most Web page objects support.

Putting Together the Puzzle

In many ways, working with JavaScript requires little more than knowing Web page object names and knowing which methods you can apply to those objects to do the things you want to do. The pieces are all there: objects and methods that work with specific objects. Your job as a programmer is to collect the object you want to manipulate and locate the methods that perform that manipulation.

Object-oriented programming (OOP) shines brightly in a graphical interface such as a Web browser. The packaged objects such as the Web page elements all come with a predefined set of characteristics (properties) that you can set to make the objects appear a certain way. They also come with a predefined set of methods that you can use to make the objects behave a certain way.

19

Variables provide a means for you to store data temporarily for calculations, data swapping, sorting, and other routines that do not lend themselves to onscreen controls. As with most languages, JavaScript supports a wide range of variables and operations on variables. You don't even have to define your variable types explicitly; JavaScript will attempt to guess the variable's type from the context of its usage.

The following section of JavaScript code defines three variables and then calculates with them. No screen object is being used to perform this calculation:

```
var hoursWorked, rate, totalPay
hoursWorked = 40
rate = 9.85
totalPay = eval(hoursWorked * rate)
```

The code is similar to Visual Basic but not quite in the same form as it would be in that language. JavaScript does not support arithmetic calculations directly. You call a built-in function named `eval()`, and JavaScript passes the formula to its internal calculator to return the result.

> In today's complicated graphical world, JavaScript is a good first program-ming language to learn. JavaScript programmers are in demand now, and JavaScript is a simpler language than most others. Although its roots are in C and C++, you don't have to tell JavaScript what a variable's type is. You can store a string in a variable at one place in a program and then store a number and perform math with the same variable. JavaScript adjusts the variable so that it holds whatever kind of data is needed at the time.

At this point in the book, it would be understandable if you were beginning to confuse methods and functions. A survey of languages can clear up a lot of questions but create even more. If all languages were identical, there would be little need for more than one. You have to keep straight not only all the languages discussed, but also how the elements work within each language.

In JavaScript code, a method is always separated from its object with a period, such as this:

```
document.write("This appears on the screen.")
```

A function call always has parentheses in which you pass a parameter that the function is to work with, such as the previous calculation being passed along to `eval()` to evaluate.

JavaScript's Events and Handlers

Like Visual Basic event procedures, JavaScript supports events and event handlers. When an event occurs, such as the user clicking the mouse, that event's handler executes if you've supplied the handler code. For example, if the user clicks the mouse over a button on a Web page form, the button's onClick event is triggered only if you have written code for it.

A rollover effect can apply to buttons or text on the Web page. If text contains a rollover, the text can change color or change in another way when the user points to the text. Often, such a rollover effect is used for menu selection. Figure 19.2 shows a Web page with JavaScript-enabled text before the user moves the mouse pointer over one of the text items. Figure 19.3 shows how the Author Links text changes when the user moves the mouse pointer over the text. This rollover effect is possible only because the scriptlet that contains code to handle the rollover comes to the user's computer inside the HTML Web page. The code must run on the user's computer to respond immediately to the mouse movement.

FIGURE 19.2

A Web page with JavaScript looks like any other until the user activates a JavaScript scriptlet.

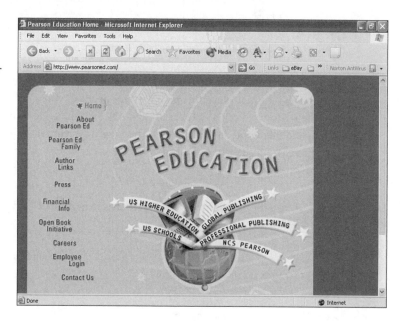

19

Figure **19.3**

When the mouse pointer moves over text with a rollover effect, the JavaScript code changes the text's appearance.

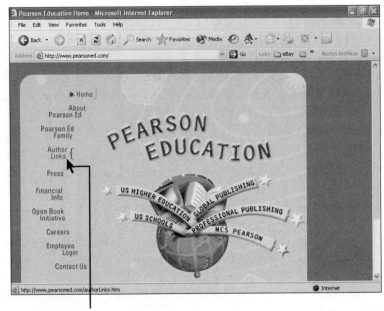

Text changes after pointing here.

Listing 19.1 contains the code that produces a command button's rollover effect. (You will not be able to reproduce this actual effect because you won't have graphics to use for the before and after rollover effects.) Not all the code will be clear even after you complete this hour; JavaScript can't be taught or learned in one short hour, but you're simply trying to grasp the fundamentals of how JavaScript activates such command buttons.

Listing 19.1 A JavaScript Script That Performs a Button Change When the User Points to the Button

```
<HTML>
<BODY>
 <A HREF="javascript:"
  onmouseover="changeOver('Img1');"
  onmouseout="changeOut('Img1');">
  <IMG NAME=Img1 SRC="Img1.gif">
 </A><BR>
 <A HREF="javascript:"
  onmouseover="changeOver('Img2');"
  onmouseout="changeOut('Img2');">
  <IMG NAME=Img2 SRC="Img2.gif">
```

continues

LISTING 19.1   Continued

```
    </A><BR>

<SCRIPT>
function changeOver(anImage) {
    if (anImage == "Img1") {
      document.images[anImage].src = "Img1over.gif";
    }
    else if (anImage == "Img2") {
      document.images[anImage].src = "Img2over.gif";
    }
}

function changeOut(anImage) {
    if (anImage == "Img1") {
      document.images[anImage].src = "Img1.gif";
    }
    else if (anImage == "Img2") {
      document.images[anImage].src = "Img2.gif";
    }
}
</SCRIPT>
</BODY>
</HTML>
```

You'll notice in the following section of Listing 19.1 that two events, onmouseover and onmouseout, trigger the execution of a function: changeOver() and changeOut(), respectively. (Uppercase and lowercase do not matter when you write JavaScript methods, functions, and event handlers.) Therefore, the programmer has supplied the handler code for those two events.

```
onmouseover="changeOver('Img1');"
onmouseout="changeOut('Img1');"
```

When the onmouseover event occurs, the changeOver() function, defined later in the script, swaps the image on the button after checking to see which picture is showing currently. The button is stored in an image array, indicated by the subscript named anImage inside these brackets: document.images[anImage]. So, the first picture (called Img1) is under the mouse, and the function displays the replacement image, Img2over.gif.

JavaScript's Language Is Complete

JavaScript supports almost as many language elements as a fully compiled language such as Visual Basic or C++. This massive vocabulary is rare for a scripting language. As you look through JavaScript code, you'll find many statements that appear in C and C++ that quickly show the roots of the JavaScript language. (Hour 17, "Programming with C and C++," contains a review of C and C++.)

19

The size of the JavaScript language is crucial to give programmers the ability to respond to the user's actions. Pictures on the Web page swap due to mouse clicks and movements, calculations are performed for financial services, and menus can appear when the user needs to select an option.

Here are some of the statements you'll find in JavaScript:

- `for` loops
- `do` loops
- `while` loops
- `if...else` statements
- Comments (comments can begin with `//`, or you can enclose multiline comments between `/*` and `*/`)
- C-like increment and decrement operators (– and ++)
- `switch` for multiple selections

Summary

JavaScript is an interpreted language that works within HTML code to activate Web pages. Not only can JavaScript manipulate objects on the screen by changing the objects' properties, but it can also interact with the user through forms by controlling and inspecting controls such as text boxes, lists, and command buttons. The object-oriented nature of JavaScript objects makes working with most onscreen objects relatively simple due to the predefined set of methods from which you can choose.

Q&A

Q Is it true that JavaScript has nothing to do with Java?

A The two languages are similar in form but operate differently and they have considerably more differences than their similar names would suggest. Both use variables, loops, and `if` statements, but most languages have these elements. Learning Java before JavaScript doesn't offer much advantage to learning any other language first.

Q If I want to place rollover effects in my HTML, do I need a JavaScript compiler?

A JavaScript is interpreted and not compiled and you don't need a development system such as Forte for Java to insert JavaScript code into your HTML. You simply start typing the JavaScript code inside the HTML. Many of today's Web design systems, such as FrontPage and Dreamweaver, automatically generate the JavaScript code for you when you want to place common JavaScript elements, such as rollover buttons and menus, on your Web page.

Workshop

The quiz questions are provided for your further understanding. For the answers, see Appendix B, "Quiz Answers."

Quiz

1. Where does JavaScript source code usually reside?

2. What is meant by an interpreted language?

3. What is a Web page client?

4. What is a Web page server?

5. What HTML command tags enclose JavaScript scriptlets?

6. Why does JavaScript support several predefined objects?

7. True or false: Since JavaScript is not compiled, you cannot define JavaScript variables.

8. True or false: When the user points to a JavaScript-enabled button, the button changes only when the user clicks the button.

9. True or false: The JavaScript language is actually closer to C than to Java.

10. True or false: The output of JavaScript code appears inside a Web browser.

19

HOUR **20**

Dynamic HTML and XML

DHTML, also called *Dynamic HTML*, is the use of HTML and other technologies, such as JavaScript and XML, to enable more effective and interactive Web sites. All of these technologies do their jobs after the Web page loads onto a user's computer. Before DHTML, the user would have to reload the Web page to see a change such as text color, but DHTML provides such changes inside the user's browser without requiring a page reload. Common Web page elements, such as buttons that change when the user moves the mouse cursor over them, are possible due to DHTML.

Most Web developers agree that XML provides the means for more advanced Web page technology and, more importantly, provides a way for companies with large Web sites to maintain those sites, create additional sites more easily, and share data with other sites.

In this hour, you will get a glimpse into the technology of XML by

- Extending HTML code with DHTML
- Using DHTML menus and rollover effects
- Describing both format and content of Web pages with XML

- Coding well-formed XML programs
- Defining XML command tags

DHTML Complements HTML Code

DHTML is not a different language from HTML but instead is a definition for add-on technologies. To create more self-activating Web sites, you piece together the tools you want to use. When you follow the DHTML standards, your Web pages become DHTML-enabled. Therefore, to master DHTML you don't learn new HTML commands or new languages necessarily; instead, you learn new ways of using existing technologies. The items you place on Web pages become more alive and interactive than before.

 This hour doesn't actually teach you many specifics of DHTML. DHTML is more of an idea than a specific, individual technology.

The following Web-based technologies all play a role in DHTML:

- HTML
- JavaScript (or VBScript, a JavaScript-like language)
- ActiveX objects
- *DOM* (*Document Object Model*)
- *CSS* (*Cascading Style Sheets*)

You had an introduction to JavaScript in the previous hour, and this hour returns to study JavaScript from the perspective of the HTML and the rest of the Web page. ActiveX objects are pre-defined objects that perform tasks such as checking user input, providing scroll bars, and displaying graphics. DOM is a set of standard objects used in Web pages such as a text box or command button. When your browser supports DOM, as most browsers in use today do, you can refer to these objects inside HTML and manipulate them to respond to the user's actions on the Web page.

With CSS, you define HTML styles that you use, such as "Boldfaced, 14-point, itali-cized, centered text," and name them. Then, instead of having to format the style's details, you simply use the style's name as a tag and the Web browser will utilize the style you've defined. If you've used Microsoft Word's named styles, you will feel com-fortable using CSS because the concept is identical. Once you define and name a style, you only have to reference the style name, which makes creating, debugging, and main-taining Web pages much simpler.

The following list provides an overview of some DHTML active elements you'll find on many of today's Web pages:

- **Menus**   Your Web page can support a system of pull-down menus that cascade out, much like the Windows Start menu.

- **Help systems**   Developers can use DHTML to provide a help system for Web pages. This same technology can be applied to company intranets and individual software packages that provide HTML-based hyperlinked help.

- **Automatic adjustment of fonts and colors**   Your Web page text and graphic sizes and colors can change, depending on your Web page user's actions. For example, you may display a catalog of items that you sell and their descriptions. When the user clicks a description, the description increases in size and becomes boldfaced so that the user can read it more easily.

- **Common database manipulations**   Web pages that display data from a database provide the user with tools to perform common sorting, filtering, and searching within the Web browser without requiring a secondary download and delay from the serving computer.

In addition, a single DHTML-based Web page is routed to all users of your Web site. The Web site behaves depending on the individual user's actions; another user who views the same site but performs different actions on that page may see something else. The most important part of a DHTML-based Web page is the page's ability to change from its original loaded state. When a user first browses to a Web page and then views that Web page inside the browser, the user's actions can change the Web page. Before DHTML technologies, a Web page was static once the page arrived at the end user's computer.

A DHTML-based Web page is known as a *client-side* Web page. A Web *server* is the computer that holds a Web page and sends the page out when someone on the Internet requests the page. The *client* software is the end user's browser that loads the Web page. With straight HTML, the Web page that the server sends looks exactly like the Web page that the user sees (although some browser subtleties may exist, such as a column of text that appears wider than was originally intended).

20

The entire process is based on the objects defined within the DOM. The following shows only a sample of the objects DOM defines:

- The current time
- The current date
- The client's browser type (such as Navigator or Internet Explorer)
- The client's browser version number
- The browser's window state (maximized, minimized, or somewhere in-between)

- The browser's window location (specified as screen coordinates such as 300, 400, which means that the window's upper-left corner begins at exactly 300 *pixels* (screen dots) from the left edge of the screen and 400 pixels from the top edge of the screen)
- The current Web page's Web address
- Tables within the Web page as well as their individual cells
- Menus and menu options embedded on the Web page
- Buttons, check boxes, and list boxes on the Web page

By assigning an object name to each of these elements, the standard DOM, combined with browsers that support the DOM standard as most currently do, enables JavaScript and other DHTML technologies on the Web page to modify or move those objects. HTML does not have such a definition of Web browser objects. A DHTML-based Web page could change its location on the screen based on the user's action due to the fact that the screen coordinates are well defined and appear to DHTML code as objects that the code can manipulate.

Looking at a DHTML-Based Page

Before discussing additional DHTML aspects, it would be useful if you visited a Web page that contains DHTML-based Web page code. When you access the following Web address, http://www.samspublishing.com/, you'll see the Sams Publishing Web page shown in Figure 20.1.

FIGURE 20.1

A DHTML-based Web page looks like other Web pages at first.

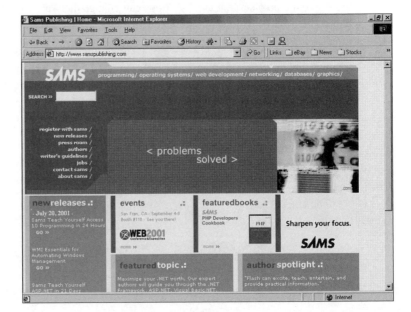

The text across the top of the screen, to the right of SAMS, is activated by DHTML code. As you point to each item, a menu drops down.

> Remember, due to client-side computing, no page reloading occurs when the page changes, because of DHTML elements. The user does not have to click a menu item to see that dropdown menu. The user only has to move the mouse cursor over the menu; that item's description instantly appears below the cursor.

Figure 20.2 shows what happens when the user points to the menu labeled web development.

FIGURE 20.2

The menu changes as a result of pointing the mouse to any other menu item.

Menu drops down

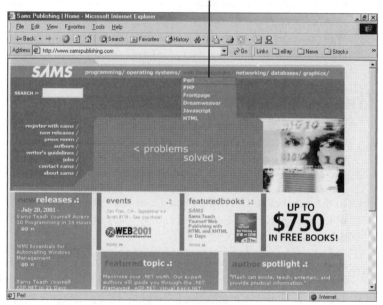

20

The Technology Behind DHTML

DOM technology is so vital to DHTML that a little more review may help shed additional light. One of the most important components of DHTML technology is the DOM designed for Web pages. The DOM is really a description that explains how to access any element on a Web page as an object. These objects, similar to Visual Basic controls and C++ objects, have properties that you can change while the user views the Web page and, in doing so, changes the object. Consider the following objects found on most Web pages: text, graphics, individual HTML tags, hyperlinks, menus, multi-media controls such as video clips, command buttons, and other controls that can appear on Web pages.

What gives the Web programmer the ability to take the DOM-defined object names and manipulate them? Since DHTML supports JavaScript, you can manipulate these objects in JavaScript code. In other words, JavaScript code could perform actions on a DHTML object, such as a command button that changes colors.

Scriptlets appear inside HTML code using the <A HREF> hyperlink tag that you learned about in the Hour 18. The anchor tag can inform the browser to expect a DHTML script-let and the scriptlet's language. The following informs HTML about a Javascript routine that appears in the Web page:

```
<A HREF="javascript:">
```

Here is what you should know so far about DHTML: A Web page based on DHTML changes in response to the user's actions. That change occurs because the objects on the Web page, defined by the DOM standard, are manipulated by scriptlets. These scriptlets are routines written in a scripting language, such as JavaScript.

The Rollover Effect

One of the most common DHTML elements in Web pages is the *rollover effect*. When the user points to a button on a Web page, that button changes color or format. By high-lighting a button this way, you help show the user that the button is being pointed to and that a mouse click will activate that button.

In the days before DHTML, when a user clicked a button, the click sent a message back to the Web page's server to fetch another page or part of a page. The user had to wait for this to occur.

Buttons that appear on Web pages often have graphic images on them. The graphic image may have the button's text and color and a design of some kind. DHTML JavaScript code can handle the rollover effect by changing the picture on the button to another picture. In other words, when the DHTML's JavaScript code senses that the mouse pointer is over the button, the code switches the graphic image to a different image. The second image might be a brighter or otherwise highlighted image of a button.

In Hour 19, "Scripting with JavaScript," you saw a listing that produced a JavaScript rollover effect. Listing 20.1 repeats that same JavaScript code.

LISTING 20.1 JavaScript Code That Replaces the Image on a Button

```
<HTML>
<BODY>
 <A HREF="javascript:"
  onmouseover="changeOver('Img1');"
  onmouseout="changeOut('Img1');">
  <IMG NAME=Img1 SRC="Img1.gif">
 </A><BR>
 <A HREF="javascript:"
  onmouseover="changeOver('Img2');"
  onmouseout="changeOut('Img2');">
  <IMG NAME=Img2 SRC="Img2.gif">
 </A><BR>

<SCRIPT>
function changeOver(anImage) {
   if (anImage == "Img1") {
     document.images[anImage].src = "Img1over.gif";
   }
   else if (anImage == "Img2") {
     document.images[anImage].src = "Img2over.gif";
   }
}

function changeOut(anImage) {
   if (anImage == "Img1") {
     document.images[anImage].src = "Img1.gif";
   }
   else if (anImage == "Img2") {
     document.images[anImage].src = "Img2.gif";
   }
}
</SCRIPT>
</BODY>
</HTML>
```

20

One of the first signs of a DHTML Web page is the `javascript` keyword. Listing 20.1 implements the `javascript` command as follows:

```
<A HREF="javascript:"
 onmouseover="changeOver('Img1');"
 onmouseout="changeOut('Img1');">
 <IMG NAME=Img1 SRC="Img1.gif">
 </A>
```

By the way, if you save this code with the `.htm` filename extension, the code will not seem to work because you will probably not have the required image files on your computer (`Img1.gif`, `Img2.gif`, `Img1over.gif`, and `Img2over.gif`). You need to have two graphic button images and two similar button images that appear when the user rolls the mouse pointer over one of the two buttons. If you want to take the time to locate four graphic images with the `.gif` filename extension, you can copy those images to the disk folder where you store Listing 20.1 and change the `.gif` filenames in the code to your files' names. Then, when you load the text file into your Web browser (use the File, Open menu option), two images will appear that will change to the other two as you run your mouse over them.

`onmouseover` is a JavaScript command that checks to see if the mouse pointer is over one of the buttons. If the mouse pointer rests over the image (named `Img1` here), then the `onmouseover` JavaScript command triggers the `changeOver` procedure that then executes. `changeOver` replaces the currently displayed image with another in this code:

```
function changeOver(anImage) {
    if (anImage == "Img1") {
      document.images[anImage].src = "Img1over.gif";
    }
    else if (anImage == "Img2") {
      document.images[anImage].src = "Img2over.gif";
    }
}
```

When the user's mouse pointer leaves the image, the `onmouseout` event triggers the `changeOut` code's execution to restore the original image as follows:

```
function changeOut(anImage) {
    if (anImage == "Img1") {
      document.images[anImage].src = "Img1.gif";
    }
    else if (anImage == "Img2") {
      document.images[anImage].src = "Img2.gif";
    }
}
```

For an example of button rollover effects, visit the Brady Games site at `http://www.bradygames.com/` to see what happens when you point to a button on the page. Figure 20.3 shows the rollover effect, which not only changes the appearance of the button but also displays a description of what clicking that button produces. (The black-and-white figure cannot show the button's color change.)

FIGURE 20.3

The button and its description change when the user points to the button.

Appears due to mouse
pointer over button

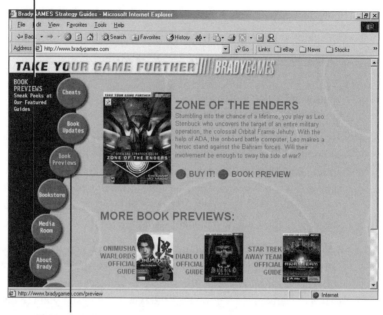

Color changes

XML and Its Impact

How important is XML? The Gartner Group, an Internet research company, says that 80% of business-to-business (also known as *B2B*) traffic uses XML. XML is much like HTML, and in many ways it is identical. The W3C has developed a standard called *XHTML* that combines both the HTML standard and XML. Generally speaking, when programmers discuss XML, however, they are including the HTML code that surrounds the specific XML also. In this light, an XML listing includes standard HTML command tags, but XML command tags are far more numerous.

An XML coder can define and use, on-the-fly, new command tag elements that are also available to other Web pages. An example of a command tag in HTML would be <BR>, as you know from Hour 18, but for XML, no pre-defined set of tags exists. You define your own, called *elements* or sometimes *tag elements* in XML terminology. In defining your own XML command elements, you are using the extensible portion of XML. Code examples throughout the rest of this hour demonstrate how the XML coder does this. The tags are programmer-defined and help to clarify and document data that the XML represents as you'll see in the rest of this hour.

20

Whereas HTML describes the format of a Web page, XML describes the data content of a Web page. XML does not tell the Web browser where and how to place Web page elements as HTML does, but instead, defines data inside the Web page.

Consider the following possible XML section from a Web page:

```
<CARMAKE>Swifty</CARMAKE>
<CARMODEL>Dove</CARMODEL>
<ENGINEPARTNO>546-32Xs</ENGINEPARTNO>
<WHOLESALE>$21,039</WHOLESALE>
<SUGGESTEDRETAIL>$32,483</SUGGESTEDRETAIL>
```

Over time, industries will begin to standardize their XML tag elements. For example, automobile Web site designers might standardize <ENGINEPARTNO> to designate any automobile manufacturer's engine part number. As other automobile Web developers standardize and use <ENGINEPARTNO> (and its corresponding ending tag of </ENGINEPARTNO>), Web pages can be combined, borrowed, and used as the basis of other Web pages that also contain such parts.

When learning XML, you would not learn a <CARMAKE> tag because no such tag exists. As soon as a Web site uses <CARMAKE>, however, the tag is in use and can then be used in that context for all pages on the site. As a Web designer, you will learn the standard XML tag elements being used for the type of Web site you are developing. Your XML elements then define data categories, not actual data specifics.

One problem at this time is that XML is too new for globally agreed upon definitions to exist. Even within industries, one company might create XML tag elements that differ greatly from those of another company. The move toward organization will come only as companies that support XML begin to agree on a standard and that standard grows. For example, if your company's Web site is to interact with a vendor's XML-based Web site, one of you will have to adopt the other's XML elements, or a combined system must be put into place. This agreement process will continue and grow as more companies begin to move to XML.

Schemas will simplify XML element-sharing

Companies are beginning to adopt a *schema* or *schemata* approach to sharing each other's XML tag elements. A schema attempts to map one company's XML elements to another's and allows for a free exchange of data between them without either company having to re-write their own XML definitions. A DTD, explained in subsequent sections, is one approach at a schema that matches XML elements between companies.

Data companies such as BizTalk are developing schema-based *frameworks* that, on a large multi-company, multi-national scale, will map the XML elements among a large number of companies. This schema approach means that a company can go ahead and define their own elements without fear of mismatching another company with whom they associate. Of course, the schema maps must constantly be updated to make this work.

For the first time, Web search engines can begin to search across industries for categories of items instead of performing time-consuming, tedious, and resource-grabbing searches for specific text embedded in Web pages. A search engine could scour Web page tags for the exact tag `<ENGINEPARTNO>` to quickly locate specific engine parts for automobile manufacturers instead of wasting search time and resources scanning nonautomobile Web site inventories.

HTML has a defined set of formatting and hyperlink tags, and you could very easily learn all of them. XML is defined as Web designers use it. You'll never learn all the XML tag elements, because new elements will continually be developed as long as the language is in use.

Multiple Platforms

Mainframes and PCs are not the only computing devices used today. On handheld palm devices that display Web content on small monochrome screens; content-limited WebTV screens; control devices wired to the Web in the home, such as security cameras and control panels; and cell phones that display 8-line Web pages, Web content is being routed to many devices other than the typical color PC screen.

If a company wants to enable its Web pages for PC users and for every other possible device that can display Web content, they will have to modify their PC-formatted, HTML-based Web pages, implementing a different HTML code to format the page for a cell phone. The company then will have to change the code again so that the page works on WebTV. With HTML, the conversion is tedious. With XML elements, the Web designers need only to transfer the XML tag elements and the content to each new format—a much simpler process. A special set of XML definitions called DTD, or *Document Type Definition,* contains the XML definitions and, as long as all Web pages adopt the same DTD, they can each interact and share data.

20

Don't discount XML's importance. Although the definition of XML may seem fuzzy (it still is), many companies are moving to convert all their Web pages from straight HTML code to XML code. Cisco, Incorporated, claims to process 95% of its business over the Internet. When Cisco converted to XML in mid-2000, it began saving $175 million annually over traditional HTML-based technology.

HTML is still, and will always be, required. Without HTML, a Web page cannot appear, no matter how many DHTML scriptlets and no matter how many XML tag elements you place in a file. HTML is the Web browser's only known language. Special extensions to HTML, supported by today's browsers, help to extend the routine HTML jobs, such as describing the format of text and graphics. The HTML still defines most of a Web page's appearance and hyperlinks. The XML is an internal layer that defines the Web page's data. As you will see in the example built in the next few sections, XML works internally on a Web page while HTML performs the external formatting.

A Complete XML Example

In spite of the freedom that a Web programmer has with XML, certain rules do apply. All XML code should conform to two requirements:

1. XML code must be well formed, meaning that there is only one root, or base, XML element and all others extend from that one, as you'll see in an example that follows. XML should begin with the `<?xml version=1.0?>` tag, which is never used in another context. Browsers do not handle poorly defined XML code as well as they do HTML. In addition, unlike HTML, case is critical so if you use uppercase XML elements once, you must continue to use uppercase. If you write badly formed HTML code, such as forgetting a terminating tag before another beginning tag, a browser will not display an error message; instead, the browser will show an incomplete sentence or a badly placed graphic image. When some of the HTML is incorrect, later HTML code is affected. Bad XML code produces actual error messages.

2. The XML code should be valid. Simple XML code cannot be validated, but by using the XML technology called Document Type Definition (DTD), you ensure that your XML code follows your own validation rules.

The next two sections explore the concepts of well-formed XML code and XML-based validity. You will see how to determine if XML code is well formed and you will see how to define the DTD. By the time you finish these sections, you will be well on your way to comprehending the goals of XML.

Using Well-Formed XML Code

Listing 20.2 contains an XML file. The file is a description of a company's personnel records. Listing 20.2 shows only one employee in the file.

LISTING 20.2   A Well-Formed XML File

```
<?XML version="1.0"?>
<LIST>
   <EMPLOYEE>
      <FIRSTNAME>James</FIRSTNAME>
      <LASTNAME>Wilson</LASTNAME>
      <EMP_CODES>
         <STARTCODE>C8</STARTCODE>
         <CURRENTCODE>B7</CURRENTCODE>
      </EMP_CODES>

      <EMPLOYEES_MANAGED>
         <EMP_MNGD>RC Collins</EMP_MNGD>
         <EMP_MNGD>Chrisy Norton</EMP_MNGD>
         <EMP_MNDG>Ted Bell</EMP_MNGD>
         <EMP_MNGD>Mavis Gray</EMP_MNGD>
      </EMPLOYEES_MANAGED>

      <REVIEW_TEXT>
James Wilson has maintained consistency as an above-average
employee of the company. He works well with his peers as
well as his subordinates.
      </REVIEW_TEXT>
   </EMPLOYEE>
</LIST>
```

The location of the starting and ending XML elements determines groups within the file. For example, this employee, James Wilson, manages four other employees. The elements `<EMPLOYEES_MANAGED>` and `</EMPLOYEES_MANAGED>` enclose the names of the four employees whom Mr. Wilson manages. If Mr. Wilson managed 20 employees, 20 names would appear between `<EMPLOYEES_MANAGED>` and `</EMPLOYEES_MANAGED>`. The name of each employee Mr. Wilson manages is enclosed between `<EMP_MNGD>` and `</EMP_MNGD>` elements. The XML element `<LIST>` is known as the root element here, just as `<HTML>` would be the root command tag of HTML code, because all other XML elements extend from the `<LIST>` element.

Listing 20.2 is well formed. No XML-compatible browser (one that understands XML by containing an *XML processor* that recognizes XML) will have a problem with the file. However, if this code's author had not grouped the tags properly, the browser would issue an error message.

Here is a badly formed section of code that would not work:

```
<EMPLOYEES_MANAGED>
   <EMP_MNGD></EMPLOYEES_MANAGED>RC Collins</EMP_MNGD>
   <EMP_MNGD>Chrisy Norton</EMP_MNGD>
   <EMP_MNGD>Ted Bell</EMP_MNGD>
   <EMP_MNGD>Mavis Gray</EMP_MNGD>
```

20

The closing </EMPLOYEES_MANAGED> tag is out of place. The employee names would not appear within the managed employees group, the goal of the grouping would be lost, and the mismatched start and end tags would cause the browser problems. The <EMPLOYEES_MANAGED> and </EMPLOYEES_MANANGED> tags should enclose the names of the employees Mr. Wilson manages.

Validating XML Code

In many ways, badly formed XML code acts like a syntax error in a regular, compiled, programming language if your browser includes an XML processor that is able to properly parse, or understand, valid XML code. As with a syntax error, badly formed XML code produces an error message. Invalid XML code acts just as a logic error acts in a regular, compiled program. That is, the browser issues no error message, but the displayed Web page will not conform to the developer's goals. Bad data is likely to appear due to the invalid XML.

Suppose you omitted a required piece of data within an XML file, such as an employee's last name. The first few lines of such a file might look like this:

```
<?XML version="1.0"?>
<LIST>
   <EMPLOYEE>
      <FIRSTNAME>James</FIRSTNAME>
      <LASTNAME></LASTNAME>
      <EMP_CODES>
         <STARTCODE>C8</startcode>
         <CURRENTCODE>B7</CURRENTCODE>
      </EMP_CODES>

      <EMPLOYEES_MANAGED>
```

Such an entry in the XML code is invalid, assuming that all employees have last names. Such an omission could be overlooked, and a search of employee records wouldn't turn up this employee because you failed to include the name.

Of course, some tags might not contain data, and such an omission could still be correct. For example, employees who are not in a supervisory position would not have any employees beneath them. The content of <employees_managed> and </employees_managed> could be left blank until the employees in question were promoted to positions in which they had subordinates.

Given the fact that XML codes are defined as you go along (until *de facto* standards are determined by a company or industry sector), you will want to eliminate all possible mistakes, such as the omission of required data.

Therefore, the second half of learning XML requires that you master DTD. DTD is simply a set of rules you make up for every XML tag element that you define.

Suppose you make a DTD entry for `<employees_managed>` that says the group may be left blank. A DTD entry for `<lastname>`, however, states that `<lastname>` can never be omitted. If you fail to list a last name, the browser will read your DTD, see the problem, and alert you to the data error.

If you write XML-based Web pages that are to be used in conjunction with another company's XML, you will want to use a uniform set of XML tag elements. Therefore, you will need access to the other company's DTD. The DTD appears right inside the Web page's source code and is open to all. Therefore, locating a Web page's DTD is as easy as looking at the Web page's HTML source code. In most browsers, you'll simply select View, Source to do just that.

Keep in mind that this XML file might contain hundreds of employees. Creating a complete set of DTD rules for one employee's entry would be overkill, but creating one set of DTD rules that covers one, ten, or hundreds of similar entries in the XML file makes a lot of sense. DTD entries ensure that you follow your own requirements.

Specifying the DTD

One requirement of a DTD is defining whether an entry requires data or can be left blank. As indicated in the previous section, the `<EMPLOYEES_MANAGED>` element can be left blank if the employee doesn't supervise others, but the employee's last name is required.

The first line in your XML's DTD code might be this:

```
<!DOCTYPE LIST [
```

The opening bracket begins the DTD. Most of the subsequent lines in the DTD will follow this format:

```
<!ELEMENT XMLelement (requiredEl1, requiredEl2, requiredEl3, ...)>
```

XMLelement is the element you are defining, and the elements between the parentheses are those that must appear between the opening and closing *XMLel* elements and the order in which they must appear. Consider the following line:

```
<!ELEMENT EMPLOYEE (FIRSTNAME, LASTNAME, EMP_CODES, EMPLOYEES_MANAGED,
[ic:ccc]REVIEW_TEXT)>
```

This DTD entry states that the tags following it must appear between the `<EMPLOYEE>` and `</EMPLOYEE>` element pair. If the XML code does not conform to the DTD's requirement, the code will be invalid and the browser can issue an error.

20

> Without any kind of DTD, your browser has no way to determine the valid-
> ity of your XML code. Therefore, you should always define a DTD for all
> XML code you write.

If the DTD contained only the single line defined so far here, it would be rather limiting. With the !ELEMENT definition just shown, the DTD provides for no optional elements or data values between the elements.

DTD uses the #PCDATA keyword to designate text. #PCDATA is a data type that your XML code will replace with a specific value. Consider this DTD entry:

```
<!ELEMENT FIRSTNAME (#PCDATA)>
```

This entry tells the browser that the <FIRSTNAME> element must have a data value. The #PCDATA tells the browser that something must appear between the <FIRSTNAME> and </LASTNAME> elements.

So far, you have seen the following lines of the DTD built:

```
<!DOCTYPE LIST [
  <!ELEMENT EMPLOYEE (FIRSTNAME, LASTNAME, EMP_CODES, EMPLOYEES_MANAGED,
[ic:ccc]REVIEW_TEXT)>
  <!ELEMENT FIRSTNAME (#PCDATA)>
```

To summarize, you (and your browser) now know the following about the XML requirements:

- A DTD is being defined that will state the format of the XML entries.
- The <EMPLOYEES> and </EMPLOYEES> elements must include (at a minimum) the following elements (their end elements are assumed): <FIRSTNAME>, <LASTNAME>, <EMP_CODES>, <EMPLOYEES_MANAGED>, and <REVIEW_TEXT>.
- A value is required for the <FIRSTNAME> element.

The next line indicates that a last name also is required for all employees:

```
<!ELEMENT lastname (#PCDATA)>
```

Assume that the <EMP_CODES> element must contain a <STARTCODE> (because all employ-ees started working at some point) and a <CURRENTCODE>. This must be some kind of pay code or years-of-service code. Therefore, depending on how long the employee has worked, the current code may be different from the start code, but both are required. The following DTD entry ensures that both elements are included:

```
<!ELEMENT EMP_CODES (STARTCODE, CURRENTCODE)>
```

Both elements require values even though the values may be identical if the employee has not worked long. The following ensures this:

```
<!ELEMENT STARTCODE (#PCDATA)>
<!ELEMENT CURRENTCODE (#PCDATA)>
```

The DTD is coming right along. No way yet exists for optional data, however. You can designate optional tags using the character *. The * represents zero or more items. An example will clarify this character.

<EMPLOYEES_MANAGED> is the first element that may or may not include other elements, such as the <EMP_MNGD> elements. You would use * to designate the optional elements:

```
<!ELEMENT EMPLOYEES_MANAGED (EMP_MNGD)*>
```

The asterisk informs the browser that <EMP_MNGD> might appear between <EMPLOYEES_MANAGED> one or more times or not at all.

Listing 20.3 shows the complete DTD with the XML code that it defines. As you can see, the DTD appears before the XML code that it defines.

LISTING 20.3   DTD and Corresponding XML

```
<?XML version="1.0"?>

<!DOCTYPE LIST [
<!ELEMENT list (employee)>
 <!ELEMENT EMPPLOYEE (FIRSTNAME, LASTNAME, EMP_CODES, EMPLOYEES_MANAGED,
[ic:ccc]REVIEW_TEXT)>
    <!ELEMENT emp_mngd (#PCDATA)>
    <!ELEMENT FIRSTNAME (#PCDATA)>
    <!ELEMENT LASTNAME (#PCDATA)>
    <!ELEMENT EMP_CODES (STARTCODE, CURRENTCODE)>
      <!ELEMENT STARTCODE (#PCDATA)>
      <!ELEMENT CURRENTCODE (#PCDATA)>
    <!ELEMENT EMPLOYEES_MANAGED (EMP_MNGD)*>
    <!ELEMENT REVIEW_TEXT (#PCDATA)*>
]>

<LIST>
   <EMPLOYEE>
      <FIRSTNAME>James</FIRSTNAME>
      <LASTNAME>Wilson</LASTNAME>
      <EMP_CODES>
         <STARTCODE>C8</STARTCODE>
```

20

continues

LISTING 20.3   Continued

```
            <CURRENTCODE>B7</CURRENTCODE>
        </EMP_CODES>

        <EMPLOYEES_MANAGED>
            <EMP_MNGD>RC Collins</EMP_MNGD>
            <EMP_MNGD>Chrissy Norton</EMP_MNGD>
            <EMP_MNGD>Ted Bell</EMP_MNGD>
            <EMP_MNGD>Mavis Gray</EMP_MNGD>
        </EMPLOYEES_MANAGED>

        <REVIEW_TEXT>
Mr. Wilson has maintained consistency as an above-average
employee of the company. He works well with his peers as
well as his subordinates.
        </REVIEW_TEXT>
    </EMPLOYEE>
</LIST>
```

Summary

DHTML activates Web pages by enabling the use of objects that can be manipulated by scripting code such as JavaScript or VBScript. DHTML is not fully supported by every browser in use today, but it will be in the future. (By then, another technology will probably replace DHTML; such is the way with these things.) Most Web sites can safely use it now because most current browsers support it, at least partially. DHTML enables you to create Web pages that are more active, adding to the user's browsing experience.

You now have an understanding of basic XML language. Perhaps more important than the language specifics is understanding why XML is so vital to the Web's future. The XML elements define data and don't format a Web page as HTML does. Your Web page will still need HTML to format the look and behavior of the page, but the underlying XML code will make your page more easily accessible by sites that recognize the XML elements you use. In the future, search engines and other processes will be able to perform more accurate searching, sorting, and manipulation of Web data.

Q&A

Q Can I learn DHTML and XML and skip right over HTML?

A No, because neither DHTML nor XML are replacements for HTML. Rather, they utilize HTML to do their jobs. Knowledge of HTML is a prerequisite to coding in either DHTML or XML.

Q How can I get a list of XML tag elements used within my industry?

A At the present, that's the question on everybody's mind. If your company plans to convert your Web pages to XML-compatible Web pages, you should contact your major vendors to see what they use. If nobody you deal with uses XML yet, then you will be the first and you can develop your own library of XML elements, so when subsequent companies want to interface to your XML, they will have to get the XML from you, or you'll both have to agree on a compromise standard. In addition, the Web site http://www.schema.org contains excellent XML element information as well as a blueprint for a replacement for DTD called *schemas* that will possibly be widely adopted as a future way to share XML elements among organizations.

Workshop

The quiz questions are provided for your further understanding. For the answers, see Appendix B, "Quiz Answers."

Quiz

1. What does the *D* in DHTML stand for?
2. True or false: DOM treats items on your Web page and your Web browser as objects.
3. How does one refer to DOM objects?
4. What is a rollover effect?
5. Which technology, XML or DHTML, controls Web page dropdown menus and rollover effects?
6. What does XML stand for?
7. What is meant by a well-formed XML document?
8. True or false: When you convert to XML, you must upgrade to an XML-compatible Web browser.
9. What is a DTD??
10. What wildcard character designates optional XML-based tags?

20

Hour **21**

.NET—The Future of Online Programming

One of the most important technologies that will affect online programming in the future is a new technology by Microsoft called .NET. .NET cannot be described in terms of a product or technology because .NET is not new technology, but a way to approach new technology. .NET consists of today's software and hardware tools as well as tomorrow's more advanced ones. Therefore, to master .NET you don't need to master one or more programming languages, a compiler, or a browser; instead, you need to understand how programming fits into the .NET environment and how .NET is poised to fit into the lives of computer users over the next decade or so.

The highlights of this hour include

- Understanding how languages you have learned fit into the framework of .NET
- Mastering the concept of .NET
- Working with multiple online platforms

- Learning the tools required for .NET integration
- Learning how .NET takes advantage of distributed computing environments

Understand What .NET Is

Throughout the earlier hours, you have seen ways to tackle online programming, including Java, HTML, and JavaScript. .NET is a new approach to online and networked technology. Microsoft has developed a new approach to online programming and encapsulated that approach into an umbrella of multiple technologies called .NET.

Microsoft's goal is for .NET to address the needs of users who will live in an always on and connected online world. The way people utilize computers should change dramatically in the next few years as technologies improve. For example, bandwidth, which is the speed and size of online data flow, will only get faster for most users. The use of distributed computing will increase as individual computers become more powerful and affordable. New hardware with online connections will appear in new places and in new forms, such as in automobiles. Web browsers aren't just for desktops anymore. The programmer inside the .NET environment must understand the goals of .NET so that programming can be understood from this new perspective.

Increased Bandwidth

The vast majority of online users still use relatively slow modems to connect to the Internet. Modem connections simply don't allow for streaming video and other high-powered services at the typical user's desktop. In the future, users will adopt faster bandwidth, and .NET attempts to redefine online computing in that faster world.

Today's tools for Web site creation, data transfers, and interacting with the local user's computer will not suffice once true bandwidth comes into focus for most users. Microsoft is positioning the .NET approach for a more standardized way of interacting in such a highly connected world.

Microsoft is not the only game in town. Other developers are trying for a similar universal programming and operating framework. *J2EE* (*Java 2 Platform, Enterprise Edition*) is a Java-based platform with goals similar to Microsoft's .NET strategy. Hewlett-Packard is developing the OpenView approach where they offer support for both Java-based and .NET technologies. In addition, Oracle has developed the Dynamic Services initiative that utilizes Oracle database technology to combine data and online connectivity for data sharing.

Obviously, Microsoft wants to profit by defining the environments and languages used. Users and other companies should also benefit, however, because when everybody is working within the same parameters, compatibility issues dwindle and product launches will occur more quickly and more accurately. As more companies adapt to the .NET way of doing things, more systems will communicate with each other, less programming and training will be required, and happier users will result more quickly.

Distributed Computing

.NET describes and defines ways to leverage *distributed computing* power. Distributed computing is the term applied to computers that are networked and share processing power. The early years of computing saw *centralized computing* where one large mainframe computer performed all calculations and data processing tasks. Users would connect to the mainframes from computer terminals and slow microcomputers with modems, the mainframe would process all the data, and the terminals and micros simply provided the input and output to the larger system.

Computing technology has advanced rapidly. Today, and even more so in the future, the following *distributed computing* environment exists: many powerful small and large computers are connected to each other, often via high-speed Internet connections. By combining the processing power of several of these computers, two or more of these computers can share the processing power to accomplish one task. In other words, a cluster of computers on the Internet might work together to solve a graphical computation, another cluster might be used to sort huge databases, and another might be used for scientific calculations such as weather forecasting. As a programmer, you will have to deal with a distributed world, where your programs will be communicating to other programs across the earth, sharing data and possibly even sharing computing power.

At the present, distributed computing exists in many forms. *Client-server computers* exist in many networked environments; the users sit at their computers and run programs served to them by a central computer on the network. The server might also hold most of the network's data.

If you've used the Internet very much, you've no doubt used a more advanced form of distributed computing called *peer-to-peer* computing. A central computer acts as a broker between other computers, acting as the traffic cop between data and programs shared between the computers. The most obvious example is *Napster* and other Napster-like systems. Users all over the world, with no direct link to one another, share files.

Another form of distributed computing is in widespread use today in chat rooms and online messaging services such as MSN Messenger, shown in Figure 21.1. Users sit at their own computers, but their communications and available resources are managed by central computers elsewhere. The two people talking with each other within the instant chat session might be thousands of miles apart.

21

In the most recent Microsoft operating system, Windows XP, MSN Messenger is more integrated than previous operating systems. Programmers in C++, C#, and Visual Basic (other languages will follow) will use a *Messenger API* (for *Application Programming Interface*), which is a set of routines that enables you to call built-in functions to send data or retrieve data from a remote Messenger connection. All of the connections will be initiated by the users and performed by the operating systems, but your programs will be able to ride on that connection by calling these API routines and sending data as arguments to these routines.

FIGURE 21.1

Distributed computing technologies include instant chat sessions such as MSN Messenger.

The problem with instant messaging and other peer-to-peer distributed systems is that there are so many technologies available. Such choice in systems is often welcomed but when one company develops a messaging system, they develop a proprietary and brand-new system, thus new standards emerge, and communication between systems gets more difficult. The API will work to reduce the confusion and complexity of different systems using the Messenger path to communicate.

A recent Microsoft ad reads, "Two competitors just merged but working together will be easy since their software plays well with others." The ad goes on to say this communication between the merged companies is made possible due to .NET. The promise is that running different systems is no longer the nightmare it used to be. Cross-platform sharing will be simpler thanks to the API routines given to programmers through supported languages. People will collaborate more easily across boundaries. That is, when .NET is finalized and fully implemented.

Changing Hardware

You have a good idea of the technology available today and the technology that will be available tomorrow. Laptops probably will become more powerful, lighter, and able to last longer on one charge as processors and battery technology improve. Palm devices, cell phones, digital cameras, wireless Internet, and MP3 players will probably converge into multicapability devices.

Although predictions can be made, nobody can foresee all future technology. Perhaps some new device will appear that stores terabytes of information in a wristwatch so the Library of Congress can accompany you wherever you go.

Getting new devices to talk to other similar devices is simple. Getting new devices to talk to other types of new devices and to older devices, and to have a path to talk to subsequently invested devices, is another story. Microsoft wants to make .NET's net wide enough to handle just about anything that comes along.

There's no way Microsoft can create .NET to handle every future new device but .NET certainly is comprehensive enough (and still undefined enough) to cover a lot of ground. New hardware and software makers don't have to conform to .NET's standards but they risk losing out on being connected to other devices and software that do conform to .NET's framework.

The .NET Approach

Although .NET is fundamentally a general approach to tomorrow's online world, .NET does encompass several specific tools. By adopting some tools today within the .NET strategy, Microsoft hopes to standardize the way developers implement technologies that will be used tomorrow.

In describing specific .NET technologies, this section shows how those technologies conform to .NET's approach. Only after adopting .NET-approved technologies, and only after adopting the .NET-approved approach for developing online technologies, can a company adhere to .NET's design.

The languages and tools described here are not always specifically linked to .NET. For example, XML is a language behind Web pages that is in great use today, and the full .NET strategy has yet to be released. Just because your company uses XML does not in any way mean that your company is adapting to the .NET way of doing things. Nevertheless, companies that do want to shift to .NET will adopt XML because XML is a useful tool for implementing .NET, and XML is a .NET-approved language for Web communications.

21

.NET's Operating Environment

To fully grasp the huge technology blanket called .NET, you must understand a plethora of online computing technologies. The following sections explore some of the more common online technologies involved with .NET.

XML Is Mainstream

XML plays a huge role in .NET because of XML's general nature. In Hour 20, "Dynamic HTML and XML," you learned about XML and saw how XML will improve the way that online systems talk with each other.

XML allows two or more companies to define their own HTML command tags that not only format text and place hyperlinks but also describe the data on the Web page. Not only can you place your inventory online and format that inventory with HTML, but you can also compose and apply XML commands to describe categories of your inventory such as <YARDTOOLS> and <LONGTERMBONDS>. When you share your XML command tag set with those who do business with you, they can utilize your XML tags to automate *data-mining* (a search for data) more quickly.

For example, without XML, a company searching your inventory will have to enter a specific part number or description and search through your entire data set to locate items that match. By issuing a search of predetermined command tags that describe the category that interests them, a vendor or another company working with yours can scan your inventory by the command tag topic and locate all items within that topic without having to search for specific data values.

SOAP Washes XML

SOAP stands for *Simple Object Access Protocol* and is a new Internet and communications *protocol*. A protocol simply determines how one computer communicates with another. Perhaps you've heard of *HTTP (HyperText Transfer Protocol)*. Actually, if you've ever typed a full Web page address, you've probably typed http, as in http://www.PearsonEd.com/. SOAP is a new protocol that better supports XML and the other .NET-enabled technologies that will transfer over the Internet and along traditional networking lines.

SOAP defines a common data path so that different parts of .NET on different pieces of computing devices can communicate with each other. When your program needs to route data to a user, if your program routes the data through a predetermined SOAP protocol–defined set of API routines, your program's output will look just as good on a SOAP-enabled cell phone Web browser as it looks on a 21-inch plasma monitor. Although the cell phone's display may not be as colorful or as detailed, the output will appear in a format suited for the device it appears on.

The Common Language Runtime

.NET will support a *Common Language Runtime* (*CLR*), whereby the .NET-compatible operating system on any device will be able to execute any program written in a .NET-supported language that compiles into the CLR's special code.

CLR might sound difficult to understand at first, but it's simple. A .NET-compatible language such as Visual Basic, Visual C++, or C# will not compile to a specific machine, as is historically the case for computer languages, but rather will compile to a common machine language. Every .NET-based operating system will emulate this common language. So, in theory, a single program written in C++ could run, unaltered, on a PC, a palm device, and on WebTV, assuming those three devices were designed to support the .NET framework.

By the way, expect .NET-based versions of Microsoft's languages to be given new names. Visual Basic will probably become VB.NET, Visual C++ will probably become Visual C++ .Net and so on. C#, however, looks to still be called C#. (As you'll see in a later section, C# is a language designed specifically for .NET applications.) All of these languages will compile into CLR code that will operate in any .NET-enabled operating environment.

> If a programmer learns a language that compiles to a CLR, that program runs on any device that supports .NET. A different compiler and a different language no longer have to be developed for each kind of computing device.

ASP.NET is a Better ASP

Getting a handle on *ASP*, *Active Server Pages*, is almost as difficult as understanding .NET. ASP does many things, including streamlining the ability to provide software-for-rent over the Internet. Instead of purchasing a Microsoft Office software license, for example, you'll simply rent Office for a specific period of time. You'll access the software via the Internet, getting key components from your online connections, and when the rental meter runs out, you either plug the meter one more time or stop using the program.

ASP is just a scripting form of a programming language that Web pages access. Instead of writing an installation routine to place your applications on a single computer, your application will come with an online ASP script that sends the program to users who have properly rented the software and the application will operate for the prepaid amount of time.

21

These programs run on the *server* (the system sending out the Web pages) and not on the end user's computer (as a Java program would). Therefore, the server's owner can have more control over the program and can check information against a central database, as might be done on a Web site with credit card processing. The user buys something and sends the card information to the server, and the server, via ASP, looks to a credit card database, checks the credit line, and processes the order while the user waits for confirmation.

ASP.NET (sometimes referred to as ASP+) takes ASP to the next step by making ASP code work in the CLR platform. Again, CLR means that any .NET device can run the program downloaded from the online connection after running the ASP script to verify that the user has the permission to get the program.

C# Could Replace Java

C# is a new language, developed specifically for .NET, to act as a scripting language for applications and Web pages.

C#, like Java, is based on the C and C++ programming languages. C# applications will be able to transfer to an end user's computer, embedded inside a Web page, and execute on the end user's machine. The end user's computer must be able to understand the CLR that the C# code will require. Hence, the need exists for *both* the developer and the end-user to have .NET tools. As mentioned earlier, the full .NET implementation will probably not be released until Blackcomb, the version of Windows slated to be released after Windows XP.

If .NET takes off the way Microsoft expects, C# could very well take over the Java programming world. Both are object-oriented and both work well in an online environment. With Microsoft's muscle, C# could gain market acceptance over Java. Microsoft has talked about producing a Java-to-C# converter, and even if Microsoft does not do this, other companies will. In addition, .NET-enabled Java engines will also allow straight Java code to work as though it were written in C#. Therefore, the large collection of currently installed Java code is not made obsolete by C# and the other .NET-based technologies.

Visual Studio and .NET

Microsoft's standard programming platform for years has been Visual Studio. Visual Studio is an integrated editor and compiler that supports Visual Basic, Visual C++, and other Microsoft languages. Visual Studio will change somewhat with the implementation of .NET. The Visual Studio .NET will support all the .NET languages, including C#, and will also provide support for a standard set of *Web forms*, or a uniform method of producing online forms and graphical pages that all .NET-based languages can access and manipulate. Therefore, you can take your knowledge of Visual Basic and use

Visual Basic .NET to compile your application for the new .NET environment. By doing so, you make it simple to change the application to use the .NET APIs and share data cross the .NET connections.

> All program development for .NET will be done from a common platform, the Visual Studio .NET. Here the learning curve is lowered; you don't have to learn a new programming editor if you learn a new language. Also, any .NET language will be able to access form-based information over the Web because access to such Web forms will be uniform.

MSN and Messenger and Hotmail

Microsoft's online Internet system, *MSN*, the *Microsoft Network* Internet Service Provider, is quickly gaining new users by promotions Microsoft is backing such as a free 2-year MSN contract with the purchase of a new PC. In addition to MSN, Microsoft also supports Hotmail.com, a free Internet-based e-mail service.Hotmail.com is the premiere Internet-based e-mail service and products such as Microsoft Outlook 2002 and Outlook Express integrate with Hotmail.com well.

Along with MSN Messenger (see Figure 21.1), Microsoft Network and Hotmail are ultimately related to .NET's framework. Microsoft is planning to leverage all three of these online products and use them as a backbone of .NET's peer-to-peer strategy. You will use these technologies to access other computers on the distributed set of networked .NET computers. Microsoft continues to merge MSN, Hotmail.com, and MSN Messenger into one central system or subscription service, all supporting and related to the .NET framework. A new buzzword has been passed around lately—*Hailstorm*—and it appears that Hailstorm will be the blanket under which these online services will be managed. Microsoft wants Hailstorm to be readily available for any device that can communicate with the Internet, including wireless handheld devices.

.NET's Framework Ties It All Together

Throughout the previous sections and in other information, you've no doubt seen the term *.NET framework* tossed around. The term, known formally in its capitalized form, *.NET Framework*, is simply the name for the overall environment of .NET products, services, and tools. The .NET Framework includes all the languages supported by the .NET initiative, such as C#, and defines a library of objects that all the .NET tools recognize.

21

COM (*Common Object Model*), a concept that has been around for a few years, is a way to refer to computer-related elements as objects. The .NET Framework also extends the COM model. COM is little more than a list of names for common objects throughout the computer's hardware and software. For example, the computer screen can be a COM object, a window on the screen can be a COM object, a toolbar can be a COM object, and a toolbar button can be a COM object. By assigning a name to each of these objects, any language that supports COM (such as Visual C++ and Visual Basic, which have provided some form of COM support for years) can interact with these objects without requiring each language's programmer to relearn new ways of approaching and working with those objects.

All of the .NET Framework's defined objects will be available for XML: the .NET-supported languages, Web-based technologies such as ASP+, and even database-related systems (such as those that currently support *ADO, ActiveX Data Objects*). The .NET Framework tries to incorporate every .NET-approved technology so that any item within the huge (and still not completely defined) umbrella of the .NET Framework can communicate with any other product that uses a technology within the .NET Framework.

Summary

The question, "What is .NET?" is difficult to answer in full simply because .NET is so comprehensive and so forward-looking that it has not been completely defined yet. Nevertheless, you can get a good idea of the trends of .NET technology. At its most fundamental level, the .NET Framework includes all the tools needed, as well as can be foreseen today, to make an integrated and online world work better in the future.

All of the products and languages described here are not, in and of themselves, .NET products; each can be used on its own to accomplish some computing or communications goal. Nevertheless, Microsoft wants every product that falls inside the .NET Framework to communicate with each other no matter what the nature of the underlying hardware happens to be. Tomorrow's hardware will certainly be different from today's, but if the hardware developers follow the .NET strategy, devices should be able to communicate and share information with much greater ease than they can today. As a programmer, it is important to pay attention to where technology is going and how changes could potentially impact your skills.

Q&A

Q Does .NET have to wait for faster and more universal bandwidth? Can't .NET be implemented today?

A Certainly, and many components of .NET are already being used. For example, XML has been in use for a few years and will continue to be used, and grow even more, as .NET matures. The fast bandwidth, especially as more and more of the world gets connected to always-on, high-speed Internet services, changes the nature of online computing in great ways that current modems cannot allow. Individual users and companies cannot take advantage of services such as video distribution and massive communication speeds with the current hardware make-up. .NET is an answer for the future; .NET describes and recommends to hardware and software makers how to design their products so those products communicate with each other once the world does get better connected.

Q What programming language is most closely tied to .NET?

A Most would probably agree that C#, Microsoft's competitor to Java, is at this time the language most closely tied to .NET's new technology. Time will tell whether or not C# becomes a leader over C++ and Java. Given that Microsoft is flexing quite a bit of muscle over .NET and that much more programming will relate, in some way, to the online world as time goes by, you might want to consider adding some knowledge of C# to your programming arsenal.

Workshop

The quiz questions are provided for your further understanding. For the answers, see Appendix B, "Quiz Answers."

Quiz

1. Is .NET a new language, a new operating environment, or a new way to communicate?
2. How has bandwidth affected system development?
3. What is the difference between distributed computing and centralized computing?
4. Need one be proficient at XML programming to be good at .NET technology?
5. True or false: As computing technologies mature, it is more important that different devices learn to talk with one another.

21

6. How do all the .NET languages work on the same device?

7. What is Microsoft's purpose for C#?

8. True or false: Microsoft has a plan to utilize a combination of Hotmail, MSN Messenger, and the Microsoft Network.

9. How does the .NET Framework extend the COM model?

10. What is the purpose for the Common Language Runtime?

PART V
The Business of Programming

Hour

Hour **22**

How Companies Program

This hour attempts to give you an idea of how companies program computers. The focus is on the larger companies with big data processing staffs working on one or more mainframes, minicomputers, and microcomputers. You will also learn about the smaller companies and how they deal with programming staff and other types of computer personnel.

Companies must coordinate their programming efforts to make the best use of their resources. This doesn't always mean that every program wanted by every person gets written. Actually, the allocation of programming talents is one of the data processing manager's primary tasks. You will learn about the different types of available jobs and their titles and how those people interface with one another. After this hour, you will better understand the wording of the employment ads for computer professionals, and you will get an idea of the experience needed to obtain the different jobs in the computer industry.

This hour's lesson is useful to you even if you want to work for a smaller company or start your own. The larger companies have honed the usage of data processing within the corporate umbrella, so seeing how larger companies take care of their programming requests will help you make decisions regarding the computer department you end up in.

Highlights of this hour include:

- Learning about various computer departments in companies
- Paying for a computer department's expenses
- Schooling behind programming: which programming degree is best
- Getting computer experience without a degree or training
- Understanding programming-related jobs
- Performing a structured walkthrough

Data Processing and Other Departments

A company's data processing department often goes by several names. It is known as *DP, Data Processing, Information Services, Information Systems, IS,* and *MIS* (but usually not, strangely enough, by that acronym's meaning: *Management Information Systems*). No matter what the company's employees call the computer department, it is commonly in the center of almost every major new project the company takes on. When a company expansion, acquisition, or merger is about to take place, the data processing department must prepare for the additional computing resources needed. When an engineering project begins, data processing supplies the analysis programs for the engineers (although some engineering departments prefer to write their own programs and keep the central DP department in charge of the business side of the company). Whatever new direction a company takes, its data processing staff is usually involved in some way.

As Figure 22.1 shows, the data processing department writes programs for every other department in the company. Unless the company itself is a software-writing company (such as Symantec or Microsoft), the company's main focus is not going to be software development. The company has other objectives, but the computer department supplies the computer systems needed to keep the other departments working as effectively as they can.

FIGURE 22.1

The data processing department writes programs for the rest of the company.

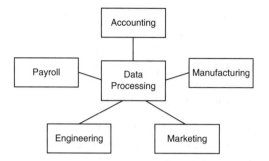

Such a corporate setup is natural. In the early years of business computing, the computer department was placed in the accounting department and governed by the accounting staff. The problem with putting the computer department under direct control of accounting is that accounting will tend to write computer systems it needs and the engineering, marketing, and upper management departments might take a back seat. This doesn't mean that the accounting department would selfishly hoard the computer resources, but the accounting bias would be natural because part of the accounting department's own budget was set aside for the computers and their people.

It was realized in the late 1960s that the data processing department was not directly tied to any one department such as accounting, but, instead, computer people worked for the entire company because they developed programs that the entire company used. Therefore, standalone computer departments started appearing on companies' organizational charts. Organizations began viewing their computer departments as individual cost centers that required their own budget and autonomy. Figure 22.2 shows how the typical data processing department fits into today's organizational charts. As you can see, the data processing department is located on the same level as accounting, payroll, engineering, and the rest of the departments.

FIGURE 22.2

The data processing department is evenly ranked with the company's other departments.

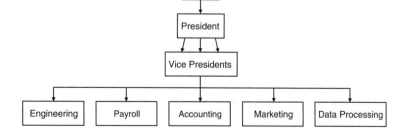

Despite the fact that the data processing department is now autonomous in most companies, that autonomy still doesn't ensure proper allocation of computer resources. A data processing department's resources consist of the hardware, peripheral material, such as paper and tapes, and people. The people are the most expensive resource in a data processing department. Their office spaces, desks, supplies, personal computer equipment, telephones, benefits, and payroll costs all add up to a tidy sum.

No matter how much money a company makes, it cannot allow unlimited spending for the computer resources just described. There must be some checks and balances applied to the money spent in data processing. Unlike other departments, whose worth is measured in dollars received by outside customers, the company itself is the only customer of its data processing department. (Many of the accounting-related departments, such as payroll, often have a similar setup where they work for the rest of the company and produce no outside income of their own.) That is, each department's budget includes a little extra for overhead expenses (lights, desks, paper, telephones, faxes, copying, secretarial, and data processing usage). By collecting some of each department's overhead budget, the company can pay for the data processing resources.

This overhead method of paying for data processing costs doesn't always work well. Overhead is fine for departments such as the accounting department's general ledger group, but the data processing department's skills are more in demand than are other departments'. Without checks and balances of some kind, all the other departments will want programs written with little regard to cost (after all, they've already paid their share of the overhead expense). The computer department can't hire an unlimited supply of programmers just because it receives endless requests for programs.

There isn't enough incentive with the overhead method to curb unreasonable data processing requests. Under this method, departments from all over the company will constantly hound the computer programmers for more programs.

Not all data processing employees work at the company's location. As technology improves, companies are learning that some jobs, such as programming, can be performed from any location, including the employee's own home. For some, telecommuting is available to staff members who want to work from home. These employees must still come into the office for meetings and team evaluation and review but the bulk of their work can be done from a PC-equipped with a modem or another connection to the Internet. Telecommuters save companies money because the company no longer has the expense of the office space and other support services for each employee.

Understanding the Chargeback Approach

22

Companies have been turning away from the overhead approach to another approach called *chargeback*. With chargeback, the data processing center is given no funds from the overhead account (which immediately lowers the overhead expenses for all the other departments). When a department needs a program written, that department requests the program from data processing. The data processing personnel estimate the cost of writing the program and send that estimate back to the original department.

It is then up to the requesting department to accept or reject the charge for the programming. If the department wants the program badly enough, and it has the funds in its budget, that department's management can then transfer those funds to the data processing department's budget. DP then begins to work on the program.

One of the biggest advantages of the chargeback method is that a department cannot ask for the world unless it is willing to pay for it. A department's own limited resources keep it from requesting more than it really needs.

The money being transferred is sometimes referred to as *funny money*. It is made up of internal funds that already belong to the company that are being passed from department to department. The company is still out the cost of the computing resources, but when it comes directly from the requesting department's budget, that department puts its own check-and-balance system in place to determine whether its data processing requests are reasonable.

The nice thing about chargeback is that the data processing department works like a miniature company within the company, supplying services as long as those services are paid for. The company doesn't have to worry about skyrocketing data processing costs; after all, if the money is already in a department's budget and that department wants to spend it on data processing, there is nothing wrong with that. The department will not have those funds to spend on other things, and departments have the right to determine how they spend their own budgets.

> **Rewarding Cost-Conscious Departments**
>
> At the end of the year, the data processing department often finds that it has made a profit from the other departments. Because the profit is really internal funds, that profit is often distributed *back* to the departments that paid for data processing services at the end of the year. The portion of the refund each department gets is proportional to the amount of data processing dollars that department spent during the year.
>
> In this way, the departments know they are spending only as much money as the DP services cost; if they went outside the company for the same services, they would surely pay more because outside DP services would have to make a profit. The profit made by the internal DP department is redistributed back to the company.

Often, the data processing department hires contract programmers when the company's requests grow. If the DP department predicts that its workload will increase for a while, such as when another company is bought by the parent company, the data processing department hires contract programmers. A *contract programmer* is hired to program for a fixed time period. Whether the time is six months, a year, or longer is negotiable.

Generally, contract programmers are paid a large salary because the company doesn't have to pay for the contract programmer's benefits and retirement. There are software companies that hire programmers full-time, giving them benefits and insurance, and then those companies do nothing but hire out their programmers to other companies who need contract programming. Don't rule out an opportunity for contract programming if you are looking for a job. The pay is good, the experience is better, and often a company eventually hires the contract programmers it uses if they turn out to be productive workers.

Computer Jobs

Several times a year, leading magazines and newspapers list the job outlook for the coming year, five years, and ten years. For the last decade, computer jobs have been high on the lists for the best job environments, highest pay, long-term stability, and so forth. That trend will continue for many years. Despite advancements, computer technology is still in its infancy because there are a lot more programs to write than those that have been written in the past.

Companies sometimes allow data processing managers and personnel to work in more relaxed conditions than other departments. Whereas a company's accounting department reports in at 8:00 a.m., clocks out for exactly 60 minutes for lunch, and leaves at 5:00 p.m. on the dot, its DP staff might not all arrive and leave at a uniform time.

22

The reason working conditions can be more relaxed is that programmers, analysts, and computer technicians often need to pursue a problem or programming task until its conclusion, even if that means staying awake in the computer room for 20 hours straight. Programmers love to burn the midnight oil. As you now know, programming is not a science yet, and it might never be one. A large part of programming reflects a person's style and involves a personal commitment to a project. There is a creative side to programming that programmers often find addictive. A programmer who drags in at 11:00 a.m. might be doing so because he stayed up until 4:30 a.m. trying to debug some code for the company.

DP managers understand that the creative spirit that programming brings often comes in spurts. When a programmer gets involved on a programming project, she spends more voluntary overtime than any other type of worker would consider. The trade-off seems to be worth the relaxed attitude in many programming organizations.

Another primary advantage of the programming field over many others is its equal opportunity. Because the business computer industry didn't really begin until the mid-1960s—when the idea of equal pay for equal work was coming into acceptance—equal opportunity was already a part of the computer industry. There are many female, minority, and handicapped employees in data processing departments, from the lowest-paid job to the highest, and the norm has always been for their job and salary to be equal to those of others among them.

Job Titles

You should understand the kinds of jobs that are out there for programmers. Then when you look at the employment ads in newspapers, you'll have an idea of the qualifications and experience needed for the different jobs that are advertised.

The titles described in this section are fairly common in the computer industry, but they are not necessarily universal. Whereas the title for a job in one company might be *Programmer Analyst*, another company might give the same duties a title of *Senior Programmer*. The specific titles mentioned here, although open to change and interpretation, are common enough to describe most of the responsibilities and titles in most computer departments.

Degrees and Certificates

Most computer jobs require some kind of degree or certification (except for the first one, Data Entry Clerk, described later in the section "Data Entry"). There is debate as to whether a two-year associate degree or a four-year bachelor's degree is best. The four-year degree is always better in one respect: you are more founded in the theory behind how computers work and will be able to learn new computer skills faster because of it. However, a four-year degree keeps you out of the work force two years longer than a two-year degree, and two years is a long time in the rapidly changing field of computers.

A two-year programming degree simply doesn't give you enough time to learn much about foundational computing theory. In two years, a college will teach you as many hands-on skills as possible. You'll pick up one or two programming languages (as opposed to four or more in a four-year curriculum). However, you'll find that you can probably enter the programming marketplace at the same job rank and get paid just as much as someone with a four-year degree. The drawback to a two-year degree is that you will not progress through the ranks as fast as someone with a four-year degree.

Perhaps the best of both worlds is possible. You can get a two-year degree, go to work for a company in an entry-level programming job, and get the last two years part-time to finish a four-year degree (most four-year colleges give credit for classes taken for a two-year degree with only a few exceptions here and there). Often a company will pay for, or at least supplement, its employees' continuing education.

> If you have time and money to spare, and who doesn't (seriously, though, there are always scholarships, grants, and loans), consider getting a second degree, either an additional two-year degree or a master's in a field other than programming. A second degree will augment your programming skills. In addition to understanding programming, you will be able to apply those programming skills more readily to an area such as accounting or engineering.

Certification

One of the newest kinds of degrees in the computing scene is not a degree at all. Instead of a degree, a technical certificate shows that you are well skilled in a specific area of computing. Microsoft, Novell, and several other companies offer certification training classes and testing sites. After you adequately pass the certification test for a specific area, you are then certified by the corporation offering the certificate. Job applicants in the computing industry are in much greater demand if they are certified. Unlike a college degree, the certificate demonstrates a specific, measurable ability in a high-demand area of computing, such as networking or operating systems.

The certification tests are rigid and difficult. That's a good thing (if you pass one) because it demonstrates true proficiency in a subject matter. With a certificate, your minimum skill level is known in advance by those hiring.

22

Data Entry

Some computer jobs don't require any programming skills. On the low end of the computer ranks are the *Data Entry Clerks* (often called *Data Entry Operators*). Data Entry Clerks typically need only a high school diploma or its equivalent and some keyboarding skills. Data Entry Clerks, except for the ones who have been with a company for a long time and have often received pay raises, make the lowest salaries of any of the computer jobs in the company.

The life of a Data Entry Clerk is simple; he sits in front of a computer screen typing data into the computer. Typically, as Figure 22.3 shows, all the Data Entry Clerks type on terminals (keyboard and screen combinations) attached to a central computer, usually a mainframe. Eight hours a day, five days a week, the data entry department enters data.

FIGURE 22.3

Data Entry Clerks normally enter data into the same computer.

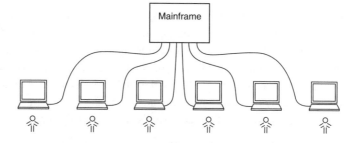

A company's data-entry requirements are massive. Payroll figures, sales figures, government figures, competing statistics, market trends, industry trends, projections, and so forth all must be factored into the company's working atmosphere. The computer programs that process a large amount of data need it to be entered somehow. The larger the organization, the larger the data needs; some companies have hundreds of full-time Data Entry Clerks.

At first glance, you might want to stay away from such a job. The data-entry position, however, can be a powerful first step into a computing career for some people. People with little or no computer training who need experience can begin as a Data Entry Operator. While with the company, they can show a positive attitude, meet others within the company, and receive the typical company insurance and benefits. If the clerk pursues the proper training, she can move into higher programming positions.

As mentioned earlier, a company will often pay for some or all of an employee's part-time education. Therefore, a Data Entry Clerk, with no programming background at all, can take night classes to begin training in programming skills. After he finishes a degree, or is trained adequately enough, the company can move him into one of the entry-level programming jobs. Such a person might never have been able to get a programming job if he had not started out in data entry.

Programming

A person with knowledge of programming, either a self-taught programmer who has a degree in another area, a person who received programming training in a two-year or four-year institution, or a certified programmer, will bypass the data-entry job and move straight into a job actually related to programming. The first job title given to a new programmer hired fresh out of college (or one with little professional programming experience) is usually *Assistant Programmer* (also known as *Junior Programmer* or *Programmer I*). Assistant Programmer is generally considered the entry-level job for anyone without experience as a programmer in another company.

A person typically doesn't remain an Assistant Programmer for more than six or eight months. The job is really a trial period so the company can determine the employee's work attitude, skills, and general benefit to the company. An Assistant Programmer does no new programming. Instead, she works on programs others have written, often doing routine program maintenance. During the trial period, an Assistant Programmer learns how the company operates, gets acquainted with the other computer personnel, and generally "learns the ropes" of the company's working environment.

After a person stays in the Assistant Programmer role for a while, he is usually promoted to *Programmer,* along with a small raise and a pat on the back. The Programmer title means that the company expects good things in the coming years and has trust in the person. It is rare for a person to hold an Assistant Programmer title for several years and still be with the same company.

The Programmer earns a respectable salary for someone with little experience. As mentioned earlier, the computer field pays well, and its titles tend to command higher pay when ranked with similar experience titles in other departments. Therefore, if a person graduates with a programming degree at the same time as someone with a different type of degree, and they both go to work for the same company, the programmer usually has a higher salary after the first year. Of course, this depends on many factors and doesn't always hold, but on the average it does.

22

The title of Programmer is a little misleading. The Programmer does little more than the Assistant Programmer. The Programmer's primary job is to work on programs written by others, maintaining them and modifying them when the need arises. The Programmer rarely gets to write a program from scratch for the first year or two.

After a year or two of success, the Programmer's supervisor will begin to have the Programmer write programs from scratch. Of course, the specifications of the program (the flowchart, output definition, and possibly pseudocode) will already be done and the programmer has to implement only those specifications into a new program. After a while, the Programmer's attitude and on-the-job learning can justify moving into a more advanced job with the title *Senior Programmer* (sometimes called a *Programmer Analyst*).

The Senior Programmer is primarily responsible for writing new programs after being given specifications to follow. The Senior Programmer doesn't have to worry much about maintaining older code because the new Assistant Programmers and Programmers take care of that. (There is nothing wrong or unfair about maintaining programs, but when you train for writing programs, you cannot wait to get your hands on new programming projects.)

The Senior Programmer title usually commands a pay raise (over the normal annual cost-of-living raise) and maybe an office of his own instead of sharing an office with another Assistant Programmer or Programmer. A person is a Senior Programmer for a few years, writing code and getting to know the workings of the company, its users' needs, and the base of programs already in existence.

After a few years of success (the time is based on an individual's abilities, but two to three years is typical), the company will probably give that programmer the next highest programming title (along with a raise): Programmer Analyst.

A Programmer Analyst begins to work more closely on the front-end of programming: the program design. Hour 3, "Designing a Program," explains a lot about the analysis and design steps that must take place before you can write a program. Although Programmer Analysts don't do a lot of design work, they work closely with those who do. By working with designers (whose jobs are described in the next section), supervisors can learn just how apt that Programmer Analyst will be at program design. The Programmer Analyst does more programming than analyzing, but she does receive on-the-job training for the next step up the organizational ladder.

Analysis and Design Staff

When you make it to the next job level, *Systems Analyst,* you know you've made the big time. You'll probably never have to write another program again; instead, you'll analyze and design programs that others will write.

> Isn't it strange that you train for a long time to be a computer programmer and work hard at programming for several years, just so you don't have to program anymore? Actually, the programming experience is a must for the high-level Systems Analyst. Without the understanding that programming brings, one cannot design systems for others to program.

The Systems Analyst is the liaison between the users and the other departments who need data processing work performed. As Figure 22.4 shows, the Systems Analyst talks to both the users and the programming staff. The users don't understand computer requirements; they only know what they want (or what they think they want). The users must work with the Systems Analyst to design the needed computer system. The Systems Analyst has worked in the company for many years. The Systems Analyst understands the needs of the programmers and the needs of the users in the company. The programmers might appear too technically oriented to the users; sometimes the users themselves don't even know what they want. The Systems Analyst must be able to produce the output definition and logic design through numerous conversations with the users.

FIGURE 22.4

The Systems Analyst is the go-between for the users and the programmers.

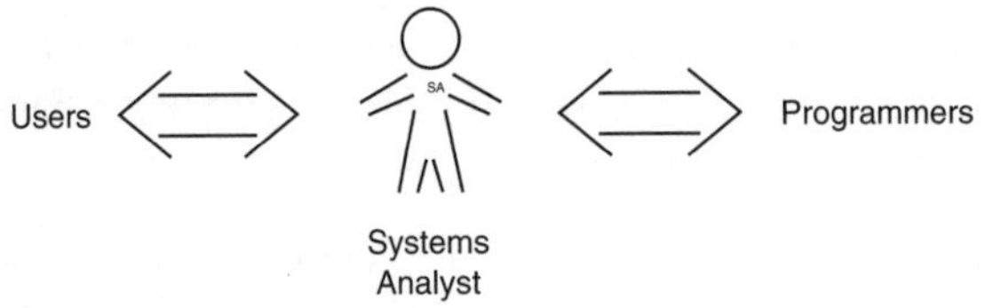

Users ⟺ Systems Analyst ⟺ Programmers

The job of the Systems Analyst is one of the most respected jobs in the computer industry. The Systems Analyst is paid a lot and often has high-level benefits available only to supervisory-level positions within the firm. Often, a person becomes a Systems Analyst and retires from that position instead of moving to another job. Some companies reward years of excellent performance by promoting a Systems Analyst to *Senior Systems Analyst.* The Senior Systems Analyst often does nothing different from the other Systems Analysts, however, and the new title is more of a "thank you" from the company than anything else.

22

In smaller programming departments, one person might wear lots of hats, but that person's job title doesn't accurately reflect the range of jobs performed. For example, some companies have only two or three people in the entire computer department. All of them might program and also perform systems analysis and design duties. Smaller companies give you the opportunity to perform a wider range of programming tasks, improve your skills, and gain an understanding of the responsibilities of lots of job titles. Larger companies, however, usually offer better benefits, pay, and job security, but it will take you longer to broaden your skills.

Internet and Network-Related Jobs

The online world has created its own set of job positions, many of which overlap those you've read about in this hour. Programmers today often create Web pages by writing HTML code to format Web pages or by writing Java applets that work on pages sent to others. The programmers who write programs for the Internet have their own specific titles, such as Web Designer, HTML Coder, and *TCP/IP* (an abbreviation for the communications protocol used by Internet programs) Analyst.

The huge collection of networked computers generates its own set of jobs as well. You will see jobs with titles such as LAN Designer and WAN Specialists as well as managers of these positions and technologies, including security officers who patrol the network for unauthorized access. *LAN* is an abbreviation for *Local Area Network,* a network that links two or more computers located in the same area, floor, or building, usually by direct wiring or wireless technology. *WAN* is an abbreviation for *Wide Area Network,* which is a network that spans more territory than the usual one-building network.

Due to the newness of these positions, most companies link these jobs to other positions. For example, a Java Specialist might have the same corporate status and pay scale as a Programmer or Programmer Analyst, although the Java Specialist would concentrate on the online Java language only.

Demand plays a big role in the pay scales and corporate level of all computer-related jobs. For example, in the last half of the 1990s, people with Internet-related skills received a bonus that boosted their pay levels higher than they would have traditionally earned based on seniority. This was due to the demand for workers with those types of skills.

The higher salaries offered in the computer field can be a mixed blessing. When you've been in data processing for a few years, your salary becomes much higher than that of others who have been with other departments for the same amount of time. A person who makes it to Systems Analyst and then decides that computers are no longer a challenge often finds it difficult to move to another position within that company. Companies rarely let people move to a position that requires a pay cut; such employees soon miss the money they were used to, and they start looking elsewhere for a job. The Systems Analysts find themselves locked into a job from which they cannot escape if they stay too long. Their only recourse when this happens is to move to a completely different company.

Often, a Systems Analyst decides that he or she is ready to move into management. One of the first management-level job titles in data processing is that of *Supervisor*. Supervisors manage a small group of programmers and analysts, directing projects from a management point of view (making sure their people have adequate resources to do their jobs, are properly evaluated for raises, and so forth). Data processing departments normally prefer their Supervisors to have data processing experience. That is why so many Supervisors are promoted from within the ranks of Systems Analysts.

From a supervisory position, you might next move into a job called *Data Processing Manager* and be responsible for several Supervisors and their projects. The head manager of a data processing department is typically called the *Director*. The Director is usually even in rank with the Vice Presidents in other departments of the firm.

> One of the advantages to moving into a supervisory or management position is that you can often move to non-DP departments within the company as a Supervisor or Manager. Before reaching a management position, your job rank and salary would make you overqualified for positions within other departments.

Structured Walkthroughs

The programming standards within the company are most often in focus during a walkthrough. A structured walkthrough has nothing to do with structured programming. A structured walkthrough is a review of a newly written program by some of the programming staff.

22

A programmer follows these steps when the programmer is finished writing a program:

1. The programmer tests the program at her desk and tries to get as many bugs out as possible.
2. The programmer passes the program on to the user for testing (often, a parallel test is performed).
3. The user puts the program into use.

Now that you are more familiar with the roles of the programming staff, you might be interested to know about an extra step that often takes place between steps 1 and 2. When the programmer is satisfied that the program is as accurate as possible, he prints listings of the program for several people and prepares for the structured walkthrough.

In the structured walkthrough, several other Programmers and Systems Analysts get together with a copy of the original listing, with the Programmer in the room, and they pick apart the program in detail, trying to find errors, weak spots, broken standards, and poor documentation. Along the way they make suggestions on how to improve the code.

A structured walkthrough often produces what is known in the industry as *egoless programmers*. Programmers are often known for their egos; a good structured walkthrough often shows that a program is not as well written as the original programmer might have first thought.

The structured walkthrough is not an attempt to point fingers. Its only purpose is to produce the best code possible. The other programmers are not going to be critical of the programmer personally; after all, they are going to be at the center of a future structured walkthrough themselves.

After a programmer implements many of the suggestions from the structured walkthrough, the programmer usually finds that he agrees that the program is better written than it was originally. After many such walkthroughs, the programmer develops better programming skills and the company acquires better programs.

Putting a Program into Production

Figure 22.5 shows all the steps needed to get a program into use by the user. When the user is finally convinced that the program works as well as originally asked for, and the user is convinced that the parallel testing went smoothly, the program is then moved into production.

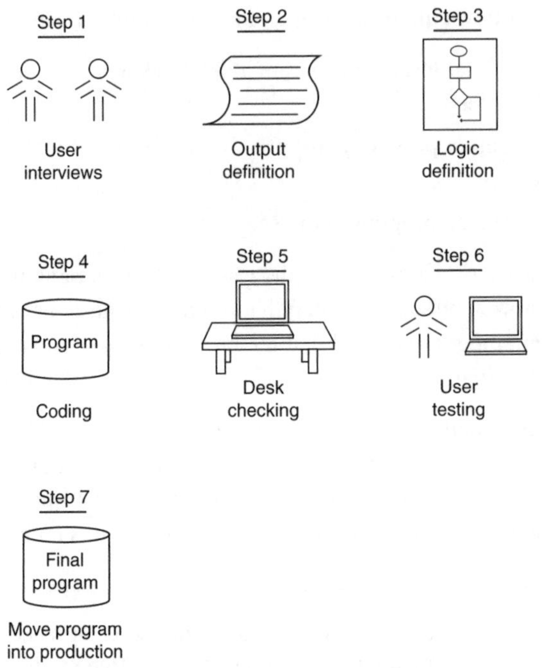

FIGURE 22.5

The steps for design-ing, writing, and installing programs.

Step 1

User
interviews

Step 2

Output
definition

Step 3

Logic
definition

Step 4

Program

Coding

Step 5

Desk
checking

Step 6

User
testing

Step 7

Final
program

Move program
into production

When a program moves into production, it is considered complete. The user begins to use the program in a working, non-test environment. The program's results are consid-ered reliable within reason. (Over time, a program's reliability improves as it is used and continues to work well.)

Being in production hardly implies that the program needs no changing and updating over the years. Nevertheless, a production program is one that is considered fixed and usable until a user makes a request to update the program or scrap it for a completely new one. If changes are made to a program that is in production, the Systems Analyst goes back to user interviews and determines what the user wants. The entire systems analysis and design stage is then repeated for the revised program. Depending on the extent of the changes, a program's revision might take more or less development time than its ancestor program took to write. As you have read throughout this entire book, the maintenance of programs is critical in our ever-changing world. If you write your code better, by supplying more documentation and closely following your company's pro-gramming standards, then you will have a better chance at locking in your career in the computer field.

22

> ### "I Want Job Security!"
>
> *Job security* is an overused term. Often, you hear programmers jokingly talk about the cryptic code they write so that "only they will be able to understand it." Modern programmers are only too aware of the fact that the better employers seek programmers who write clear, clean code, are more concerned with proper programming, and follow as many of the company's programming standards as possible.
>
> Some people can write programs very quickly, but the spaghetti code they produce is unreadable for future maintenance. Don't fall into the trap of thinking that speed is more important than clear programs.

Many companies have formal procedures for moving programs into production. When a program is ready to be moved into production, the programmers finalize the program's documentation and prepare a source code file with a filename added to the production program list's records. That program is then stored on tapes and disks in what are known as production areas.

> PC programming languages sometimes come with *version-control modules* that keep strict track of versions that programs go through as programmers update them and release new versions of the software.

Some mainframe systems don't enable programmers to change a program once the system is instructed to treat that source program as a production program. Programmers are able to make copies of the program's source code, but the program is read-only and cannot be changed. If an update has to be made, the programmer copies the source code and makes changes to the copy. After the updates are made and the new version is ready for production, the production records are changed to reflect the new source code. From that point, the production system treats the new version of the code as the production version, but the original remains in place as a backup.

This tight control over production source code enables a company to ensure that it always has an unmodified copy of every program used by every user in the company. Without such control, a programmer could write a program, compile and test it, and install it on the user's system. When installed, the programmer might inadvertently change the program. Because it is virtually impossible to reproduce source code from compiled code, the data processing department would have no way to generate the original source code if the users wanted a change made to the program they are using.

Consulting

Many programmers find an enriching life as a computer consultant. Too many businesses and individuals buy a computer thinking all their problems will be solved, and they don't realize the amount of training that is often needed to use the computer effectively. There has been a growing niche for computer consultants over the last several years, and you might find success as a consultant yourself.

As a consultant, you can be a hero or a heroine to your clients. So many times, computer consultants rush to help someone with a problem getting a report completed, only to find that the client is inserting a disk upside-down or forgetting to press the online button on the printer. The computer is still a mystery to a vast number of people.

As a consultant, you can take on as much or as little work as you want. Many programmers moonlight as consultants, sometimes finding that their consulting business grows enough to do it full time. They might give up the benefits that a company can provide, but they like having full say over what they do.

Getting started as a consultant takes little more than word-of-mouth coverage. Offer to help your accountant, attorney, or anyone you know who uses a computer. Tell them that you'd like to start doing some consulting and that you'd be glad to give them an hour or two free of charge just to see how they like the work (and how you like the work). Often, these initial free calls turn into a long-term proposition that is good for both you and your clients.

Summary

You now have an understanding of computer departments and their people. There are many jobs in the computer industry, both for entry-level and advanced programmers. A computer job is a fun, well respected, and needed occupation; you'll be glad you're a part of the computer industry.

Understanding the job levels and job promotions can be confusing, especially because many companies follow a unique promotion and title scheme. Nevertheless, the general order of jobs that a programmer follows from the beginning to the end of her career is similar across many companies. The online and networking worlds have increased the nature of jobs and improved demand to further complicate the industry and make the roles of programmers even more interesting.

The next hour describes the tools and policies available to distribute programs to users.

Q&A

Q Why is the concept of production programs so important?

A The company knows that all programs in production are the final versions of each software release for each program ever written and used within the company. In other words, the production programs are those programs actually used by the company. Other programs might be in process and are still being written. Other programs might be used by individuals but not sanctioned by the company's data processing department and, therefore, not part of the released software.

Q When a company makes a change to a production program's source code, does the compiled and revised program replace the current program being used?

A The revised program will also go into production but not replace the original program. The original program version is never removed from the production set in case the revision has problems and the company has to revert back to the original program.

Workshop

The quiz questions and exercises are provided for your further understanding. See Appendix B, "Quiz Answers," for answers.

Quiz

1. What does MIS stand for?

2. Who do the data processing department's programmers write programs for?

3. What is the most entry-level computer-related position found in large organizations?

4. What do entry-level programmers typically do?

5. What does a Systems Analyst do?

6. What is a structured walkthrough?

7. True or false: A company should keep all source code for all programs that it moves into production.

8. How can computer-programming personnel ensure job security?

9. What is the difference between a LAN and a WAN?

10. Why is the pay for Internet-related jobs usually better than for other DP jobs even though the jobs' ranks might be the same as more conventional computer positions?

HOUR 23

Distributing Applications

After you write a program, test it, and debug it, you must get your program into the hands of those who will use it. One of the problems with the software industry is a lack of installation standards for new software. Although Windows provides some uniformity for installing software, not all software producers conform to that standard and not all software could even be made to conform to the Windows control panel's Add/Remove Programs feature.

This hour introduces you to the problems associated with software distribution. You want to be sure that your users have an easy time installing the programs you write. In addition, those programs have to work after they are installed. Today's distribution tools help a lot when it comes to creating distributable software. This hour takes a look at how one software product, Visual Basic, creates a customized installation for you.

The highlights of this hour include

- Learning why installation issues can be complex
- Using wizards to simplify the creation of installation routines
- Understanding why compiling the application is so critical to proper installation

- Using version control
- Making an installation wizard work for you
- Mastering the installation wizard's file storage of its generated files
- Using an uninstall routine

Issues Surrounding Software Distribution

One of the easier aspects of software distribution is finding an outlet to sell the product. More computer-related stores and software Web sites are now open than ever before. Even discount stores and warehouse chains carry software, as if software were a staple item for our daily lives. Software companies are looking for new titles to distribute and new programmers to write the code. Software mail-order catalogs are numerous. The business of computers today gives you many avenues in which to market your product.

Just because you wrote a program that works on your computer with your software settings certainly does not mean that the program will work on others' computers. For happy users, you must make sure that the program installs on the user's computer and that the program will run after it's installed.

Windows Application Distribution

This section walks you through one of the most common distribution methods of Windows software in use today. The Microsoft Visual Studio supports a standard distribution system that collects all files related to a Windows *project* (a project is a collection of files that comprise a Windows application) and packages those files into a distributable set of disks or CD-ROMs or into a set of files for distribution over a network of computers. The Visual Studio even creates an *installation script* that controls the entire program installation when the user installs the program.

The Microsoft Visual Studio is certainly not the only product that creates standard installation scripts for the Windows programs that you write. Nevertheless, almost all Microsoft languages, including Visual Basic, Visual C++, and Visual J++, use the Visual Studio interface and the distribution system. If you end up using a non-Microsoft language or a different installation distribution system, the steps you go through will not match those of this hour exactly but the general nature of the system will mimic that of the Visual Studio system.

Your First Step: Compilation

As mentioned earlier, you will need to compile whatever Windows application you distribute. The compiled file is a final executable file with the .EXE filename extension. All the related Windows application modules and forms work together to form the executable file. Although auxiliary files might still be necessary, such as a Microsoft Access database file used for initial data, most of your project's files combine into the executable to make distribution easier.

23

A compiled application is more secure than a distributed source project. If you distribute the source code (the project and its related files), anyone with a Visual Studio language, such as Visual Basic, can modify your work. However, most people won't be able to run the source code because most do not have Visual Basic. Therefore, a compiled file is not only secure, but it is also necessary so that all can use your application.

Your compiled application runs much faster than the application running within Visual Basic's development environment. You want your application to run as quickly and smoothly as possible without your users doing more than necessary. The compiled executable file makes the application's execution simple.

Before you finish compiling your application for distribution, make sure that you've debugged the application as much as is feasible to eliminate as many bugs as possible.

When you're satisfied that you have your program running as accurately as possible, Visual Studio's File, Make option actually performs the compilation. Other programming platforms use a similar, if not identical, menu option for the compile function. Visual Studio then displays a Make Project dialog box that is little more than a File Open dialog box. You need to select the folder where you want to store the compiled application and the name for the executable file. (The project will have the executable filename extension .EXE.)

Before clicking OK to start the compilation, you can set compilation options by clicking an Options button to display the Project Properties dialog box (see Figure 23.1). The dialog box lets the programmer specify version information for the compiled application that is common information needed by developers. If you plan to release several versions of the software, the version numbers let you determine the order of versions. You can specify the version information from the development environment's Project Properties dialog box so you don't have to specify versions just at compile time. The version numbers and description information stay with the project's source code.

FIGURE 23.1

Set the compiled project's options in the Project Properties dialog box.

The Icon entry designates the icon that indicates the application on the Windows Start menu and on a taskbar button. Generally, you leave the primary form name in the Icon field. The form's Properties window contains an Icon entry from which you can select an icon for the form and, therefore, for the compiled application.

A Compile tab (also common among all companies' compilers) displays the Compile Options page shown in Figure 23.2. To optimize the compiled project to make it run as quickly as possible, you could set options such as the Compile to Native Code option. (If you compile to *p-code*, a special intermediate language used by some compilers such as Visual Basic, the application requires that your users keep a runtime Visual Basic–based DLL file in their System folder. Native code runs faster and requires fewer files.)

FIGURE 23.2

You can control the compile options.

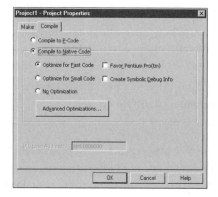

If you select any of the options that appear when you click the Advanced Optimizations button, you forsake some of the runtime error checking but gain execution speed.

When you close the Project Properties dialog box and click OK, Visual Studio compiles your code. Assuming that no compile errors exist, Visual Studio creates the `.EXE` file (you'll see the compilation status in the upper right corner). You can exit Visual Studio and run the application by selecting the Start menu's Run option after locating the `.EXE` file. The form's icon that you selected appears in the taskbar when you run the program.

Of course, your users will not, at first, be able to run your application as easily as you can because the application is already loaded on your system. The next section shows one tool that automatically creates an installation script for your users so they can install your application with minimal trouble.

Deploying Your Application

In Visual Studio, beginning with release 6, a special wizard exists that walks you through the creation of a Windows-based installation for your application. Although you might not have a Visual Studio-based product now, and although you might use a different vendor's product in the future, you can learn a lot about such products by following the walk-through described here.

Visual Studio's Package and Deployment Wizard does a lot of work for you, including the following:

- Compiles the application and compresses the files.

- Creates a setup program that your users can use to install the application.

- Determines the best fit for the installation of floppy disks, creates the numerous setup disks, and splits extra large files across multiple floppy disks. The Package and Deployment Wizard tells you in advance how many floppy disks the setup requires.
- Copies your compiled application to a hard disk so that you can install the application over a network or onto a CD-ROM creator.
- Sets up your application for distribution across the Internet for Internet Explorer users.

The Package and Deployment Wizard generates a list of several files needed for the setup. A single `Setup.exe` doesn't come out of the setup routine. Often, a Windows application requires `.DLL` and `.ocx` files, and those files reside in the targeted setup area (floppy disks or a hard disk) with the compiled program and the `Setup.exe` program.

> Most installation programs that contain the installation script for any given application are named `Setup.exe`.

Starting the Package and Deployment Wizard

Before you can run the Package and Deployment Wizard, you must load your application's project into the Visual Studio environment. Therefore, if you use Visual Basic, you would load your Visual Basic project files as if you were going to work on the application.

Only after you have debugged and compiled your project are you ready to create the installation module. The installation routine, the Package and Deployment Wizard, will compile your code one final time if you've made an edit since your most recent compilation. Figure 23.3 shows the opening screen of the Package and Deployment wizard.

FIGURE 23.3

Use the Package and Deployment Wizard to create a `Setup.exe` *file.*

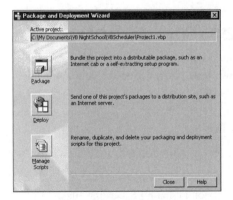

The first Package and Deployment Wizard option, which is the option you'll probably select most of the time, creates a standard Setup.exe program that your users can install. The Package and Deployment Wizard can prepare this installation routine on a disk, floppy disks, CD-ROM writer, or in special .CAB files that you can send out over the Internet for online distribution. The second option sends the install routine to an Internet server that can install the application remotely.

During the installation-creation routine, the Package and Deployment Wizard creates a script file that describes the setup routine. In subsequent sessions, you can either modify a setup script that you've already created or create the setup from the original project. The third option on the Package and Deployment Wizard's opening window lets you manage your installation scripts.

> Due to the size of most Windows applications today and to the abundance of CD-ROM recorders, few applications come on disks.

The Wizard's Options

The first option generates the most common forms of an installation routine for most applications. It is this option that most other software installation routines follow. After you click the first option, you'll see the window shown in Figure 23.4. Unless your application requires external ActiveX controls or database files, you can keep the first option selected.

FIGURE 23.4

Determine the kind of setup package to create.

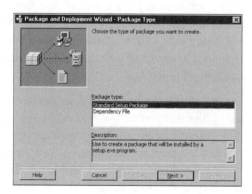

> If you want to set up an ActiveX control, you need to select the Dependency File option so the wizard can collect the proper files in the order the application needs them. Without telling the wizard that other dependent files must appear in the project, the wizard would be unable to collect all the necessary files.

The Installation Location

You'll need to specify a folder on your own computer where you want the distribution files saved. The Package and Deployment Wizard needs to know where your final setup application should go. The directory you select should be empty so that other installation routines don't get in the way. Therefore, as a developer, you will have many folders on your disk drives with each folder holding one complete set of installation files for each application that you write. You should document these folders so that you can later go back and collect the proper files you need for applications that you distribute to others.

> By saving the installation to a new and empty folder, you'll know when the wizard finishes that all the files in the directory are there as the result of the wizard.

The Dependency Files

One of the most powerful features of an installation-creation system, such as the Package and Deployment Wizard, is that the wizard can scan your project file to determine which program files your application needs. (The wizard can't determine which database drivers are needed if your application contains any data-related controls, so you'll have to select them from a dependency-file screen.)

A dialog box such as the one shown in Figure 23.5 appears after the wizard finishes collecting all the application's files that you've specified. Make sure that you look through the files to determine that every file your application requires is listed. You might need to add (by clicking Add) more files, such as Readme.txt or a database file. Additional database support files might be needed, and you would need to add those database files to the file list so the installation routine stores the database files along with the installation files in the setup package.

FIGURE 23.5

Look through the files to make sure the Package and Deployment Wizard collected the files your project needs.

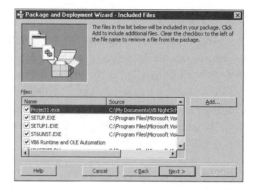

Selecting the Location

The Package and Deployment Wizard's next dialog box requests distribution information. You can create a single distribution file or request that the setup routine be placed across multiple floppy disks or other kinds of media. After you determine how you want the Package and Deployment Wizard to divide your installation routine, you can display the Installation Title screen to type your installation project's title, which appears in the installation dialog box that the user sees. After clicking Next, the Start Menu Items dialog box appears, as shown in Figure 23.6.

FIGURE 23.6

You can determine the way the application will appear on the end-user's Windows Start menu.

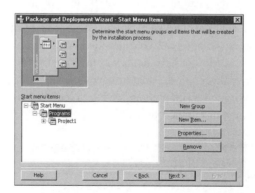

From the Start Menu Items dialog box, create the submenu that will appear on the installed PC's Start menu. Clicking the New button and displaying the Add Group dialog box enables you to add new menus to the user's Start menu group of menus. You can specify the application's submenu items, which might include a `Readme` file you want to add to the project or an auxiliary program, such as a system utility. By clicking the New Icon button, you can even specify a new icon that will appear on each menu option.

Completing the Wizard

Several additional screens might appear, depending on your installation options. A screen called Install Locations determines the locations of each of the installed files. Although you'll want the majority of the files installed in the folder that the user selects during the installation procedure, as specified by a system variable called AppPath, you can select individual files in the Package and Deployment Wizard's list and send those files to an alternative folder, such as the user's Program Files folder (specified by a system variable called ProgramFiles).

> As you can see, installation systems such as Visual Studio's Package and Deployment Wizard require numerous decisions. With those decisions, however, comes complete control over how and where your application arrives on the user's system.

Click Next to select any files that you want to designate as shared files. A file might be shared not only by other users (as would be the case for a database file the application might access) but also by other programs on the computer, as might be the case for ActiveX controls that your project contains. Designate which files are shared by clicking next to each shared file and placing a check mark in the box next to that file.

One of the finishing touches of the Visual Studio Package and Deployment Wizard is a screen that asks what you want to call your installation's script file (see Figure 23.7). By creating a script file, you will not have to answer the long list of wizard queries that you've had to answer to this point the next time you create the installation routine. In addition, you can modify the script without having to redo the installation screens if something changes in the installation process, such as the removal of a shared file.

FIGURE 23.7

Save your installation script so you do not have to re-create it later.

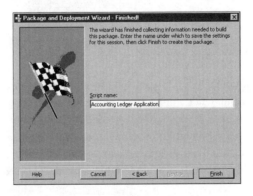

When finished, the Package and Deployment Wizard builds the installation script, creates the installation routine, and places that routine in one or several files depending on the options you selected. When finished, a Setup file will reside on your PC that you can distribute in one or several files, which will install and re-create your application on other computers.

After Generating the Setup

23

After your installation wizard generates a setup routine, test it. To test the routine, run the generated Setup program to make sure that no bugs appear and the final application runs smoothly on the computer.

> If you really want to test the setup routine, run the Setup program on a computer that has never contained your application. Even better, make sure that the computer doesn't even have a copy of the Visual Studio language you are using. By testing your application on such a *clean machine*, you help ensure that your application will install properly on a user's computer. Some business copier centers allow you to rent PCs and such PCs are good candidates for installing your software if you are allowed to install new software on the computers there.

The simplest way to test the generated setup routine is to choose Run from the Windows Start menu and find the `Setup.exe` file. Click the Run button to start the application's setup. A typical setup installation will occur. The Setup program will analyze the target computer to ensure that no programs are running that might conflict with a file that is about to be installed.

> If you cancel the Setup program at any time before it completes, it closes after removing any files copied up to that point. Therefore, if you cancel the process at any time, Setup removes all traces of the application's setup.

Uninstalling the Application

Installation wizards such as the Package and Deployment Wizard not only generate the installable setup routine, but also an application uninstaller that lets users uninstall all the application's files at any time. The Package and Deployment Wizard works in conjunction with the system Control Panel's Add/Remove Programs icon. Therefore, if users want to remove the application from the system, they only have to follow these steps:

1. From the Start menu, choose Settings, Control Panel.

2. Double-click the Add/Remove Programs icon.

3. Select the application from the list of installed applications. After verifying that the user wants to remove the application, the uninstall routine takes over and removes the program and all its related files from the user's computer.

The Package and Deployment Wizard stores the uninstall information in the same directory as the application. The file that contains the removal instructions is named ST6UNSTLOG and holds the necessary details for the Add/Remove Programs system utility to do its job. Not all files should be removed, especially system files that might be shared by other programs. Before removing such potentially needed files (such as ActiveX controls), the removal utility displays a warning dialog box that lets users decide how to remove such files.

Summary

This hour's lesson was more technical than many of the previous ones but creating an installation script is not actually straightforward. Fortunately, Windows utility programs such as the Visual Studio Package and Deployment Wizard make the work simpler. Not only can you specify the files needed to install, but also the wizard handles auxiliary files such as database and ActiveX files your application needs as well as creates an uninstall program so your users can properly remove the application from their systems.

The next hour concludes your 24-hour introduction to programming by discussing some of the issues related to the world of computing and exploring some of the tasks you'll face as a programmer.

Q&A

Q Should I always offer an uninstall routine?

A By providing a way for your users to uninstall your application, you help your users get rid of old versions of the software when new ones come out. In addition, the user knows that all traces of the program go away when the user implements the uninstall routine. All traces of a Windows application rarely go away when a user has to attempt to remove an application without the automated help of an uninstaller.

Workshop

The quiz questions are provided for your further understanding. For the answers, see Appendix B, "Quiz Answers."

Quiz

1. Name some places that sell software.
2. Why is a standard installation routine critical for software success?
3. What is a software project?
4. What is an installation script?
5. What filename extension do compiled programs use?
6. What filename is often used for the primary installation file of an application?
7. What kind of media (such as disks) can an installation system often use for distributing the application?
8. Why do installations rarely come on disks these days?
9. Why is testing the installation on a clean machine so important?
10. How do you create an uninstall routine?

23

HOUR 24

The Future of Programming

What's in store for you as a programmer? One thing is certain and that's *change*. Change occurs rapidly in computing. The face of programming has dramatically changed since computers were first invented, and the rate of change is increasing. Today's programming tools were not even dreamed of ten years ago. New languages such as Java often crop up to handle new technology like the Internet.

This final hour shows you what tools are available to help you become a better programmer. More important than the tools, however, is proper coding that is easily maintained later.

The highlights of this hour include

- Improving your programs with the proper tools
- Profiling for improving your program's efficiency
- Keeping efficiency and retaining maintainability

- Tracking with version control
- Understanding Windows resource management
- Finding other resources available to improve your programming skills

Some Helpful Tools

As you develop more programming skills and work with more programming language environments, you will run across tools that you will want to add to your bag of coding tricks. The following sections briefly describe tools that you might run across as a programmer that you'll want to look into.

Profilers

Hour 8, "Structured Techniques," introduced you to profiling tools. A profiler analyzes parts of your program and determines exactly which parts are sluggish. It is thought that 90% of a program's execution time is spent in less than 10% of the code. Of course, this rule of thumb is probably not scientifically provable but its concept is understandable.

Perhaps a sorting algorithm is inefficient and needs looking into to speed it up. Perhaps you are performing a sequential search when a binary search might be faster. Perhaps a calculation is inefficient and you can combine operations to make the program compute results more quickly. A profiler can analyze the execution of your program and tell you where the time is being spent during the execution.

Speed and efficiency are great factors, but don't forsake proper programming techniques if doing so means eking out a microsecond or two of machine time. Clear code should be paramount in your coding. Computers are getting faster, not slower, so you know that your program will never run *slower* than it runs today. Some scientific and financial calculations, for example, get extremely complex. To clarify your code, you could break such calculations into several statements, storing intermediate calculation results along the way. Although it might be more efficient and execute a few microseconds faster, if you combined all the calculations into one long expression, this expression would later be difficult to debug or change if a problem arises. Therefore, unless a system's speed is critical (as might be the case in some medical or space exploration programs), don't make your code too tricky to be maintained later.

Many of the major programming languages on the market either have a profiler or their authors are producing one. A balance can be met between efficient code and clear, maintainable code. Sadly, programmers don't use profilers enough. Often, a program contains a sluggish section that could use some honing that would not risk the code's maintainability. The backlog of programming jobs right now and in the foreseeable future also keeps programmers from taking the time needed to check the execution profile of their applications.

Version Controllers

Version control used to be important only in the mainframe world where programming teams wrote computer information systems for large groups of people within the company. Perhaps one department might use a version of the software that contains more features than the other department programs contain. The programming staff developed a way to keep the versions straight. They assigned unique version numbers to each program sent into production that was used by the company.

Now, PC languages are getting into the act by providing version control software that enables programming departments to track versions of software. The version control tracks versions of distributed programs and keeps track of all source code that goes out to end users. Companies are seeing the need for such control on their PC software because so many data processing chores are being ported to the PC for client/server computing, where the data might be stored on a networked mainframe, but processed on the PCs connected to the mainframe. Such a distributed system of programs can get confusing, so the version tracking software keeps things in order.

When the programmers complete an application for a department, the programmer can use the version control software to log every file related to the project. Software such as Visual Basic includes version control called *SourceSafe* as an option every time you save a source program. A dialog box such as the one in Figure 24.1 appears asking if you want to add the program to the source code version control, which means that you want to track the software in the version control system and assign a unique version number to the files in the project.

FIGURE 24.1

PC software requires version control tracking just as mainframe software does.

24

Generally, not just anyone can, or should, add software to the version control system. Usually, a System Administrator or a DP Security Officer will control the adding of programs to version-tracking systems, such as SourceSafe, to maintain integrity and to make sure that all the software in the version-tracking system has been approved for storage there.

By requiring the proper authority, programming departments can help keep incorrect software out of the version library so that a user is not assigned the wrong program during the program's distribution.

Keep in mind that version control is *not* the same version-tracking value that you saw in Hour 23, "Distributing Applications," when compiling a program (see Figure 24.2). Although you can assign major and minor version numbers to a compiled program, it is the source code that must be monitored with secure version-control software. The source code is the only sure way that a company has of modifying the program at a later date. The proper version of source code must always be tracked to ensure that the source code ends up assigned to the proper department that uses the compiled version of the code.

FIGURE 24.2

Monitoring compiled software is less important than monitoring source code.

Major version number

Minor version number

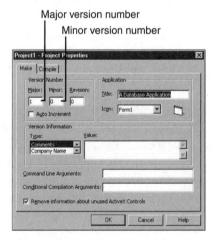

One of the advantages of version control is that you can release a new version of an application and, if the user finds serious bugs, you can restore an older version of the software. The version tracking system will keep track of each version you release and will enable you to easily retrieve previous versions when needed.

Resource Editors

A Windows programming language brings its own requirements to the table. Tools exist to help the Windows programmer that were not needed in the DOS environment and make no sense in the mainframe world.

One such tool is called a *resource editor*. A Windows resource is just about anything used in Windows. A resource might be an icon, a text string, a bitmap image, a menu, or a dialog box. As you work with programming languages, you will manipulate such resources. Resources appear in an application's project in a file that ends with the file-name extension .RES.

Several ways exist for you to use resources in your Windows applications. You can, for example, designate an icon to use for the end user's installation of your application. The user can click that icon to start the application. You might want to create your own icon. A tool called the *resource editor* can help you create and edit icons and other Windows resources. Visual Studio contains a resource editor that appears as a dialog box, as shown in Figure 24.3, which lets you add, delete, and edit resources in your application's project.

24

FIGURE 24.3

The Visual Studio resource editor keeps track of your project's resources.

Will Programming Go Away?

For several years, people have been predicting the demise of programmers. As those predictions get older and more numerous, the demand for programmers has grown tremendously. The need for programming seems to be increasing at a rapid pace.

In the mid 1970s, *Management Information Systems* (*MIS*) were going to be the answer to all computing needs. Each company would have MIS in place and all data needed by the company would be at each computer user's fingertips. That kind of data filtering was to be so vast and efficient that ordinary and more specific programs would not be needed. Obviously, the promise of MIS was not only over-predicted, but also never materialized.

CASE Tools

In the late 1980s, *CASE (Computer-Aided Software Engineering)* was going to replace programmers. Instead of having coders who knew one or more programming languages, programming teams would master CASE tools. CASE is like a program generator, only instead of helping programmers write programs, CASE tools help the DP staff create programs starting at the initial design level. A Systems Analyst can use CASE from the inception of a program request to the program's movement into production.

CASE is a massive program on the computer that the Systems Analyst can use for the initial output design, data definitions, logic definition (some CASE programs even draw flowcharts from a flowchart description entered by the Systems Analyst), and program generation. CASE often produces code based on the Analyst's logic definition, but heavy programmer intervention is needed to implement any but the most general of programs and to ensure the project's overall success.

CASE's proponents promised that it would revolutionize the programming environment and decrease the time and resources needed to produce a finished program. (Most of the newer programming advances promote quicker development time and easier maintenance as their primary goals.) The promise of CASE, however, never materialized. Although CASE has achieved some success, it has yet to produce the advances in software development that were originally hoped.

The CASE products of the 1980s were not bad tools. The problems that resulted from them were due to the fact that CASE helped Systems Analysts and programmers do faster what the Systems Analysts and programmers already did incorrectly. Pre–object-oriented programming (OOP) methods suffer from difficult maintenance and documentation problems that OOP does not introduce. CASE could not eliminate the inherent problems that non-OOP programming contains. (OOP has its own set of problems as well, however, but it is viewed as an improvement over other traditional methods.)

Think of CASE as a program that helps you and others design and write programs. CASE is good for handling the minute details throughout the system's development, so you and the other programmers and Systems Analysts can work on implementing all the user's requests.

In recent years, programmer's tools have certainly become sophisticated, as you've seen throughout this entire 24-hour tutorial. Some even feel that wizard technology, such as the Visual Basic Application Wizard, will become so powerful that programming will become little more than answering a series of questions.

The reason that programmers are needed more than ever is that computer technology keeps changing along with the programming tools. The early PCs brought new challenges to programs because of their lack of speed and their high demand. As PCs got faster, people networked them together and to mainframes, so distributed client/server programs were needed. Windows required much more effort to program than the simpler, text-based DOS mode. The Internet brought a new set of requirements for programmers that was not dreamed of before.

As you can see, programming demand keeps increasing because the nature of computing keeps changing and becoming more complex. That's the trend that will probably continue for years to come. Programming language developers are recognizing that new tools are needed not to replace programmers but to help them perform their ever-complex jobs.

UML: Data Modeling

Microsoft has joined several other vendors to solidify a program-modeling language called *UML*, or the *Unified Modeling Language*. The UML provides a uniform definition of modeling a program. Therefore, a company that models one program can share that model with companies that are writing similar programs. The models are not code but are definitions of the applications.

The UML is extremely useful, initially, for database designers and database application writers to share the components of each database and to transfer those components between computers. The concepts in the UML, however, are also being applied to program designs.

UML benefits the following five areas of computing:

1. Reuse: After a company completes a design, that design can be reused.
2. Tool interoperability: The UML design uses different programming and database systems. Therefore, a UNIX-based HotJava programmer will be able to use the same UML model as a Visual Basic programmer.
3. Team development: The UML tools are usable in a team-programming environment.
4. Data resource management: Resources that appear along with the required data in the UML design are tracked along with the UML's objects.
5. Dependency tracking: If files are required by other files in the design, the UML keeps track of those dependents.

As with the other design tools of the past, the UML will not replace programming, but should enhance programming and enable the design of a system to be used with other systems to improve programmer productivity.

Your Training Needs

Only if you keep up with industry changes can you help ensure that computer problems do not occur in the future. Programmers continually hone their skills to keep up with the changing technology in languages, operating systems, software, and hardware. As you learn more about programming, you should consider sharing your knowledge with others through training, consulting, writing, or teaching. You will find that your own programming skills improve when you teach them to someone else.

The need for training is never as apparent as it is in virtually every programming department in the world. Programmers are often called to offer a training class for others who do not possess some needed skills. In-house training enables a company to keep a cap on its training costs and control the material being covered.

Your own computer training does not stop. The computer industry changes rapidly. The skills you have today can be obsolete in five years, so part of your job is to continue your own training. It is incumbent upon you to stay up with current trends if you want to secure your computer position in the future.

Industry Standards

Not every new breakthrough in computer hardware and software becomes an industry standard. You do not have to be on the *bleeding edge* of technology (a programmer's pun describing very new and unproved technology), learning everything there is to learn. You do not even have to be on the *leading edge* of computer programming innovations. For instance, object-oriented programming is now considered by the industry as the best way to program, yet the majority of computer programmers haven't learned how to program with objects. They might or might not have to master OOP depending on where their jobs take them and the language they must master in their companies. The future seems to be heading towards using OOP languages in most situations, however. While it is a good idea to stay on top of the latest trends, it isn't necessary to learn them all because today's breakthrough might be tomorrow's flop.

You will find your own niche in the computer field. Specialization is almost a must these days. It is so very difficult to master everything. Some people choose to specialize in networking, Internet programming, Web page design, object-oriented programming, or graphical user interfaces. As you learn more about programming, you will find the area that best fits your own interests and you will master that area.

Each month, take a trip to your local library or bookstore to scan the shelves for the latest computer magazines. Try to read one good computer book every month or two. Every six months, research a new topic of computer programming to improve your skill levels. Most computer people find that self-study is not a job they balk at; the field of programming is exciting. It never gets old. The new innovations everywhere you look are always exciting and hold the promise of powerful computing power in the future.

Now that you have a more solid foundation than almost any other beginning programmer has ever had, you are ready to direct your education toward more specific goals. You should now begin tackling a programming language in depth. Mastering a programming language takes a while, and people learn at different rates. Nevertheless, the biggest problem budding programmers face is that they jump in too fast. After reading *Teach Yourself Beginning Programming in 24 Hours*, you will not have that problem; you will be surprised at how well this book's concepts prepare you for your programming future, whether that future is just for fun or for a career.

24

 Computer books are known for their series approach. As you already know, the *Sams Teach Yourself in 24 Hours* series is designed to teach you the basics of a subject in as little time as possible. The *Sams Teach Yourself in 21 Days* series is also designed to teach a topic to a newcomer but the topic is taught in more depth due to the added time. In addition to the highly successful *Sams Teach Yourself* series, you'll want to use the *Unleashed* books to master the advanced aspects of a programming language.

The following Sams Publishing titles are a sampling of some books that you might want to look at to improve your skills as a programmer. These books were specifically chosen to get you up to speed in a specific area of programming:

- *Sams Teach Yourself HTML in 24 Hours*; *Sams Teach Yourself Visual Basic .NET in 24 Hours*; *Sams Teach Yourself Java 2 in 24 Hours, Second Edition*; *Sams Teach Yourself JavaScript in 24 Hours*; and *Sams Teach Yourself C++ in 24 Hours, Third Edition*: These books are the perfect next step from this book to take you more deeply into the language of your choice.

- *Sams Teach Yourself XML in 21 Days, Second Edition*; *Sams Teach Yourself Visual Basic 6 in 21 Days*; *Sams Teach Yourself Java 2 in 21 Days*; and *Sams Teach Yourself C++ in 21 Days, Fourth Edition*: These books take you far into the languages to prepare you for your career or hobby.

- *Visual C++ 6 Unleashed*: The *unleashed* family of books assumes some familiarity with the languages and they digdeep into the language to provide you with a comprehensive reference and study aid.

To keep up with the latest in programming titles, regularly check out Sams Publishing's Web site at www.samspublishing.com.

Summary

Programming tools go far beyond just the languages themselves. Throughout this 24-hour tutorial, you've seen examples of languages and programming tools that help you be a better programmer. You've seen tools for both standalone computing as well as online programming, and you learned about the future .NET technology in Hour 21 that coincides well with this hour's material. This hour showed you additional tools that programmers can use to become more productive programmers. The most important part of programming is writing clear and concise code so that others can maintain your programs when needed.

After you've mastered programming, what's next? Keep mastering! Continuing education is almost as vital in the field of computers as it is in the medical profession. The rapidly changing computer technologies require that programmers stay on top of current trends by reading books and magazines and taking courses when possible. Share your knowledge with others to help improve the programming community and reduce the backlog that the computer industry faces. Knowledge shared is knowledge improved.

Q&A

Q Are CASE tools available for PCs?

A Some CASE tools exist for PCs, but they are primarily used on mainframes where a huge program that is used by hundreds or thousands of users must handle the company needs. Although extremely advanced programming is now being done at the PC level, especially enterprise computing that is made possible by client/server models, CASE hasn't found a good foothold in the door of PC programmers. Probably the failure of CASE in the 1980s has made PC programmers afraid to try it. Other tools, such as UML, are more common in the arena of PC development.

Workshop

The quiz questions are provided for your further understanding. For the answers, see Appendix B, "Quiz Answers."

Quiz

1. How can a profiler improve program efficiency?

2. Which is more important: program efficiency or program maintainability?

3. Why is the version control library important to a programming department?

4. What are two possible Windows resources?

5. What is a resource manager?

6. What does a resource editor do?

7. Why does the demand for programmers increase even though tools become more powerful?

8. True or false: The computer industry changes often so you must continually hone your skills to maintain your competence and stay in demand.

9. What is *CASE*?

24

PART VI
Appendixes

APPENDIX **A**

Glossary

2's complement   An internal method that computers use to represent negative values.

7-bit ASCII   An older ASCII system that represents only 128 different characters.

absolute value   The positive representation of a positive number, zero, or a negative number.

abstraction   The name given to an object's details that are hidden from the view or use of other parts of the program that use the object.

accumulator   A variable that is updated as a program executes.

Active Server Pages   See *ASP*.

ActiveX   Prewritten objects that work as controls that you can embed in a Web page.

algorithm   A common procedure or step-by-step methodology for performing a specific task and producing desired results.

anchor tag   A tag that creates a link to another Web page location.

animation   The movement of graphic images on your screen.

API   A set of prewritten routines, which often interact with the operating system, that your programs can call. API is the abbreviation for *application programming interface*.

applet   A small program that travels with a Web page and executes on the end-user's computer to add interaction to a Web page.

appletviewer   A program with which you can view an applet without the use of a Web browser.

application   A program.

Application Wizard   A Visual Basic wizard that generates an initial application according to your specifications.

argument   A value passed to a function. Sometimes called a *parameter*, although technically one passes arguments to a function and receives parameters in a function.

arithmetic assignment operators   Operators that update the values stored in variables.

array   A list of variables that have the same name and data type.

array element   An individual variable from an array.

ascending order   Items sorted from a low value to a high value.

ASCII   A system that assigns a unique character to the numbers 0 through 256.

ASP   A primary method whereby software companies will be able to lease software to users over the Internet. ASP is an acronym for *Active Server Pages*.

Assembly language   A language just above the machine language level that assigns codes to machine language instructions to help people read machine language listings a little more easily.

Assistant Programmer   An entry-level programming position. Also called a *Junior Programmer* or *Programmer I*.

bandwidth   The speed and efficiency of an online connection.

BASIC   One of the early programming languages written for introductory programmers. BASIC stands for *Beginner's All-purpose Symbolic Instruction Code*.

beta testing The process of testing a program before you release the program to the end user.

binary An on or off state of a computer switch often represented by a 1 (for on) or a 0 (for off).

binary search A search that continually splits a sorted list in the middle until a value is located.

bit A binary value, the smallest data value that a computer can represent.

block A section of code grouped together by braces that sets apart a section of code in a smaller area than a full procedure. A procedure might contain several blocks of code.

boolean A data type that accepts only a true or false value.

bottom-up design A system design that looks at a system's details first and gradually completes the rest of the system, interlocking the details toward the end.

branching Transferring control from one program location to another.

breakpoints Locations designated during the debugging of a program where the program's execution will halt temporarily.

bubble sort A type of sort that swaps values throughout the sorting process where the low values rise slowly to the top of the sorted list.

bugs Program errors.

byte A single character of memory, containing a total of 8 bits that represent any of 256 different possibilities.

bytecode The language that Java programs compile into and that requires a Java virtual machine emulator to run. If Java compiled into machine language, the virtual machine would not be needed, but the bytecode allows Java to run on any computer as long as that computer has a Java virtual machine.

C An efficient, small language that uses a large number of operators, originally designed for writing operating systems.

C++ An OOP-based version of the C programming language.

C# Microsoft's competing language to Java, supported in the .NET environment.

call stack A list of all functions executed so far in a program, used during the debugging of a program.

call-by-value Calling a function and passing only the value of the arguments and not passing the actual arguments themselves.

cascading style sheets   See *CSS*.

CASE   A rather extensive programming tool that was to take the user from the design stage to the finished application stage, eventually without the need of a Programmer. The promise of CASE has yet to materialize. CASE is an acronym for *Computer-Aided Software Engineering*.

centralized computing   A computing environment where one large computer system is the repository of information and programs that users across the network or online connection can use.

certification   A means of specifying that a computer worker has a certain skill level.

CGI   A programming language that provides interaction between a Web page user and the Web page server. CGI stands for *common gateway interface*.

character string   See *string*.

character string function   A function that processes character string data.

chargeback   A method where a corporation pays for computer services by transferring department funds directly to the computer department.

check boxes   Small, square boxes that provide one or more choices for users. The user clicks a box to indicate a choice, thereby placing an *X* in the box. Another click removes the *X* to deselect the choice.

class   A description of an object and its properties.

client   The computer that views a Web page.

client-server computers   An environment where users on networked computers run programs sent to them (or served to them) by a server computer.

CLR   A virtual machine for the .NET environment where compilers will be able to produce programs that run on any computer that supports the CLR standard.

code   The instructions inside a program.

code module   A Visual Basic file that contains only Visual Basic programming language instructions and no graphic elements.

collision detection   The ability to detect when one graphic image overlaps another in some way.

COM   A standardized list of objects found in a computer's hardware and software, such as the screen, that COM-compatible languages can reference by name. COM is an acronym for *Common Object Model*.

comments See *remarks*.

Common Language Runtime See *CLR*.

compiler A program that converts source code into machine language.

concatenate To combine one data value to another.

conditional operators Operators that compare one value to another, also called *relational operators*.

construct A programming language's way of performing a certain kind of task.

constructor Methods that initialize a new object.

Contract Programmer A programmer who works temporarily for a company for a fixed charge or rate.

control An element with which you control the operating of a Windows program, such as a command button or text box.

conversion characters Characters used in C I/O functions such as `printf()` that format output.

coordinates Measurements that represent the number of pixels from the left edge (the *x*-coordinate) and the top edge (the *y*-coordinate) of a screen or window.

counter A variable that tracks how many times a process has occurred.

CSS An HTML option that enables you to create named styles that define the way part of your Web page looks, such as a headline area. CSS is an acronym for *cascading style sheets*.

data Facts and figures used in computer programs.

Data Entry Clerk A person who works in the Data Entry Department.

Data Entry Department The department in a large organization that enters data into the computer.

data hiding The ability of an object to hide its members from other parts of a program to protect those members from accidental change.

data member See *member*.

data processing The act of turning raw data into meaningful output, generally associated with computers.

debugging The process of removing the bugs from a computer program.

A

decision symbol   A diamond on a flowchart that represents a decision being made in the logic.

decrementing   Subtracting from a value.

default   A value that appears or that is assumed if the user does not change the value.

default text   Text that appears inside a text box that the user can keep or change.

descending order   Items sorted from a high value to a low value.

desk checking   The process of checking all paths of a computer program to test the program's accuracy.

destructor   Methods that erase a new object and free the memory that was used.

device context   A representation of a device, to which Windows writes, that might represent your screen, a window, or a printer.

dimension   Reserve storage for elements in an array.

distributed computing   A computing environment where computers are not close together but work together across a network or through an online connection.

document object model   See *DOM*.

document type definition   See *DTD*.

DOM   A classification that assigns names to elements on a Web page and to the browser's controls. DOM is an acronym for *document object model*.

DP   See *data processing*.

DTD   A set of XML definitions and what each represents. DTD is an acronym for *document type definition*.

Dynamic HTML   HTML that supports the use of JavaScripts and other special effects.

EBCDIC   A character representation, similar to ASCII, used on mainframe computers.

editor   A text processor programmers use to type program instructions and save those instructions in a source code file.

electronic signatures   The legal ability to agree to documents online as though you had physically signed the documents in person.

empty string   A string that contains no characters.

end-user   See *user*.

endless loop   See *infinite loop*.

escape sequence   A character literal that represents another character or that performs an action such as a newline character.

executable content   A Java-enabled program applet embedded in a Web page.

Explorer-style   A style of displaying data in a tree structure similar to the way Windows Explorer displays a disk's folder structure.

extraction operator   A C++ operator, >>, that fills a variable with input.

field   A place where a user can enter data, such as a text box on a form.

final class   A class that contains absolutely no code that an inherited class can use.

floating-point value   A number that includes a decimal point and an optional fractional portion.

flowchart   A pictorial representation of the flow of logic.

flowchart template   A plastic outline of common flowchart symbols that helps you draw better-looking flowcharts.

Forte for Java   A Java development system that contains an editor and a compiler.

free-form   You can start program instructions in any column and place blank lines throughout the code.

friendly class   A class that makes its members and methods available to any inheriting object.

function   A routine that processes data inside a program.

global variable   A variable that is available to all routines inside a program.

graphical user interface   An operating environment, such as Windows, where objects and controls appear on the screen graphically.

graphics box control   A region on your screen, appearing inside a window, where graphics may appear.

GUI   See *graphical user interface.*

Hailstorm   A collection of online services that Microsoft has defined that includes Hotmail and MSN Messenger.

handle   A pointer to a device that Windows can access.

hot spot   See *links.*

A

Hotmail   A Microsoft-based free, online e-mail service.

HTML   The formatting and hyperlinking language that forms Web pages. HTML stands for *HyperText Markup Language*.

hypertext link   See links.

I/O   Abbreviation for input and output.

incrementing   Adding to a value.

infinite loop   See *endless loop*.

information   Usable, processed data, typically output from a computer program.

inheritance   The ability of one data object to gain characteristics from another object.

input   The data that goes into a computer program. The source of the data might be a keyboard, disk file, or online connection.

input verification   The checking of a user's input for validity.

insertion operator   A C++ operator, <<, that outputs a value from a variable to an output stream such as the screen.

installation script   A set of specifications that determines how an application is to be installed on a computer.

integer   A whole number.

iteration   The cycle that repeats inside a loop.

J2EE   Sun Microsystems' competition to Microsoft's .NET initiative. J2EE is an abbreviation for *Java 2 Platform, Enterprise Edition*.

Java   An OOP-based language used in Web applets and standalone applications.

JavaScript   A scripting language that enables users to place active elements such as menus and rollover buttons on a Web page.

label   A named location in a program that one can branch to.

LAN   See *local area network*.

leading blanks   Blank spaces that appear before character data to pad the data value with extra positions.

Liberty BASIC   A programming development system based on the BASIC programming language.

links Locations found inside HTML-based documents, such as Web pages, that trigger an action, such as the display of a different Web page, when the user clicks the link. Also called *hypertext links* and *hot spots*.

literal Fixed data that does not change.

local area network A small network that links two or more computers together within a short distance of each other.

local variable A variable available only to the block or routine in which it's declared.

logic error An error in the logic used in a program. Often, a program continues running because logic errors, unlike syntax errors, do not cause the program to quit.

loop Program instructions that are repeated during a program's execution.

looping The process of repeating statements in a program.

machine language Compiled, computer-readable instructions that are compacted into nonhuman terms that only the computer can understand.

mainframe computers Large computers used by organizations to handle many hundreds of users and to house much online and offline storage.

maintainability The ease of maintenance that a program's author puts into the program by writing clear code.

maintenance The process of changing and updating a program's code with new features and bug fixes.

MDI See *multiple document interface*.

member An object's data value.

member functions An object's functions.

Menu Editor A tool found in Visual Basic and other Microsoft Visual programming language development systems that helps you build and test menus for your applications.

message A command that acts upon a specific object.

metatags Special HTML code placed inside Web pages that the user does not see but that search engines can locate to link to the site.

methods Procedures embedded in an object.

A

MIS   A term used primarily in the 1970s to describe the projected, central repository of data that organizations thought would transpire. Distributed computing, thanks primarily to the proliferation of the PC, all but destroyed the MIS concept. MIS is an abbreviation for Management Information System.

MSN Messenger   Microsoft's instant chat service whereby two or more users can type real-time messages to each other over a network or online connection.

multiple document interface   An application scheme whereby more than one window with data can be open at the same time.

.NET   Microsoft's plan to define the way that information and programs will interact in a more online world.

.NET Framework   The overall environment of the .NET system.

newline   A carriage return and line feed combination that effectively moves the cursor to the start of the next line on a screen or printer.

nonprinting characters   Characters that cause an action, such as a line feed or a computer beep, but that do not display on a printer or screen.

null   A value that represents nothing when stored in a variable to indicate that the variable has not yet been initialized.

null string   See *empty string*.

object   An active data value that has characteristics and properties.

object-oriented design   The process of designing a computer application that utilizes OOP concepts in the design to show active objects that are to be developed.

object-oriented programming   Programming that utilizes objects and supports inheritance and data hiding.

OOD   Acronym for *object-oriented design*.

OOP   Acronym for *object-oriented programming*.

operator   A symbol or word, such as a plus sign, that manipulates numbers or strings in some way.

operator overloading   The ability to give an operator different meanings, depending on what the operator is working with at the time.

operator precedence   The order in which a language executes multiple operators that appear in the same expression.

option buttons   Small, round buttons that provide mutually-exclusive choices for users. When the user clicks a circle to indicate a choice, a dot is placed in the circle. If a dot was already placed in another choice, that other dot is removed. Also called *radio buttons*.

output   The information produced from a program and sent to the printer, screen, an online connection, or a disk file.

output definition   The specification of all of a program's output.

overhead   A method of paying for a company's computer services through a general company overhead expense account instead of each department transferring department funds to the computer department as is the case with the chargeback method.

overloading   The ability to write multiple abilities for the same function or operator.

parameter   A value received by a function. Sometimes called an *argument,* although technically one passes arguments to a function and receives parameters in a function.

parallel testing   Testing a new program, or a new version of a program, while still using the old system to verify results.

people years   The amount of time it takes, in years, for a person to complete a computer program.

peer-to-peer computing   Users loosely connected through online connections that enable them to share data and programs.

picture element   See *pixel.*

pixel   A dot on the screen that represents the smallest area you can draw. From the words *picture element.*

polymorphism   Literally, from the Greek for *many forms*, and refers to the ability of different objects to respond differently to the same commands.

portable   The ability of a language or program to work across a wide range of computer hardware.

private class   A class that hides its members and methods available from all parts of the program.

private key   A key that deciphers an encrypted code known only to the sending and receiving party.

preprocessor directive   A command that the compiler performs before the compiler compiles the source code into machine language.

procedures   Routines, such as subroutines and functions you write, which perform a task within a program.

profiler   A software-based tool that analyzes a program and determines whether inefficiencies exist.

program   Detailed instructions that tell the computer what to do.

program editor   See *editor*.

Programmer   A person who authors computer programs.

Programmer Analyst   An advanced programmer who begins to learn to design systems as well as programs. Also called a *Senior Programmer*.

project   A collection of files that make up a Windows application.

protocol   The way in which two computers transfer data between each other.

prototype   A model.

prototype screen   A representation of what a program's screen will look like.

pseudocode   A written description of the flow of program logic. Sometimes called *structured English*.

public class   A class that makes its members and methods available to any part of the program that declares objects of that class.

public key   A key that deciphers an encrypted code available to anyone who might be viewing a Web site.

RAD   See *rapid application development*.

radio buttons   See *option buttons*.

radius   The distance from the center to the edge of a circle.

Rapid application development   A tool than enables you to design and build a complete application quickly.

relational operator   An operator that compares data values.

remarks   Comments placed inside a program's source code to provide information to other programmers. Also called *comments*.

resolution   The density of dots on your screen; the higher the resolution, the better your screen graphics and text will look.

resource editor A programming tool that helps a Programmer build and test Windows resources such as icons, menus, dialog boxes, or text strings.

reuse The ability of an object to be used by several procedures and even separate programs without recoding.

rollover effect The ability of a command button or other screen element to change shape, size, or color when the user points to the item with the mouse.

runtime error An error that occurs during the execution of a program.

scriptlet A JavaScript program.

selection Making a decision in logic.

Senior Programmer A programmer who has passed the entry-level stage by maintaining programs and writing new routines, and who has shown an understanding of programming concepts needed.

sequence The execution of a program, one statement after another.

sequential search Looking through a list of items one value at a time.

server The computer that sends a Web page to a client computer.

single document interface An application scheme whereby only one window with data can be open at any one time.

single-stepping The process of executing one line of a program at a time, slowly, to see the results of each statement.

site certificate An electronic statement that your Web browser sometimes checks to ensure that a Web page is secure.

SOAP An internet and communications protocol that defines the way computers talk to each other and share information. SOAP is an acronym for Simple Object Access Protocol.

software Programs that run on computers.

software license The right to run a program.

source code The program instructions that a programmer writes.

spaghetti code An unstructured program that branches often, back and forth, in an unclear, difficult-to-follow manner.

sprite animation Animation that you can program to make objects move and respond when collision detection occurs.

A

statements Instructions inside a computer program.

static text On-screen text that the user cannot change.

stream A flow of data, usually input or output, to or from a C or C-based language's program.

string Textual data that you cannot calculate with.

structured English See *pseudocode*.

structured programming A system of writing computer programs so they are clear, easy to follow, and simple to maintain.

structured walkthrough A team review of a programmer's work.

subroutine A section of code that you can call from another part of code one or more times.

subscript A numbered value that represents an array element.

Swing A Java add-on that most modern Java compilers support that provides Windows-like controls for Java applets and applications.

syntax The grammar rules of a programming language.

syntax error An error in the spelling or grammar of a computer language.

systems analysis and design The process of creating a complete computer application from its early design stages to a finished product.

Systems Analyst An employee who designs systems that will be computerized.

tag commands HTML commands, surrounded by angled brackets < and >, that determine how a Web page is formatted. Also called *tag references*.

TCP/IP The communications protocol used by the Internet.

temporary variable A variable that you store a value in for a short time.

top-down design A system design that looks at the overall picture first and gradually refines the details.

twip A screen measurement that equals approximately 1/20th of a point of type, typically used as the smallest addressable screen measurement for placement of text and graphics.

UML Specifies a uniform method for defining the requirements of a program. UML is an abbreviation for *Unified Modeling Language*.

user The person who uses the programs that programmers write.

user-defined functions Functions that you write as opposed to built-in functions supplied by a programming language.

variable A named storage location for data in a program.

VBScript Microsoft's scripting language that competes with JavaScript.

version controller Tracks and maintains version numbers of programs so an organization can keep track of which programs are in use and which should be discarded.

virtual machine An imaginary computer that runs compiled Java programs. Your computer or Web browser must emulate a virtual machine to run a Java applet or application.

Visual Basic A development system that enables you to use a BASIC-like language to create Windows applications.

XML An language that works inside HTML and that is similar in form to HTML whereby the user can create unique tag elements that describe data on the Web page.

WAN See *wide area network.*

watch variables Variables whose values appear in a window during the debugging of a computer program.

web forms A set of defined standards for creating forms on .NET-based Web pages and applications.

whitespace Extra blank lines and spaces inside programs to make the code more readable.

wide area network Two or more computers networked together over a long distance, often through fiber or satellite communications.

Win32 The general name for operating systems based on a 32-bit memory location such as Windows 95, Windows 98, Windows ME, Windows 2000, and Windows XP.

wizard A step-by-step routine that walks you through a process such as the creation of a program.

A

APPENDIX **B**

Quiz Answers

Hour 1

1. Data consists of raw facts and figures, and information is processed data that has more meaning.

2. A program is a set of detailed instructions that tells the computer what to do.

3. A programming language is a set of commands and grammar rules with which you write programs that give computers instructions.

4. False; a computer might make a mistake, but it's rare that it does so. In the vast majority of cases where a computer is blamed, a person entered bad data or typed a bad program.

5. Computers increase jobs, not replace them. The information industry is one of the reasons for the past two decades of economic growth.

6. Programmers use editors to type programs into the computer.

7. Liberty BASIC automatically compiles and runs your program.

8. True.

9. Liberty BASIC halts the program's execution and displays the line suspected of containing the bug.

10. `.bas` is the filename extension for most languages based on BASIC.

Hour 2

1. You can buy a program that's already written, buy a program with source code and modify the program, or write your own program from scratch.

2. Companies want their programs to conform to the way they do business.

3. Programmers must use programming languages to create programs.

4. Computers only understand a very low-level machine language and are not advanced enough to recognize higher languages.

5. Human language has more ambiguity than computer language.

6. False; a programmer might only know one or two languages and still be extremely useful and productive.

7. The more RAM your computer contains, the more of your program and data that can fit into memory at the same time and the faster your program executes.

8. C++ and C# are derived from the C language.

9. Visual Basic and Liberty BASIC are derived from BASIC. Others also exist.

10. A programmer might specialize in only one programming language because the programmer's company may use only one language. Also, the more specialized the programmer is, the better the programmer will be in that skill. Nevertheless, most programmers are familiar with several languages and prosper more because of that knowledge.

Hour 3

1. The more thorough the design, the more quickly the programming staff can write the program.

2. A programmer often begins defining the output of the proposed system.

3. True.

4. Top-down design enables a program designer to incrementally generate all aspects of a program's requirements. Pseudocode is a way to specify the logic of a program once the program's design has already been accomplished with tools such as top-down design.

5. RAD provides a way to rapidly develop systems and move quickly from the design stage to a finished product. RAD tools are not yet advanced enough to handle most programming tasks, although RAD can make designing systems more easy than designing without RAD tools.

6. False; RAD requires quite a bit of programming in many instances once its work is done.

7. A flowchart uses symbols.

8. True.

9. True.

10. The final step of programming is writing the actual code.

Hour 4

1. Use `Print` to display words in an output window.

2. `Print 10 + 20`

3. A semicolon at the end of a `Print` statement ensures that the next printed item appears right beside the one you're printing now.

4. False; `Print`, not `Output`, is the command for displaying output.

5. A variable is a named storage location.

6. Use the `Print` statement followed by a variable's name to print the contents of a variable.

7. A prompt describes the information that a user is to type.

8. The question mark completes the prompt and indicates that input is needed from the user.

9. `LPT1` is your primary printer.

10. Use `Close` when you're through using the printer in a Liberty Basic program.

Hour 5

1. `6`

2. `7`

3. A function is a routine that returns a value.

4. `-6`

5. `2`

B

6. `Len()` works with both string and numeric data.

7. The three trigonometric functions are `Sin()`, `Cos()`, and `Tan()`.

8. True.

9. `A`

10. The `Mid$()` function returns part of a string from the middle of a string, whereas `Instr$()` returns the position of one string found inside another.

Hour 6

1. A conditional operator tests how two values compare, whereas a mathematical operator calculates an answer based on the values.

2. A loop is a set of instructions that repeat.

3. True.

4. False; if the `For` loop's counter variable is already past the limit before the loop begins, the `For` loop will not execute and control passes to the statement that follows the loop's `Next` statement.

5. Use a negative `Step` value to make a `For` loop count down.

6. The loop executes six times.

7. Use the `For...Next` loop when you want to execute a loop a fixed number of times.

8. The conditional appears after the `While` command.

9. Set the conditional to true before entering the loop.

10. A loop is simpler to code that setting up a counter to control a loop.

Hour 7

1. The first computer bug appeared in a printer.

2. A logic error is a mistake in program logic, whereas a syntax error is a mistake in program grammar or spelling.

3. The programming language locates syntax errors.

4. A programming language cannot locate logic errors.

5. To single-step means to walk through the program's execution one statement at a time, analyzing the results of each statement.

6. The Debugging window shows variable contents and the next statement that will execute in your program.

7. The Step window enables you to single-step through a program at the speed you designate, whereas the Walk button slowly executes your program one line at a time.

8. Watch variables are variables you set up to monitor during a program's debugging session.

9. Just because a program compiles and runs does not mean that you have fully debugged the program. Sometimes, an error appears long after the program is in use due to a special set of data values that are entered.

10. A Windows environment enables you to set up multiple debugging windows and resize and move them so that you can analyze all code and variables easily.

Hour 8

1. Computers are used more and more, and new programs need to be written while older programs need to be updated.

2. Flowcharts can consume far too much space on paper for large systems and are cumbersome to draw.

3. Clean, easily maintainable, well-structured code is the opposite of spaghetti code.

4. The three structured programming constructs are sequence, decision, and looping.

5. The Goto statement branches to another part of the program.

6. A label specifies the target of a branch.

7. Too much branching makes a program difficult to follow and maintain.

8. Desk checking must precede beta testing.

9. When one parallel tests, the old system is used in conjunction with the new system and the results are compared.

10. A profiler analyzes a program for inefficient code.

B

Hour 9

1. An accumulator is a variable whose value is updated.

2. False; although the statement might actually be using an accumulator variable, the statement happens to be decreasing the value stored there, whereas accumulators are usually added to.

3. An ascending sort puts lists in order from low to high and a descending sort puts lists in order from high to low.

4. The third variable is needed to hold one of the values temporarily.

5. The bubble sort is one of the simplest sorts to write and understand.

6. True.

7. A sequential search is the simplest search technique.

8. The binary search is far more efficient than the sequential search.

9. A `Goto` branches unconditionally, whereas a `Gosub` is a temporary branch to execute a subroutine, returning to the statement following the `Gosub` upon completion.

10. True.

Hour 10

1. Resolution refers to the density of the screen's dots; the higher the resolution, the better the screen will look.

2. Pixel is another name for picture element.

3. The Liberty BASIC home position is a window's center pixel.

4. A handle is a pointer to a device or window.

5. Use `Cls` to erase a graphics window.

6. True.

7. The `Goto` graphics command moves the position of the next pixel to draw.

8. A coordinate pair specifies the row and column of the next pixel to draw.

9. Liberty BASIC's sprite programming forces the background of one image to become transparent. When you place the image with the transparent background on top of another image, they combine into one image.

10. You must mask an image's background to make the image fully transparent for proper sprite animation.

Hour 11

1. True.

2. Only one window can be active at once.

3. These values specify the *x*-coordinate and the *y*-coordinate pairs of a graphic's position and size in a window.

4. Build the button before opening the button's window.

5. Use `UL`, `LL`, `UR`, or `LR` to set a button's orientation inside a window.

6. A combo box retains a smaller size until the user opens it, whereas a list box's size remains constant.

7. The user's selection will be highlighted.

8. The `singleclickselect` or `doubleclickselect` value determines whether the user must single-click or double-click a list box item to select that item.

9. A check box may be checked or unchecked, so the programmer must handle both options.

10. The previous radio button will automatically be deselected.

Hour 12

1. True.

2. False; the bandwidth and size of the Java applet determines how fast the Java applet loads.

3. HTML is the language that formats Web pages.

4. Bytecode is the language into which Java compiles Java code.

5. By emulating a virtual machine, any computer in the world can run any compiled Java program.

6. Java handles security in many ways. For example, Java must receive proper security clearance from the user before accessing a network, cannot access memory space that it has no right to, cannot create, read, rename, copy, or write files on the end user's computer, and Java applets cannot call internal system routines on the end user's system.

7. The `import` command brings object libraries into the Java program.

8. The `drawString()` function writes characters to the screen.

9. The `paint()` method determines what happens when a window is redrawn.

10. Java comments begin with `//` or are enclosed inside a `/*` and `*/` pair.

B

Hour 13

1. False; you cannot change a literal.

2. Store the escape character for the quotation mark.

3. Java supports four integer data types: `byte`, `short`, `int`, and `long`.

4. The first subscript in a Java array is `0`.

5. A Boolean variable can hold one of two possible values.

6. The modulus operator returns the integer remainder of a division between two integers.

7. `sum*=18;`

8. `11`

9. The semicolon at the end of the `for` statement causes the loop to execute without ever doing anything but looping. Once the loop finishes, the `System.out.println()` executes one time.

10. False; you can increment, decrement, or change the loop variable by whatever value you want.

Hour 14

1. You can enclose comments in `/*` and `*/`.

2. Arguments are values passed between a calling procedure and a called procedure.

3. The `main()` argument list is there so that users can pass arguments from the operating system environment to the program.

4. Swing adds Windows-like controls to a program.

5. The `import` command brings Java object libraries into programs.

6. A class defines the way objects will look and behave.

7. True.

8. The program builds an object based on the class definition.

9. The extended object inherits the data and methods from the parent object.

10. False; keep the argument list empty if the argument list requires no arguments. (You'll learn that you do place `void` inside empty argument lists in C and C++.)

Hour 15

1. Keep Java applets small so they load quickly.

2. The appletviewer enables you to test Java applets without using a Web browser.

3. The Swing library enables you to add command buttons, list boxes, text boxes, and other Windows controls to your Java applets and programs.

4. The Swing library can add overhead and size to an applet.

5. `resize()` determines the applet's window size.

6. `init()` is always the first procedure that an applet executes.

7. Java applet source code uses the `.java` extension.

8. Compiled Java applets use the `.class` extension.

9. The <OBJECT> tag (or the <APPLET> tag) embeds Java applets in Web pages.

10. The two commands specify the width and height of the applet's window and often match the applet's `resize()` arguments.

Hour 16

1. You don't have to write any extra code to add Internet access to a Visual Basic application.

2. True.

3. The default names are not meaningful, and when your application uses several controls, you should name those controls with names that you will recognize when maintaining the program so you modify correct controls when needed.

4. The Toolbox control appears in the center of your Form window.

5. The Menu Editor helps you build and test menus.

6. The control you place on the form determines which properties appear in the Properties window.

7. You can debug the application inside the Visual Basic environment.

8. A compiled Visual Basic application is faster than one run inside the Visual Basic environment.

9. The procedure is private, which means only the enclosing program can access the procedure, the procedure is a subroutine so it does not return any values, and no arguments are passed to the procedure.

10. False; some procedure code can appear in Code modules.

B

Hour 17

1. C compiles into a more efficient language than Liberty BASIC, often because of its heavy use of operators instead of commands.

2. A header file brings in extra routines and library definitions and is brought in with the `#include` statement, not unlike the Java `import` command.

3. All C programs start with `main()`.

4. True.

5. The semicolon should not appear after the `if`'s closing parentheses.

6. `<iostream.h>` defines the I/O routines for most C++ programs.

7. Define an object's data members and member functions inside the object's class definition.

8. C++ programmers often use `cin>>` and `cout<<` for input and output.

9. Polymorphism allows for operator overloading.

10. Programmers do not have to repeat all the code when defining inherited objects; programmers only have to write code that adds or changes functionality.

Hour 18

1. HTML is used by Java programmers, as well as programmers of other languages, and the Web is integrated into many programming environments today.

2. FrontPage creates a Web page based on your design and generates all the HTML code for you, although most Web page programmers modify and add to FrontPage's HTML code once the Web page is generated.

3. A command tag is an HTML command.

4. An HTML command begins with `<!–` and ends with `–>`.

5. These tags define the title that appears inside the Web page window's title bar.

6. Use the `<Hn>` tag to increase headline text, replacing *n* with a larger number to indicate a larger headline size.

7. Use the `<font size=n>` tag to increase normal Web page text, replacing *n* with a smaller number to indicate a larger text size.

8. So the alternative text appears if the user has turned off the Web browser or if a visually impaired user is using a voice-enabled Web browser.

9. True.

10. Unless the underlined text is a link to another element, underlines imply that a link exists where there is none.

Hour 19

1. JavaScript code resides inside the HTML source code file.

2. An interpreted language executes without compilation, one line at a time.

3. A Web page client is the computer viewing the Web page.

4. A Web page server is the computer sending the Web page to a client computer.

5. The `<Script>` and `</Script>` tags enclose JavaScript code.

6. The pre-defined objects enable the JavaScript code to more easily control elements such as windows, command buttons, and the Web browser.

7. False; you can use variables in JavaScript scriptlets.

8. False; if you've defined a rollover effect, the button changes as soon as the user points to the button.

9. True.

10. True.

Hour 20

1. The *D* stands for *Dynamic*.

2. True.

3. The DOM objects have common names that all DOM-compatible languages and compilers recognize.

4. DHTML controls dropdown menus and rollover effects.

5. A rollover effect causes a button or other screen element to change when the user points to that element.

6. XML stands for *eXtended Markup Language*.

7. The XML tags are defined properly.

8. True.

9. The DTD defines each XML tag.

10. The asterisk, *, defines optional XML-based tags.

Hour 21

1. .NET is a definition that describes how future online environments will communicate with each other.

2. The faster the bandwidth, the more likely users are to use the Internet for video and audio content as well as for other data-intensive transfers.

3. In a distributed computing environment, users sit at powerful computers and execute programs and process data sent to them over the network from other computers. In a centralized computing environment, one or more large computers usually serve programs and data to the smaller computers connected to the network.

4. .NET technology encompasses much more than XML, but it is true that XML plays a large role in the .NET initiative.

5. True.

6. The SOAP protocol enables different devices to communicate as long as they adhere to SOAP's standards.

B

7. C# is Microsoft's response to Java, providing an efficient language that works with Web pages as well as a stand-alone application language.

8. True.

9. .NET uses the COM model in all its facets to improve the way programs communicate with common objects.

10. The Common Language Runtime allows all computers with a CLR compiler to be .NET compatible.

Hour 22

1. MIS stands for *Management Information Systems*.

2. A DP staff writes programs for the company's own users and, sometimes, to sell to other companies.

3. Data Entry is generally the most entry-level computer-related position in a company.

4. Entry-level programmers often maintain programs others have written.

5. A Systems Analyst designs new systems.

6. A structured walkthrough occurs when a team analyzes a team member's code to look for bugs and inefficiencies.

7. True.

8. Computer programming personnel can help ensure their own job security by writing clean, structured, and easily maintained programs.

9. A LAN usually exists with computers connected close to each other by direct wiring or, sometimes, by wireless technology. A WAN can connect computers across towns and even continents using cables and satellites.

10. Internet-related jobs often demand higher pay due to the newness of the technology and the ever-changing aspects that require constant upkeep to maintain skills.

Hour 23

1. Software and computer stores, mail-order outlets, office supply stores, and online vendors are just a few of the places where you can purchase software.

2. Your users should understand your application's installation so the user has no problem installing your program.

3. A software project is a collection of all files related to an application.

4. An installation script installs an application for the user and specifies the name and location of all files that are to be installed.

5. Compiled programs use the `.exe` filename extension.

6. The primary installation file is often called `Setup.exe`.

7. Applications can be downloaded from an online connection or installed from a CD-ROM or networked disk drive.

8. Due to the size of most applications these days, applications normally will not fit on a regular diskette.

9. The clean machine ensures that files needed for the installation don't appear on the computer prior to the installation. If the installation omits a needed file, you're more likely to realize that the file is missing than if you installed the application on a machine that you created the application on or on a machine to which you've installed the application at least once before.

10. A good installation-creation program, such as Visual Studio's Package and Deployment Wizard, will create the uninstall routine for you so that all files are properly removed when the user wants to remove the application.

Hour 24

1. A profiler locates inefficiencies in code.

2. Program maintainability is more important than efficiency.

3. The version control library ensures that proper versions are accounted for and installed.

4. A Windows resource might be a bitmap image, icon, window, or menu.

5. A resource manager is a program that helps you manage Windows resources by selecting them for applications.

6. A resource editor is a program that helps you create Windows resources.

7. More programmers are needed for new technologies and the online communications that have changed so much of the computing world.

8. True.

9. CASE is a rather complex design tool to help organizations design, build, test, and implement complete computer systems.

10. By designing the Unified Modeling Language, or UML, Microsoft helps to ensure that program designs are consistent.

B

APPENDIX C

ASCII Table

ASCII Character	Binary Code	Decimal Equivalent
Null	0000 0000	0
A	0000 0001	1
B	0000 0010	2
C	0000 0011	3
D	0000 0100	4
E	0000 0101	5
F	0000 0110	6
G	0000 0111	7
H	0000 1000	8
I	0000 1001	9
J	0000 1010	10
K	0000 1011	11
L	0000 1100	12
M	0000 1101	13
N	0000 1110	14

ASCII Character	Binary Code	Decimal Equivalent
O	0000 1111	15
P	0001 0000	16
Q	0001 0001	17
R	0001 0010	18
S	0001 0011	19
T	0001 0100	20
U	0001 0101	21
V	0001 0110	22
W	0001 0111	23
X	0001 1000	24
Y	0001 1001	25
Z	0001 1010	26
a	0001 1011	27
b	0001 1100	28
c	0001 1101	29
d	0001 1110	30
e	0001 1111	31
space	0010 0000	32
!	0010 0001	33
"	0010 0010	34
#	0010 0011	35
$	0010 0100	36
%	0010 0101	37
&	0010 0110	38
'	0010 0111	39
(	0010 1000	40
)	0010 1001	41
*	0010 1010	42
+	0010 1011	43
,	0010 1100	44
-	0010 1101	45
.	0010 1110	46
/	0010 1111	47

ASCII Character	Binary Code	Decimal Equivalent
0	0011 0000	48
1	0011 0001	49
2	0011 0010	50
3	0011 0011	51
4	0011 0100	52
5	0011 0101	53
6	0011 0110	54
7	0011 0111	55
8	0011 1000	56
9	0011 1001	57
:	0011 1010	58
;	0011 1011	59
<	0011 1100	60
=	0011 1101	61
>	0011 1110	62
?	0011 1111	63
@	0100 0000	64
A	0100 0001	65
B	0100 0010	66
C	0100 0011	67
D	0100 0100	68
E	0100 0101	69
F	0100 0110	70
G	0100 0111	71
H	0100 1000	72
I	0100 1001	73
J	0100 1010	74
K	0100 1011	75
L	0100 1100	76
M	0100 1101	77
N	0100 1110	78
O	0100 1111	79
P	0101 0000	80

C

ASCII Character	Binary Code	Decimal Equivalent
Q	0101 0001	81
R	0101 0010	82
S	0101 0011	83
T	0101 0100	84
U	0101 0101	85
V	0101 0110	86
W	0101 0111	87
X	0101 1000	88
Y	0101 1001	89
Z	0101 1010	90
[	0101 1011	91
\	0101 1100	92
]	0101 1101	93
^	0101 1110	94
_	0101 1111	95
`	0110 0000	96
a	0110 0001	97
b	0110 0010	98
c	0110 0011	99
d	0110 0100	100
e	0110 0101	101
f	0110 0110	102
g	0110 0111	103
h	0110 1000	104
i	0110 1001	105
j	0110 1010	106
k	0110 1011	107
l	0110 1100	108
m	0110 1101	109
n	0110 1110	110
o	0110 1111	111
p	0111 0000	112
q	0111 0001	113

ASCII Character	Binary Code	Decimal Equivalent
r	0111 0010	114
s	0111 0011	115
t	0111 0100	116
u	0111 0101	117
v	0111 0110	118
w	0111 0111	119
x	0111 1000	120
y	0111 1001	121
z	0111 1010	122
{	0111 1011	123
		0111 1100	124
}	0111 1101	125
~	0111 1110	126
f	0111 1111	127
Ç	1000 0000	128
ü	1000 0001	129
é	1000 0010	130
â	1000 0011	131
ä	1000 0100	132
à	1000 0101	133
å	1000 0110	134
ç	1000 0111	135
ê	1000 1000	136
ë	1000 1001	137
è	1000 1010	138
ï	1000 1011	139
å	1000 1100	140
ç	1000 1101	141
é	1000 1110	142
è	1000 1111	143
ê	1001 0000	144
ë	1001 0001	145
í	1001 0010	146

C

ASCII Character	Binary Code	Decimal Equivalent
ì	1001 0011	147
î	1001 0100	148
ï	1001 0101	149
ñ	1001 0110	150
ó	1001 0111	151
ò	1001 1000	152
ô	1001 1001	153
ö	1001 1010	154
õ	1001 1011	155
ú	1001 1100	156
ù	1001 1101	157
û	1001 1110	158
ü	1001 1111	159
†	1010 0000	160
°	1010 0001	161
¢	1010 0010	162
£	1010 0011	163
§	1010 0100	164
•	1010 0101	165
	1010 0110	166
ß	1010 0111	167
ß	1010 1000	168
®	1010 1001	169
©	1010 1010	170
™	1010 1011	171
´	1010 1100	172
¨	1010 1101	173
•	1010 1110	174
Æ	1010 1111	175
Ø	1011 0000	176
¤	1011 0001	177
¤	1011 0010	178
¤	1011 0011	179

ASCII Character	Binary Code	Decimal Equivalent
•	1011 0100	180
¥	1011 0101	181
µ	1011 0110	182
•	1011 0111	183
•	1011 1000	184
•	1011 1001	185
•	1011 1010	186
•	1011 1011	187
ª	1011 1100	188
º	1011 1101	189
•	1011 1110	190
æ	1011 1111	191
ø	1100 0000	192
¿	1100 0001	193
¡	1100 0010	194
	1100 0011	195
•	1100 0100	196
ƒ	1100 0101	197
+	1100 0110	198
•	1100 0111	199
«	1100 1000	200
»	1100 1001	201
…	1100 1010	202
g	1100 1011	203
À	1100 1100	204
Ã	1100 1101	205
=	1100 1110	206
Œ	1100 1111	207
œ	1101 0000	208
–	1101 0001	209
—	1101 0010	210
"	1101 0011	211
"	1101 0100	212

C

ASCII Character	Binary Code	Decimal Equivalent
'	1101 0101	213
'	1101 0110	214
÷	1101 0111	215
•	1101 1000	216
ÿ	1101 1001	217
Ÿ	1101 1010	218
•	1101 1011	219
¤	1101 1100	220
‹	1101 1101	221
›	1101 1110	222
•	1101 1111	223
•	1110 0000	224
‡	1110 0001	225
·	1110 0010	226
'	1110 0011	227
„	1110 0100	228
‰	1110 0101	229
Â	1110 0110	230
Ê	1110 0111	231
Á	1110 1000	232
Ë	1110 1001	233
È	1110 1010	234
Í	1110 1011	235
Î	1110 1100	236
Ï	1110 1101	237
h	1110 1110	238
Ó	1110 1111	239
Ô	1110 0000	240
•	1111 0001	241
Ò	1111 0010	242
Ú	1111 0011	243
Û	1111 0100	244
Ù	1111 0101	245

ASCII Character	Binary Code	Decimal Equivalent
•	1111 0110	246
^	1111 0111	247
~	1111 1000	248
‾	1111 1001	249
•	1111 1010	250
•	1111 1011	251
•	1111 1100	252
ˏ	1111 1101	253
•	1111 1110	254
•	1111 1111	255

C

INDEX

JAVA™ 2 SOFTWARE DEVELOPMENT KIT STANDARD EDITION VERSION 1.3 SUPPLEMENTAL LICENSE TERMS

These supplemental license terms ("Supplemental Terms") add to or modify the terms of the Binary Code License Agreement (collectively, the "Agreement"). Capitalized terms not defined in these Supplemental Terms shall have the same meanings ascribed to them in the Agreement. These Supplemental Terms shall supersede any inconsistent or conflicting terms in the Agreement, or in any license contained within the Software.

1. **Internal Use and Development License Grant**. Subject to the terms and conditions of this Agreement, including, but not limited to, Section 2 (Redistributables) and Section 4 (Java Technology Restrictions) of these Supplemental Terms, Sun grants you a non-exclusive, non-transferable, limited license to reproduce the Software for internal use only for the sole purpose of development of your Java™applet and application ("Program"), provided that you do not redistribute the Software in whole or in part, either separately or included with any Program.

2. **Redistributables**. In addition to the license granted in Paragraph 1 above, Sun grants you a nonexclusive, nontransferable, limited license to reproduce and distribute, only as part of your separate copy of JAVA™ 2 RUNTIME ENVIRONMENT STANDARD EDITION VERSION 1.3 software, those files specifically identified as redistributable in the JAVA™ 2 RUNTIME ENVIRONMENT STANDARD EDITION VERSION 1.3 "README" file (the "Redistributables") provided that: (a) you distribute the Redistributables complete and unmodified (unless otherwise specified in the applicable README file), and only bundled as part of the Java™ applets and applications that you develop (the "Programs"); (b) you do not distribute additional software intended to supersede any component(s) of the Redistributables; (c) you do not remove or alter any proprietary legends or notices contained in or on the Redistributables; (d) you only distribute the Redistributables pursuant to a license agreement that protects Sun's interests consistent with the terms contained in the Agreement, and (e) you agree to defend and indemnify Sun and its licensors from and against any damages, costs, liabilities, settlement amounts, and/or expenses (including attorneys' fees) incurred in connection with any claim, lawsuit, or action by any third party that arises or results from the use or distribution of any and all Programs and/or Software.

3. **Separate Distribution License Required**. You understand and agree that you must first obtain a separate license from Sun prior to reproducing or modifying any portion of the Software other than as provided with respect to Redistributables in Paragraph 2 above.

4. **Java Technology Restrictions**. You may not modify the Java Platform Interface ("JPI", identified as classes contained within the "java" package or any subpackages of the "java" package), by creating additional classes within the JPI or otherwise causing the addition to or modification of the classes in the JPI. In the event that you create an additional class and associated API(s) which (i) extends the functionality of a Java environment, and (ii) is exposed to third party software developers for the purpose of developing additional software which invokes such additional API, you must promptly publish broadly an accurate specification for such API for free use by all developers. You may not create, or authorize your licensees to create additional classes, interfaces, or subpackages that are in any way identified as "java," "javax," "sun," or similar convention as specified by Sun in any class file naming convention. Refer to the appropriate version of the Java Runtime Environment binary code license (currently located at `http://www.java.sun.com/jdk/index.html`) for the availability of runtime code which may be distributed with Java applets and applications.

5. **Trademarks and Logos**. You acknowledge and agree as between you and Sun that Sun owns the Java trademark and all Java-related trademarks, service marks, logos and other brand designations including the Coffee Cup logo and Duke logo ("Java Marks"), and you agree to comply with the Sun Trademark and Logo Usage Requirements currently located at `http://www.sun.com/policies/trademarks`. Any use you make of the Java Marks inures to Sun's benefit.

6. **Source Code**. Software may contain source code that is provided solely for reference purposes pursuant to the terms of this Agreement.

7. **Termination**. Sun may terminate this Agreement immediately should any Software become, or in Sun's opinion be likely to become, the subject of a claim of infringement of a patent, trade secret, copyright or other intellectual property right.

JAVA™ DEVELOPMENT TOOLS FORTE™ FOR JAVA™, RELEASE 3.0, COMMUNITY EDITION SUPPLEMENTAL LICENSE TERMS

These supplemental license terms ("Supplemental Terms") add to or modify the terms of the Binary Code License Agreement (collectively, the "Agreement"). Capitalized terms not defined in these Supplemental Terms shall have the same meanings ascribed to them in the Agreement. These Supplemental Terms shall supersede any inconsistent or conflicting terms in the Agreement, or in any license contained within the Software.

1. **Software Internal Use and Development License Grant**. Subject to the terms and conditions of this Agreement, including, but not limited to Section 3 (Java(TM) Technology Restrictions) of these Supplemental Terms, Sun grants you a non-exclusive, non-transferable, limited license to reproduce internally and use internally the binary form of the Software complete and unmodified for the sole purpose of designing, developing and testing your [Java applets and] applications intended to run on the Java platform ("Programs").

2. **License to Distribute Redistributables**. In addition to the license granted in Section 1 (Redistributables Internal Use and Development License Grant) of these Supplemental Terms, subject to the terms and conditions of this Agreement, including but not limited to Section 3 (Java Technology Restrictions) of these Supplemental Terms, Sun grants you a nonexclusive, nontransferable, limited license to reproduce and distribute those files specifically identified as redistributable in the Software "README" file ("Redistributables") provided that: (i) you distribute the Redistributables complete and unmodified (unless otherwise specified in the applicable README file), and only bundled as part of your Programs, (ii) you do not distribute additional software intended to supersede any component(s) of the Redistributables, (iii) you do not remove or alter any proprietary legends or notices contained in or on the Redistributables, (iv) for a particular version of the Java platform, any executable output generated by a compiler that is contained in the Software must (a) only be compiled from source code that conforms to the corresponding version of the OEM Java Language Specification; (b) be in the class file format defined by the corresponding version of the OEM Java Virtual Machine Specification; and (c) execute properly on a reference runtime, as specified by Sun, associated with such version of the Java platform, (v) you only distribute the Redistributables pursuant to a license agreement that protects Sun's interests consistent with the terms contained in the Agreement, and (vi) you agree to defend and indemnify Sun and its licensors from and against any damages, costs, liabilities, settlement amounts and/or expenses (including attorneys' fees) incurred in connection with any claim, lawsuit or action by any third party that arises or results from the use or distribution of any and all Programs and/or Software.

3. **Java Technology Restrictions**. You may not modify the Java Platform Interface ("JPI", identified as classes contained within the "java" package or any subpackages of the "java" package), by creating additional classes within the JPI or otherwise causing the addition to or modification of the classes in the JPI. In the event that you create an additional class and associated API(s) which (i) extends the functionality of the Java platform, and (ii) is exposed to third party software developers for the purpose of

developing additional software which invokes such additional API, you must promptly publish broadly an accurate specification for such API for free use by all developers. You may not create, or authorize your licensees to create, additional classes, interfaces, or subpackages that are in any way identified as "java," "javax," "sun," or similar convention as specified by Sun in any naming convention designation.

4. **Java Runtime Availability**. Refer to the appropriate version of the Java Runtime Environment binary code license (currently located at `http://www.java.sun.com/jdk/index.html`) for the availability of runtime code which may be distributed with Java applets and applications.

5. **Trademarks and Logos.** You acknowledge and agree as between you and Sun that Sun owns the SUN, SOLARIS, JAVA, JINI, FORTE, STAROFFICE, STARPORTAL and iPLANET trademarks and all SUN, SOLARIS, JAVA, JINI, FORTE, STAROFFICE, STARPORTAL and iPLANET-related trademarks, service marks, logos and other brand designations ("Sun Marks"), and you agree to comply with the Sun Trademark and Logo Usage Requirements currently located at `http://www.sun.com/policies/trademarks`. Any use you make of the Sun Marks inures to Sun's benefit.

6. **Source Code**. Software may contain source code that is provided solely for reference purposes pursuant to the terms of this Agreement. Source code may not be redistributed unless expressly provided for in this Agreement.

7. **Termination for Infringement**. Either party may terminate this Agreement immediately should any Software become, or in either party's opinion be likely to become, the subject of a claim of infringement of any intellectual property right.

For inquiries please contact: Sun Microsystems, Inc., 901 San Antonio Road, Palo Alto, California 94303

SAMS
Teach Yourself
in 24 Hours

When you only have time for the answers™

Other Sams Titles

**Sams Teach Yourself XML
in 21 Days, Second Edition**
   Devan Shepherd
   0672320932
   $39.99 US/$59.95 CAN

**Sams Teach Yourself C++
in 24 Hours Starter Kit**
   Jesse Liberty
   0672322242
   $29.99 US/$44.95 CAN

**Sams Teach Yourself UML
in 24 Hours, Second Edition**
   Joseph Schmuller
   0672322382
   $29.99US /44.95 CAN

**Sams Teach Yourself
Visual Basic 6 in 24 Hours**
   Greg Perry
   0672315335
   $19.99 US/$28.95 CAN

**Sams Teach Yourself OOP
in 21 Days**
   Anthony Sintes
   0672321082
   $39.99 US/$59.95 CAN

**Sams Teach Yourself Java 2
in 24 Hours, Second Edition**
   Rogers Cadenhead
   06723206363
   $24.99US /$37.95 CAN

**Sams Teach Yourself HTML
in 24 Hours, Fourth Edition**
   Dick Oliver
   0672317249
   $19.99 US/$28.95 CAN

**Sams Teach Yourself C
in 24 Hours, Second Edition**
   Tony Zhang
   067231861X
   $24.99 US/$37.95 CAN

**Sams Teach Yourself JavaScript
in 24 Hours, Second Edition**
   Michael Moncur
   0672320258
   $24.99 US/$37.95 CAN

SAMS

www.samspublishing.com

What's on the CD-ROM

The companion CD-ROM contains Sun Microsystem's Java Software Development Kit (SDK) version 1.3, Forte 3.0 Community Edition, Liberty BASIC v2.02 Shareware, plus the source code from the book.

Windows Installation Instructions

1. Insert the disc into your CD-ROM drive.
2. From the Windows desktop, double-click on the My Computer icon.
3. Double-click on the icon representing your CD-ROM drive.
4. Double-click on the icon titled START.EXE to run the installation program.
5. Follow the on-screen prompts to finish the installation.

> If you have the AutoPlay feature enabled, the START.EXE program starts automatically whenever you insert the disc into your CD-ROM drive.

Use of this software is subject to the Sun Microsystems, Inc. Binary Code License Agreement contained on page 481 of the accompanying book. Read this agreement carefully. By opening this package, you are agreeing to be bound by the terms and conditions of this agreement.

By opening this package, you are also agreeing to be bound by the following agreement:

You may not copy or redistribute the entire CD-ROM as a whole. Copying and redistribution of individual software programs on the CD-ROM is governed by terms set by individual copyright holders.

The installer and code from the author(s) are copyrighted by the publisher and the author(s). Individual programs and other items on the CD-ROM are copyrighted or are under an Open Source license by their various authors or other copyright holders.

This software is sold as-is without warranty of any kind, either expressed or implied, including but not limited to the implied warranties of merchantability and fitness for a particular purpose. Neither the publisher nor its dealers or distributors assumes any liability for any alleged or actual damages arising from the use of this program. (Some states do not allow for the exclusion of implied warranties, so the exclusion may not apply to you.)

NOTE: This CD-ROM uses long and mixed-case filenames requiring the use of a protected-mode CD-ROM Driver.